Bibliography of

New Religious Movements

in Primal Societies

Volume 4

Europe and Asia

Other Volumes

1. Black Africa
2. North America
3. Oceania
5. Latin America
6. The Caribbean

Bibliography of

New Religious Movements

in Primal Societies

Volume 4

Europe and Asia

HAROLD W. TURNER

G.K. Hall & Co.
70 Lincoln Street • Boston, Mass.

First published 1991
by G.K. Hall & Co.
70 Lincoln Street
Boston, Massachusetts 02111

10 9 8 7 6 5 4 3 2 1

Library of Congress Cataloging-in-Publication Data

(Revised for vol. 4)
Turner, Harold W.
    Bibliography of new religious movements in primal societies.

    (v. 1: Bibliographies and guides in African Studies)
    Includes indexes.
    Contents: v. 1. Black Africa. – v. 2. North America – [etc.] –
v. 4. Europe and Asia.
    1. Developing countries – Religion – Bibliography. 2. Margiuality,
Social – Bibliography. 3. Cults – Bibliography. 4. Sects – Bibliography.
I. Title. II. Series: Bibliographies and guides in African Studies.
Z7835.C86T87 1977 [BP603]   016.2919   77-4732
ISBN 0-8161-7930-1 (v. 4)   CIP

MANUFACTURED IN THE UNITED STATES OF AMERICA

For our eldest daughter, Alison.
In appreciation of her fascination with the
art of Asian peoples

Contents

	Entries	Page
Introduction		ix
THEORY	1-288	1
GENERAL	289-356	45

EUROPE

North (Scandinavia)	357-386	57
East (Russian Europe, Balkans)	387-399	62
West, Central, and South	400-401	64

ASIA

Theory	402-416	65
General	417	67
North Central		
(Mongolia, Siberia, etc.)	418-433	68
West	434	70
East		
China and Taiwan	435-452	70
Korea	453-532	73
South (Indian subcontinent)		
India	533-782	83
Nepal	783-784	119
Southeast		
Burma	785-823	120

Contents

Indonesia...824-986   126
Kampuchea...987-988   149
Laos..989-1003   149
Malaysia...1004-1018   152
The Philippines..1019-1301   154
Singapore...1302-1304   194
Thailand..1305-1332   194
Vietnam 1333-1397   199

PARTICULAR MOVEMENTS

Iglesia ni Cristo (The Philippines) 1398-1509   209
Philippine Independent Church
    (The Philippines) 1510-1708   221
Unification Church (Korea).....................................1709-1741   247

Index of Authors and Sources...   253

Index of Main Movements and Individuals.............................   269

Introduction

This volume, the fourth in the series on new religious movements in primal societies, differs from earlier and later volumes in not being confined to one major cultural-geographical area. While it does include one such area, Asia, it also covers Europe, where, as may be expected, movements of this kind are marginal; there is also a General section on materials connected with this subject that are not focused on one of our major areas but are more world-ranging in scope. The volume opens with a section titled Theory, containing materials that are not primarily field-oriented but that deal with the more theoretical issues raised by these movements in all areas; this section should be used in conjunction with the introductory sections on theory at the beginning of the other volumes and at the beginning of sections on specific geographic areas; a certain amount of duplication has been allowed across these theoretical sections to make each volume a little more self-contained.

In the case of Europe especially, it should be remembered that the subject of these volumes is related to the new movements arising from some relation to the primal religions of tribal cultures; therefore it does not include the so-called sects and cults that have been a new feature of the European scene for several decades and that arise within a different set of dynamics. Nor, although for a different reason, does the section on Europe include movements such as Kimbanguism or the Celestial Church of Christ from Africa, or the Rastafarians from Jamaica, that have appeared in Europe by immigration of their members or, less often, by conversion; any items on their history or forms in European countries are to be found along with the main body of materials in the relevant country of origin in the other volumes. European items are confined to movements that have originated in Europe and against a tribal background.

The larger part of this volume is on Asia, and here it should be noted that materials are confined to items in European languages, with some exceptions in the case of Indonesia and the Philippines. Without this limitation these volumes would never have appeared, nor would they serve a wide range of readers and disciplines. Scholars in particular areas who find them inadequate at this point have, for the most part, their own remedy. There is no section on Japan for two reasons: as yet the aborigines, or tribal Ainu people, do not seem to have produced movements of this kind, although some expect this will yet occur; and the great range of "new religions" in Japan, like the "sects" and "cults" in the West, are sufficiently different in kind and especially in dynamics to be excluded from our category and to require the special treatment they receive in their own voluminous literature.

Likewise there are no sections on Tibet or on Sri Lanka, which have been deeply Buddhist for so long and do not appear to exhibit our phenomena. Similarly, Afghanistan and other West Asian countries that have long been Islamicized are absent, for reasons akin to those applying in northern Africa. Again, China and Taiwan, with their sophisticated Confucian and Taoist traditions, as well as Buddhist and Islamic populations, might not be expected to appear here; they do come within our scope, however, on account of their little-known and marginal tribal minorities or because of similarities between peasant millennial revolts and our tribal movements, as explained in the introduction to the China section.

The inclusion of Korea is explained in the introductory note. Special thanks are due to Dr. James H. Grayson of the Institute for Korean Studies at the University of Sheffield, without whose careful checking of the Korean and Unification Church items and advice about spelling and capitalization we should not have ventured to include these materials on an area so beyond our own competence.

Similar thanks are tendered to Dr. William A. Smalley of New Haven, Connecticut, whose knowledge of Southeast Asia was employed to survey our materials, especially those on Laos and Thailand, and to suggest new items. Dr. Smalley agrees that there are many messianic movements among the more tribal peoples of this whole area that have either not been documented or else have been very inadequately reported.

Inadequate information also applies to the many small independent or semi-independent Christian churches in the Asian countries, especially in areas such as Indonesia. Some of these appear in the country sections of David B. Barrett's remarkably comprehensive *World Christian Encyclopaedia* (see entry 293), although his criteria do not always coincide with our own. Dr. Stan Nussbaum, director of the Centre for New Religious Movements at the Selly Oak Colleges, Birmingham, G.B., has drawn attention to the contrast between the fascination for African independent movements exhibited by scholars and by the Christian ecumenical movement and neglect of similar developments in China and other parts of the world (see entry 175, last part). These are not on the scale of some of the African movements and have not caught the attention of the social scientists or of missionary writers as have the more politically involved or more millennial and syncretist movements. It is inevitable that these disparities should be reflected in our bibliographical volumes, which must report the literature rather than the actual phenomena themselves.

Disparities of a different kind appear in the variant spellings of proper names to be found in our text; some of these merely reflect variations in the originals or in current practice, although doubtless some, as with other inconsistencies of format or style, derive from our own inadequacies. It is hoped, however, that none provides a barrier between the user of these volumes and the information desired.

Theory

This material should be used in conjunction with the collections of more theoretical materials that begin each of the major areas – North America, Latin America and the Caribbean, Africa, Europe, Asia, and Oceania – in the various volumes. There is no sharp distinction between the theoretical items associated with these different areas. They have been distributed partly because they were written or published in, or had some special relevance to the area concerned. A few basic theoretical items have been repeated in one or more areas.

Some of the material here concerns religious or social change in general, without any special application to new religious movements in primal or any other societies. It has been selected from a vast literature because of some important focus that is relevant. Similarly there is some general material on millennialism or messianism without specific reference to our kind of new religious movement. It is hoped that this varied collection of theoretical materials will offer a working basis for the understanding of these movements.

By way of introduction to this division a few items may be identified here. There are two of the series of extended book reviews found in *Current Anthropology* – that on W. La Barre's bibliographic essay, in 1971 (entry 125), and that on V. Lanternari's world survey, in 1965 (entry 128). Others that may be mentioned are A. J. P. Köbben's 1959 article, translated into English in 1960 (entry 119), W. E. Mühlmann's symposium of 1961 (entry 171), and H. W. Turner's identification of this new field of study in 1971 (entry 242).

1 Aberle, David F[riend]. "A note on relative deprivation theory as applied to millenarian and other cult movements." In *Millennial dreams in action,* edited by S. L. Thrupp. The Hague: Mouton, 1962, pp. 209-14. Reprinted in *Cultural and social anthropology,* edited by P.

1

Hammond. New York: Macmillan, 1964, pp. 338-42. Reprinted in *Reader in comparative religion*, edited by W. A. Lessa and E. Vogt. 3d ed. Harper & Row, 1972, pp. 527-31.

2 Aberle, David F[riend]. *The Peyote religion among the Navaho.* Viking Fund Publications in Anthropology, 42. Chicago: Aldine Publishing Co., 1966, xxvi + 454 pp.
   Chap. 19, classification of social movements; "transformative" and "redemptive" movements, in relation to the "relative deprivation" of the situations in which they occur.

3 Aberle, David F[riend]. "The prophet dance and reactions to white contact." *Southwestern Journal of Anthropology* 15, no. 1 (1959): 74-83.
   On the causes of movements and the contact/precontact issue. See reply by L. Spier, et al., pp. 84-88.

4 Ames, Michael M. "Reaction to stress: A comparative study of nativism." *Davidson Journal of Anthropology* (Seattle) 3, no. 1 (1957): 17-30. Mimeo.
   Examples illustrating a conceptual framework.

5 *Archives de Sociologie des Religions* (Paris), no. 5 [3] (January-June 1958).
   Special issue on messianism and millenarianism; see especially G. Balandier, pp. 91, 95. See also articles in no. 4 [2] (July-December 1957) and 6 [3] (July-December 1958).

6 Baal, Jan van. "The political impact of prophetic movements." In *International Yearbook for the Sociology of Religion. Westdeutscher Verlag* (Cologne and Opladen) 5 (1969).
   Includes a six-group typology, and examines the relation to colonialism and nationalism; by a former colonial governor, later an anthropologist.

7 Baal, Jan van. "De Westerse beschabing als constante factor in het hedendaagse acculturatie-proces." *Indonesië* 2 (1948): 102-39.
   An attempt to explain why Western culture is dominant in interaction situations. See also comment by H. Th. Fischer, pp. 470-74, and reply by van Baal, pp. 556-58.

8 Balandier, Georges. *Anthropologie politique.* Paris: Presses Universitaires de France, 1967. English translation. *Political Anthropology.* London: Penguin Books, 1970, 214 pp.

English translation, pp. 99-122, messianic movements as providing hope for a threatened society rather than as interaction movements. Chap. 5 (pp. 99-122), religion and power.

9 Banton, Michael [Parker]. "L'afrique coloniale: Du réflexe religieux." In *Sociologie des relations sociales*. Paris: Payot, 1971, pp. 211-28.
   Kimbanguism and other movements; their causes (not primarily as social protest); the role of prophets.

10 Barber, Bernard. "Acculturation and messianic movements." *American Sociological Review* 6 (October 1941): 663-69.
   American Indian movements as examples, especially the Ghost Dance and Peyote.

11 Barker, Eileen. "Appendix: Characteristics which can be compared between new religious movements or the same movement in different times and societies." In *New religious movements: A perspective for understanding society*, edited by E. Barker. New York and Toronto: Edwin Mellen Press, 1982, pp. 325-29.

12 Barker, Eileen. "From sects to society: A methodological program." In *New religious movements: A perspective for understanding society*, edited by E. Barker. New York and Toronto: Edwin Mellen Press, 1982, pp. 3-15.

13 Barkun, Michael. *Disaster and the millennium*. New Haven: Yale University Press, 1974, 246 pp., bib.
   See index for "millenarian movements," "Taiping" rebellion, and "cargo cults"; p. 94, Indian Shakers; p. 109, Handsome Lake; pp. 174-75, Rastafarians – all set in a theoretical context.

14 Barkun, Michael, ed. "Millenarian change: Movements of total transformation." *American Behavioral Scientist* 16, no. 2 (1972): 143-288, bib.
   Special theme for whole issue; see especially his introduction, pp. 145-51, on the questions involved.

15 Barnett, H[omer] G[arner]. "Personal conflicts and culture change." Report S. F. 20, 1941, pp. 160-71. Reprinted in *Acculturation abstracts: North America*, edited by B. J. Siegel. Stanford: Stanford University Press, 1955, pp. 166-67.

Personal conflict as the primary motive for innovation. The Tsimshian people of Canada in contact with William Duncan as case study.

16 Bartlett, F[rederick] C. *Psychology and Primitive Culture*. Cambridge: Cambridge University Press, 1923, 294 pp.
Chap. 5 (pp. 133-59), the psychological study of the contact of peoples.

17 Bastide, Roger. "Conclusion d'un debat récent: La pensée obscure et confuse." *Le Monde Non-chrétien*, n.s., nos. 75-76 (1966), pp. 137-56.
His support for an anthropological method akin to that of M. Leenhardt, in order to discover the inner logic of primal societies.

18 Bastide, Roger. "Messianisme et développement économique et sociale." *Cahiers Internationaux de Sociologie*, n.s., no. 31 [8] (July-December 1961): 3-14. Reprinted in *Le prochain et le lointain*. Paris: Cujas, 1970, pp. 275-86. English translation. "Messianism and social and economic development." In *Social change: The colonial situation*, edited by I. Wallerstein. New York: J. Wiley, 1966, pp. 467-77.
An important theoretical article on the role of messianic movements in modernization, with examples from Zaïre.

19 Bastide, Roger. "Les métamorphoses du sacré dans les sociétés en transition." *Civilisations* 9, no. 4 (1959): 432-43.

20 Bastide, Roger. "Sociologies (au pluriel) des missions protestantes." In *Les missions protestantes et l'histoire: Actes du IIe colloque (4-9 Octobre 1971)*, by Centre d'Histoire de la Réforme et du Protestantisme, Université Paul Valéry-Montpellier. Études des Colloques, 2. Paris: Société de l'Histoire du Protestantisme Français, [1972], pp. 47-62.
Distinguishes three kinds of sociology of religion.

21 Bates, E. S. "John Alexander Dowie." In *Dictionary of American Biography*. Vol. 5. New York: Scribner, 1930, pp. 413a-413b.
Included in view of Dowie's influence in South Africa, Nigeria, the Philippines, and a number of other countries.

22 Bateson, Gregory. "Culture-contact and schismogenesis." *Man*, article 199, 35 (December 1935): 178-83.
A critique of the memorandum of the Social Science Research Council (*idem*, article no. 162) on the study of culture contact, with his own methodological suggestions.

23 Beckford, James A. "Beyond the pale: Cults, culture, and conflict." In *New religious movements: A perspective for understanding society*, edited by E. Barker. New York and Toronto: Edwin Mellen Press, 1982.

Criticism reveals stereotypes of both the cults and what a normal person or religion is assumed to be. This analysis can be applied to the assumptions about the older churches or "mission Christianity" that are implied in criticism of new movements in primal societies.

24 Beckford, James A. "Explaining religious movements." *International Social Science Journal* (New York) 29, no. 2 (1977): 235-49.

Discusses three new perspectives, including that of "movement organization," which draw on general sociological theory; refers primarily to movements in Western society. Pp. 236-37, on conventional sociological assumptions, are widely relevant.

25 Benz, Ernst. "Traum, hallucination, vision." In *Offene Tore*. Zurich: Swedenborg Verlag, 1966. English translation. *Dreams, hallucinations, visions*. New York: Swedenborg Foundation, 1968, 46 pp.

An eminent historian of religion surveys dreams and visions from the viewpoint of religious experience, examines revelatory potential, and distinguishes them from the pathological and the hallucinatory emphasized in medical and psychological studies; of theoretical importance.

26 Bourguignon, Erika. "The effectiveness of religious healing movements: A review of recent literature." *Transcultural Psychiatric Research Review* 13 (1976): 5-21.

27 Bourguignon, Erika. "Introduction: A framework for the comparative study of altered states of consciousness." In *Religion, altered states of consciousness, and social change*, edited by E. Bourguignon. Columbus: Ohio State University Press, 1973, pp. 3-35; see also pp. 321-39, etc., for an assessment of some comparisons and implications.

28 Bourguignon, Erika. "The self, the behavioural environment, and the theory of spirit possession." In *Context and meaning in cultural anthropology*, edited by M. E. Spiro. New York: Free Press, 1965, pp. 39-60.

Ritual possession in certain societies as a normal rather than an abnormal phenomenon; based on Haïtian Vodou.

29 Bourguignon, Erika. "World distribution and patterns of possession states." In *Trance and possession states*, edited by R. Prince.

Proceedings of the 2d annual conference of the R. M. Bucke Memorial Society, Montreal, 1966, pp. 3-34, bib.

30 Brown, Peter [Robert Lamont]. *Religion and society in the age of St. Augustine*. London: Faber & Faber, 1972, 352 pp.

Avoids oversimplifying reductions, either sociological or religious (e.g., re Donatism as merely sociopolitical movement); Manichaeism was a genuinely missionary religion. Also good on magic in late Roman Empire.

31 Budd, Susan. *Sociologists and religion*. London: Collier-Macmillan, 1973, viii + 196 pp.

Pp. 68-73, millenarianism and syncretism.

32 Burger, Henry G. "Syncretism, an acculturative accelerator." *Human Organization* 25, no. 2 (1966): 103-15.

Syncretism analyzed into seven types or degrees – "quantitative, supplementary, substitutive, phasic, simulative, simulative-trending, and simulative-enhancing."

33 Bürkle, Horst. "Die missionstheologische Relevanz der Motive und Erscheiningsformen neuerer religiöser Bewegungen in Übersee." *Ordensnachrichten* (Vienna) 20, no. 5 (1981): 380-93.

34 Burridge, Kenelm O[swald] L[ancelot]. "Millennialisms and the recreation of history." In *Religion, rebellion, revolution*, edited by B. Lincoln. London: Macmillan, 1985, pp. 219-35.

35 Burridge, Kenelm O[swald] L[ancelot]. *New heaven, new earth: A study of millenarian activities*. Pavilion Series. Oxford: Basil Blackwell, 1969, 191 pp., bib.

A critical survey of cargo cults, etc., theories (see index) with reference to examples – Melanesian, Polynesian, Plains Indians, and Asian Indian tribals; pp. 153-64, the prophet figure. One of the best studies of the whole subject.

36 Burridge, Kenelm O[swald] L[ancelot]. "Revival and renewal." In *The encyclopedia of religion*, edited by M. Eliade. Vol. 12. New York: Macmillan, 1987, pp. 368a-374b.

On millennialism (including in a primal context), morphology, and theories.

37 Burridge, Kenelm O[swald] L[ancelot]. *Someone, no one: An essay on individuality*. Princeton: Princeton University Press, 1979, 270 pp.

Renewal in religion and its relation to individuals; pp. 208-12, on Christian influences through missionaries and on new movements in history.

38 Chenu, Marie Dominique. "Libération politique et messianisme religieuse." *Parole et Mission* (Paris), 19 October 1962, pp. 529-42.

The religious transformations involved in modernization, with reference to V. Lanternari's survey (entry 128).

39 Chéry, H.-Ch. "Visage des sectes et motif de dissidence." *Devant les sectes non-chrétiennes*. Muséum Lessianum, Section Missiologique, no. 42. Louvain: Desclée de Brouwer, [1962], pp. 28-51.

40 Clemhout, Simone. "The psycho-sociological nature of nativistic movements and the emergence of cultural growth." *Anthropos* 61, nos. 1-2 (1966): 33-48.

Classification system; mainly China and Japan referred to. The common factor in most movements is "a situation of contrast between cultures in contact."

41 Clemhout, Simone. "Typology of nativistic movements." *Man*, article 7, 64 (January-February 1964): 14-15.

Continues the anthropologists' discussion begun by R. Linton, A. F. C. Wallace, M. W. Smith, and F. W. Voget and incorporates categories from several of these earlier attempts.

42 Clemmer, Richard O. "Resistance and the revitalization of anthropologists." In *Reinventing Anthropology*, edited by D. Hymes. New York: Random House, 1969, pp. 213-47.

Movements resisting acculturation seen in terms of their own dynamiscs, ideologies, and values rather than from the viewpoint of the dominant culture; Hopi Indian revival of identity and culture as a case study.

43 Colless, Brian. "The religion of Moses as the first cargo cult in history." In *The religious dimension*, edited by J. C. Hinchcliff. Auckland: Rep Print, 1976, pp. 72-75.

See Deut. 6:10ff. for the Israelite version of the cargo; uses S. Fuchs's "Messianic movements in primitive India," *Asian Folklore Studies* (Tokyo) 24, no. 1 (1965), fourteen characteristics, and K. O. L. Burridge (entry 35), as basis of an analysis of Israelite religion as new religious movement. Demonstrates an approach to biblical material other than those of literary criticism and theology.

44 Colpe, Carsten. "Krisenkulte und prophetische Bewungen, und Messianismus und Millenarismus." In *Handbuch der Religionsgeschichte,* edited by J. P. Asmussen, et al. Vol. 3. Göttingen: Vandenhoeck & Ruprecht, 1975, pp. 495-523, bib.
Includes area surveys in all continents, in a theoretical context.

45 Colpe, Carsten. "Das Phänomen der nachchristlichen Religionen in Mythos und Messianismus." In *Der Christliche Glaube unde die Religionen,* edited by C. H. Ratschow. Hauptvortrag des evangelischen Theologen-Kongresses. Berlin: Topelmann, 1967, pp. 42-76.

46 Colpe, Carsten. "Syncretism and secularization: Complementary and antithetical trends in new religious movements." *History of religions* 17, no. 2 (1977): 158-76.

47 Covar, Prospero R[eyes]. "A perspective on revitalization." *Philippine Sociological Review* 21, nos. 3-4 (1973): 283-87.
Rejecting "value-loaded explanations of cultural deprivation, social unrest, mazeway resynthesis," for a more positive view of movements as creative synthesis. Reviews the theories from R. Linton (entry 153) to A. F. C. Wallace (entry 261).

48 Crespy, Georges. "Sociologie et théologie des messianismes." *Études Théologiques et Religieuses* (Montpellier) 54, no. 2 (1976): 189-210.
A theological analysis of the introduction to *Dieux d'hommes,* by H. Desroche, et al. (entry 54).

49 Deltgen, Florian. "Was kann unter einer 'Bewegung' verstanden werden?" In *Aspekte der Entwicklungs-soziologie,* edited by R. König, et al. Köln and Opladen: Westdeutscher Verlag, 1969, pp. 410-29.

50 Desroche, Henri [Charles]. "Les messianismes et la catégorie de l'échec." *Cahiers Internationaux de Sociologie,* n.s. 35 (July-December 1963): 61-84.
An historical and theoretical survey.

51 Desroche, Henri [Charles]. *Les religions de contrabande: Essai sur les phénomènes religieux en époques critiques.* Collection Repères Sciences Humaines-Idéologies, 12. Paris: Mame, 1974, 230 pp.

Pp. 189-220, theoretical analysis of forms of religious innovation, in terms of common functions, structures, and meanings.

52 Desroche, Henri [Charles]. *Sociologie de l'espérance*. Archives de Sciences Sociales. Paris: Calman-Levy, 1973, 253 pp. English translation. *The sociology of hope*. London: Routledge & Kegan Paul, 1979, 209 pp.
   Pp. 94-101 (English translation, pp. 69-79), Messianism – Oceania, sub-Saharan Africa, North America, etc. A comprehensive theoretical study of millennialism, and of the relation of religious messianism to revolutionary ideologies.

53 Desroche, Henri [Charles]. "Syncrétisme et messianisme en Afrique noire." *Archives de Sociologie des Religions*, no. 16 [8] (July-December 1963): 105-8.

54 Desroche, Henri [Charles], et al. *Dieux d'hommes: Dictionnaire des messianismes et millénarismes de l'ère chrétienne*. Paris and The Hague: Mouton, 1969, 281 pp.
   Pp. 1-41, important theoretical discussion of origins, typologies, etc., of messianism.

55 Douglas, [Margaret] Mary. *Natural symbols: Explorations in cosmology*. London: Barrie & Rockliff, 1970, 177 pp.
   Pp. 12-14, Peyote among the Navajo, based on Aberle (entry 2); pp. 136-39, cargo cults as millennial; chap. 8, witchcraft, and pp. 121-22, on witch-cleansing movements as not truly millennial; passim, a typology of social structures and their relation to millennialism, especially pp. 103-6, 150-55.

56 Dozon, Jean-Pierre. "Les mouvements religieux de type messianique." In *Encyclopaedia universalis: Le grand atlas des religions*. Paris: Encyclopaedia Universalis France, 1988, pp. 142-43, illus.
   A sociological approach, relating messianism to social crises and especially to the colonial situation, and giving a very wide meaning to the term.

57 Du Toit, B[rian] M[urray]. *Beperkte Lidmaatskap: N'Anthropologies – Wetenschaplike Studie van Geheime organisasies*. Cape Town: John Malherk, 1965, 193 pp.
   Includes similarities between Afrikaner Broederbond and "revitalization movements" of "restricted membership" societies.

58 Eckert, Georg. "Das Propheentum und sein Einfluss auf Geschichte und Kulturentwicklung der Naturvölker." *Forschung und Fortschritte* 17, no. 6 (1941): 59-60.

59 Edmonson, Munro S. "Nativism, syncretism, and anthropological science." In *Nativism and syncretism*, by M. S. Edmonson, et al. Middle American Research Institute Publication 19. New Orleans: Tulane University, 1960, pp. 183-202.
   Focused on Central America but of general importance.

60 Eister, Allan W. "Culture crisis and new religious movements." In *Marginal religious movements in America today*, edited by I. I. Zaretsky and M. P. Leone. Princeton: Princeton University Press, 1974, pp. 612-27.
   Shorter, revised version of entry 61. Confined to cults in a Western milieu.

61 Eister, Allan W. "An outline of a structural theory of cults." *Journal for the Scientific Study of Religion* 14, no. 4 (1972): 319-33.

62 Eliade, Mircea. "Dimensions religieuses du renouvellement cosmique." *Eranos Jahrbuch* (Zurich) 28 (1959): 241-75.
   An evaluation of millennial movements in primitive societies; all have the general character of renewal, and should be classed with New Year festivals and initiations.

63 Elkin, A[dolphus] P[eter]. "The reaction of primitive races to the white man's culture: A study in culture contact." *Hibbert Journal* 35 (1936-37): 537-45.
   Discussed with special reference to Aborigines in eastern Australia, and revival of their own religion after disillusionment with whites' Christianity.

64 Emmet, Dorothy [Mary]. "Prophets and their societies." *Journal of the Royal Anthropological Institute* 86, no. 1 (1956): 13-23.
   Examines M. Weber's charismatic theory of the prophet type; describes the social role of prophets, and offers a typology.

65 Ertle, Brigitte. "Über Ursachen messianischer Bewegungen unter Natur-völkern." *Zeitschrift für Ethnologie* 97, no. 1 (1972): 61-73.
   Good survey of causal theories, with South American illustrative examples.

66 Espín[d]ola, Julio César. "On the classification of crisis cults." *Current Anthropology* 14, nos. 1-2 (1973): 168 (and brief reply by W. La Barre).

A clarification of his distinction between endogenous and exogenous (with reference to the Guarani), and W. La Barre's comments on Espindola's 1961 article; brief reply by La Barre.

67 Estruch, Juan. *La innovación religiosa: Ensayo téorico de sociología de la religión*. Barcelona: Ed. Ariel, 1972, 183 pp.

68 Fabian, Johannes. "The anthropology of religious movements: From explanation to interpretation." *Social Research* 46, no. 1 (1979): 4-35.

The guest editor's introduction to this special issue, critical of over-classification and over-conceptualization, and of stress on colonialism and acculturation as interpretive ideas.

69 Fabian, Johannes. "Genres in an emerging tradition." In *Changing perspectives in the scientific study of religion*, edited by A. Eister. New York and London: John Wiley & Sons, 1974, pp. 249-72.

The relation of hermeneutics to methodology in social anthropology, illustrated from Jamaa African materials.

70 Fabian, Johannes. "Ideology and content." *Sociologus*, n.s. 16, no. 1 (1965): 1-18.

The importance of cultural, historical, or meaning aspects of ideologies, and of theories of social change; as preparation for explaining "prophetic-messianic movements" (pp. 16-17).

71 Fabian, Johannes. "Language, history, and anthropology." *Journal for the Philosophy of the Social Sciences* 1 (1971): 19-47.

On methodology, with special reference to his study of the Jamaa movement in Zaïre.

72 Fabian, Johannes. "Taxonomy and ideology: On the boundaries of concept classification." In *Linguistics and anthropology: In honour of C. F. Voegelin*, edited by M. D. Kinkade, et al. Lissie, Netherlands: Peter de Ridder Press, 1976.

Jamaa in Africa used to illustrate his theory of cultural knowledge as ideology.

73 Fabian, Johannes, ed. "Beyond charisma: Religious movements as discourse." *Social Research* 46, no. 1 (1984): 1-203.

74 Fallaize, E. N. "Some examples of collective hysteria." *Discovery Magazine* (London), no. 38 [4] (1923): 49-50.
   Represents the explanation sometimes used in this period to explain new religious movements such as the "Vailala Madness" in Papua.

75 Farb, [Stan] Peter. "Ghost dance and cargo cult." *Horizon* (New York) 11, no. 2 (1969): 58-65.
   Using A. F. C. Wallace's revitalization theory to analyze millenarian movements–Ghost Dance, cargo cults, African Watch Tower, Handsome Lake, and Peyote religion.

76 Farb, [Stan] Peter. *Man's rise to civilization as shown by the Indians of North America from primeval times to the coming of the industrial state.* London: Secker & Warburg, 1969, 332 pp. London: Paladin, 1971, 332 pp.
   Chap. 15, Borrowed cultures.

77 Flanagan, Thomas. "Social credit in Alberta (A Canadian cargo cult?)." *Archives de Sociologie des Religions*, no. 34 [17, no. 2] (1972): 39-48.
   Discussed as a secular millennial movement within an advanced society, with patterns similar to those in primal societies.

78 Flasche, Rainer. "Vom Wandel und den Chancen der Religionen." *Zeitschrift für Religions-und Geistesgeschichte* 29, no. 2 (1977): 105-13.
   The dynamic and innovative nature of religion in the contemporary world is illustrated by the new movements (Umbanda, Kitawala, Black Muslims, Soka Gakkai) and by revivals within Christian, Hindu, and Islamic traditions.

79 Flusser, David. "Salvation, present and future." *Numen* (Leiden) 16, no. 2 (1969): 139-55.
   Chiliastic movements within Semitic religions, especially Black Muslims, Seventh Day Adventists, and Jehovah's Witnesses; inverse relation between strength of Christology and millennial emphasis; effects of nonfulfillment of hopes – as parallels to movements in primal societies.

80 Ford, J[osephine] Massingberd. "Was Montanism a Jewish-Christian heresy?" *Journal of Ecclesiastical History* 17, no. 2 (1966): 145-58.
   Useful as an early Christian millennial movement similar to modern ones, with prophecy, women leaders, holy city, etc.

81 Fourquin, Guy. *Les soulèvements populaires au Moyen Âge*. Paris: Presses Universitaires de France, 1972. English translation. *The anatomy of popular religion in the Middle Ages*. Europe in the Middle Ages, 9. Amsterdam: North-Holland Publishing Co., 1978, 181 pp., bib.

    Pt. 2, chap. 1, Messianic movements, including English peasants' revolt of 1381 and Taborite uprising (1420-ca. 1434).

82 Friesen, J. Stanley. "The significance of indigenous movements for the study of church growth." In *The challenge of church growth: A symposium*, edited by W. R. Shenk. Missionary Studies, 1. Elkhart, Ind.: Institute of Mennonite Studies, 1973, pp. 79-106.

    Tests "Church Growth" theory of D. M. McGavran against four examples of growth in independent African movements and concludes that the theory needs modification to embrace these.

83 Fuchs, Stephen. "Messianic movements." In *Anthropology for the missions*. Allahabad: St. Paul Society, 1979, 198 pp.

    Chap. 12 (pp. 158-69) presents fourteen characteristics of such movements, arising in the tensions between cultures in very different stages of development. By an S. V. D. missionary.

84 Gensichen, Hans-Werner. "Der Syncretismus als Frage an die Christenheit heute." *Evangelische Missions Zeitschrift*, n.s. 23, no. 2 (1966): 58-69.

    Pp. 61ff., discusses African separatist groups and the "new religions" of Japan.

85 Gerlach, Luther P., and Hine, Virginia H. *People, power, change: Movements of social transformation*. Indianapolis: Bobbs-Merrill Co., 1970, 257 pp., bib.

    Chaps. 1-2 et passim, the Pentecostal and Black Power movements, in terms of organization, recruitment, commitment, ideology, opposition, and new perspectives.

86 Goodman, Felicitas D. "Belief systems, millenary expectations and behaviour." In *Symbols and society: Essays on belief systems in action*, edited by C. E. Hill. Proceedings of the Southern Anthropological Society, 9. Athens: University of Georgia Press, 1975, pp. 130-38.

87 Goody, Jack. "Religion, social change, and the sociology of conversion." In *Changing social structure in Ghana*, edited by J. Goody. London: International African Institute, 1975, pp. 91-106.

Examples of religious scepticism and successions of innovative cults, demonstrating the dynamic character of religion in conservative, relatively isolated African societies; hence new movements are not dependent on culture contact or the colonial situation. His examples may lie in the borderline between developments within primal religions and what we call neo-primal movements.

88 Grotanelli, Christiano. "Archaic forms of rebellion and their religious background." In *Religion, rebellion, and revolution*, edited by B. Lincoln. London: Macmillan, 1985, pp. 15-45.

In agricultural, preindustrial societies, lacking secular ideologies, all revolt was necessarily religious, and since linear views of time were absent, was also seeking restoration of some previous better era. Focuses on Mediterranean and European areas, with some other data.

89 Guariglia, Guglielmo. "Gli aspetti etno-sociologici della fame nel mondo." In *Il problema della fame nel mondo*. Milan: Vita e Pensiero, 1964, 248 pp.

Pp. 57-61, prophetic-salvation movements, in Africa as elsewhere, as reactions to economic distress.

90 Guariglia, Guglielmo. "Les grandes caractéristiques des sectes modernes (mouvements prophético-salvifiques) dans les terres des missions." In *Devant les sectes non-chrétiennes*, by Muséum Lessianum. Louvain: Desclée de Brouwer, 1962, pp. 13-27.

91 Guariglia, Guglielmo. "Movimenti profetico-salvifici a livello etnologico: Appunt storico culturali ad un' interpretazzione storicistica." *Studi e Materiali per la Storia della Religioni* (Rome) 32, no. 2 (1961): 248-84.

A critique of *Religions of the oppressed*, by V. Lanternari (London: MacGibbon & Kee, 1963).

92 Guariglia, Guglielmo. "Pour une nouvelle typologie des 'mouvements prophétiques' au niveau ethnologique." In *Actes du VIe Congrès International des Sciences Anthropologiques et Ethnologiques*. Vol. 2, pt. 2. Paris: Musée de l'Homme, 1964, pp. 393-98.

93 Guariglia, Guglielmo. "Prophetismus und Heilserwartungs-Bewegungen bei den Niedrigen Kulturen." *Numen* (Leiden) 5, no. 3 (1958): 180-98.

A classification into seven classes; p. 197, eight "theses" applicable to such movements.

94 Gusfield, Joseph R. "The study of social movements." In *International encyclopedia of the social sciences*. Vol. 14. New York: Collier-Macmillan, 1968, pp. 445-52.

95 Hadaway, Christopher Kirk. "Life satisfaction and religion: A reanalysis." *Social Forces* 57, no. 2 (1978): 636-43.
  Does religion compensate for deprivations, or help toward greater happiness? Recent research supports the latter – religion is not something people seek out because of their misery; correlation between faith and sense of well-being.

96 Harrison, Michael I. "The maintenance of enthusiasm: Involvement in a new religious movement." *Social Analysis* (De Kalb, Ill.) 36, no. 2 (1975): 150-60, bib.
  How movements focus and sustain the participants' experiences of inspiration; based on a study of pentecostalism among Catholics in the U.S.

97 Hassan, Riffat. "Messianism and Islam." *Journal of Ecumenical Studies* 22, no. 2 (1985): 261-91.
  While apparently incompatible with Quranic teaching, messianism is seen as essential by Shi'a Islam and is widespread in the Islamic world; the Shi'a theory of the imamate and the "Mahdi"; relevance to dialogue between the Semitic religions.

98 Heberle, Rudolf. *Social movements: An introduction to political sociology*. New York: Appleton-Century, 1951, 478 pp.
  Includes comprehensive bibliography of earlier works. Pp. 6-11, the concept of social movement; pp. 350-54, religious models for political orders.

99 Herskovits, Melville J[ean]. "Some comments on the study of cultural contact." *American Anthropologist* 43, no. 1 (1941): 1-10.
  An introduction to the five papers on the subject in this issue, including relation of acculturation to diffusion and cultural borrowing.

100 Herskovits, Melville J[ean]; Linton, Ralph; and Redfield, Robert. "A memorandum on the study of acculturation." *Man*, article 162, 35, (October 1935): 145-48.
  An early program for this study outlining types and situations of contact, the processes and psychological mechanisms involved, and the various types of response or result.

101 Hesselgrave, David J. "What causes new religious movements to grow?" In *Dynamic religious movements*, edited by D. J. Hesselgrave. Grand Rapids: Baker Book House, 1978, pp. 297-326.

A "church growth" study, seeking to learn from a variety of new religious movements.

102 Hill, Frances R. "Nationalist millenarians and millenarian nationalists." *American Behavioral Scientist* 16, no. 2 (1972): 269-88.

Millenarianism and nationalism are neither sequentially related nor mutually exclusive, although often opposed; examples from Taiping, Cao Dai, and Hoa Hao (Vietnam), Lenshina's Lumpa Church (Zambia), Soka Gakkai (Japan), and Iglesia ni Cristo (Philippines).

103 Hine, Virginia H. "The deprivation and disorganization theories of social movements." In *Religious movements in contemporary America*, edited by I. I. Zaretksy and M. P. Leone. Princeton: Princeton University Press, 1974, pp. 646-61.

Deprivation and disorganization, as tested in the spread of pentecostalism, prove to be facilitating rather than causal factors.

104 Hoeckman, Remi. "Overview of Vatican document: The pastoral challenge of new religious movements." *Origins: NO Documentary Service* 17, no. 9 (1987): 136-43.

A summary and comment (together with summary of H. W. Turner's address at the WCC/LWF Consultation on NRMs, September 1986, in the margins of pp. 136-39) and comments on the relation between the Vatican and the WCC/LWF reports.

105 Hoeckman, Remi. "The Roman Catholic Church, the World Council of Churches, and the new religious movements." *Angelicum* (Rome, Pontifical University of St. Thomas Aquinas) 29, no. 1 (1987): 562-82.

Paper presented at the Ecumenical Conference on NRMs, Washington, D.C., 27 March 1987. Also reports Amsterdam Consultation, September 1986.

106 Hollenweger, Walter J. "Roots and fruits of the charismatic renewal in the third world: Implications for mission." *Theological Renewal*, no. 14 (February 1980), pp. 11-28. Also in *Occasional Bulletin of Missionary Research* 4, no. 2 (1980): 68-75 (with comment by J. A. Forbes, Jr., pp. 75-76).

Pp. 69-70, Brazilian messianism – a movement since the 1950s that joined the Assemblies of God; p. 70, Prophet Do's healing movement at Etodome, Ghana; pp. 72-73, glossolalia.

107 Hopper, Rex D. "The revolutionary process: A frame of reference for the study of revolutionary movements. *Social Forces* 28, no. 3 (1950): 270-79.

An analysis of stages in the process, which closely resembles those of A. F. C. Wallace for revitalization movements.

108 Horton, Robin. "Judaeo-Christian spectacles: Boon or bane to the study of African religions?" *Cahiers d'Études Africaines*, no. 96 [24, no. 4] (1984): 391-436.

Discussed with reference to Africa but applicable to new religious movements in all areas; supports the "bane" view.

109 Hultkrantz, Åke, ed. *International dictionary of regional European ethnology*. Vol. 1, *General ethnological concepts*. Copenhagen: Rosenkilde & Bagger, 1961, 281 pp.

See articles on Acculturation, Assimilation, Culture, Folk, Folk Culture, Transculturation.

110 Isenberg, Sheldon R. "Millenarism in Greco-Roman Palestine." *Religion: Journal of Religion and Religions* 4 (Spring 1974): 26-46.

Applies social science models as used by K. O. L. Burridge, P. M. Worsley, and the writers in S. L. Thrupp's symposium (entry 228) to Palestinian movements in antiquity.

111 Jeffreys, M. D. W. "Role of the native prophet in a vanishing culture." *Forum* (Johannesburg) 5, no. 6 (1956): 17-18.

Nativistic movements, revivalist and passive types, illustrated from African prophetesses Mai Chaza and Alice Lenshina.

112 Jones, A. H. M. "Were ancient heresies national or social movements in disguise?" *Journal of Theological Studies*, n.s. 10, no. 2 (1959): 280-297.

Denies that the "sects" were determined by sociopolitical factors, rather than religious (i.e., rejects reductionist interpretations).

113 Jones, Rufus M[atthew]. *The church's debt to heretics*. London: James Clark & Co., [1925], 256 pp.

Chap. 1 (pp. 11-28), "Who are the heretics?"; chap. 2 (pp. 28-60), "The Gnostic complex"; chap. 6 (pp. 131-61), "Heresies of the Spirit" (Montanism, etc.).

114 Jules-Rosette, Bennetta. "The veil of objectivity: Prophecy, divination, and social inquiry." *American Anthropologist* 80, no. 3 (1978): 549-70, photo of author.

Pp. 558-62, on prophecy in the Apostles of John Maranke; compared with traditional divination as alternative systems of knowledge and then with scientific forms of discovery; a certain rapprochement between these and the two folk forms is examined.

115 Justinger, Judith Marie. "Reaction to change: A holocultural test of some theories of religious movements." Ph.D. dissertation (cultural anthropology), State University of New York (Buffalo), 1978, 296 pp.

Examines fifteen hypotheses cross-culturally; concentrates on millennial movements; finds no support for theories based on stress, relative deprivation, oppression, natural disasters, collapse of traditional values or authorities.

116 Kaufman, Robert. "Le millénarisme." In *Religions de salut*, edited by A. Abel, et al. Brussels: Institut de Sociologie Solvay, 1962, pp. 81-98.

Pp. 94-96, Jehovah's Witnesses in Central Africa; otherwise on Jehovah's Witnesses in general, and theory of millenarism.

117 Kehoe, Alice B[eck]. "Revitalization movements and the hope of peace." *Zygon* 21, no. 4 (1986): 491-500.

118 Keskitalo, Alf Isak. *Newsletter, Nordic Institute of Folklore* (Turku) 2, no. 4 (1974) : 12-13.

On the "assymetric" nature of research in interethnic relationships, where the majority group tends to have a suppressive or distortive effect on the minority, which does not meet on equal terms.

119 Köbben, A[ndré] J. F. "Profetische bewegingen als uiting van sociaal protest." *Sociologisch Jaarboek* 13 (1959): 5-72. English translation. "Prophetic movements as an expression of social protest." *International Archives of Ethnography* (Amsterdam) 14, no. 1 (1960): 117-64, bib. Revised and updated in *Van primitieven tot wereldburgers*. Assen: Van Gorcum & Co. n.v., 1964, chapt. 6 (pp. 94-154). Reprint. 1974, with addendum updating and correcting earlier ed. and 1959 article.

Discusses typology in terms of variations of content and form; criticism of R. Linton's and A. F. C. Wallace's classifications; extensive bibliography.

120 Koppers, Wilhelm. "Prophetism and messianic beliefs as a problem of ethnology and world history." In *Proceedings of XIth International*

Congress for the History of Religions, Tokyo and Kyoto, 1958. Tokyo: Maruzen, 1960, pp. 39-50. German translation. *"Prophetismus und Messianismus als völkerkundliches und universalgeschichtliches Problem." Saeculum* (Freiburg) 10, no. 1 (1959): 38-47.

Includes brief survey of each culture area; based on *Prophetismus und Heilserwartungs-Bewegungen* . . . , by G. Guariglia (entry 312), with some general theory.

121 Kopytoff, Igor. "Classifications of religious movements: Analytical and synthetic." In *Symposium on new approaches to the study of religion: Proceedings of the American Ethnological Society 1964*, Seattle: American Ethnological Society 1964, pp. 77-90.

An analytical profile approach, illustrated by the Suku Holy Water movement, Zaïre.

122 Kraeling, Carl H. "Method in the study of religious syncretism." *Journal of Bible and Religion* 9 (1941): 23-34, 66.

123 Kuby, David Joseph. "Elitism and holiness in Swazi conversion." Ph.D. dissertation (anthropology), University of California (Los Angeles), 1979, 266 pp.

Includes the "Afro-Christian (Zionist)" as one end of the spectrum of response to Christianity, with "Evangelical absolutism" at the other end, and Catholicism and Pentecostalism in between.

124 La Barre, Weston. *The Ghost Dance: The origins of religions*. Garden City, N.Y.: Doubleday & Co., 1970, 677 pp.

Chap. 9 (pp. 277-98), culture and acculturation.

125 La Barre, Weston. "Materials for a history of studies of crisis cults: A bibliographic essay." *Current Anthropology* 12, no. 1 (1971): 3-44.

"World survey of 'crisis cults' and theories about their causes," together with fifteen comments by scholars in various disciplines. An important survey.

126 Lanternari, Vittorio. "L'acculturazione dei popoli ex-coloniali." *Sapere* (Milan), Aprile 1964, pp. 201-7.

127 Lanternari, Vittorio. "Ancora sui movimenti profetici: Una replica necessaria." *Studi e Materiali di Storia delle Religioni* 33, no. 1 (1962): 108-28.

128 Lanternari, Vittorio. "A CA book review: The religions of the oppressed: A study of modern messianic cults." *Current Anthropology* 6, no. 4 (1965): 447-65.
An important discussion with other scholars.

129 Lanternari, Vittorio. "Désintégration culturelle et processus d'acculturation." *Cahiers Internationaux de Sociologie* 41 (July-December 1966): 117-32.

130 Lanternari, Vittorio. "Dinamica culturale e nuove religioni dei popoli arretrati." *Atti, I Congresso di Scienze Antropologiche, Etnologiche e di Folklore (Torino 1961)*. Turin: 1964, pp. 289-93.

131 Lanternari, Vittorio. "Discorso sul messianismo." *Nuovi Argomenti* (Rome) 46 (1960):13-36. English translation. "Messianism: Its historical origin and morphology." *History of Religions* 2, no. 1 (1962): 52-72.
A major survey, with frequent reference to messianic aspects of new religious movements and the relation to traditional or primal culture and mythology.

132 Lanternari, Vittorio. "Explanation of the new cults among primitive peoples and the problem of conciliation between two different approaches." *Proceedings of the XIth International Congress of the International Association for the History of Religions . . . 1965*. Vol. 3. Leiden: E. J. Brill, 1968, pp. 48-56.
The anthropological and historical methods.

133 Lanternari, Vittorio. "Messia." *Enciclopedia IX: Mente operazioni*. Turin: Einaudi, 1980, pp. 118-40.
Section 3 (pp. 132-39), movements in the third world.

134 Lanternari, Vittorio. "Millennio." *Enciclopedia IX: Mente operazioni*. Turin: Einaudi, 1980, pp. 312-31.
Section 92 (pp. 316-21), Melanesian millennial movements; Section 93 (pp. 321-27), millennial movements in other areas— North America, Garvey and Rastafarians, Black Muslims, South America, with brief references to Kitawala (Africa) and Taiping (China).

135 Lanternari, Vittorio. "I movimenti millenaristi e il comparativismo storico-religioso." *Revista Storica Italiana* (Naples) 76, no. 3 (1964): 760-73.

Review article on *Millennial dreams in action*, edited by S. L. Thrupp (entry 228).

136 Lanternari, Vittorio. "Movimenti profetico-salvifici a livello etnologico." *Studia e Materiali di Storia della Religioni* 32, no. 2 (1961): 284-308.
Review article on "Prophetismus und Heilserwartungs-Bewegungen . . . ," by G. Guariglia (entry 93).

137 Lanternari, Vittorio. "Nouveaux syncrétismes religieux." *Actes du Congrès International des Sciences Anthropologiques et Ethnographiques, Paris 1960.* Paris: 1964, pp. 647-48.

138 Lanternari, Vittorio. "Reconsiderando i movimenti social-religiosi nel quandro dei processi di acculturazione." *Religioni e Civilta* 1 (1972): 31-68. English translation. "Nativistic and socio-religious movements: A reconsideration." *Comparative Studies in Society and History* 16, no. 4 (1974): 483-503.

139 Lanternari, Vittorio. "Religione popolare e contestazione: Riflessioni storico-sociali sul dissenso religioso." *Testimonianze* (Florence), no. 118 [12] (October 1969), pp. 708-29.

140 Lanternari, Vittorio. [The science of religions and the new religious movements, problems of methodology]. *Euhemer – Prezeglad Religionznawczy* 24, no. 2 (1980): 23-30, English summary.
In Polish. On the importance of considering the social and economic factors conditioning these movements.

141 Lanternari, Vittorio. "Sonzo/visione." *Enciclopedia.* Vol. 13. Turin: Einaudi, 1981, pp. 94-126.
Dreams and visions.

142 Lanternari, Vittorio. "Syncrétismes, messianismes, néo-trditionalismes: Postface à une étude des mouvements religieux de l'Afrique Noire." *Archives de Sociologie des Religions,* no. 21 [11, no. 1] (1966): 101-10.

143 Laplantine, François. "Les trois voix de l'imaginaire: Le messianisme, la possession, et l'utopie." *Étude Psychiatrique* (Paris), 1974, pp. 112-48.

144 Laughlin, Charles D., Jr., and d'Aquili, Eugene G. "Ritual and stress." In *The spectrum of ritual,* edited by E. G. d'Aquili, et al. New York: Columbia University Press, 1979, pp. 280-317.
Pp. 307-15, revitalization processes.

145 Leach, Edmund. "Melchisedech and the emperor: Icons of subversion and orthodoxy." *Proceedings of the Royal Anthropological Institute of Great Britain*, 1972, pp. 5-14, illus.
       Ambiguities in the early Christian iconography of Melchizedek as either a conservative or a revolutionary figure, i.e., as representing orthodoxy upholding the established political order, or heresy (Arianism) seeking justification for rebellion and arising from the bottom of society in the form of new millenarian, etc., cults. Cf. A. H. M. Jones (entry 112).

146 Leavitt, John. "Towards a general theory of visionary experience." *Anthropology Tomorrow* 12, no. 1 (1979): 64-88, bib.
       On dreams and visions: neglected by anthropology; value of a Freudian approach for analysis of particular cases.

147 Lebra, Takie Sugiyama. "Millenarian movements and resocialization." *American Behavioral Scientist* 16, no. 2 (1972): 195-217.

148 Lewis, I[oan] M[yrddin]. *Ecstatic religion: An anthropological study of spirit possession and shamanism*. Harmondsworth: Penguin Books, 1971, 221 pp., illus.
       References to many movements – Islamic, in Haïti, cargo cults, in Brazil, in Africa, passim.

149 Lewis, I[oan] M[yrddin]. *Religion in context: Cults and charisma*. Cambridge: Cambridge University Press, 1986, 139 pp.

150 Lewis, I[oan] M[yrddin]. "Spirit possession and deprivation cults." Malinowski Memorial Lecture, 1966. *Man*, n.s. 1, no. 3 (1966): 307-29.
       P. 323, brief reference to new prophet movements stressing notions of "rewards in heaven" and sustaining the moral order; final assimilation of such movements into ordinary social life.

151 Lewy, Guenter. *Religion and revolution*. New York: Oxford University Press, 1964, 674 pp.
       Chap. 26 (pp. 583-90, 674), Conclusion – on conservative and radical dimensions of religion.

152 Lex, Barbara W. "Physiological aspects of ritual trance." *Journal of Altered States of Consciousness* 2 (1975): 109-22.

153 Linton, Ralph. "Nativistic movements." *American Anthropologist* 45, no. 2 (1943): 230-40. German translation in *Religionsethnologie*, edited by C. A. Schmitz. Frankfurt, 1964, pp. 390-403.

An influential discussion with an anthropological typology in terms of revivalist or perpetuative, and magical or rational features.

154 Ljungdahl, Axel. *Profetrörelser, deras orsaker, innebörd och föratsattninger.* Stockholm: Almqvist & Wiksell, 1969, 278 pp., English summary (pp. 245-51).

Prophet movements, their causes, import and the conditions under which they arise.

155 Lowie, Robert H. "Primitive messianism and an ethnological problem." *Diogenes* 19 (Fall 1957): 62-72.

Diffusion or independent evolution?

156 Luzbetak, Louis J. *The church and cultures: An applied anthropology for the religious worker.* Techny, Ill.: Divine Word Publications, 1963, 417 pp., illus. Pp. 239-48 reprinted in *Practical Anthropology* 13, no. 3 (1966): 115-21, 128.

Pp. 239-48, "Christo-paganism"–on syncretisms in various cultures: Caribbean, Central and North America (Peyote cult); the causes and controls, from a Christian viewpoint.

157 McAyley, J. "We are men–what are you?" *Quadrant* (Sydney), no. 15 (1960), pp. 73-79.

On myths of racial superiority or, alternatively, of moral relativism.

158 Maier, Norman R. F. "The role of frustration in social movements." *Psychological Review* 49 (1942): 586-99.

No reference to religious movements, but shows the place of frustration in originating and uniting movements, and the apparently irrational behavior resulting, without relation to positive goals.

159 Mair, Lucy P[hilip]. "The study of culture contact as a practical problem." *Africa* 7 (1938): 415-22.

160 Masson, Joseph. "Le dialogue avec les syncrétistes." *Bulletin: Secretariatus Pro Non-Christianis*, no. 30 [10, no. 2] (1975): 311-14.

161 Masson, Joseph. "Liminaire"; "Conclusions." In *Devant les sectes non-chrétiennes*, by Muséum Lessianum. Louvain: Desclée de Brouwer, 1962, pp. 7-11, 292-98.

By the Jesuit editor of the report of the 31st Missiology Seminar at Louvain, 1961.

162 Maurier, H. "The religious movements [RMs]." *Petit Echo* (Rome), nos. 9-10 (1986): 559-72, 625-42; no. 3 (1987): 167-79.

Pt. 1: "Their nature and how they work"; Pt. 2: "The contents and typology of the RMs"; Pt. 3: "Discernments." A White Father on "Sects" of all kinds, as commonly defined comprehensively by Roman Catholics to include Jehovah's Witnesses, Unification Church, and African independent churches.

163 Mbon, Friday. "A new typology for Africa's new religious movements." *Update* (Aarhus) 8, nos. 3-4 (1984): 35-42.

Offers the term "protectionist" as a general description; really a new terminology rather than a typology, as no range of forms is described.

164 Megged, Nahum. "A social and religious revolution among the Mayan tribes as suggested by mythology." In *Gilgul*, edited by S. Shaked, et al. Leiden: E. J. Brill, 1987, pp. 138-68.

Religious change in the course of Mayan history; Central America, including the factors of conquest by other cultures, intracultural class relations, and popular or folk level religious conservation.

165 Melton, J[ohn] Gordon, with Geisendorfer, James V. *A dictionary of religious bodies in the United States compiled from the files of the Institute for the Study of American Religion.* New York: Garland Publishing, 1977, 305 pp.

Chap. 1 (pp. 1-24), primary religious groups; chap. 2 (pp. 25-74), classification of American religious bodies. Notes, pp. 280-85.

166 Merton, Robert King. *Social theories and social structure.* Glencoe: Free Press, 1949. Rev. and enl. ed. 1957, 645 pp.

Chaps. 4-5 (pp. 131-94), on typology of individual adaptations: conformity, innovation, ritualism, retreatism, and rebellion.

167 Miller, D. E. "Sectarianism and secularization: The work of Bryan Wilson." *Religious Studies Review* 5, no. 3 (1979): 161-74.

A detailed analysis with complete bibliography; "millennialism" and non-Western forms are included.

168 Montgomery. Robert L. "Domination versus an alternative route of change." *Bulletin: Christian Institute for Ethnic Studies in Asia* 3, nos. 3-4 (1969): 13-18.

Orthodox Western Christianity–with inbuilt appeal to oppressed minorities–as alternative focus for acculturation in primal societies dominated by a non-Western culture; compare new religious movements as alternative to domination by Western Christian forms.

169 Moreau, A. Scott. "An introduction to cults." *East Africa Journal of Evangelical Theology* 6, no. 2 (1987): 3-12.

170 Mühlmann, Wilhelm E[mil]. "Chiliasmus, Nativismus, Nationalismus." In *Soziologie und Moderne Gesellschaft*, edited by A. Busch. Stuttgart: Enke, 1959, pp. 223-42.

171 Mühlmann, Wilhelm E[mil], ed.. *Chiliasmus und Nativismus: Studien zur Psychologie, Sociologie, und historischen Kasuistik der Umsturzbewegungen*. Berlin: D. Reimer, 1961. Reprint. 1964, 472 pp. French translation. *Messianismes révolutionnaires du tiers monde*. Paris: Gallimard, 1968, 389 pp. (Some case studies in the German original not included.)

Pt. 1, case studies; pt. 2, comparative analysis. Includes modern millennial phenomena in Africa, with roots both in frustrations consequent on culture contact and in the "mutation" from mythic to historical thought resulting from the impact of the biblical viewpoint.

172 Mühlmann, Wilhelm E[mil], ed. *Rassen-Ethnien-Kulturen: Moderne Ethnologie*. Soziologische Texte, 24. Neuwied and Berlin: Hermann Luchterhand, 1964, 389 pp.

Pp. 323-39, Chiliasmus, Nativismus, and Nationalismus–similar to entry 171.

173 Nicholas, Ralph W. "Social and political movements." *Annual Review of Anthropology* 2 (1973): 63-84.

A theoretical discussion of terms such as "movement" (and in relation to time and space), "deprivation" and the etiology of movements, "culture," "ideology," "charismatic authority"–with illustrations drawn from Paliau, Handsome Lake, Jamaa, east and west Bengali and other movements.

174 Nida, Eugene A. "New religions for old: A study of culture change." *Practical Anthropology* 18, no. 6 (1971): 241-53. Also in *Solidarity* (Philippines) 6, no. 3 (1971): 7-20 and in *Church and culture change in Africa*. Lux Mundi, 3. Pretoria: N. G. Kerk-Boekhandel, 1971, pp. 9-44, bib.

On religious change, with insights from various models – economic and linguistic.

175 Nussbaum, Stan. "New religious movements: (1) The neglected component of missionary preparation. (2) Partnership and dialogue. (3) Contextualization and church growth. (4) Missiological surprises." *Mission Focus* (Elkhart, Ind., Mennonite Board of Missions) 16, no. 2 (1988): 29-32; no. 3 (1988): 58-61; 17, no. 1 (1989): 11-14; no. 2 (1989). Reprinted as a pamphlet, *New Religious Movements*. Elkhart, Ind.: Mission Focus Publications, 1989, 36 pp.

A four-part series on the missiological implications of these new religious movements, by the director of the Centre for New Religious Movements, Selly Oak Colleges, Birmingham. Part 4 includes the "New Age" range of movements.

176 Obeyesekere, Gananath. "Social change and the deities: Rise of the Kataragama cult in modern Sri Lanka." *Man*, n.s. 12, nos. 3-4 (1977): 377-96.

On the increase in "spirit cults" simultaneously with modernizing change, and with a large patronage among the elites or the most modernized, contrary to expectations. Primal religions are not involved, but the process described occurs widely.

177 Oosterwal, Gottfried. *Modern messianic movements as a theological and missionary challenge*. Elkhart, Ind.: Institute of Mennonite Studies, 1973, 55 pp.

A good introduction to theoretical and theological aspects, by a Seventh Day Adventist scholar.

178 Peel, J[ohn] D[avid] Y[eadon]. "Understanding alien belief systems." *British Journal of Sociology* 20, no. 1 (1961): 69-84.

With illustrations from Nigerian *aladura* movements, and various theories of African and similar movements.

179 Piddington, Ralph [O'Reilly]. "Psychological aspects of culture contact." *Oceania* (Sydney) 3, no. 3 (1933): 312-24.

A useful discussion.

180 Pillay, Gerald J. "The use of functional-type theories in the study of independent Christian movements: A critique." *Neue Zeitschrift für Missionswissenschaft* 2 (1968): 124-35.

181 Posern-Zielínski, Aleksander. "Antropologiczna interpretacja ruchow spolenczno-religijnych trzeciego swiata: Oceny i propozycje [An anthropological interpretation of socio-religious movements in the third world: Evaluation and comments]. *Lud* (Warsaw) 55 (1971): 83-113.
    Problems of research into socio-religious movements in the third world.

182 Poulat, Emile, et al. "Contrôle et production des mouvements religieux." *Archives de Sciences Sociales des Religions*, no. 50 [25, no. 1] (1980): 129-41, English summary.
    Summaries of eight papers at a workshop at Versailles, 1979.

183 Pye, E. Michael. "The transplantation of religions." *Numen* 16, no. 3 (1969): 234-39.
    A phenomenology of the dynamics, as well as of the statics of religion; with Van der Leeuw, identifies syncretism, transposition, mission (renamed transplantation), revival, and reformation. Transplantation is analyzed into three aspects, with five differentia, thus providing eight questions to be raised.

184 Queiroz, Maria Isaura Pereira de. "Aspectos gerais do messianismo." *Revista da Antropologia* (São Paulo) 8, no. 1 (1960): 63-76.
    A general account of messianism, prophets, etc.

185 Queiroz, Maria Isaura Pereira de. "Book review: *The religions of the oppressed* by Vittorio Lanternari." *Current Anthropology* 6, no. 4 (1965): 452-54.
    A criticism of Lanternari's exogenous/endogenous classification of causes and movements, of the failure to identify messianism with this-worldly concerns, and of the inapplicability of his interpretations to Brazilian peasant messianisms.

186 Queiroz, Maria Isaura Pereira de. "Maurice Leenhart [*sic* for Leenhardt] ou les démarches de la pensée ethnologique." *Archives Internationales de Sociologie de la Coopération et du Développement*, no. 28 (July-December 1970), pp. 3-23.

187 Queiroz, Maria Isaura Pereira de. "Messianic myths and movements." *Diogenes* (Paris), no. 90 (Spring 1975), pp. 78-79. French ed., pp. 90-114.

Brazilian, etc., illustrations for a theory of the origins of messianic movements in oppression or anomie; a typology of crises, from materials in all world areas, and mainly nineteenth century; the importance of the messiah figure.

188 Queiroz, Maria Isaura Pereira de. "Millénarismes et messianismes." *Annales: Économies, Sociétés, Civilisations* (Paris) 19, no. 2 (1964): 330-44.

A theoretical survey from a sociological viewpoint, reviewing the contributions of W. D. Wallis, G. Guariglia, V. Lanternari, N. Cohn, E. Hobsbawm, and the symposium of S. L. Thrupp (entry 228).

189 Queiroz, Maria Isaura Pereira de. "On materials for a history of studies of crisis cults." *Current Anthropology* 12, no. 3 (1971): 387-90.

A detailed critique of W. La Barre's bibliographic essay (entry 125) – its bibliographic omissions, ethnographic inaccuracies, and conceptual inadequacy; her own restatement of the problem in terms of messianic cults and their functions in traditional societies.

190 Queiroz, Maria Isaura Pereira de. *Réforme et révolution dans les sociétés traditionelles: Histoire et ethnologie des mouvements messianiques*. Paris: Éditions Anthropos, 1968, 394 pp., illus., bib. Spanish translation. *Historia y etnologia de los movimentos messiánicos: Reforma y revolución en las sociedades tradicionales*. Mexico City: Siglo XXI Editores, 1969, 355 pp. German translation. *Reform und Revolution in traditionalen Gesellschaften*. Geissen: A. Achenbach, 1974, 320 pp.

Surveys messianic movements in North America, Africa, Oceania, and especially South America; pp. 245-375, theoretical section on the social dynamics of messianism. By a senior Brazilian scholar.

191 Ranger, T[erence] O[sborn]. "*Magic and the millennium*." *African Religious Research* (Los Angeles, African Study Center) 3, no. 2 (1973): 27-33.

A historian's review of *Magic and the millennium* by B. R. Wilson (entry 277); highly critical of his theory and methodology as ethnocentric, identifying magic and religion, and overworking the basic category of "thaumaturgy" to the point of uselessness.

192 Reich, Wendy. "The uses of folklore in revitalization movements."
Folklore 82 (1971): 233-44.

On the functions of folklore in periods of rapid social changes:
new functions of helping society to adjust – examples from Tangu cargo
cults, Peyote cult, Sikhism, and the Sepoy rebellion in India.

193 Robertson, Roland. *The sociological interpretation of religion.* Oxford:
Basil Blackwell, 1970, 255 pp.

Pp. 163-67, millennial movements, as usually without long-term
influence.

194 Rosen, George. "Social change and psychopathology in the emotional
climate of millennial movements." In *Millenial change: Movements of
total transformation. American Behavioral Scientist* 16, no. 2 (1972):
153-67.

Millennialisms as the natural outcome of social change rather
than as exotic, fringe movements; illustrated mainly from Europe and
ancient near East.

195 Roszak, Theodore. *Unfinished animal: The Aquarian frontier and the
evolution of consciousness.* New York: Harper & Row, 1975, 271 pp.
Reprint. London: Faber, 1976.

A mutation in human consciousness is beginning and is seen in
the plethora of off-center cultural movements.

196 Russo, Antonio. "Profetismo e movimenti salvifico-messianici." *Revista
di Etnografica* (Naples) 14 (1960): 78-85.

Based largely on G. Guariglia, V. Lanternari, and W. E.
Mühlmann.

197 Ryan, Bryce. "Die Bedeutung der Revitalizationbewegegungen für den
Sozialen Wandel in den Entwicklungsländern." In *Aspekte der
Entwicklungssoziologie*, edited by R. König. Kölner Zeitschrift für
Soziologie und Sozialpsychologie, Sonderheft 13. Cologne and Opalen:
Westdeutscher Verlag, 1969, pp. 37-65.

198 Ryan, Michael Timothy. "New worlds of pagan religion in the
seventeenth century." Ph.D. dissertation (modern history), New York
University, 1974, vi + 519 pp., bib.

European attempts to come to terms with newly-discovered
paganism, by assimilation to the classical pagan or Judeo-Christian
traditions – hence see especially pp. 317-34, "Savage Jews or Chosen
Indians?" Useful background for "Hebraist" movements, especially

among Maori and African peoples regarding themselves as descended from the Jews. Extensive bibliography.

199 Sanford, Margaret. "Revitalization movements as indicators of completed acculturation." *Comparative Studies in Society and History* 16, no. 4 (1974): 504-18.
Black Caribs as case study. Return to older practices is not necessarily regressive or nativistic.

200 Sawatsky, Rod. "New religious movements: What was Turner sent to teach us?" *Mennonite Reporter* (Waterloo, Ontario) 11, no. 23 (1981): Section A, p. 5.
Reflections by the academic dean of Conrad Grebel College on Mennonite involvement both in Africa and in North America among Indians and also in the new "cults."

201 Schapera, I. "Field methods in the study of modern culture contacts." *Africa* 8 (1935): 315-28, French summary (pp. 327-28).
Based on experience of the Kxatla in Botswana, but of general application.

202 Schlosser, Katesa. "Der Prophetismus in niederen Kulturen." *Zeitschrift für Ethnologie* (Berlin) 75 (1950): 60-72.

203 Schreike, B. "Native society in the transformation period." In *The effect of Western influence on native civilization in the Malay archipelago*, edited by B. Schreike. Batavia: G. Kolff & Co., 1929, pp. 237-47.

204 Schreiter, Robert J. "Syncretism and dual religious systems." In *Constructing local theologies*. Maryknoll, N.Y.: Orbis Books, 1985, pp. 144-58, 169-70.

205 Schwarz, Hillel. "The end of the beginning: Millenarian studies 1969-1975." *Religious Studies Review* 2, no. 3 (1976): 1-15.
Millenarianism in all religions, including new movements in primal societies; of theoretical value.

206 Segal, Robert A. "Eliade's theory of millenarianism." *Religious Studies* 14, no. 2 (1978): 159-73.
On the question of return of the past or entry into a new future: seen as a normal phenomenon, continuous with ordinary life.

207 Seumois, André. *Théologie missionaire IV: Église missionaire et facteurs socio-culturels*. Rome: Casa Generalizia O.M.I.; Università Urbaniana, 1978, 192 pp.
Pp. 137-54, "The missionary problem of Christo-pagan syncretisms"–this term is chosen to describe alll new religious movements; the references are mainly African.

208 Seunarine, J. F. *Reconversion to Hinduism through Suddhi*. Madras: Christian Literature Society, 1977, 105 pp.
Pp. 90-93, A. F. C. Wallace's revitalization theory applied to the Arya Samaj movement in India, as example of its wide usefulness.

209 Shank, David A. "The shape of mission." *Mission Focus* (Elkhart, Ind.; Mennonite Board of Missions) 8, no. 4 (1980): 69-74.
Pp. 71-73, on new religious movements as one of three major realities now shaping Christian mission responsibilities. By a Mennonite with experience of independent churches in Ivory Coast.

210 Sharma, Arvind. "An exploration into the possibility of prehistoric messianism." *Journal of Religious History* 10, no. 1 (1978): 86-94.
By study of the Tasada people discovered in the Philippines in 1971, concludes that messianism could have existed in the Palaeolithic period–but this has since been shown to be an organized fake discovery of people who were not primitives.

211 Shepperson, George. "The comparative study of millenarian movements." In *Millennial dreams in action*, edited by S. L. Thrupp. Comparative Studies in Society and History, Supplement 12. The Hague: Mouton, 1962, pp. 44-52.

212 Sierksma, Fokke. *Een nieuwe hemel en een nieuwe aarde: Messianische en eschatologische bewegingen en voorstellingen bij primitieve volken*. The Hague: Mouton, 1961, 312 pp. (bib., pp. 302-12).
An important theoretical study.

213 Sierksma, Fokke. Review of *Chiliasmus und Nativismus*, edited by W. E. Mühlmann (entry 171). *Sociologus* (Berlin) 12 (1962): 80-83.

214 Simpson, George E[aton], and Aberle, David F[riend]. "Cultural deprivation and millennial movements: A discussion." In *Cultural and social anthropology*, edited by P. B. Hammond. New York and London: Collier-Macmillan, 1964, pp. 334-42.

215 Smith, Marian W. "Towards a classifcation of cult movements." *Man*, article 2, 59 (January 1959): 8-12.

Surveys the anthropological contributions to this problem between 1943 (R. Linton, entry 153) and 1958; suggests three basic classifications as nativistic, vitalistic, or synthetist.

216 Smith, Wilfred Cantwell. "Traditional religions and modern culture." In *Proceedings of the XIth International Congress of the International Association for the History of Religions*. Vol. 1, *The impact of modern culture on traditional religions*. Leiden: E. J. Brill, 1968, pp. 55-72.

Criticizes above terms, "impact" and "traditional," and discusses meaning and location of religion.

217 Social Science Research Council, Summer Seminar on Acculturation, 1953. "Acculturation: An exploratory formulation." *American Anthropologist* 56 [6, no. 1] (1954): 973-1002.

An important statement from a seminar at Stanford University, 1953.

218 Spencer, R. F. Review of *Prophetismus und Heilserwartungs-Bewegungen als völkerkundliches und religionsgeschichtliches Problem*, by G. Guariglia (entry 312). *American Anthropologist* 63, no. 3 (1961): 596-98.

Criticizes the typological/phenomenological approach.

219 Spier, Leslie; Suttles, Wayne; and Herskovits, Melville J[ean]. "Comment on Aberle's thesis of deprivation." *Southwestern Journal of Anthropology* 15, no. 1 (1959): 84-88.

220 Stark, Rodney, and Bainbridge, William Sims. "Networks of faith: Interpersonal bonds and recruitment to cults and sects." *American Journal of Sociology* 85, no. 6 (1980): 1376-95.

Focused on movements in Western societies but generally useful.

221 Stipe, Claude E[dwin]. "Religion and culture crises." *Anglican Theological Review* 55 (July 1973): 289-304.

Discusses the new importance given to religion by anthropology; revitalization of cultures exemplified in cargo cults, Handsome Lake religion, and African independent churches.

222 Stipe, Claude E[dwin]. "The role of religion in culture change." *Christian Scholar's Review* 10, no. 2 (1981): 116-31.

Pp. 116-24, neglect and distortions of religion in anthropological studies; pp. 124-30, examples from four continents of the role of religion in acculturation; p. 131, conclusion, that indigenous belief systems are needed to explain these movements, and not merely nonreligious factors.

223 Symons-Symonolewicz, Konstantin. "Nativistic movements and modern nationalism." *Transactions, Illinois State Academy of Science* (Springfield, Ill.) 59, no. 3 (1966): 236-40.

224 Talmon, Yonina. "Millenarism." *International encyclopedia of the social sciences*. Vol. 10. New York: Macmillan, 1968, pp. 349-62, bib.
    History, characteristics, functions.

225 Talmon, Yonina. "The millennial dream." In *Protest, reform, and revolt: A reader in social movements*, edited by J. R. Gusfield. New York: Wiley, 1970, 576 pp. Abridged from *European Journal of Sociology* 2 (1962): 130-44.

226 Theobald, Robin. "The role of charisma in the development of social movements: Ellen G. White and the emergence of the Seventh Day Adventists." *Archives de Sciences Sociales des Religions*, no. 49 [25, no. 1] (1980): 83-100.

227 Thomas, M[adathipilparamil] M[ammen]. *Man and the universe of faiths*. Madras: Christian Literature Society, 1975, 161 pp.
    Pp. 49, 58-62, modern religious movements in primal societies as significant for dialogue between the "unitive, primal" world view and modernizing "messianic" views.

228 Thrupp, Sylvia L. "Millennial dreams in action: A report on the conference discussion." In *Millennial dreams in action*, edited by S. L. Thrupp. Comparative Studies in Society and History, Supplement 12. The Hague: Mouton, 1962, pp. 11-27.

229 Tiryakian, Edward A. "A model of societal change and its lead indicators." In *The study of total societies*, edited by S. Z. Klausner. Garden City, N.Y.: Doubleday, 1967, pp. 69-97.
    Pp. 92ff., one of three indicators that "seem to be significantly related to the outbreak of a revolution"; with a lead time of about ten to thirty years, involves "significant increases in the outbreak of non-institutional religious phenomena," with specific mention of African independent movements.

230 Tiryakian, Edward A. "Le sacré et le profane dans la destruction coloniale et la construction nationale." *Revue de l'Institut de Sociologie* (Université Libre de Bruxelles) 2-3 (1967): 203-16.

Spiritual renewal as basic to decolonization, assisted by independent religious movements as early modernizers and Africanizers, illustrating the theses of Durkheim and Weber in an African context; economic effects especially treated; parallels drawn with the Reformation and nineteenth century American revivals.

231 Toch, Hans. *The social psychology of social movements*. Indianapolis: Bobbs-Merrill Co., 1965, 257 pp.

Chap. 2 (pp. 28-44), Illusions as solutions; pp. 30-33, 43, Ras Tafari movement; pp. 33-38, 43, A. C. Sam's back-to-Africa movement, Oklahoma, 1914; pp. 39-42, cargo cults. All based on standard sources.

232 Trompf, Garry W[inston]. "The future of macro-historical ideas." *Soundings* 62, no. 1 (1979): 70-89.

See especially pp. 80-84 on a predicted increase in millenarianism – "more than at any other time in world history."

233 Trompf, Garry W[inston]. "Missiology, methodology, and the study of new religious movements." *Religious Traditions* 10 (1987): 95-106.

The methodological stances of the social sciences and of missiology and theology – their language, assumptions, and interrelationships.

234 Turner, Harold W[alter]. "Articulating theology through relations with new religious movements." *Discernment* (London, British Council of Churches) 1, no. 2 (1986): 4-15.

An autobiographical account of theoretical reflections on varied personal experience over a period of fifty years.

235 Turner, Harold W[alter]. "The contribution of studies on religion in Africa to Western religious studies." In *New Testament Christianity for Africa and the world: Essays in honour of Harry Sawyerr*, edited by M. E. Glasswell and E. W. Fashole-Luke. London: SPCK, 1974, pp. 169-78.

As exemplified in study of African independent churches, but with similar issues and potential in other regions.

236 Turner, Harold W[alter]. "Further comments on *Survival*'s philosophy." *News from Survival International* (London), no. 8 (October 1974), p. 9.

On pessimistic or optimistic interpretation of new religious movements, especially Hallelujah in Guyana and the Peyote cult in the U.S.

237 Turner, Harold W[alter]. "A further dimension for missions (new religious movements in the primal societies)." *International Review of Mission*, no. 247 [62] (July 1973): 321-37.

238 Turner, Harold W[alter]. "The hidden power of the whites: The secret religion withheld from the primal peoples." *Archives de Sciences Sociales des Religions*, no. 46 [23, no. 1] (1978): 41-55. Hungarian translation. "A fehérek rejtett hatalma: A titkos vallás, amelyet nem osztanak meg a törzsi népekkel." *Világosság* (Budapest) 6 (1978).
On the widespread misunderstandings of the source and nature of the superior powers of the whites, including belief that they have a different Bible kept secret because of its power.

239 Turner, Harold W[alter]. "Keeping up with recent studies 1: Understanding the new world of religious movements in primal societies." *Expository Times* 89, no. 6 (1978): 167-72.

240 Turner, Harold W[alter]. "A methodology for modern African religious movements." *Comparative Studies in Society and History* 8, no. 3 (1966): 12-25.
The location and identification of the phenomena and the allocation to the most relevant disciplines; applies as much to other areas as to Africa.

241 Turner, Harold W[alter]. "Monogamy: A mark of the Church?" *International Review of Missions* 219 [55] (1966): 313-21. Reprinted in *Religious innovation in Africa*. Boston: G. K. Hall, 1979, pp. 215-23.
Theological refutation of the view that polygamy in new religious movements disqualifies them from acceptance as forms of Christian church.

242 Turner, Harold W[alter]. "A new field in the history of religions." *Religion: Journal of Religion and Religions* 1, no. 1 (1971): 15-23.
New movements related to tribal or primal societies have sufficient distinctive features in common to be regarded as a new and coherent area of study.

243 Turner, Harold W[alter]. "New mission task: Worldwide and waiting." *Missiology* 13, no. 1 (1985): 5-21.

A theoretical view of the place in missiology of new religious movements in primal societies.

244 Turner, Harold W[alter]. "New religious movements and syncretism in tribal cultures." In *Dialogue and syncretism: An interdisciplinary approach*, edited by J. D. Gort, et al. Currents of Encounter Series. Grand Rapids: W. B. Eerdmans; Amsterdam: Editions Rodopi, 1989, pp. 105-13.

A paper presented at a symposium, Free University of Amsterdam, May 1988.

245 Turner, Harold W[alter]. "New religious movements in primal societies." In *Australian essays in world religions*, edited by V. C. Hayes. Adelaide: Australian Association for the Study of Religions, 1977, pp. 38-48. Reprinted in *Religious innovation in Africa*. Boston: G. K. Hall, 1979, pp. 3-13.

A general survey of features and significance.

246 Turner, Harold W[alter]. "The place of independent religious movements in the modernization of Africa." *Journal of Religion in Africa* 2, no. 1 (1969): 42-63. For similar statement see "African independent churches and economic development." *World Development*. Vol. 8. Oxford: Pergamon Press, 1980, pp. 523-33; also in *Religious values and development*, edited by K. P. Jameson and C. K. Wilbur. Oxford: Pergamon Press, 1980, pp. 523-33.

Analysis of the necessary changes in world view that apply as much elsewhere as in Africa.

247 Turner, Harold W[alter]. "Prophetism." In *Concise dictionary of the Christian world mission*, edited by S. Neill. Nashville: Abingdon, 1971, 500a-501a. German translation. *Lexicon zur Weltmission*. Wuppertal: R. Brockhaus, 1975.

248 Turner, Harold W[alter]. "The relationship between development and new religious movements in tribal societies of the third world." In *God and global justice*, edited by F. Ferre and R. H. Mataragnon. New York: Paragon House, 1985, pp. 84-110.

Similar to entry 246 and the associated items.

249 Turner, Harold W[alter]. "Two kinds of new religious movement." In *The future of religion: A tribute to G. C. Oosthuizen*. Pretoria: Serva Publishers, 1989, pp. 183-202.

A theoretical account of the relations between the "sects and cults" found in the West and new movements related to tribal cultures – their similarities and differences.

250 Turner, Harold W[alter], ed. "New primal religious movements." *Missiology* 13, no. 1 (1985): 128 pp.
Special theme for the whole issue, with articles by D. A. Shank on Africa, K. D. Scott on Latin America, T. Ahrens on Melanesia, and C. F. Starkloff on North America, as well as a survey and a separate bibliography by the editor. Contains theoretical discussions at many points.

251 Turner, Victor W[itter]. "Passages, margins, and poverty: Religious symbols of communitas." Part 1. *Worship* 46, no. 7 (1972): 390-412.
Pp. 405-8, millenarian and nativistic, etc., movements in connection with his views on "liminality" and "communitas."

252 Turner, Victor W[itter]. *The ritual process: Structure and anti-structure.* Chicago: Aldine Publishing Co., 1969, 213 pp.
Pp. 111-12, egalitarian and communal features of millenarian movements; pp. 188-91, South African separatism and Melanesian millenarianism as examples of "religions of humility and status reversal."

253 Valjavek, Friedrich. "Über die Selbstorganisation von Krisenkulten." Parts 1, 2. *Sociologus*, n.s. 33, no. 1 (1983): 1-24; no. 2 (1983): 131-51, English synopsis, p. 151.
Crisis cults are dynamic processes of self-organization.

254 The Vatican. "Documentation supplement: Sects or new religious movements: Pastoral challenge." *Secretariat for Promoting Christian Unity: Information Service* 61, no. 3 (1986): 145-54.
The first official Catholic world survey of all kinds of new religious movements, displaying an eirenic outlook.

255 Waal Malefijt, A. de. "Religious change." In *Religion and culture.* New York and London: Collier-Macmillan, 1968, pp. 329-59.

256 Walker, Sheila S. *Ceremonial spirit possession in Africa and Afro-America.* Leiden: E. J. Brill, 1972, 179 pp.
Especially chap. 11 (pp. 126-45), "The normality or abnormality of spirit possession." An important study by a black anthropologist.

257 Wallace, Anthony F. C. *Culture and personality.* Studies in Anthropology, 1. New York: Random House, 1961, 213 pp.
　　Chap. 4, the psychology of culture change, especially pp. 143-52, revitalization processes in five stages: steady state, increased individual stress, cultural distortion, revitalization (six functions distinguished, from formulation of a new code to routinization), new steady state.

258 Wallace, Anthony F. C. "Mazeway disintegration: The individual's perception of socio-cultural disorganization." *Human Organization* 16, no. 2 (1957): 23-27. (Special issue, Human adaptation to disaster.)

259 Wallace, Anthony F. C. "Mazeway resynthesis: A biocultural theory of religious inspiration." *Transactions of the New York Academy of Sciences,* 2d ser. 18, no. 7 (1956): 626-38.
　　Pp. 626-31, specifically on Handsome Lake, especially on the question of the change in the participant's whole view of his culture during his eight-hour trance; this is discussed in terms of the reorganization of the individual's mental "mazeway."

260 Wallace, Anthony F. C. "Nativism and revivalism." *International encyclopedia of the social sciences.* Vol. 11. New York: Macmillan, 1968, pp. 75-80, bib.
　　History of their study, present theories, current research.

261 Wallace, Anthony F. C. *Religion: An anthropological view.* New York: Random House, 1966, xv + 300 pp.
　　Pp. 157-66, "religion as revitalization," with a typology of revitalization movements; pp. 209-15, "functions of revitalization rituals."

262 Wallace, Anthony, F. C. Review of *Magic and the millennium,* by B. R. Wilson (entry 277). *American Anthropologist* 77, no. 3 (1975): 99-101.

263 Wallace, Anthony F. C. "Revitalization movements." *American Anthropologist* 58, no. 2 (1956): 264-81. Reprinted in *Studies in social movements,* edited by B. McLaughlin. New York and London: Free Press; Collier Macmillan, 1969, pp. 30-52. German translation in *Religionsethnologie,* edited by C. A. Schmitz. Frankfurt, 1964, pp. 404-27.
　　An influential theoretical framework, interpreting movements as attempts to relieve strain by remaking culture.

264 Wallace, Anthony F. C. "Revitalization movements in development." In *The challenge of development theory and practice*, edited by R. J. Ward. Chicago: Aldine Publishing Co., 1967, pp. 448-54.

A succinct account of his revitalization theory; pp. 451-53, Handsome Lake movement as an example.

265 Wallace, Anthony F. C. "Stress and personality changes." *International Record of Medicine*, no. 2886 [169, no. 12] (1956): 761-74.

266 Wallace, Anthony F. C. "Study of process of organization and revitalization of psychological and socio-cultural systems, based on a comparative study of nativistic revivals." In *American Philosophical Society Year Book, 1957*. Philadelphia: American Philosophical Society, 1958, pp. 310-11.

Outlines of mathematical theory of organization applicable beyond the problem of revitalization movements.

267 Wallace, Anthony F. C.; Voget, F. W.; and Smith, M[arian]. "Towards a classification of cult movements: Some further contributions." *Man*, articles 25-27, 59 (February 1959): 25-28.

Continues the discussion from M. W. Smith in the previous month's issue; Voget distinguishes cultural, sociopsychological, and sociological "referents."

268 Wallis, Roy. "Relative deprivation and social movements: A cautionary note." *British Journal of Sociology* 26, no. 3 (1975): 360-63.

Critique of use of this theory, in relation to G. Allan's article in *idem* 25, no. 3 (1974): 291-311.

269 Wallis, Roy. *Salvation and protest: Studies of social and religious movements*. London: Frances Printer, 1979, 231 pp.

Includes Scientology, Children of God, National Festival of Light, National Viewers' and Listeners' Association, etc. Chap. 10 (pp. 174-92), a theory of propensity to schism.

270 Wallis, Wilson D[allam]. *Messiahs: Christian and pagan: Their role in civilization*. Boston: Richard G. Badger, 1918, 276 pp. Reprint. Washington, D.C.: American Council on Public Affairs, 1943.

271 Welbourn, F[rederick] B[urkewood]. "A metaphysical challenge." *African Ecclesiastical Review* 12, no. 4 (1970): 301-4.

Comments on D. B. Barrett's views on causes of independent churches, and on the influence of cultural forms on all religions.

272 Werblowsky, R[aphael] J[ehadah] Zwi. "Messianism in primitive societies." *Listener* (London): 64, no. 1647 (20 October 1960): 684-86, illus.

As a sign of dissatisfaction with the present; examples from North American and Pacific cargo cults.

273 Werblowsky, R[aphael] J[ehadah] Zwi. "'A new heaven and a new earth': Considering primitive messianisms." *History of Religions* 5, no. 1 (1965): 164-72.

Review article on *Een nieuwe hemel en een nieuwe aarde: Messianische en eschatologische bewegingen en voorstellingen bij primitieve volken*, by Fokke Sierksma (entry 212), with theoretical discussion.

274 Werbner, R[ichard] P., ed. *Regional cults*. A.S.A. Monographs, 16. London, New York, and San Francisco: Academic Press, 1977, 257 pp., maps.

Pp. ix-xxxvii, introduction by Werbner; essays by E. Colson, M. Schoffeleers, W. J. van Binsbergen, Thoden van Velzen, etc.

275 Wilson, Bryan R[onald]. "An analysis of set development." *American Sociological Review* 24, no. 1 (1959): 3-15. French translation. "Typologie des sectes dans un perspective dynamique et comparative." *Archives de Sociologie des Religions* 16 [8] (July-December 1963): 49-63. German translation. "Ein analyse der Sektenentwicklung." In *Religionssoziologie*, edited by H. Maus and F. Furstenberg. Soziologische Texte, 19. Neuwied and Berlin: Luchterhaus, 1964, pp. 279-304.

Sects as organizations attempting to preserve their original value orientations; four types of sects distinguished.

276 Wilson, Bryan R[onald]. *Contemporary transformations of religion*. Riddell Memorial Lectures. Oxford: Oxford University Press, 1976, 132 pp.

Pp. 46-47, "nativistic new religious movements in the third world ... have no future"; pp. 47-63, movements with a new social ethic contributing to a new culture – Kimbanguism (pp. 47-52), Chilean Pentecostalism (pp. 52-56), Jehovah's Witnesses in Kenya (pp. 56-60), etc.

277 Wilson, Bryan R[onald]. *Magic and the millennium: A sociological study of religious movements of protest among tribal and third-world peoples*. London: Heinemann Educational Books; New York: Harper & Row,

1973, 547 pp. Reprint. Frogmore, St. Albans: Grenada Publishing, Paladin Books, 1975.

A world survey using a theoretical sociological framework, based on his earlier studies of sects in Western societies; "revolutionist" and "thaumaturgical" as the two main forms in third-world movements; special attention to the latter form, interpreted as "magical" (i.e., the same as religious); pp. 484-504, conclusions, with summary. Extensive bibliographies. See T. O. Ranger (entry 191) for critical review.

278 Wilson, Bryan R[onald]. "Millennialism in comparative perspective." *Comparative Studies in Society and History* 6, no. 1 (1963): 93-114.

Review article on *Millennial dreams in action*, edited by S. L. Thrupp (entry 228) and *Chiliasmus und Nativismus: Studien zur Psychologie, Sociologie, und historischen Kasuistik der Umsturzbewegungen*, edited by W. E. Mühlmann (entry 171).

279 Wilson, Bryan R[onald]. *The noble savages: The primitive origins of charisma and its contemporary survival.* Berkeley and London: University of California Press, 1975, 131 pp.

Considers the cases of Pontiac (pp. 38-46), Tecumseh and Tenskwatawa (pp. 47-58), the prophet W. W. Harris of West Africa (pp. 58-69), and S. Kimbangu in Zaïre (pp. 70-82) in terms of Weber's view of charismatic leadership; pp. 82-92, "movements in search of leaders."

280 Wilson, Bryan R[onald]. *Religious sects.* World University Library. London: Weidenfeld & Nicholson, 1970, 256 pp., illus.

Pp. 22-25, the problem of definition (discusses Troeltsch, then various attributes – voluntariness, exclusivity, merit, self-identification, elite status, expulsion, conscience, legitimation; pp. 212-18, South African examples (seen in B. G. M. Sundkler's categories); pp. 218-25, Japanese new religions.

281 Wilson, Bryan R[onald]. "Time, generations, and sectarianism." In *The social impact of new religious movements*, edited by B. R. Wilson. New York: Rose of Sharon Press, 1986, pp. 217-34.

Reasons for the greater "visibility" of current movements; the urgency of the message for the present time; emphasis on the "modern" in methods used and in interpreting the situation as different from the past; generational transmission and its effect on the beliefs and practice of movements. Useful suggestions of wide application.

282 Wilson, John. "Making inferences about religious movements." *Religion* 7, no. 2 (1977): 149-66.

Stresses the distinctively religious factors, operating through symbols, as against sociological or other reductionisms.

283 Wilson, John. Review of *Magic and the millennium: A sociological study of religious movements of protest among tribal and third-world peoples*, by Bryan R. Wilson (entry 277). *Scientific Study of Religion* 13, no. 3 (1974): 366-73.

284 Wolf, Eric R. "Peasant rebellion and revolution." In *National liberation, revolution, and the third world*, edited by N. Miller and R. Arya. New York: Free Press, 1971, pp. 48-67.

On the place of peasants in the Mexican (1910), Russian (1905, 1917), Chinese (1920-21), Vietnamese (post-World War II), Algerian (1954), and Cuban (1958-59) revolutions.

285 Wolf, Eric R. *Peasants*. Foundations of Modern Anthropology Series. Englewood Cliffs, N.J.: Prentice Hall, 1966, 116 pp., illus.

Pp. 100-109, "Levels in religious traditions" – on peasant religion, its protest or millennial movements (mentioning only Taiping in China in particular).

286 Worsley, Peter M[aurice]. "The analysis of rebellion and revolution in modern British social anthropology." *Science and Society* (New York) 25 (1961): 26-37.

On the change from static, normative, structuralist views of society to more dynamic views recognizing time and change in social processes.

287 Wuthnow, Robert. "World order and religious movements." In *New religious movements: A perspective for society*, edited by E. Barker. New York and Toronto: Edwin Mellen Press, 1982, pp. 47-65. Reprinted from *Studies in the modern world system*, edited by A. Bergsen. New York: Academic Press, 1980.

Movements arise in the changing interrelations of power *between* the group of "dominant core areas" of the world, and the group of "dependent, peripheral areas" – rather than in the changing situations *within* societies of any one kind.

288 Yinger, J[ohn] Milton. *The scientific study of religion*. New York: Macmillan; London: Collier, 1970, x + 593 pp., illus.

Chap. 15, Religion and minority status; includes sections on revitalization movements, cargo cults (pp. 317-19), North American Indian movements (pp. 319-24), and among Afro-Americans (pp. 324-26).

General

This division includes items that deal with these new religious movements either in general or across the world, or that span several of the cultural-geographical areas represented by the separate volumes. On occasion an item covering only two of these cultural-geographical areas has been placed in the volumes for both of these areas or in only one of them, according to the weight of the material.

It is sometimes difficult to classify an item as either "general" or "theoretical," so that items placed here as belonging to the former category may also contain useful material in the latter category.

This General division also contains items that are not easily located in other main divisions. An example is the *Sixth and Seventh Books of Moses*, which does not deal with any new religious movements but which is fairly widely used in some of these movements.

Extracts are included from some of the few world surveys, such as those of G. Guariglia (entry 312), V. Lanternari (entry 320), B. R. Wilson (entry 354), and the symposium edited by H.-C. Puech (entry 337). Some area materials from these works have also been included in the relevant regional volumes – North America, Africa, etc. Two shorter items giving a systematic overview from different perspectives are G. Oosterwal (entry 332) and H. W. Turner (entry 352).

289 Adas, Michael. *Prophets of rebellion: Millenarian protest movements against the European colonial order*. Chapel Hill: University of North Carolina Press, 1979, 243 pp.

> The causes and interpretation of five rebellions: Java War (1825-30), Pai Marire movement (New Zealand, 1860s), Birsa (India, 1899), Maji Maji (Tanzania, 1905), Saya San (Burma, 1930-32), all with religious dimensions.

290 Amstutz, Josef; Collet, Giancarlo; and Zurfluh, Werner, eds. *Kirche und Dritte Welt im Jahr 2000*. Zurich: Benziger Verlag for Schweizerischen Katholischen Mission Rates, 1974, 252 pp.

Pp. 105-59, the Church and religious movements; pp. 106-8, 127-29, Africa; pp. 109-11, Kardecism; pp. 111-15, 130-31, Umbanda; pp. 115-18, Pentecostalism; pp. 119-21, 131, cargo cults; pp. 121-24, 132-33, Japan; pp. 134-59, various features of such movements.

291 *Anthropological Quarterly* 37, no. 3 (1964): 73-155.

New religious cults and movements – special issue. Articles by W. H. Hodge (Navaho Pentecostalism), S. Leacock (Afro-Brazilian), F. Moos (Korea), L. Plotnicov (Nigeria), I. Rubin (Jewish), and A. de Waal Malefijt (Surinam). See further in these areas.

292 Barkun, Michael. *Disaster and the millennium*. New Haven: Yale University Press, 1974, 246 pp.

See index for millenarian movements, and especially pp. 12-17 ("Vailala Madness," Papua), pp. 116-19, 140-43, 194-97 (Taiping and similar movements).

293 Barrett, David Brian, ed. *World Christian encyclopedia: A comparative study of churches and religions in the modern world, A.D. 1900-2000*. New York, Nairobi, etc.: Oxford University Press, 1982, 1010 pp.

See sections on independent or indigenous churches and other religious movements in entries for relevant countries.

294 Bates, E. S. "John Alexander Dowie." *Dictionary of American biography*. Vol. 5. 1930, pp. 413a-414b.

On the founder of the Christian Catholic Apostolic Church with its Zion City near Chicago, who was widely influential in other new movements in South Africa, the Philippines, Nigeria, etc.

295 Benz, Ernst. *Neue Religionen*. Stuttgart: E. Klett Verlag, 1971, 179 pp.

With chapters on Cao Dai (Vietnam), Peyote and Black Muslims (U.S.), cargo cults (Melanesis), and African movements. See further in these areas.

296 Brézault, Alain, and Clavreuil, Gérard. *Missions en Afrique: Les Catholiques face à Islam, aux sectes, au Vatican*. Paris: Éditions Autrement, 1987, 188 pp.

Pp. 133-42, Rosicrucians and other "sects" in Cameroon and Congo; pp. 143-53, Vodou in Haïti and Benin with discussion of the church's approach to "syncretism."

297 Butler, John F. *Christianity in Asia and America after A.D. 1500.* Iconography of Religions, 24, no. 13. Leiden: E. J. Brill, 1979, xxiv (bib.) + 45 pp. + 48 plates.

   P. 21 and Pl. 36 (3) with p. 42 note (from Moihen's notebooks), cargo cults in Papua New Guinea; pp. 26-27 and Pl. 43 (2) with p. 44 note, Vodou (Sea-goddess).

298 Camps, Arnulf. "Christian togetherness in non-Western countries." In *International yearbook for the sociology of religions,* edited by J. Matthes, no. 5 (1969), pp. 182-94.

299 Chéry, H.-Ch. "Sectes en pays de mission." *Parole et Mission* 5, no. 17 (1962): 286-92.

   A detailed account of the 31st Semaine de Missiologie, Louvain, 1961.

300 Chesneaux, Jean. "Hérésies coloniales et millénarismes de libération nationale." In *La naissance des dieux.* Paris: Édition de l'Union Rationaliste, [1966], pp. 237-71.

   Similar to his 1958 item (entry 301).

301 Chesneaux, Jean. "Les hérésies coloniales: Leur rôle dans le développement des mouvements nationaux d'Asie et d'Afrique. ..." *Recherches Internationales à la Lumière du Marxisme* (Paris) 6 (March-April 1958): 170-88.

   Pp. 172-74, Taiping; pp. 174-76, cargo movements in Melanesia; pp. 176-78, Philippine peasant movements; pp. 178-80, African movements.

302 Comhaire, Jean L. "Religious trends in African and Afro-American urban societies." *Anthropological Quarterly* 1, no. 4 (1953): 95-108.

   Pp. 95-98, Kimbanguism in Congo; p. 99, Kenyan and South African independent movements; pp. 100-103, Lagos "native churches"; pp. 103-4, other parts of West Africa; pp. 104-8, Haïtian vodou. All assessed as having little future prospects.

303 Crumrine, N. Ross. "Folk drama in Latin America: A ritual type characterized by social group unification and cultural fusion." *Canadian Journal of Latin American Studies,* n.s. 6, no. 12 (1981): 103-25.

   Death and resurrection in Easter folk dramas of the Mayo (N.W. Mexico), Catacaos (N. Coastal Peru), and on Marinduque island (Philippines) – a comparative study.

304 Dammann, Ernst, ed. *Nachchristliche Bewegungen in Neuguinea und Brasilien*. Stuttgart: Evang. Missionsverlag, 1968, 52 pp.

Includes J. F. Wagner on New Guinea, E. Fulling on Brazil, and R. Flasche on Brazil.

305 Desroche, Henri. *Sociologie de l'espérance*. Archives des Sciences Sociales des Religions. Paris: Calmann-Levy, 1973, 253 pp. English translation. *The sociology of hope*. London: Routledge & Kegan Paul, 1979, 209 pp.

Pp. 94-106 (English translation, pp. 69-77), millennialism in the third world – brief outlines on Oceania, Africa, and Latin America.

306 Dorsinfang-Smets, Annie. "La recherche du salut chez les Indiens d'Amérique." *Réligions du salut: Annales du Centre d'Étude des Religions* (Brussels, Institut de Sociologie Solvay) 2 (1962): 113-25, illus.

Pp. 114-16, Guarani, Tupinamba, and Taino (Caribbean) search for paradise; pp. 117-18, Ghost Dance; pp. 119-25, Midewiwin and other societies: all as examples of indigenous millennial traditions.

307 Eckert, Georg. "Das Prophetentum und sein Einfluss auf Geschichte und Kulturentwicklung der Naturvolker." *Forschungen und Fortschritte* (Berlin) 17, no. 6 (1941): 59-63.

308 Ellenberger, Henri F. "Les mouvements de libération mythique." *Critique* (Paris), no. 190 [19] (March 1963), pp. 247-67.

A review article on *Chiliasmus und Nativismus*, edited by W. E. Mühlmann (entry 171), *Les mouvements religieux … des peuples opprimés*, by V. Lanternari (entry 320), and *The trumpet shall sound: A study of "cargo" cults in Melanesia*, by Peter M. Worsley (London: MacGibbon & Kee, 1957).

309 Gill, Sam D. *Beyond "the primitive": The religions of nonliterate peoples*. Englewood Cliffs, N.J.: Prentice-Hall, 1982, 120 pp., illus.

Chap. 7 (pp. 98-109), "Confronting and affirming modernity"; pp. 99-103, summary of K. O. L. Burridge on Mambu; pp. 103-4, Vailala Madness; pp. 104-106, Ghost Dance; p. 107, Maji Maji in Tanganyika – all seen as "crisis cults."

310 Gratus, Jack. *The false messiahs*. London: Victor Gollancz, 1975, 285 pp.

Pp. 202-8, examples of new movements in Africa, North and South America, and Melanesia.

311 Guariglia, Guglielmo. "I movimenti profetico-salvifici e le missioni." *Le Missioni Cattoliche* (Milan) 89, nos. 8-9 (1960): 258-69.

312 Guariglia, Guglielmo. *Prophetismus und Heilserwartungs-Bewegungen als völkerkundliches und religionsgeschichtliches Problem*. Vienna: F. Berger, 1959, xvi + 332 pp., maps, bib.

General world survey, in terms of syncretism, millennialism, vitalism, etc.; extensive bibliography.

313 Halsey, John J. "The genesis of a modern prophet." *American Journal of Sociology* 9, no. 3 (1903): 310-28.

John Alexander Dowie and his Christian Catholic Apostolic Church and Zion City, which has been influential in the origins of new movements in southern Africa and several other areas.

314 Hesselgrave, David J., ed. *Dynamic religious movements*. Grand Rapids: Baker Book House, 1978, 326 pp.

Twelve rapidly growing movements; includes M.-L. Martin summarizing her book on Kimbanguism, P. Steyne on African Zionist movements, Iglesia ni Cristo (Philippines), Cao Dai (Vietnam), Umbanda (Brazil), Unification Church (Korea), Soka Gakkai (Japan); pp. 297-326, discussion of their growth and the lessons for Christianity (by the editor).

315 Hollenweger, Walter J. "Le livre oral: Portées sociales, politiques, et théologiques des religions orales." In *Les cultures populaires*, edited by G. Poujol and R. Labourie. Sciences de l'Homme. Institut National d'Éducation. Toulouse: Privat, 1979, pp. 123-34.

Pp. 127-28, S. Kimbangu; pp. 128-30, Antonio José dos Santos.

316 Houtart, François. "Mouvements religieux du tiers-monde, formes de protestation contre l'introduction des rapports sociaux capitalistes." Parts 1, 2. *Civilisations* 27, nos. 1-2 (1977): 81-98; nos. 3-4 (1977): 245-58.

Pt. 2 (pp. 245-58) examines three such movements: in India (the Izhavas of Kerala–a low-caste movement), in Brazil (messianic movements, northeast and south), and in South Africa (independent churches).

317 Ihrman, Claire. "Chocolate, the third world, and mission." *Church Herald* (Grand Rapids, Reformed Church in America) 41, no. 11 (1984): 14-15, 20.

A general account of the Selly Oak Colleges and its Centre for New Religious Movements, by a former student intern from Hope College (Holland, Mich.).

318 La Barre, Weston. *The Ghost Dance: Origins of religion*. Garden City, N.Y.: Doubleday & Co., 1970, 677 pp.

Asian movements: pp. 234-35 (Burkhan, etc.); pp. 261-75, 279, 317, Pau Cin Hau in Burma. Oceanic movements: pp. 238-45, 250-52, cargo cults; pp. 239-45, Vailala Madness; pp. 247-48, 252, 263-65, Marching Rule; pp. 246-47, 252, 316, Naked Cult; pp. 247, 252, 316, John Frum; pp. 233-34, 250, Maori King movement; p. 236 Mansren. See also index, "cult leaders." An idiosyncratic work, seeing all movements as "crisis cults," but with valuable bibliographies.

319 Lanczkowski, Günther. "Einige systematische Erwägungen zu neuzeitlichen Religionsstiftungen." *Kairos* (Salzburg) 6, nos. 3-4 (1964): 209-19.

A general world survey of the main features, including Mormonism, Japanese new religions, etc.

320 Lanternari, Vittorio. *Movimenti religiosi di libertà e di salvezza dei popoli oppressi*. Milan: Feltrinelli, 1960, 366 pp., bib. 2d ed. 1974, xxix + 366 pp. French translation. *Les mouvements religieux de liberté et de salut des peuples opprimés*. Paris: Maspero, 1962, 399 pp. English translation. *The religions of the oppressed: A study of modern messianic cults*. London: MacGibbon & Kee, 1963, xx + 343 + xiii pp. Toronto: New American Library of Canada, 1963. New York: Knopf, 1963. New York: Mentor Books, 1965, xvi + 286 pp. Spanish translation. *Movimientos religiosos de libertad y salvación de los pueblos oprimados*. Barcelona: Ed. Seix Barrel, 1965. German translation. *Religiöser Freiheits-und Heilsbewegungen unterdruckter Völker*. Soziologische Texte, 33. Neuwied and Berlin: Hermann Luchterhard Verlag, 1966, 538 pp. Hungarian translation. *Gyarmatosítás és Vallási Szabadság-mozgalmak*. Budapest: Kossuth, 1972, 405 pp.

Chap. 1, "Nativistic-religious movements in Africa"; pp. 22-39, the Congo; pp. 39-49, South Africa; pp. 49-50, Nyasaland; pp. 50-56, West Africa; pp. 56-58, "other movements." Religious movements in colonial areas are reactions against oppression, anxiety, and frustration, aggravated by alienation of lands and race relations. New Italian impression, 1974, has new preface and updated bibliography. See also *Current Anthropology* 6, no. 4 (1965): 447-65, fifteen reviews of *Religions of the oppressed* together with a précis of the book, and reply to the reviewers by Lanternari.

321 Larsen, Egon. *Strange sects and cults: A study of their origins and influence*. London: Arthur Barker, 1971, 202 pp.

Pp. 125-34, Father Divine (U.S.); pp. 135-44, Soka Gakkai (Japan); pp. 144-50, 153-58, (Nigerian) Cherubim and Seraphim in London, and Nigerian background during the Biafran civil war; pp. 151-53, Alice Lenshina (Zambia); pp. 159-61, Peyote cult (U.S. Indians); pp. 184-86, Cao Dai (Vietnam); pp. 186-87, Spiritism in Brazil; pp. 187-90, cargo cults in Melanesia.

322 Latourette, Kenneth Scott. *Christianity in a revolutionary age*. Vol. 5, *The twentieth century outside Europe*. London: Eyre & Spottiswoode, 1963, 568 pp.

P. 156, brief references to Shouters, Shango, Obeah; pp. 254-55, New Zealand Maori movements; pp. 257-58, "Bantu sects" in South Africa; pp. 361-62, 365, Philippine Independent Church; p. 367, Iglesia ni Cristo; pp. 446-47, cargo cults in Melanesia.

323 Laugeson, Helen. "New mission fields beckon." *Outlook* (Wellington, N. Z.), November 1980, pp. 14-15, photo, also cover photo of prophet Rua and missionary J. G. Laughton.

On the churches' relations to new religious movements; based on interview by H. Laugeson with H. W. Turner, and on his experiences.

324 Lewy, Guenter. *Religion and revolution*. New York: Oxford University Press, 1974, 674 pp.

Pp. 194-200, African messianism; pp. 221-36, Cargo cults; pp. 338-341, Saya San (Burma); pp. 618-25, 640-41, notes.

325 Luzbetak, Louis J. *The Church and cultures*. Techny, Ill.: Divine Word Publications, 1963, 417 pp.

Pp. 248-58 (and notes, pp. 262-63), nativistic movements, with examples from North America (including Black Muslims), Latin America, Africa, and especially Oceania; by a Catholic scholar.

326 Mair, Lucy P[hilip]. "Independent religious movements in three continents." *Comparative Studies in Society and History* 1, no. 2 (1959): 113-36.

An important early survey.

327 Meek, George W., ed. *Healers and the healing process: A report on ten years of research by 14 world famous investigators*. Wheaton, Ill., London, and Madras: Quest Books, Theosophical Publishing House, 1977, 304 pp.

Pp. 41-47, Andrija Puharich, Arigo, and paranormal healing in Brazil; pp. 59-127, paranormal healing in the Philippines–based on seven healers.

328 Mitterhöfer, Jakob. "Neue Religionen: Zur Themenstellung." *Ordensnachrichten* (Viennna) 20, no. 5 (1981): 299-305.

329 Monge, F. "Movimientos mesianicos y identidad indígena: Estados Unidos y Nueva Zelanda." *Revista Española de Antropologia Americano* (Madrid) 15 (1985): 261-81.

330 [Moses.] *The sixth and seventh books of Moses, or Moses' magical spirit-art*. N.p., n.d. "Published for the trade. Printed in the U.S.A." Sometimes published as edited by Horst, or Johan Scheible, 190 pp., illus.
    An influential and widely distributed book of mediaeval and earlier magic, found in use in some new movements.

331 Nida, Eugene A[lbert]. *Message and mission: The communication of the Christian faith*. New York: Harper & Bros., 1960, 253 pp., illus.
    Pp. 139-143, "nativistic" and "indigenous Christian" movements–with brief examples from Africa, North America, and Melanesia.

332 Oosterwal, Gottfried. *Modern messianic movements*. Missionary Studies, no. 2. Elkhart, Ind.: Institute of Mennonite Studies, 1973, 54 pp.
    A very good theological introduction by a Seventh Day Adventist missiologist with much field experience.

333 Oosterwal, Gottfried. "New religious movements: A challenge to mission." *Mission Focus* (Elkhart, Ind.) 3, no. 5 (May 1975): 11 pp. Reprinted in *Mission Focus: Current issues*. Scottdale, Pa.: Herald Press, 1980, pp. 244-64.
    A general survey similar to his 1973 booklet (entry 332).

334 Poggi, Vincenzo. "Libertà e movimenti profetico-salvifici." *Gentes LMS* (Rome) 45 (1971): 83-90.

335 Pollak-Eltz, Angelina. "Marginal religious movements in the world today." *Bulletin, International Committee on Urgent Anthropological and Ethnological Research*, no. 18 (1976), pp. 93-97.

New "cults and sects" – syncretist, pentecostal, occult, spiritist, etc. – mostly marginal to established society and religions.

336 Posern-Zielinska, Miroslawa, and Posern-Zielinski, Aleksander. "Charismatic leader in American Indian socio-religious movements. *Etnologia Polona* 2 (1976): 63-85.
   Covers North and Latin American leaders.

337 Puech, Henri-Charles, ed. *Histoire des religions*. Encyclopédie de la Pléiade, vol. 3. Paris: Gallimard, 1976, 1460 pp., maps.
   See N. Traan Huan (S.E. Asia: Caodism); L. Ogg (Korea); H. O. Rotermund (Japan); W. La Barre (North America); R. Bastide (Afro-American); E. Schaden (South America); J. M. van der Kroef (Indonesia); K. O. L. Burridge (Oceania); C. Wauthier (southern Africa); G. Balandier (Black Africa) – all important surveys.

338 Schlosser, Katesa. "Der Prophetismus in niederen Kulturen." *Zeitschrift für Ethnologie* (Berlin) 75 (1950): 60-67.

339 Shank, David A. "The shape of mission." *Mission Focus* (Elkhart, Ind.) 8, no. 4 (1980): 69-74.
   Pp. 71-72, emergence of new religious movements.

340 Sierksma, Fokke. *Een nieuwe hemel en een nieuwe aarde: Missianistische en eschatologische bewegingen en voorstellingen bij primitieve volken*. The Hague: Mouton, 1961, 312 pp., illus., bib.
   Messianic ideas among primitive peoples – Africa mentioned, pp. 211-12. Chap. 1 (pp. 13-37), Hawaii (Kalakau); chap. 2 (pp. 38-65), the whites as both gods and men, "Vailala Madness"; chap. 6 (pp. 142-70), American Indian Ghost Dance; chap. 7 (pp. 171-85), Yaruro Indian movement in Venezuela; chap. 8 (pp. 186-210), Australian examples – Kurangara, Unambul; chap. 9 (pp. 211-41), Melanesian examples, especially Paliau.

341 Smalley, William Allen, comp. *Readings in missionary anthropology*. Vol. 2. Enl. ed. South Pasadena, Calif.: William Carey Library, 1978, 912 pp.
   Replaces the 1967 edition. Seven articles reprinted from *Practical Anthropology*, 1957-72.

342 Smart, [Roderick] Ninian. *Background to the long search*. London: British Broadcasting Corporation, 1977, 316 pp., illus.

P. 230, Paviotso's Ghost Dance and Isatai's Sun Dance; pp. 235-36, 246, "New African Christianities" – Kimbanguism and Shembe's church; pp. 246-47, Cao Dai – all popular treatments, with a few inaccuracies.

343 Thompson, [T.] Jack. "New religious movements among primal peoples." In *The encyclopedia of world faiths*, edited by P. Bishop and M. Darton. London: Macdonald; Maryknoll, N.Y.: Orbis, 1987, pp. 307-11.
General descriptive survey of the field.

344 Turner, Harold W[alter]. "A further frontier for mission: A general introduction to new religious movements in primal societies." *Missionalia* 11, no. 3 (1983): 103-12.

345 Turner, Harold W[alter]. "New religious movements among primal peoples: Repercussions of the Christian contact." *Milligan Missiogram* (Milligan College, Tenn.) 2, no. 1 (1974): 13-16.

346 Turner, Harold W[alter]. "New religious movements in primal societies." In *A handbook of living religions*, edited by J. R. Hinnells. Harmondsworth and New York: Penguin Books, Viking, 1984, pp. 439-49, 454 (bib.).

347 Turner, Harold W[alter]. "New religious movements in primal societies." *Point*. Series 2, *Religious movements in Melanesia today (1)*, edited by W. Flannery. Goroka: Melanesian Institute, 1983, pp. 1-6.

348 Turner, Harold W[alter]. "New religious movements in the primal societies." *World Faiths* (London), no. 95 (1975), pp. 5-10.

349 Turner, Harold W[alter]. "New religious movements related to primal religions." In *Shap handbook on world religions and education*. London: Commission for Racial Equality, 1987, pp. 97-98.

350 Turner, Harold W[alter]. "New vistas: Missionary and ecumenical. Religious movements in primal (or tribal) societies." *Mission Focus* (Elkhart, Ind.) 9, no. 3 (1981): 45-55. Shorter version in *AACC Bulletin* (Nairobi) 12, no. 1 (1982): 7-18. Reprinted as pamphlet, *Religious movements in primal societies*. Elkhart, Ind.: Mission Focus Publications, 1989, 31 pp.
A general survey related to the interests of the North American Mennonite community.

351 Turner, Harold W[alter]. "Nouveaux mouvements religieux et cultures tribales." In *Encyclopaedia universalis: Le grand atlas des religions.* Paris: Encyclopaedia Universalis France, 1988, pp. 140-41, illus.
A world survey with a five-part classification system.

352 Turner, Harold W[alter]. "Tribal religious movements, new." *Encyclopaedia Britannica*, 15th ed., 1974. Micropaedia, vol. 10, p. 115, and references for 11 brief articles on African movements; Macropaedia, vol. 18, pp. 697-705.
Pp. 697-700, theory; pp. 701-4, historical outlines by main areas.

353 Watkins, June E. "Messianic movements: A comparative study of some religious cults among the Melanesians, Maoris, and North American Indians." M.A. dissertation, University of Sydney, 1951.

354 Wilson, Bryan R[onald]. *Magic and the millennium: A Sociological study of religious movements of protest among tribal and third-world peoples*. London: Heinemann Educational Books; New York: Harper & Row, 1973, 547 pp. Reprint. Frogmore, St. Albans: Granada Publishing, Paladin Books, 1975.
Pp. 50-53, Aiyetoro; pp. 54-57, Tigare; pp. 61-63, Mgijima; pp. 84-91, anti-witchcraft; pp. 94-100, Lenshina; pp. 136-41, Shembe; pp. 152-54, Deima cult; pp. 176-95, Church of the Lord, Aladura; pp. 236-40, Makanna and Xhosa prophets; pp. 241-42, Yakan cult; pp. 264-68, Mau Mau; pp. 368-73, 456-58, Kimbanguism; pp. 374-75 Matswa; pp. 376-79, Mpadi; and many lesser references – see index of movements.

355 Wilson, Bryan R[onald]. "New religious movements." *Man, Myth, and Magic* 5, no. 71 [1971-72]: 1977-81, illus.
Popular outline.

356 Zaretsky, Irving I., and Shambaugh, Cynthia. *Spirit possession and spirit mediumship in Africa and Afro-America: An annotated bibliography.* Garland Reference Library on Social Science, vol. 56. New York: Garland Publishing Co., 1978. Reprint of the 1966 ed., 1978, xxiv + 443 pp. Previously published as *Bibliography on spirit possession and spirit mediumship*. Evanston: Northwestern University Press, 1966.
Good for annotations.

Europe

Some may be surprised to find Europe represented in these materials, but in the north and east, primal religions may be identified in modern times. It might be asked whether there were not new religious movements according to our definition accompanying the expansion of the Christian faith into tribal Europe in the first millennium of the Christian era. There were certainly many cultural expressions of the new faith, and developments called heretical or syncretist by the main Christian movement, but it is not yet clear that the kinds of new movements associated with the expansion of the European peoples and the Christian faith after Columbus were also present in the earlier expansion into Europe. We have remained satisfied with the inclusion under northern Europe of A. V. Strom's article on North Germanic pre-Christian syncretism, which, despite its title does include discussion of Christian influence, and under eastern Europe of V. G. Marinich's article on Kievan Russia.

NORTH (Scandinavia)

In Northern Europe we are confined to the Lapps (now preferably called Sami) of northern Scandinavia, in recent centuries. Here the only identifiable movement is not a very clear example of our type for it was started by a white pastor, L. L. Laestadius, and its main expansion has been in white Lutheran churches, especially in Finland and among emigrants in the United States. Insofar, however, as it did spread among the Sami it has much in common with this kind of movement among other primal or tribal peoples. We have therefore included a selection of materials, even though in some cases the reference to the Sami is slight.

North (Scandinavia)

357 Boreman, Per. *Laestadianismen*. Fennoskandiens märkligaste väckelse och dess förhållande till kyran. Stockholm, 1953, 291 pp.

358 Boreman, Per, and Dahlback, Gustav, eds. *Lars Levi Laestadius och hans gärning: Festskift till hundraårsminnet av hans od, den 21 februari 1861*. Stockholm, 1965, 454 pp., portraits.

359 Brännström, Olaus. "Om laestadianska själavärdstraditionen i Sverige under 1800-talet." Th.D. dissertation, Uppsala University, 1962, with English summary.
    By the Bishop of Lulea. On the Laestadian pastoral tradition.

360 Castrén, Kaarlo. *Kiveliön suuri herättäjä Lars Levi Laestadius*. Helsinki, 1934, 277 pp.
    On the personality of Laestadius.

361 Engh, Arne. "Stockfleth og Samene." *Norsk Tidsskrift for Misjon* 3, no. 3 (1949): 177-87.
    Stockfleth's labors on behalf of Christianity and civilization amongst the Lapps of northern Norway. Pp. 184-86, activities at Kautokeino, and L. L. Laestadius.

362 Gjessing, Gutorm. *Changing Lapps: A study in culture relations in northernmost Norway*. Monographs on Social Anthropology, 13. London: Department of Anthropology, London School of Economics and Political Science, 1954, 67 pp.
    Chap. 4, Laestadianism: as a revivalistic Lutheran movement.

363 Gjessing, Gutorm. "Culture contact in a Lapp (Sami) community: Karasjok in eastern Finnmark, Norway." *Man*, article 174, 53 (1953):116-17.

364 Haetta, Lars Jacobsen. "En beretning om de religiøse og moralske forhold i Kautokeino før den laestadianske vaekkelse." Bidrag til Finmarkens Kirkehistorie, 2. *Norvegia Sacra* (Oslo) 3 (1923): 68-89.
    Laestadianism.

365 Holmio, Armas K. E. "Apostolic Lutheran Churches in America." In *The encyclopedia of the Lutheran Church*, edited by J. Bodensieck. Minneapolis: Augsburg, 1965.
    Vol. 1, p. 97, on Laestadian church.

366 Kantonen, Taito A. "Laestadius, Lars Levi." In *The encyclopedia of the Lutheran Church*, edited by J. Bodensieck. Minneapolis: Augsburg, 1965.
Vol. 2, pp. 242b-245a, + photo; very sketchy.

367 Kostet, Oskar. "Korpelarörelsen: Studier i en nutida primitivorgiastik sekt." Kandidatsavhandling till Religionhistoriska Proseminariet Stockholms Högskola September 1950. Mimeo.
On Torvio Korpela's revivalist "sect" derivative from Laestadianism in the 1930s.

368 Lindgreen, E. J. "Divination by 'magic' drums. Rare relics of the ancient Lapp religion (finally abolished in the 18th century) which were destroyed in thousands by Christian missionaries: Two examples preserved at Cambridge." *Illustrated London News*, 4 January 1936, pp. 14-16, illus.
P. 14, Southern Swedish Lapps escaped the fanatical revivalist movement which spread over northern Lapland in the 19th century, as well as earlier missionaries; i.e. a "negative instance."

369 Manker, Ernst Mauritz. *Över vidderna: Skisser och studier från landet i norr*. Stockholm: LTs Förlag, 1952, 303 pp., illus.
Pp. 218-20, 225-26, Lapp ecstatic "dancing."

370 Mühlmann, Wilhelm Emil. "Hyperboräische eschatologie." In *Chiliasmus und Nativismus*, edited by W. E. Mühlmann. Berlin: D. Reimer, 1961. Reprint. 1964, pp. 197-221, bib.
Pp. 198-202, The Lapps and Laestadianism.

371 Paine, Robert [Patrick Barten]. *Coast Lapp society*. 2 vols. Tromsø Museums Skrifter, 4. Tromsø: Universitetsforlaget, 1:1957; 2:1965.
Vol. 1: Study of neighborhood in Revsbotn Fjord; pp. 85, 238, 248 on Laestadianism. Vol. 2: Study of economic development and social values. See index and pp. 120-37, 160-61, 180-83, Laestadianism.

372 Raittila, Pekka. *Laestadiolaisuuden matrikkeli ja bibliografia: Biographia et bibliographia laestadiana*. Suomen Kirkkohistoriallisen Seuran Toimituksia, vol. 74. 1967, 366 pp.

373 Saarnivaara, Uuras. *Amerikan Laestadiolaisuuden eli Apostolisluterilaisuuden historia*. Ironwood, Mich.: National Publishing Co., 1947, 364 pp., illus.

North (Scandinavia)

In Finnish. The Apostolic Lutheran Church in America (1879-1962) – formerly Finnish A.L.C.A.

374 Saarnivaara, Uuras. *The history of the Laestadian or Apostolic-Lutheran movement in America*. Ironwood, Mich.: National Publishing Co., 1947, 98 pp., illus.
A summary of his "excellent history in Finnish." The only account Whitaker (entry 384) could trace in English. Pp. 7-19, before arrival in America.

375 Sandewall, Allan. "Separatismen i övre Norrland 1820-1855." 2 vols. Skrifter i Utgivna av Svenska Kyrkhistoriska Föreningen, Ny följd, no. 4. Uppsala and Stockholm, 1952, xiii + 312 pp. Published as *Separatismen i övre Norrland efter 1855*. Uppsala Universitets årsskrift, no. 1. Uppsala and Weisbaden, 1954, 149 pp., English summary.
A thesis. Includes Laestadianism.

376 Silvertsen, Dagmar. *Laestadianismen i Norge*. Oslo, 1955, 500 pp.

377 Spencer, Arthur. *The Lapps*. This Changing World. New York: Crane Russak; Newton Abbot: David & Charles, 1978, 160 pp., illus.
Pp. 34-36, spread of Christianity, including pp. 35-36 on Laestadianism from 1845 – "the new doctrine, now moderated, retains an essential role in the Lutheran religion as practiced by the Lapps, not least because it helps to preserve the old values and the traditional social structure" (p. 36); pp. 84-100, traditional religion including bear cult and cult sites.

378 Ström, Åke Victor Ored. "Tradition und Tendenz: Zur Frage des christlichvorchristlichen Synkretismus in der nordgermanischen Literatur." In *Syncretism*, edited by S. S. Hartmann. Stockholm: Almquist & Wiksell, 1969, pp. 240-62.
Despite its title, this does include Christian influence.

379 Suolinna, Kirsti. "Den laestadianska väckelserörelsen i Tornedalen." In *Studier kring gränsen i Tornedalen*, edited by E. Haavio-Mannila and K. Suolinna. Nordisk Udredningsserie. Nordisk Betaenkninger 7. Stockholm: Fritzes Hovbokhandel, 1971, 183 pp., illus.
Sociology of Laestadianism in the Tornio river valley.

380 Suolinna, Kirsti. "The relationship between social change and religious movements." In *Dynamics and institution ... Symposium at Åbo ...*

1976, edited by H. Biezais. Stockholm: Almquist & Wiksell International, 1976, pp. 45-55.

Religious groups expressing the social interests more indirectly than political groups in the course of group conflict. Laestadianism provides the case study, especially as in northern Finland in 1976. Passing mention of the Lapps as an ethnic minority being represented by Laestadianism. The inner tensions in on-going Laestadianism.

381 Suolinna, Kirsti. "Yhteiskunnan ja uskonnollisten liikkeitten suhteista." *Helsingin yliopiston sosiologian laitoksen tutkimuksia* (Helsinki) 119 (1969): 1ff.
Sociology of Laestadianism; Tornio river valley area, Finnish-Swedish border.

382 Thulin, Henning. *Lars Levi Laestadius och hans förkunnelse.* Stockholm: Förlaget Filadelfia, 1949, 232 pp.
Laestadius.

383 Vorren, Ørnulv, and Manker, Ernst. *Same kulturen.* Oslo: Oslo University Press, 1958. English translation. *Lapp life and customs: A survey.* London: Oxford University Press, 1962, 183 pp.
Pp. 118-28 (English translation), Lapp shamanism; pp. 128-30, conversion to Christianity, from the seventeenth century; p. 130, Lars Laestadius and Laestadianism as the Lapp form of Christianity, shared with whites.

384 Whitaker, Ian R. *Social relations in a nomadic Lappish community.* Samiske Samlinger 2, Redaksjon Asbjorn Nesheim. Oslo: Norsk Folkemuseum, 1955, 178 pp., map.
Chap. 12 (pp. 105-11), "The social aspects of religion in Karesuando," is entirely on Laestadianism.

385 Zidbäck, Aulis. *Lars Levi Laestadiuksen kristillisyydennäkemys.* Turku, 1937, 243 pp.
A thesis on Laestadius.

386 Zidbäck, Aulis. *Pohjolan suurin maallikkosaarnaaja Juhani Raattamaan.* Helsinki: Kustannusosakeyhtiö Otava, 1941, 270 pp., illus.
Laestadianism.

East (Russian Europe, Balkans)

EAST (Russian Europe, Balkans)

For general comments on the question of these new religious movements in Europe see the introductory note to the Europe section, above.

In eastern Europe the kinds of movements with which we are concerned may be identified in at least two areas. The item by V. G. Marinich (entry 389) describes "revitalization movements in Kievan Russia" from the tenth to the twelfth centuries. Other items describe the Kuga Sorta or "Big Candle" movement among the Cheremis people from the later nineteenth century. This is important because of its lateness in history for a European context, and for the presence of Eastern Orthodoxy as one of the partners in the interaction. Unfortunately, little information as to the later history of this movement has been available since the Russian Revolution; we are dependent chiefly on the work of T. A. Sebeok in the 1950s.

387 Kuznetsov, S. K. [The Cheremis sect Kuga Sorta.] *Ethnograficheskoe Obozrenie* 29, no. 4 (1908) (appeared 1909): 1-59.
In Russian. A detailed sympathetic account: new domestic beeswax-candle cult replacing traditional groves and animal sacrifices; moral reforms; history of founding brothers Yakmanov and of the persecution of the movement.

388 Lanternari, Vittorio. *The religions of the oppressed: A study of modern messianic cults*. London: MacGibbon & Kee, 1963, xx + 343 + xiii pp. Toronto: New American Library of Canada, 1963. New York: Knopf, 1963. New York: Mentor Books, 1965, xvi + 286 pp.
Pp. 229-32 (London ed.), the Kuga Sorta (Big Candle) movement among the Cheremis, a Finnish-stock people in the Upper Volga region of Russia, from the 1870s.

389 Marinich, V. G. "Revitalization movements in Kievan Russia." *Journal for the Scientific Study of Religion* 15, no. 1 (1976): 61-68.
Contra-acculturative religious movements from the tenth to twelfth centuries, after conversion of ruling classes to Christianity.

390 Sebeok, Thomas A[lbert]. *The Cheremis*. Studies in Cheremis, vol. 5. New Haven: Human Relations Area Files, 1955.
Includes Kuga Sorta.

391 Sebeok, Thomas A[lbert]. "Cow swallows book: An instance of Cheremis nativism." *Ural-Altaische Jahrbucher* 28 (1956): 215-19.

On the alleged "lost book" of the Cheremis – a story developed in reaction against Russian and Christian pressures.

392 Sebeok, Thomas A[lbert]. "Eighteenth century Cheremis: The evidence from Pallas." In *American Studies in Uralic Linguistics*. Bloomington: Indiana University Publications, 1960, pp. 289-345.
On the Cheremis before the Kuga Sorta.

393 Sebeok, Thomas A[lbert]. "The seventeenth century Cheremis: The evidence from Witsen." In *On language, culture, and religion: In honor of Eugene A. Nida*, edited by M. Black and W. A. Smalley. The Hague: Mouton, 1974, pp. 301-14, illus.
On the Cheremis before the Kuga Sorta movement, but after a few had become Christians or Muslims. As background to the Kuga Sorta movement.

394 Sebeok, Thomas A[lbert], and Ingemann, Frances J. *"Big candle": A nativistic movement*. Indiana University, [1953?], 78 leaves, bib. (pp. 75-77).

395 Sebeok, Thomas A[lbert], and Ingemann, Frances J. *Studies in Cheremis: The supernatural*. Studies in Cheremis, vol. 2. Viking Fund publications in Anthroplogy, 22. New York: Wenner-Gren Foundation, 1956, 357 pp.
Pp. 320-37, Kuga Sorta "nativistic sect" – from ca. 1870, in Jaransk district of the Mari Soviet Republic.

396 Sebeok, Thomas A[lbert], and Raun, Alo. *The first Cheremis grammar*. Studies in Cheremis, vol. 3. Chicago: Newberry Library, 1956, 136 pp.
Includes Kuga Sorta. A facsimile of 1775 edition with introduction and analysis.

397 Vasiljev, V. M. [The Cheremis religious sect Kuga Sorta.] Krasnokokshaisk, 1927.
In Russian. Cited by T. A. Sebeok and F. J. Ingemann (entry 395).

398 Wallace, Donald MacKenzie. *Russia*. Rev. and enl. ed. London: Cassell & Co., 1912, 788 pp., map.
Pp. 152-68, on the "Russification" of Finnish and Tartar villages, including Cheremis people, and on religious interaction, but no mention of Kuga Sorta.

East (Russian Europe, Balkans)

399 Zykov, N. V. [Religious trends among the Mari.] Nizhni Novgorod, 1932.

      In Russian. Cited by T. A. Sebeok and F. J. Ingemann (entry 395).

WEST, CENTRAL, AND SOUTH

There are no tribal peoples with a primal type of religion (unless the Gypsies be so regarded) in these European areas, and any movements within our categories found in this region are nonindigenous entries from elsewhere–especially from Latin America and the Caribbean (e.g., Rastafarians), black Africa (independent churches such as Kimbanguism and the Celestial Church of Christ), Vietnam (Cao Dai), the Philippines (Iglesia ni Cristo), and Korea (Unification Church). All such movements are dealt with in the bibliographies in the country of origin. At the same time, there are indigenous new religious movements in this region that have more in common phenomenologically with those of our category than with many of the so-called sects and cults–they are folk religions with prophets (as with prophet Lou among fisher people in the Netherlands), healing, millennialism, etc. Here we can no more than call attention to this further range of religious developments.

400 Van Fossen, Anthony Belgrano. "Disciples of the living God: The origins, prophetic failures, hierarchies, and survival of a contemporary French messianic movement." Ph.D. dissertation, Princeton University, 1982, 303 pp.

      The Église-Chrétienne Universelle–a messianic and millennial healing movement near Avignon from 1947; how it changed to deal with failed prophecies, and the founders' successive claims to be Christ, God, and "an ever more ethereal God." 1980 had been set as the date of the millennium.

401 Zaal, Wim. *Gods onkruid: Nederlandse sekten en messiassen.* Amsterdam: Meulenhoff, 1972, 150 pp.

      Pp. 97-144, Lou de Palingboer in the Netherlands.

Asia

THEORY

This is admittedly somewhat of a "hold-all" group for items that are predominantly theoretical but usually related more specifically to one particular part of Asia, especially to India. There are, however, so few that it did not seem practicable to form a separate theoretical group for individual Asian countries. Those interested in one country should also refer to this initial Asian section on theory for relevant material.

402 Bhatt, Gavri Shankar. "Brahmo Samaj, Arya Samaj, and the church-sect typology." *Review of Religious Research* 10, no. 1 (1968): 23-32.

   A testing of the Western typology in a non-Western religious context: it fails to apply, since these movements are more like castes than sects, denominations, or churches, and orthodox Hinduism does not fit the church category.

403 England, John C. "The shape of theological reflection – using people's movements as resource." *Ching Feng* (Hong Kong) 28, no. 4 (1985): 207-20.

   Presenting the method, contents, and aims of a theology that takes people's movements as a resource in Asia.

404 Fuchs, Stephen. "Applied anthropology in India." In *Anthropology and archaeology*, edited by M. C. Pradhan, et al. Bombay and London: Oxford University Press, 1969, pp. 258-71.

   Background for acculturation, with some account of Hindu influences.

Theory

405 Fuchs, Stephen. "Messianic movements: A new missionary method for India?" *Verbum SVD* (Rome) 13, nos. 3-4 (1972). Reprinted in *Catalyst* (Goroka, Papua New Guinea) 6, no. 1 (1976): 3-17.

The use of messianic mass movements as instruments of conversion to Christianity. P. 5, two late nineteenth-century examples; p. 7, similar earlier Bengali movements towards Islam; pp. 12-13, two lost opportunities for the churches; the possibility of encouraging or even providing charismatic messiahs in certain situations.

406 Houtart, François, and Lemercinier, Genevieve. "Le rôle des mouvements religieux dans le passage d'une société de caste à une société de classe à Kerala (Inde du sud)." *Annual Review of the Social Sciences of Religion* (The Hague), no. 1 (1977), pp. 185ff.

407 Jay, Edward J. "A comparison of tribal and peasant villages in India." *Journal of the Indian Anthropological Society* 9, no. 1 (1974): 36-69.

Suggesting that they belong to the same socio-cultural continuum.

408 Klimkeit, Hans-Joachim. *Anti-religiöse Bewegungen in modernen Südindien: Eine religionssoziologische Untersuchungen zur Säkularisierungsfrage.* Untersuchungen zur allgemeinen Religionsgeschichte, n.s. 7. Bonn: Ludwig Röhrscheid, 1971, 155 pp.

Chap. 1 discusses current theories as applicable to India – "nativism," "messianism," "acculturation," etc.

409 Klimkeit, Hans-Joachim. "Das Kreuzsymbol in der Zentralasiatischen Religionsbewegung." *Zeitschrift für Religions- und Geistsgeschichte* 31, no. 1 (1979): 99-115.

Background for Burkhanism.

410 Lindgren, Ethel John. "An example of culture contact without conflict: Reindeer Tungus and Cossacks of northwestern Manchuria." *American Anthropologist* 40, no. 4 (1938): 605-21.

A "negative instance": The Cossacks were nonmissionary, respected Tungus shamanism, and lived in harmony with the Tungus; no new movements appeared.

411 Redfield, Robert. "Culture contact without conflict." *American Anthropologist*, n.s. 41, no. 3 (1939): 514-17.

Ladinos and Indians in Lake Atitlan region of Guatemala, discussed in relation to E. J. Lindgren's article on the Cossacks-Tungus contact (entry 410). A "negative instance."

412 Sachchidananda. *Culture change in tribal Bihar: Munda and Oraon.* Calcutta: Bookland, 1964, 158 pp., illus.

On failure of recent efforts at deliberate assimilation and development.

413 Scheiner, Irwin. "The mindful peasant: Sketches for a study of rebellion." *Journal of Asian Studies* 32, no. 4 (1973): 579-91.

414 Schreike, B. "Native society in the transformation period." In *The effect of Western influence on native civilizations in the Malay Archipelago,* edited by B. Schreike. Batavia: G. Kolff & Co., 1929, pp. 237-47.

415 Scott, James C. *The moral economy of the peasant: Rebellion and subsistence in Southeast Asia.* New Haven: Yale University Press, 1976, 246 pp.

Includes revolts with religious forms; see pp. 91-100, 149-56, 219-25, 233-40. Movements referred to include Iglesia ni Cristo (pp. 219-20, 221, 224) and Sakdalista (Philippines), Samin (Java), and Saya San (Burma – pp. 99-100, 149-57, etc.).

416 Seunarine, J. F. *Reconversion to Hinduism through Suddhi.* Madras: Christian Literature Society, 1977, 105 pp.

Pp. 90-93, applying A. F. C. Wallace's revitalization theory to the Hindu Arya Samaj movement.

GENERAL

In view of the cultural and religious diversity of Asia, it is not surprising that there should be only one item with anything like a general survey, and even that somewhat limited.

417 Moritzen, Niels-Peter. "Gibt es asiatische unabhängige Kirchen." *Ökumenische Rundschau* 32, no. 3 (1983): 318-34.

Are there independent churches as in Africa? Examples proposed from Japan (Mukyokai and Mayuka), Korea (the Unification Church is not Christian), China (Watchman Nee's "Little Flock," True Jesus Church), the Philippines (Philippine Independent Church, Iglesia ni Cristo), Indonesia (Coolen's Church, Muhdi-Akbar, Huria Kristen Indonesia, etc.), India (various guru and Pentecostal groups, but none of those related to the tribal peoples is mentioned); the difficulty in securing information that is embarrassing to the older churches.

North Central (Mongolia, Siberia, etc.)

NORTH CENTRAL (Mongolia, Siberia, etc.)

There is a paucity of recorded movements in this vast area and a dearth of information since the Russian Revolution. It is suspected that there may be much still to learn about movements among these peoples, although the absence of a major stimulus from Christian missions and other contacts may be a factor in the situation. The main movements seem to be Samojeden and the Burkhan, the latter among the Altai Turks in 1904 having Buddhist and some Christian aspects.

418 A[ckerblom], B. "Eine religiöse Bewegung im Altai." *Globus* 89 (1906): 220-21.
   On Burkhanism among the Kalmuck, from personal observation in 1904.

419 Adelman, Fred. "Kalmyk cultural renewal." Ph.D. dissertation (anthropology), University of Pennsylvania, 1960, 338 pp.
   Includes a Kalmuck Mongol nativistic Buddhist-related cult.

420 Anokhin, A. V. "Burkhanizm v Zapadnom Altae." *Sibirskie Ogni* 5 (1927): 162-67.
   Burkhanism in the western Altai.

421 Bakai, N. "Legendarnyi Oirot-Khan." *Sibirskie Ogni* 4 (1926): 117-24.
   Materials from the Tomsk Archival Bureau 44, 1904, on the legendary figure featured in the Burkhan movement; see L. Krader (entry 426).

422 Castrén, Matthias Alexander. *Reiseerinnerungen aus der Jahren 1835-44.* Nordische Reisen und Fordschungen, vol. 1. St. Peterburg: Buchdruckerei der Kaiserlichen Akademie der Wissenschaften, 1853, 308 pp.
   Pp. 169f. the Samojeden movement – cited by W. E. Mühlmann (entry 171), p. 221.

423 Diâkonova, V. P. "Religioznye kul'ty tuvintsêv." *Sbornik* (Leningrad Akademiiâ nauk SSSR, Muzei Antropologii i Etnografii) 33 (1977): 172-216.
   Religious cults of the Tuvintsy.

North Central (Mongolia, Siberia, etc.)

424 Guariglia, Guglielmo. *Prophetismus und Heilserwartungs-Bewgungen als völkerkundliches und religionsgeschichtliches Problem*. Vienna: R. Berger, 1959, xvi + 332 pp., maps, bib.
Pp. 239-41, general; pp. 241-42, Oirot-Khan (Altai Turks); pp. 247-48, Kesar-Sage (Tibet).

425 Heissig, Walter, and Klimkeit, Hans-Joachim, eds. *Synkretismus in den Religionen zentral-asiens: Ergebnisse eines Kolloquium vom 24,5 bis 26,5.1983 in St. Augustin bei Bonn*. Studies in Oriental Religions, 13. Weisbaden: O. Harrassowitz, 1987, 226 pp.
Fifteen papers, not specifically on named movements, but highly relevant to the issues.

426 Krader, Lawrence. "A nativistic movement in western Siberia." *American Anthropologist* 58, no. 2 (1956): 282-92.
Among Altai-Turks, 1904 – the Oirot-Khan or Burkhan movement under prophet Chot Chelpan; part of nativistic responses to Western impact, anti-Russian, messianic, with Buddhist and Christian elements.

427 La Barre, Weston. *The Ghost Dance*. Garden City, N.Y.: Doubleday, 1970, 677 pp.
Pp. 234-35, on Burkhan movement in the Altai area from 1904 until World War II.

428 Lanternari, Vittorio. *The religions of the oppressed: A study of modern messianic cults*. London: MacGibbon & Kee, 1963, xx + 343 + xiii pp. Toronto: New American Library of Canada, 1963. New York: Knopf, 1963. New York: Mentor Books, 1965, xvi + 286 pp.
Pp. 285-88 (London ed.), Burkhan.

429 Laufer, Berthold. "Burkhan." *Journal of the American Oriental Society* 36 (1917): 390-95.
On etymology of the name "Burkhan," which denotes the Buddha in Mongol literature, but also deities in general. Nothing on Burkhan movement as such.

430 Mänchen-Helfen, Otto. *Reise ins Asiatische Tuwa*. Berlin: Verlag der Bücherkreis, 1931, 172 pp., illus., map.
Pp. 95-96, outline of Burkhanism among the Altai and neighboring Tuwa, and its continuance underground.

North Central (Mongolia, Siberia, etc.)

431 Mühlmann, Wilhelm Emil. "Hyperboräische eschatologie." In *Chiliasmus und Nativismus*, edited by W. E. Mühlmann. Berlin: D. Reimer, 1961. Reprint. 1964, pp. 197-221, bib.

   Pp. 202-5, Samojeden movement; pp. 205-10, Burkhan (based on L. Krader, entry 426).

432 Schmidt, Wilhelm. *Der Ursprung der Gottesidee*. Vol. 9, *Die Primäre Histenvolk der Alt-Türken, der Altai-und Abakan-Tatarn*. Munster: Verlag Aschendorff; Freiburg in der Schwiez: Paulusverlag, 1949.

   Pp. 118f., 172f., Turk tribes influenced by Islam added a holy book of wisdom, "Nom," after they had developed a kind of runic script by the seventh century A.D.

433 Schrenk, A. G. *Reise nach dem Nordosten des europäischen Russlands durch die Tundren der Samojeden zum Arktischen Uralgebirge*. 2 vols. Dorpat, 1848, 1854.

   Vol. 1, pp. 409ff., Samojeden movement. Cited by W. E. Mühlmann, *Chiliasmus und Nativismus* (entry 171).

WEST

434 Isenberg, Sheldon R. "Millenarianism in Greco-Roman Palestine." *Religion: Journal of Religion and Religions* 4 (Spring 1974): 26-46.

   Applies models used by social scientists (especially K. O. L. Burridge, P. M. Worsley), and the writers in *Millennial dreams in action*, edited by S. L. Thrupp [entry 228] to Palestinian movements in antiquity.

EAST

CHINA AND TAIWAN

This section includes Hong Kong (but not Singapore or the Chinese diaspora) and also Taiwan, but without any reference to its recent or future political history. Strictly speaking, Chinese movements do not arise within the milieu of a primal religion, unless it were to be among the tribal peoples to the far west. A small selection of items on peasant revolts, often with syncretist or millennial features, such as the White Lotus sects, and especially the Taiping movement, have, however, been included. A separate bibliography on the religious aspects of the Taiping movement is planned by the Centre for New Religious Movements. Chinese sects in general are not covered. Some items on independent churches in Hong Kong (M. Berndt, 435) and Taiwan are included for comparative purposes with other areas, and because the hill or aboriginal peoples of Taiwan do fall within our stricter category. A further item on Taiwan by C.-F. Hsiao (entry 442) also serves comparative purposes.

435 Berndt, Manfred Helmuth. "The Diakonia function of the Church in Hong Kong." S.T.D. dissertation, Concordia Seminary (St. Louis), Dept. of Practical Theology, 1970, 400 pp.

Chap. 10 (pp. 268-301), on para- and non-Christian religions; chap. 11 (pp. 302-8), conclusions; Appendix E. (pp. 345-48), membership of churches in Hong Kong.

436 Bolton, Robert. "South of the clouds: Church planting in Yunnan Province through Lisu people movements (1906-1949)." Research paper, Fuller Theological Seminary, School of World Mission (Pasadena), 1974. Revised, 1981, 16 pp. Typescript.

On "people movements" in relation to Assemblies of God missionaries.

437 Dardess, John W. "The transformations of messianic revolt and the founding of the Ming dynasty." *Journal of Asian Studies* 29, no. 3 (1970): 539-58.

438 Forbes, Andrew D. W. "The Muslim national minorities of China." *Religion* 6, no. 1 (1976): 67-87.

Pp. 73-77, "New Sect" and "Old Sect" Islamic movements in central Asia; New Sect founded 1762; both involved in rebellions against the Ching dynasty in the nineteenth century.

439 Glüer, Winfried. "The New Confucian – a modern religious movement." *Ching Feng* (Hong Kong) 15, no. 3 (1972): 138-43.

The New Confucian Church in Taiwan and the Chinese diaspora from the 1950s, based on revelation to Ch'en Chien-fu, and with both traditional and Christian elements.

440 Grootaers, Willem A. Review of *The religions of the oppressed*, by V. Lanternari (entry 428). *Current Anthropology* 6, no. 4 (1965): 451.

I-Koan-Tao, etc., mediumistic cults since 1939 as messianic Christian-Chinese syncretisms reacting against Japanese occupation and later the Communist government, and embracing the majority of north China peasants. Valuable for scarce sources.

East: China and Taiwan

441 Grootaers, Willem A. "Une société secrète moderne, I-Koan-Tao: Bibliographie annotée." *Folklore Studies* (Catholic University of Peking) 5 (1946): 316-52.

442 Hsiao, Ching-fen. "The current situation of new religions in Taiwan." *Theology and the Church* (Tainan) 10, nos. 2-3 (1971): 1-28. Shorter version in *New religions of the east Asia region – Korea, Japan, Taiwan: Reports of the Study Commission, Tokyo, 1972.* Korea Christian Academy, 1972, pp. 13-32.

From Japan: Tenrikyo, Nichirenkyo; from Korea: Tong-i-shen-ling-chiao (neo-Confucian with Christian elements); Coscino-mancy (planchettes, etc.); neo-Taoist movements, charismatic leaders, and unity-of-all-religions movements. Not related to primal religions but as examples of popular religious innovation.

443 Naquin, Susan. *Millenarian rebellion in China: The Eight Trigrams uprising of 1813.* New Haven: Yale University Press, 1976, 384 pp.

Arising within, and in partial reaction against a "great" religious tradition. A White Lotus set of peasant origin, as a late example of this continuing religious tradition.

444 Overmyer, Daniel L. "Folk-Buddhist religion: Creation and eschatology in medieval China." *History of Religions* 12, no. 1 (1972): 42-70.

Buddhist syncretist popular movements, which often had political or rebel aspects; the White Lotus Sect – its history, mythology, and eschatology.

445 Perry, Elizabeth J., and Chang, Tom. "The mystery of Yellow Cliff." *Modern China* (Beverly Hills and London) 6, no. 2 (1980): 123-60.

A religious rebellion in central Shandong province in 1866, on a remote mountain top, Yellow Cliff – a rural elite with a peculiar religious doctrine and incorporating outlaws.

446 *Religion in the People's Republic of China.* Documentation, no. 18 (December 1985), pp. 29-30.

The Shandong Independent Church.

447 Seaman, Gary North. "Temple organization in a Chinese village." Ph.D. dissertation (anthropology), Cornell University, 1974, 179 pp.

The historical development of a new religious cult using the sand planchette in séances: its ideology, organization, and interaction with village factions.

448 Seiwert, Hubert. "Religious response to modernization in Taiwan: The case of I-Kuan Tao." *Journal of the Hong Kong Branch of the Royal Asiatic Society* 21 (1981): 43-70.

449 Shek, Richard. "Millenarianism: Chinese millenarian movements." In *The encyclopedia of religion*, edited by M. Eliade. Vol. 9. New York: Macmillan, 1987, pp. 532-36.

450 Shek, Richard. "The revolt of the Zaili, Jindan Sects in Rehe (Jehol), 1891. *Modern China* (Beverly Hills and London) 6, no. 2 (1980): 161-96.
      White Lotus.

451 Thaxton, Ralph. "Some critical comments on peasant revolts and revolutionary politics in China." *Journal of Asian Studies* 33, no. 2 (1974): 279-88.
      Review article on J. Chesneaux, *Peasant revolts in China, 1840-1949* (London: Thames & Hudson, 1973), 180 pp., illus., maps. An important theoretical article.

452 Welch, Holmes, and Yü, Chün-fang. "The tradition of innovation: A Chinese new religion." *Numen* 27, no. 2 (1980): 222-46.
      "The Holy Teaching of Heaven's Virtue," founded in 1899 and flourishing in the New Territories and in Taiwan, as it did in Hong Kong in the 1960s. A syncretism of Buddhist, Taoist, and other Chinese systems.

KOREA

There have been influential immigrant religions in Korea, especially Confucianism from China, which was important at all levels in society; Pure Land Buddhism, a popular form from the seventh century; and Christianity, spreading widely since the later nineteenth century. The autochthonous religion was an unusual form of shamanism (more like spirit possession) that may be treated as within the family of primal religions. From about the middle of the last century, about 200 new religions have appeared, usually by interaction with one of the immigrant traditions (increasingly, with Christianity) to form new syncretisms. The best-known in the West, but not the largest, is Tŏngil-gyo, or the Unification Church, which is summarily presented here as one of the Particular Movements at the end of the Asian series.

East: Korea

453 Bieder, Werner. "How I experienced South Korea theologically." *Northeast Asia Journal of Theology* (Tokyo), no. 10 (March 1973), pp. 1-14.
Pp. 12-13, questions that the new religions present to the Christian Church in Korea.

454 Chang Byung-il. *Religions in Korea.* Seoul: Korean Overseas Information Service, 1984, 66 pp., illus.
Pp. 27-35, new religions – 14 listed in a table; p. 55, "Bahaism"; pp. 55-57, Chinese (Taoist) and Japanese new religions introduced. Note: no mention even of the Unification Church of S. M. Moon.

455 Ch'oe Chae-sŏk. "A sociological survey of Sindonae." *Transactions of the Korea Branch, Royal Asiatic Society: The New Religions of Korea* (Seoul) 43 (1967): 129-56.
Includes new religions – Sangje-gyo, Ilsim-gyo, Kwansŏng-gyo, Ch'ŏndo-gyo, etc.

456 Ch'oe Sin-dŏk. *A comparative study of the new religious groups in Korea.* Seoul: Christian Seminary Press, 1965.

457 Ch'oe Sin-dŏk. "A comparative study of two new religious movements in the Republic of Korea: The Unification Church and the Full Gospel Central Church." In *New religious movements and rapid social change*, edited by J. A. Beckford. Beverly Hills: Sage Publications, 1986, pp. 113-45.

458 Ch'oe Sin-dŏk. "Korea's Tong-il movement." In *Transactions of the Korea Branch, Royal Asiatic Society: The New Religions of Korea* (Seoul) 43 (1967): 167-80.

459 Ch'oe Sin-dŏk. "A sociological study of the S. Church." *Journal of the Korean Sociological Association* (Seoul) 13:49-77.

460 Cho Yong-il. "Arrière-plan de la pensée du Tong-Hak." In *Collection d'articles sur la pensée coréenne.* Vol. 3. Seoul, 1973, pp. 156-81.
Denies the influence of Catholicism.

461 Chung Chai Sik. "Korea: The continuing syncretism." In *Religion and societies: Asia and the Middle East*, edited by C. Calderola. Religion and Society, 22. The Hague: Mouton Publishers, 1982, 688 pp.
Pp. 622-24, the "new religions" – mainly on Tonghak.

462 Chung Chai Sik. "Religion and cultural identity–the case of 'Eastern Learning.'" In *International Yearbook for the Sociology of Religion*, edited by J. Matthes, 5 (1969): 118-32, German summary.
On Tonghak, 1860s-.

463 Clark, Charles A[llen]. *Religions of old Korea*. New York: Fleming H. Revell, 1932, 245 pp. Seoul: Christian Literature Society, 1961, 295 pp., illus.
Pp. 130-31, Poch'ŏn-gyo (spiritualism); pp. 140-43, Tan'gun-gyo, of Kim Yum Paik; pp. 144-72, "the most complete English language discussions of Ch'ŏndo-gyo as a religious cult"; pp. 258-76, the Bible of the Ch'ŏndo-gyo (text).

464 "La Corée du Sud, record mondial des religions nouvelles: plus de 200." *Missi* (Lyons), no. 10 (December 1976), pp. 318-22.
Of these 200, 90 religions are officially registered.

465 Earhart, H. Byron. "The new religions of Korea: A preliminary interpretation." *Transactions of the Korea Branch, Royal Asiatic Society* (Seoul) 49 (1974): 7-25.

466 Henderson, Gregory. *Korea: The politics of the vortex*. Cambridge: Harvard University Press, 1968, 479 pp.
Pp. 63-65, 68-71, Tonghak as new syncretic revealed religion, which supported Japan in 1904-5, and was renamed Ch'ŏndo-gyo in 1905.

467 Hong Sŏn-gyŏng. "Tonghak in the context of Korean modernization." *Review of Religious Research* (North Newton, Kan.) 10, no. 1 (1968): 43-51.

468 Hulbert, Homer C. "The Religion of the Heavenly Way." *Korea Review: A Monthly Magazine* (Seoul), November 1906, pp. 460-65.

469 Hyon Sidong. "Tayonggyo." In *Korea, its land, people, and culture in all ages*, edited by Korean Government. Seoul: Hakwon-sa, 1960, pp. 348-51.

470 Ikche, O. "The Tonghak movement." In *Korea, its land, people, and culture in all ages*, edited by Korean Government. Seoul: Hakwon-sa, 1960, pp. 342-48.

East: Korea

471 Ji, Won-yong. "Christian churches and sects." In *Korea struggles for Christ*, edited by H. S. Wong. Seoul: Christian Literature Society of Korea, 1966, pp. 113-32.

472 Junkin, William N. "The Tonghak." *Korean Repository* 2, no. 2 (1895): 56-61.
Outline of founder's vision and call; his sources for his new religious and magical practices; uprising, and suppression of the movement in 1894.

473 Kang Wi Jo. "Belief and political behavior in Ch'ŏndo-gyo." *Review of Religious Research* (North Newton, Kan.) 10, no. 1 (1968): 38-43, bib.

474 Kim Han-gu. "Religious protest and revitalization movements among minorities." *Korea Journal* 20, no. 9 (1980): 17-25.

475 Kim Han-gu. "Tonghak: Revitalization movement in Korea." Ph.D. dissertation (anthropology), University of Toronto, 1970, xi + 370 pp.
Analyzes the historical development of the movement and its social effects.

476 Kim Myung H. "Prayer, revival, and evangelization of the church in Korea." *World Evangelization* (Singapore), no. 50 [15] (January-February 1988), pp. 9-13, illus.
P. 12, Prayer Mountain movements from 1910 and increasingly from 1945, as a "nursery of pseudo-religious movements and heretical sects" – often "legalistic, superstitious, or blessing pursuing," as well as nationalistic.

477 Kim Ui-hwan. "L'arrière-plan historique de la pensée du Tonghak." In *Collection d'articles sur la pensée coréenne*. Vol. 3. Seoul, 1973, pp. 87-156.

478 Kim Yong-bock. "Historical transformation: People's movement and messianic koinonia: A study of the relationship of Christian and Tonghak religious communities to the March First Independence movement in Korea." Ph.D. dissertation (religion), Princeton Seminary, 1976.

479 Kim Yong-bock. "Messiah and Minjung: Discerning politics over against political messianism." In *Minjung theology: People as the subjects of history*, edited by Y. B. Kim. Singapore: Christian Conference of Asia, 1981, pp. 185-96.

Donghak religion, etc.

480 Kim Yong-choon. "An analysis of early Ch'ŏndo-gyo thought." *Korea Journal* (Seoul) 17, no. 10 (1977): 41-46.
A paper presented at the International Association for the History of Religions Congress, Lancaster, 1975.

481 Kim Yong-choon. "Ch'ŏndo-gyo (Religion of the Heavenly Way)." In *The encyclopedia of religion*, edited by M. Eliade. Vol. 3. New York: Macmillan, 1987, pp. 336-37.

482 Kim Yong-choon. *The Ch'ŏndo-gyo concept of man: An essence of Korean thought*. Seoul: Pan Korea Book Corporation, 1978, 151 pp.

483 Kim Yong-choon. "The Ch'ŏndo-gyo concept of the nature of man." *International Philosophical Quarterly* 13, no. 2 (1973): 209-28.

484 Kim Yong-choon. "The Ch'ŏndo-gyo concept of the origin of man." *Philosophy East and West* 22, no. 4 (1972): 374-84.

485 Kim Yong-choon. "Ch'ŏndo-gyo eschatology." *Numen* 21, no. 2 (1974): 141-53.

486 Kim Yong-choon. "Ch'ŏndo-gyo thought and its significance in Korean tradition." *Korea Journal* (Seoul) 15, no. 5 (1975): 47-53.

487 Kim Yong-choon. "The concept of man in Ch'ŏndo-gyo." Ph.D. dissertation (religion), Temple University, 1969, 429 pp.

488 Kim Yong-choon. "The essence of man in Ch'ŏndo-gyo philosophy." *Journal of Social Sciences and Humanity* (Korean Research Center), June 1972, pp. 1-11.

489 Kim Yong-choon. *Oriental thought: An introduction to the philosophical and religious thought of Asia*. Springfield, Ill.: Thomas, 1973, 129 pp.
Includes Ch'ŏndo-gyo, pp. 95-106.

490 *Korea: Its people and culture*. Seoul: Hakwon-sa, 1970, 471 pp., illus.
Pp. 162-68, Tonghak; pp. 168-74, Taejong-gyo.

491 Korea Christian Academy. *Dialogue* (Korean Christian Institute) (Special issue) 1, no. 4 (30 April 1973): 47-67.

East: Korea

Not on new religions but establishes Korean folk religion as a continuation of the autochthonous religion and so somewhat equivalent to a primal religion: this gives Korean new movements a certain parallel to those in other "primal societies."

492 Korea Study Committee (East Asia Christian Conference). "New religions in Korea." A summary of research papers. Seoul: Korea Christian Academy, 1971. 2d printing, 1973, 52 pp. Mimeo.
Seven papers by T. S. Ryu, M.-H. Tak (2), S. H. Mun, D.-H. Lee, P.-Y. Lee, and K.-I. Kim, representing demographic, doctrinal, anthropological, psychological, sociological, and missiological approaches.

493 Korea Study Committee (East Asia Christian Conference). "New religions of the east Asia region." [Seoul: Korea Christian Academy], 1972, 36 pp. Mimeo.
Three papers, introduction, and discussion report; includes one paper on Taiwan.

494 Korean Overseas Information Service. *A handbook of Korea.* Seoul: K.O.I.S. (Ministry of Culture and Information), 1978. Reprint. 1979, 825 pp.
P. 207, new religions.

495 *Korean Repository* (Seoul): "Confessions of a Tonghak chief," 5, no. 6 (1898); "A retrospect" (editorial), 2, no. 1 (1895); "Seven months among the Tong Haks," 2, no. 6 (1895).
All as cited by R. E. Speer (entry 524), p. 362, n1, and see further references in his later footnotes. See also the article on Tonghak by W. M. Junkin (entry 472).

496 Leverrier, Roger. "Arrière-plan socio-politique et caractéristiques des nouvelles religions en Corée: Le cas de Tong Hak." *Social Compass* 25, no. 2 (1978): 217-37.
An important survey.

497 McCully, Elizabeth A. *A corn of wheat or the life of Rev. W. J. McKenzie of Korea.* 2d ed. Toronto: Westminster Co., 1904, 290 pp. illus.
Pp. 163-98, Tonghak.

498 Mok Chong-gyun. "The centipetal and centrifugal functions of the Tonghak movement with reference to communication of Tonghak group." *Korea Journal* (Seoul) 18, no. 5 (1978): 50-63.

A study of a mass movement from the viewpoint of communications – how it rallied the masses in so short a time.

499 Moos, Felix. "Leadership and organization in the Olive Tree movement." *Transactions of the Korea Branch, Royal Asiatic Society: The New Religions of Korea* (Seoul) 43 (1967): 11-27.

Comparisons between new religions in Korea and Japan; the Pak Changno-gyo or Olive Tree movement with its "Christian towns," extensive industries, and two million followers by 1964. For comment, see A. D. Shupe, Jr., comp., in *Six perspectives on new religions* (New York: Edwin Mellen Press, 1987), pp. 103-6.

500 Moos, Felix. "Some aspects of Park Chang No Kyo–a Korean revitalization movement." *Anthropological Quarterly* (Washington, D.C.) 37, no. 3 (1964): 110-20. Reprinted in entry 499, pp. 15-27.

Comparisons between new religions in Korea and Japan; Olive Tree, or Pak Changno-gyo, with "Christian towns" and industries.

501 Mun Sang-hi. "Fundamental doctrines of the new religions in Korea." In *New religions in Korea*, edited by Korea Christian Academy. Seoul: The Academy, 1971, pp. 13-28.

502 Mun Sang-hi. "Fundamental doctrines of the new religions of Korea." *Korea Journal* (Seoul) 11, no. 12 (1971): 18-24, illus.

Research report by a theological professor at the Korean Christian Academy, an introduction to eleven groups identified – syncretistic, salvific, paradisiacal, apocalyptic-prophetic, shamanistic, and those with beliefs in Koreans as a chosen people.

503 Mun Sang-hi. "Openness in religion: A must for survival and self-transcendence." *Korea Journal* 18, no. 10 (1978): 15-19.

A general survey of Korean religions, with shamanism penetrating all; pp. 17-18, the new religions, from Tonghak in 1860.

504 Mun Sang-hi. "The phenomenon of the new religion." *Yonsei Chun-chu Weekly* (Yonsei University), 19 June 1972.

505 Na, John D. K. "The nature and significance of a new religious movement for the oppressed: A study of Eastern Learning 1860-1919." Ph.D. dissertation (theology), University of Birmingham, 1988, 334 pp.

Extensive bibliography of Korean items, with English translation of titles and excerpts of the texts.

East: Korea

506 Ogg, Li. "Les religions de la Corée." In *Histoire des religions*. Vol. 3. Encyclopédie de la Pléiade. Paris: Gallimard, 1976, pp. 474-94, bib.
Pp. 488-90, Tonghak, as derived from Confucian, Buddhist, and Taoist sources, but of uncertain relation to shamanism.

507 Paik, L. George [Paek Nak-chun]. *The history of Protestant missions in Korea 1832-1910*. P'yŏngyang: Union Christian College Press, 1929, 438 pp. Reprint. Seoul: Yonsei University Press, 1970.
Pp. 161-63, 247-48, brief accounts of Tonghaks. A Yale University Ph.D. thesis, 1927.

508 Palmer, S[pencer] J. *Korea and Christianity: The problem of identification with tradition*. Monograph Series no. 2, Royal Asiatic Society, Korea Branch. Seoul: Hollym Corporation Pub., 1967, 174 pp.
Pp. 93-94, compares the appeal of Christianity and Tonghak.

509 Palmer, S[pencer] J. *Transactions of the Korea Branch, Royal Asiatic Society: The New Religions of Korea* (Seoul) 43 (1967).
See Chae-sŏk Ch'oe (entry 455), Sin-dŏk Ch'oe (entry 458), and F. Moos (entry 499).

510 Park, Paul. "A study of the relation of shamanism to other religions in Korea." *Korean Religions* (Seoul) 2, no. 1 (197): 12-24.
Pp. 19-23, shamanism and Christianity; pp. 21-22, Tonghak; pp. 22-23, Sich'ŏn-gyo.

511 Park Pong Bae. "The encounter of Christianity with traditional culture and ethics: An essay in Christian understanding." Ph.D. dissertation, Vanderbilt University, 1970, 315 pp.

512 Pattisson, Peter R. M. "False Christs." In *Crisis unawares*. Sevenoaks, Kent: Overseas Missionary Fellowship, 1981, pp. 230-37.
The "religious boom" in Korea: the sects, with a case study of the Unification Church and briefer accounts of the Olive Tree Church, Mormons, and Jehovah's Witnesses.

513 Prunner, Gernot. "The birthday of a god: A sacrificial service of Chungsan'gyo." *Korea Journal* (Seoul) 16, no. 3 (1976): [15 pp.], illus.
The history, pantheon of gods from Chinese popular religion, doctrines, and sacrificial rites of a sect of Chungsan-gyo, founded 1924.

514 Prunner, Gernot. "Current trends in the new religions of the world and the thought of Chungsan-gyo." *Chungsan sasang yon'gu* (Seoul) 4 (1978): 242f.

515 Prunner, Gernot. "The new religions in Korean society." *Korea Journal* (Seoul) 20, no. 2 (1980): 4-15. Also in *Papers of the 1st International Conference on Korean Studies*. Seoul: Academy of Korean Studies, 1980, pp. 1079-97.

516 Prunner, Gernot. "New religions – new eras: A preliminary inquiry into the nature of chronological systems used by the new religions of Korea." *Proceedings of the 2nd International Symposium on Asian Studies, 1980*. Hong Kong: Asian Research Service, 1981, pp. 337-56.
    The systems are grouped in relation to the accepted twelve-part classification system for Korea's new religions in the nineteenth and twentieth centuries; the various factors at work in choosing the inauguration date for the new era.

517 "The Religion of the Heavenly Way." *Korean Religions* (Seoul) 2, no. 1 (1970): 60-63.
    The beliefs, rites, and history of Ch'ŏndo-gyo, since 1860.

518 Rha Young Bok. "An analysis of the terms used for God in Korea in the context of indigenization." Th.D. dissertation (theology), Boston University School of Theology, 1977, 214 pp.
    Pp. 76-87, analysis of God in Korean shamanism; pp. 87-96, God in Taejong-gyo (Great Shaman Religion, a developed urmonotheism); pp. 96-111, Ch'ŏndo-gyo (Heavenly Way Religion, or Tonghak, or Eastern Learning) as an indigenized Catholicism on a shamanistic foundation.

519 Ryu Tong-shik. "Ch'ŏndo-gyo: Korea's only indigenous religion." *Japanese Religions* (Kyoto) 5, no. 1 (1967): 58-77.

520 Ryu, Tong-shik. "Religion and the changing society of Korea." *East Asian Cultural Studies* 11, nos. 1-4 (1972): 6-17, statistical tables.
    Christianity and the new religions since 1945 – the latter as a "reactionary mass movement"; characteristic features, with Olive Tree Church and Unification Church as case studies.

521 Ryu, Tong-shik. "Some problems raised by the newly-risen religions in Korea." *Korean Religions* 2, no. 1 (1970): 38-43.

East: Korea

The doctrines, social implications, and appeal of The Holy Spirit Association for the Unification of World Christianity; Chŏndo-gwan, the Church of Elder Pak Taisŏn; Sokagakkai and Tenrikyo from Japan; and Taejong-gyo, a shamanistic sect.

522 Shim Il-sup. "The new religious movements in the Korean church." *International Review of Mission*, no. 293 [74] (January 1985), pp. 103-8.

523 "Small sectarian religions in Korea." *Korean Religions* (Seoul) 2, no. 1 (1970): 64-66.

Tan'gun-gyo, Ch'ŏnsung-gyo, Nichiren Masumane (Buddhist), Chŏnjin-gyo or "Real Truth" – brief notes and bibliography of their own publications for these four sects, out of more than 80 bodies known to the National Police.

524 Speer, Robert E[lliot]. *Missions and modern history*. 2 vols. New York and London: Fleming H. Revell, 1904.

Vol. 2, pp. 359-92, the Tonghak new monotheistic religion from 1860 as a synthesis of Confucian, Buddhist, and Taoist elements under Christian influence, similar to Taiping, except in being antiforeign.

525 T'ak Myŏng-hwan. *Les nouvelles religions de Corée*. 3 vols. Seoul, 1976.

526 T'ak Myŏng-hwan. "Therapeutic phenomena of new religions." *Korea Journal* (Seoul), 1 December 1971, pp. 27-30, illus.

Healing is dominant feature; Christian-derived movements use prayer, fasting, laying on of hands or massage, and holy water (e.g., Chŏndo-gwan of Elder Pak); "water worship" movements (Yonghwa samdŏk-to and Sŏngdŏk-to); Tan'gun-connected movements use "rectification of the mind"; Japanese-originated movements (e.g., Tenri-gyo and Sokagakkai). Disease-curing is both a "development factor" and an "impediment to maturity."

527 Vos, Frits. *Die Religionen Koreas*. Die Religionen der Menschheit, 22.1. Stuttgart: W. Kohlhammer, 1977, 264 pp. (pp. 227-34, bibliographies in Korean, Japanese, Chinese and European languages).

Chap. 8 (pp. 189-202), Tonghak; chap. 9 (pp. 203-17), new religions – according to dominant content, etc., as shamanist, Buddhist, Confucian, Tonghak, Christian, etc.

528 Wasson, Alfred W[ashington]. *Church growth in Korea*. New York: International Missionary Council; Concord, N.H.: Rumford Press, 1934, 175 pp.

Pp. 36-39, 47, 99, the Tonghak rebellion.

529 Weems, Benjamin B. "Ch'ondogyo enters its second century." *Transactions of the Korea Branch, Royal Asiatic Society: The New Religions of Korea* (Seoul) 43 (1967): 157-66.

530 Weems, Benjamin B. *Reform, rebellion, and the Heavenly Way.* Association of Asia Studies Monographs and Papers, 15. Tucson: University of Arizona Press for Association of Asia Studies , 1964, xi + 122 pp., illus., bib.

    Ch'ŏndo-gyo reform movements; emphasis on political aspects. The author was born in Korea; a Georgetown University M.A. thesis, 1955.

531 Yi Pu-yong. "A psychological study." *Korea Journal* 11, no. 12 (1971): 24-27, illus.

    The new religions of Korea–their general common characteristics, psychological dynamics, and religious symbols.

532 Yi Sŏn-kun. "Le mouvement Tong-Hak et la modernisation de la Corée." *Collection d'articles sur la pensée coréenne.* Vol. 3. Seoul, 1973, pp. 208-22.

    Asserts that Tonghak explored traditional religion and was not a response to Western influences.

SOUTH

INDIA

The Indian section refers to some 400 "scheduled tribes," comprising nearly 40 million people, mainly of the hills and forests, not absorbed into Hindu or Islamic cultures or Sanskritized. Many of their primal or Dravidian forms continued into the nineteenth or twentieth centuries remarkably intact, although some have been Hinduized at a lower caste level, and a few (such as the Mizo) have been completely Christianized. Of the new religious movements, some have developed in interaction with Hindu influences, others with the Christian presence, and a few with both; Islam, however has seldom been involved. It is often difficult to distinguish the religious forms of village Hinduism, especially in the lower castes, from those of the primal religions. A few items are included on religious reform and revitalization movements in the Hindu context, as well as on Hebraist and independent

South: India

church forms other than that among the tribal peoples. There is also material on Sikh millennialism and on the general acculturation problem and self-image of the tribal peoples.

Since the eighteenth century, tribal religious movements have been associated with peasant or tribal revolts, not only against British imperial control, but also against the oppression of Hindu landlords. The prominence of social and economic grievances helps to explain the shift by the mid-twentieth century away from religious to political activist movements; some movements reveal both aspects still. The only major general survey is *Rebellious prophets*, by S. Fuchs (entry 595), on 44 movements since 1816. There is probably much that has remained unreported.

533 Ahmed, Akbar S. *Millennium and charisma among Pathans: A critical essay on social anthropology*. London and Boston: Routledge & Kegan Paul, 1976, 173 pp.

Pp. 103-11, Islamic millenarian movements in Malakind; pp. 111-15, institutionalization of charisma in Swat; pp. 115-18, rival religious challenge; pp. 118-19, colonial interaction. Pp. 105-7, relation to Melanesian cargo cults, viewed as mainly economic (Fiji Tuka movement wrongly placed in New Guinea).

534 Appasamy, Paul. *The centenary history of the C.M.S. in Tinnevelly*. Palamcottah Printing Press, 1923, xxi + 304 pp.

Pp. 88-89, Muttukutty's movement (a Nadar movement), neo-Hindu, early 1840s; pp. 90-91, Alagappa Nadan anti-Christian movement among low-caste Nadars, 1844.

535 Archer, W[illiam] G[eorge]. "The Santal rebellion, II." *Man in India* (Ranchi) 25, no. 4 (1945): 223-39.

Comments on Culshaw's article in same issue (entry 561), with further material.

536 Baago, Kaj. *The movement around Subba Row*. Madras: Christian Literature Society, 1968, i-vi, 1-32.

Sort analysis of an independent Hindu-Christian group.

537 Banerji, M. G. "A nationalist hero of Chota Nagpur." *Journal of Historical Research* (Ranchi) 1 (1959): 1-4.

On Birsa.

538 *Bengalee* (Calcutta). Various editiorials, reports, etc., in 1900 on the Birsa uprising.

For list of items, see K. S. Singh (entry 733), p. 67 of notes.

539 Berquist, James A., and Manickam, P. Kambar. *The crisis of dependency in third world ministries: A critique of inherited missionary forms in India*. Madras: Christian Literature Society, 1974, 174 pp.

Chap. 4 (pp. 65-71), "The modified model": ministry in some independent churches. Based on selected churches from 72 identified in Madras city; some features in common with African independent churches.

540 Bhadra, Ranajit K. "Revitalization movements among the Gonds of Madhya Pradesh." *Eastern Anthropologist* (Lucknow) 30, no. 3 (1977): 131-38.

Brief survey of messianic movements of revolt – Muria and Maria (1910), Bhausing Rajnegi (1929), Raj Gond (1936), Raj Mohini (1951), and fuller account of Pravir Chandra Bhanjodeo (1955-66).

541 Bhandari, J. S. "Changing emphasis in the religious beliefs – a study in ideological conflict among the Mishing." In *Studies in social change*, edited by K. S. Mothur, et al. Lucknow: Ethnographic and Folk Culture Society University Press, 1973.

542 Bhardwaj, Gopal. "Socio-political movements among the tribes of India." In *Ethnicity, identity, and interaction*. Tribal Heritage of India, vol. 1, edited by S. C. Dube. New Delhi: Vikas Publishing House, 1977, pp. 141-60.

Pp. 141-47, theoretical discussion of "social movements" and their classification; pp. 147-52, survey of the study (and neglect of study) of Indian tribal movements; pp. 152-54, eastern region movements; pp. 154-58, Chota Nagpur and other central area movements; p. 158, other areas; pp. 159-60, the contemporary scene.

543 Bihar, Government of. *Ranchi, Bihar district gazetteers*. Edited by N. Kumar. Patna: Government of Bihar, Gazetteers' Branch, Revenue Department, 1970, xxviii + 674 pp.

P. 73, "Tana Bhagart movement," of 1914.

544 Biswas, Prophilla Chander. *Santals of the Santal Parganas*. Delhi: Bharatiya Adimjati Sevak Sangh, 1956, 230 pp., illus.

Pp. 7-12, on religious revolts; pp. 214-18, "culture contact," on Hindu and Christian influences; p. 215, the Kherwar movement.

545 Boal, Barbara M[ather]. "Centuries of change and resistance to change among the Konds of Orissa." In *Aspects of tribal life in south Asia I: Strategy and survival. Proceedings of an international seminar ... Berne*

South: India

1977, edited by R. R. Moser and M. K. Gautam. Studia Ethnologica Bernensia, 1. Berne: Institute of Ethnology, University of Berne, 1978, pp. 135-51.

Especially pp. 145-50, on preservation of tribal identity, first by reform of their primal religion, and then by independent corporate decision to become Christians.

546 Bodding, P[aul] O[laf]. "The Kharwar movement among the Santals." *Man in India* (Ranchi) 1, no. 3 (1921): 222-32.
An authoritative statement.

547 Bodding, P[aul] O[laf]. "A Santal sect." *Modern Review* (Calcutta), 13 March 1922, p. 358.

548 Bodding, P[aul] O[laf]. *Traditions and institutions of the Santals*. Oslo: A. W. Broggers Boktrykheri, 1942, 198 pp.
Santal religious movements.

549 Bower, Ursala Graham. *Naga path*. London: John Murray, 1950, 260 pp., illus., maps.
Pp. 45-49, millennial Kach Naga movement of Gaidiliu (1929-); by an English amateur anthropologist.

550 Bradley-Birt, F[rancis] B[radley]. *Chotanagpore, a little known province of the Empire*. London: Smith Elder & Co., 1903, 310 pp., illus., map. 2d enl. ed. 1910, 327 pp.
Pp. 75-77 (1903 ed.), The Birsa rising.

551 Bradley-Birt, F[rancis] B[radley]. *The story of an Indian upland*. London: Smith Elder & Co., 1905, 354 pp., illus., map.
Chap. 7 (pp. 159-206), the "Santal rebellion"–a scholarly, sensitive account. Pp. 184-92, the religious aspects.

552 Briggs, George W[eston]. *The Chamars*. The Religious Life of India. London: Oxford University Press; Calcutta: Association Press, 1920, 270 pp., illus.
Pp. 27, 29, 219-23, Satnami.

553 Campbell, A. "Santal Kherwarism in Chutia Nagpore and the Santal Pergannas." *Indian Evangelical Review* (Madras), July 1881, pp. 83-92.
By a missionary.

554 Campbell, J[ames] M[acnabb], ed. *Gazetteer of the Bombay Presidency: Kaira and the Panch Mahals*. Bombay, Miscellaneous Public Documents, 1879.
> Pp. 223-28, on Joria's revolt among the Narkdas.

555 Carstairs, R[obert]. *Harma's village, a novel of Santal life*. Pokhwria, Manbhum: Santal Mission Press, 1935, 320 pp.
> Fiction, inspired by the Santal revolt, written by a Deputy Commissioner of the Santal Parganas, 1885-98, but little on religious aspects.

556 Carter, H. W., ed. *Chhim Bial Kahhran Chanchin*. Lungleh: South Lushai Mission Press, 1945.
> History of the South Mizo Church. P. 57, Puma Zai anti-Christian song movement, about 1908.

557 Chatterji, Saral K. "A note on the study of religion and society, mission and transformation." *Religion and society* (Bangalore) 28, no. 3 (1981): 2-8.
> Especially pp. 2-5, on popular protest movements.

558 Chattopadhayaya, K. P. "Diffusion of a religious cult." In *Anthropology on the march*, edited by B. Ratham. Madras: Book Centre, 1963, pp. 325-33.
> The Cadak cult among the Santal of West Bengal, and also found in East Bengal; with Hindu influence.

559 Chaudhuri, Sashi Bhusan. *Civil disturbances during the British rule in India (1765-1857)*. Calcutta: World Press, 1955, 231 pp., map.
> On communal revolts, peasant, tribal, and other, with military and sociopolitical aspects only–almost nothing on religion.

560 Choudhury, Nirendra Chandra. "Acculturation of the Munda: A study in differential change and caste formation." Ph.D. dissertation (anthropology), Northwestern University, 1963, 180 pp., map.
> On Chota Nagpur and southern Bengal–in the latter there were greater changes through Hinduization. See pp. 156-69 for tables for comparison of religious changes, with Munda in southern Bengal becoming syncretized as a Hindu caste, but without deliberate Hindu proselytizing.

561 Culshaw, W[esley] J[ames]. "The Santal rebellion, I." *Man in India* (Ranchi) 25, no. 4 (1945): 218-23.

South: India

A "review from a new angle."

562 Das, Amal Kumar. "Religions of the scheduled tribes of West Bengal." *West Bengal Cultural Research Institute Bulletin* (Calcutta) 12, nos. 1-2 (1976): 123-29.
    Pp. 128-29, census returns for members of Sari Dharma ("True Religion"), Marang buru ("Principal Deity"), Chandobonga, Santal, Tirkia, and Paharia religions.

563 Das, Anthony. "Guru Ghasi Das, founder of the Satnami sect in Chhattisgarh." M.Th. dissertation, St. Albert's College (Ranchi), 1986-87. Abstract in *Sevartham* (Ranchi, St. Albert's College) 13 (1988): 119-20.
    A monotheistic movement from the late eighteenth century in Madhya Pradesh among low-caste Chamars or tanners – a revolt movement that later became a religious sect, Satnami.

564 Das, N. K., and Guptia, Pabitra. "The Abom movement." In *Seminar on contemporary tribal movements in India*. Calcutta: Anthropological Survey of India, 1976.
    In Assam state.

565 Das, T. C. "Nature and extent of social change in tribal society of Eastern India." *Sociological Bulletin* (Bombay) 11 (1962): 221-38.
    P. 231, great influence of Christian missions; p. 232, five groups of Bhagat movements among the Oraons, with some detail on Tana Bhagat; p. 232, Alekh cult of Khond poet Bhima Bhoi. Whole article useful as background of acculturation.

566 Datta, K. K. [Kalikinkar]. *History of the freedom movement in Bihar.* 3 vols. [Patna]: Government of Bihar, 1957-58, illus.
    Vol. 1, pp. 96-105, the Birsa movement (p. 97, religious aspect); vol. 3, pp. 185-95, 288, Sapha Hor revival in the revolution of 1942-43: mainly on military/police action against them.

567 Datta, Kalikinkar. "Original records about the Santal insurrection." *Bengal Past and Present* (Calcutta) 48, no. 1 (1934): 32-37.

568 Datta, Kalikinkar. *The Santal insurrection of 1855-57.* Calcutta: University of Calcutta Press, 1940, 103 pp.
    Pp. 10-19, 66-73, religious aspects.

569 Datta-Mujumder, Nabendu. *The Santal: A study in culture change.* India: Department of Anthropology Memoir 2, 1955. Delhi: Manager of Publications, 1956, xvi + 150 pp., illus., maps.

Pp. 24-30, the Santal rebellion, 1855; chap. 7 (pp. 98-108), Santal religion.

570 Datta-Mujumder, Nabendu. "The Santal: A study in culture change." Ph.D. dissertation (anthropology), Northwestern University, 1948, 209 pp.

571 Derne, S. "Religious movement as rite of passage: An analysis of the Birsa movement." *Contributions to Indian Sociology* (Bombay), n.s. 19, no. 2 (1985): 251-68.

572 Devanandan, P. D. *The Dravida Kazhagam: A revolt against Brahminism.* Bangalore: Christian Institute for the Study of Religion and Society, 1959, 30 pp.

Tamil cultural renewal movement, rejecting Hinduism and seeking return to Dravidian forms. Rationalist in attitude to religion (pp. 22-27 especially), but with moral reforms.

573 Dhan, Rekha O. "The problems of the Tana Bhagats of Ranchi district." *Bulletin, Bihar Tribal Research Institute* (Ranchi) 2, no. 1 (1960): 136-86.

On the millenarian monotheistic movements and revolts from 1914 known under this name, which still claim some 10,000 adherents in the 1970s.

574 Dietrich, Gabriele. *Religion and peoples' organization in East Thanjavur.* Social Concern Series, 19. Madras: Christian Literature Society, for the Christian Institute for the Study of Religion and Society, 1977, 169 pp.

Pp. 17-24, "ritual upgrading" (usually Sanskritization) and anti-ritual upgrading movements in relation to development; pp. 166-67, non-Sanskritizing borrowings from Hindu culture by tribals in defense against the latter.

575 Diwakar, R[anganath] R[amachandra], ed. *Bihar through the ages.* Bombay: Orient Longmans, 1959, 891 pp.

Includes the Santal rebellion.

576 Dokhuma, James. *Zoram Kohhran Tualto Chanchinte.* Aizawl: D. Buanga at Tlangnuam Press, 1975.

South: India

Pp. 11-29, on the Thiang Lau "pawl" or Mizo "All Free Group," about 1947; pp. 30-35, 38, 40, 51f., Khuangtua "pawl" movement, about 1950; pp. 56-61, Zakaia "pawl," which revived the Puma Zai anti-Christian songs; pp. 61-81, Mizo Israel, a Hebraist movement identifying with the Israelites. All were short-lived Mizo syncretist and nativistic movements with a background in the Christian revivals.

577 Doshi, S[hambhu] L[al]. *Bhils: Between societal self-awareness and cultural synthesis*. New Delhi: Sterling Publishers (P), 1971, 284 pp.
Pp. 166-75, Oraon Bhagat movements' influence on the Bhils.

578 Downs, Frederick S. "Christianity as a tribal response to change in northeast India." *Missiology* 8, no. 4 (1980): 407-16.
Christianity as the best option for acculturation towards modernization by peoples long resistant to Sansritization.

579 Dube, S[hyama] C[haran], ed., *Ethnicity, identity, and interaction*. Tribal Heritage of India, vol. 1. New Delhi: Vikas Publishing House, 1977, 212 pp., bib.
See essays by K. N. Sahay (entry 722) and G. Bhardwaj (entry 542).

580 Ekka, Philip. "Messianic movements among the Chotanagpur tribes." *Sevartham* (Ranchi, St. Albert's College), no. 4 (1979), pp. 21-33.
Background and description of the Birsa rising (pp. 26-29) and Tana Bhagats (pp. 29-32), with short analysis and conclusion. By a Jesuit.

581 Ekka, Philip. "Revivalist movements among the tribes of Chotanagpur." In *Tribal situations in India*, edited by K. S. Singh. Simla: Indian Institute for Advanced Study, 1972, pp. 424-34.
On the Tana Bhagats of the Oraons and Birsa movements of the Mundas, whose related people, the Hos or Larka Kols, present a "negative instance" of immunity to such cults.

582 Ekka, Philip. "The Tana Bhagats: A study in social change." D. Phil. thesis, University of Oxford, 1966.

583 Elmore, Wilber Theodore. "Dravidian gods in modern Hinduism: A study of local and village deities of southern India." *University Studies* (Lincoln, University of Nebraska) 15, no. 1 (1915): 1-149. Reprint. *Dravidian gods in modern Hinduism*. Madras: Christian Literature Society for India, 1925, xiv + 163 pp.

Pp. 75, n16-p. 76, Verabramham in Madavaram, deified by villagers in a cult with many Christian forms; legends of Verabramham recalling the life of Christ.

584 Elwin, [Harry] Verrier [Holman]. *The Barga*. London: John Murray, 1939, 550 pp.
Pp. 513-14, a Raj Gond Hinduizing reformer in 1936.

585 Elwin, [Harry] Verrier [Holman]. *The tribal world of Verrier Elwin*. Bombay: Oxford University Press, 1964, 356 pp.
Pp. 117-18, a reformer establishing a "New Gond religion" near Dindori, 1936-38.

586 Enchakkalody, Th. *Keralathile Cristava Sahhakal*. Tiruvalla, 1962.
P. 279, Pratyaska Raksha Sasha–the "Church of Revealed Salvation" among outcastes in the early 1920s, Travancore and Cochin.

587 *Englishman* (Calcutta). Various editorials and letters on the Birsa movement in Chota Nagpur between 1899 and 1901, including: 10 January 1900, official statement; also 13, 15, 16, 17, 18, 20, 22, 23, 24, and 31 January and 17 and 18 April, 1900.
Cited by S. P. Sinha (entry 746), pp. 94-97; see also L. O. Skrefsrud (entry 749).

588 Feys, J. "A godless religion: The Deva Dharma." *Studia Missionalia* 34 (1985): 181-211.
Deva Samaj, founded in 1887 by a guru influenced both by nineteenth century Hindu movements and Western post-Enlightenment writers. Became atheistic in 1895. The guru then gradually assumed the position of God.

589 Fuchs, Stephen. *Aboriginal tribes of India*. Delhi: Macmillan Co. of India, 1973, 308 pp.
Pp. 143-46, increased acculturation currently producing new prophets and messianic movements; pp. 288-97, on tribals' welfare, with overtones of the American Indian situation.

590 Fuchs, Stephen. "The concept of salvation in tribal religions." *Indian Missiological Review* 4, no. 4 (1982): 361-71.
Pp. 364-67, various movements and prophets among the Santals, Oraons, Bhils, etc.; pp. 367-71, messianic movements during economic distress, including Birsa.

South: India

591 Fuchs, Stephen. "The conversion of the tribals." *Indian Missiological Review* 8, no. 2 (1986): 102-14.

592 Fuchs, Stephen. *The Gond and Bhumia of eastern Mandla*. New York: Asia Publishing House (printed in Bombay), 1960, x + 584 pp., illus.
Pp. 189-92, Raj-Gond Hinduizing movements. Pt. 4 (pp. 371-540), religious beliefs and magic.

593 Fuchs, Stephen. "Messianic and chiliastic movements among Indian aboriginals." In *Hinduism*. Studia Missionalia, 13. Rome: Gregorian Pontifical University, 1963, pp. 85-103.
See extended version of same material (entry 595).

594 Fuchs, Stephen. "Messianic movements in primitive India." *Asian Folklore Studies* (Tokyo) 24, no. 1 (1965): 11-62.
His best outline; see p. 62, analytic table of 14 movements.

595 Fuchs, Stephen. *Rebellious prophets*. Publication of the India Branch of the Anthropos Institute, 1. Bombay and London: Asia Publishing House, 1965, 304 pp., bib.
An important survey of messianic movements in all forms of Indian religions, including especially the low Hindu castes and the tribal peoples. The only major survey, by a Jesuit.

596 Fuchs, Stephen. Review of *The theology of a South African messiah*, by G. C. Oosthuizen (Leiden: E. J. Brill, 1967). *Religion and Society* (Bangalore) 16, no. 4 (1969): 90-93.
Makes comparison with Indian tribal movements.

597 Fuchs, Stephen. "A royal 'Saviour' of the Bastar tribals." *Journal of the Anthropological Society of Bombay*, n.s. 14, no. 1 (1969): 36-50.
Maharaja Pravir Chandra (1929-66), who exhibited most of Fuchs's characteristics of a messiah (entry 595, pp. 1-15) for the tribals of the former Bastar state.

598 Fürer-Haimendorf, Christoph von. "Aboriginal rebellion in the Deccan." *Man in India* (Ranchi) 25, no. 4 (1945): 208-17.
Pp. 209-12, the Rampa rebellion, 1879-80, by Hill Reddis of the Eastern Ghats; pp. 212-16, the revolt of Gonds and Kolams under Kumra Bhimu in Hyderabad district, 1940–brief references in both cases to prophet-type leaders (pp. 211, 216).

599 Fürer-Haimendorf, Christoph von. "Comparing the fortunes of tribal populations in Nagaland, Arunachal Pradesh, and Andhra Pradesh." In *Eastern Himalayas*, edited by T. C. Sharma and D. N. Majumdar. Delhi: Cosmo Publications, 1980, pp. 206-21.

Nothing on religion but useful account of the relations with Hindu society of the Apa Tanis (of Arunachal Pradesh) and of the Raj Gonds (of Andhra Pradesh) since the 1940s, as background for cultural interaction.

600 Ganguly, P. G. "Separatism in Indian society." In *Anthropology and Archaeology*, edited by M. C. Pradhan, et al. Bombay: Oxford University Press, 1969, pp. 70-73.

Ranchi area Mundas and Oraons and their forms of voluntary self-help organization after the Birsa's failure.

601 Gautam, Mohan K. "Tradition, modernization, and the problem of identity among the Santal." In *Aspects of tribal life in south Asia I: Strategy and survival. Proceedings of an international seminar . . . Berne 1977*, edited by R. R. Moser and M. K. Gautam. Studia Ethnologica Bernensia, 1. Berne: Institute of Ethnology, University of Berne, 1978, pp. 105-21.

Tribal revitalization by rejection of the option of becoming low-caste Hindus, by restoration of Santal identity, and (p. 115) restoration of primal religion (e.g., Sarna, "the sacred grove" and R. Murmu's Sarna Dharam Samlet, "sacred grove religious organization").

602 *Ghar Bandhu* (Ranchi, Gossner's Evangelical Lutheran Mission Press). Edited by A. Nottrott.

A fortnightly received by every literate Christian family. Issues of 1899-1900 contain full information on the Birsa movement from the German missionary viewpoint. Cited in S. P. Sinha (entry 746), pp. 93-94, etc.

603 Ghurye, Govind Sadashiv. *The scheduled tribes*. Bombay: Popular Prakashan, 1952. Reprint. 1963, xii + 287 pp. (Originally publishd as *The aborigines so-called and their future*.)

Pp. 28-31, 46-61 represent useful sections of the introductory chapters on acculturation, with mention of Birsa movement (p. 46).

604 Goswami, B[inod] B[ehari]. "By-product of Christianity on the hill tribesmen of north-east India." *Review of Ethnology / Revue Etnologique* (Vienna) 7, nos. 1-3 [Newsletter 3] (1979): 42-46, bib.

South: India

> Two movements among Mizo people of Assam: Zakia Pawl (1937-) and Khuangtua Pawl (1960s-).

605 Goswami, B[inod] B[ehari]. "Hill tribesmen of north-east India: The impact of Christianity." In *The tribal world and its transformation*, edited by B. Singh and J. S. Bandhari. New Delhi: Concept Publishing Co., 1980, pp. 124-29.

> Pp. 124-25, Pentecostal revivals and Takia Pawl; pp. 125-28, Khuangtua Pawl or Thiangzau; pp. 128-29, Nagaland revivalism.

606 Goswami, B[inod] B[ehari]. *The Mizo unrest: A study of politicisation of culture*. Jaipur: Aalekh Publishers, 1979, 220 pp.

> Pp. 122-27, new Christian movements and the earlier revivals; pp. 167-69, ritual and values; pp. 191-95, "religion" – Presbyterian, and the *hmilims*.

607 Goswami, B[inod] B[ehari]. "Spirit possession in a hill tribe of Assam." In "Proceedings of the Summer School in Anthropology, Darjeeling," edited by N. C. Choudhary. Calcutta: Anthropological Survey of India, 1966. Mimeo.

> On the "possession dancers" in the revivals among the Christian Mizo of the Welsh Presbyterian Mission.

608 Gough, Kathleen. "Indian peasant uprisings." *Economic and Political Weekly* (Bombay) 9, nos. 32-34 (1974): 1391-1412, bib. in footnotes.

> On violent revolts during British rule, and since independence, including those with religious and millenarian features, whether by tribal, Hindu (often low-caste), or Muslim groups. See especially pp. 1395, 1396, 1397 for tribal religious movement (often based on S. Fuchs [entry 595]).

609 Griswold, Harvey DeWitt. *The Chet Rami sect*. Cawnpore: Christ Church Mission Press, 1904, 26 pp.

> A paper read at the Mussoorie Conference, 1904.

610 Guariglia, Guglielmo. *Prophetismus und Heilserwartungs-Bewegungen als völkerkundliches und religionsgeschichtliches Problem*. Vienna: F. Berger, 1959, xvi + 332 pp. , maps, bib.

> Pp. 242-43, Birsa-Bhagoan; pp. 245-46, Lushai hills movement.

611 Gupta, A. K. Sen. "Hinduisation and tribalisation: Two case studies." *Folklore* (Calcutta) 8 (1967): 427-32.

Hinduization of tribals and tribalization of castes as two opposite processes at work, tested by case studies of the Pan caste of Orissa, which is now better seen as a tribe, and of nearby Bagatas, etc. of Andhra Pradesh, which may now be more a Hindu caste than a tribe. Of theoretical value.

612 Hardgrave, Robert L., Jr. *The Nadars of Tamilnad: The political culture of a community in change*. Publications of the Center for South and Southeast Asia Studies. Berkeley: University of California Press, 1969, 314 pp., maps.

Low-caste toddy-teppers in Madras state; pp. 43-55, conversion; pp. 36-38, Madar "demonolatry" and deity; pp. 38-42, missionary view of Madars; pp. 71-90, Hindu Church of Lord Jesus.

613 Hewitt, Gordon. *The problems of success: A history of the Church Missionary Society, 1910-1942*. Vol. 2. London: S.C.M. Press for Church Missionary Society, 1977, 424 pp.

Vol. 2, pp. 75-76, Alvaneri schism of Tinnevelly C.M.S. Evangelical Church, 1925; p. 78, National Church of Madras (1886) and Hindu Church of the Lord Jesus in Tinnevelly (1890s) – brief mentions; pp. 113-21, C.M.S. missions among Santals, Gonds, and Bhils, as useful background.

614 Hminga, Changte Lal. "Christianity and the Lushai people." M.A. thesis, Fuller Theological Seminary, 1963.

Pp. 93-95, 102, revivalism from 1907, including during the 1918 epidemic, and Pentecostal "prophets" in 1961; pp. 94-95, a Hebraist or "Zionist" movement.

615 Hodne, Olaf. *L. O. Skrefsrud, missionary and social reformer among the Santals of Santal Parganas*. Oslo: Egede Institute, 1966, 362 pp.

Pp. 265-87, Santal Kherwarism. Skrefsrud (1840-1910) had opposed the movement and the story is in this vein.

616 Hodson, T[homas] C[allan]. *India: Census ethnography, 1901-1931*. Delhi: Government of India Press, 1937, 118 pp., illus., maps.

Pp. 95, 98-99, 108, on the Mata, Kherwar, Bursait, and Ahmadia movements.

617 Hoerschelmann, Werner. *Christliche Gurus: Darstellung von Selbstandnis und Funktion indigen Christseins durch unabhangige charismatisch gefuhrte Gruppen in Sudindien*. Studies in the

South: India

Intercultural History of Christianity, 12. Frankfurt: Peter Lang, 1977, 589 pp.

Independent preachers and charismatics of varying relationships to Christianity who develop clienteles rather than movements, and in folk Hinduism resemble some developments more related to primal religions. Pp. 126-31, Muttukutti; pp. 152-55, Yohannan.

618 Hoffmann, Johannes B. *37 Jahre Missionar in Indien*. Innsbruck: Verlagnastalt Tyrolia, 1923, 64 pp.

Pp. 8-9, a Jesuit's popular account of the Birsa movement.

619 Hrach, Hans-Georg. "From 'regulated anarchy' to 'proto-nationalism': The case of the Santals." In *Aspects of tribal life in south Asia I: Strategy and suvival. Proceedings of an international seminar ... Berne 1977*, edited by R. R. Moser and M. K. Gautam. Studia Ethnologica Bernensia, 1. Berne: Institute of Ethnology, University of Berne, 1978, pp. 97-101.

620 Hunt, W[illiam] S[aunders]. *The Anglican Church in Travancore and Cochin, 1816-1916*. Vol. 2. Kottayam: Church Missionary Society, 1920, 277 pp.

Vol. 2, pp. 154-69, the revival in Travancore from 1873, and Rev. Justus Joseph's secession "Revival Church" (1875); pp. 234-35, Poyikayil Yohannan, a "Pariah convert" as a prophet and independent preacher.

621 Hunter, W[illiam] W[ilson]. *Imperial gazetteer of India*. 9 vols. London: Trubner & Co., 1881.

Vol. 1, p. 364, Satnami religion; vol. 2, pp. 139-40, Mangal's messianic movement among Panka untouchables in Raipur district, ca. 1860-.

622 Jay, Edward. "Revitalization movements in tribal India." In *Aspects of religion in Indian society*, edited by L. P. Vidyarthi. Meerut City: Kedar Ram Nath, [1961], pp. 282-315. Earlier form published in *Anthropology Tomorrow* (University of Chicago students' anthropological journal), 1959.

1. The Mundas: Sardar movement, 1870s, a semi-Christian sect; pp. 286-88, Birsar movement, 1895-; 2. the Santals: Bir Singh and other "prophets"; 3. the Oraons: Bhagat movements (Kabirpanthi and Tana; Nemha and Bhachhi-dan); 4. the Bhumij: Kshatriya movement; 5. theoretical considerations.

623   Jha, Aditya Prasad. "Nature of the Santal unrest of 1871-75 and origin of the Sapha Hor movement." *Proceedings of the Indian Historical Records Commission* 35, no. 2 (1960): 103-13.

Pp. 103-4, the Santal Rising, 1855-57; pp. 106-13, Bhagirath Manjhee's Hinduizing Sapha Hor Kherwar movement, with reprint of much of L. O. Skrefsrud (entry 750).

624   Jha, Jagdish Chandra. Review of *The dust storm and the hanging mist: A study of Birsa Munda and his movement in Chotanagpur (1874-1901)*, by S. K. Singh (entry 733). *Journal of the Bihar Research Society* (Patna) 52, nos. 1-4 (1966): 222-25.

625   Josson, H[enri]. *La mission du bengale occidental ou archdiocese de Calcutta*. Vol. 2. Bruges: Imprimerie Sainte-Catherine, 1921, 479 pp., illus., maps.

Vol. 2, chaps. 21-22 (pp. 130-211), and pp. 205-6, 240-44, Birsa'a movement. By a Jesuit.

626   Juliusson, Per. *The Gonds and their religion: A study of the integrative function of religion in a present pre-literary and pre-industrial culture in Madhya Pradesh*. Stockholm Studies in Comparative Religion / Acta Universitatis Stockholmiensis, 2. Stockholm: University of Stockholm, 1974, 248 pp., illus., maps.

Pp. 202-6, Bhagat movements; pp. 205-6, Raj Mohini Devi from 1950s.

627   Kalia, S. L. "The Raj Mohini Devi movement in Surguja." *Bulletin, Tribal Research Institute* (Chhindwara), no. 2 (1962), pp. 49-61.

From 1950s, founded by a Gond woman, Raj Mohini, after a revelation in 1951, under Hindu and Christian influence – an anti-alcohol Bhagat movement.

628   Kandulna, Anselm. "Christianization as a legitimate alternative to Sanskritization." *Indian Missiological Review* 6, no. 4 (1984): 307-31.

629   Kandulna, Anselm. "The Sarna religion and the Birsa reform." M.Th. dissertation, St. Albert's College, Faculty of Theology (Ranchi), 1986, iv + 119 pp.

The religion of the Munda and the new, eclectic Birsa religion, rejecting spirit-worship and animal sacrifices, and borrowing from Hindu and Christian sources.

South: India

630 Khurana, B. K. "Bhagti movements." *Bulletin, Tribal Research Institute* (Chhindwara), nos. 2-3 (1959), pp. 68-76.
   On theories of why these movements develop; considers Oraons and Mundas, and movements of Birsa, Raj Mohini, and especially Mahua Dev as a case study.

631 Khurana, B. K. "Bhagti movements." In *The changing tribes of Madhya Pradesh*, edited by T. B. Naik. Indore: Government Regional Press, 1961, pp. 44-48.
   Mainly on the Mahua Dev movement from ca. 1945, mostly in the Chhattisgarh area.

632 Klimkeit, Hans-Joachim. "Dayananda Sarasvati: Ein indische nativistischer Prophet." *Anthropos* 74, nos. 5-6 (1979): 889-907.
   A late nineteenth-century nativistic movement borrowing from Islam and Christianity to remodel Vedic religion in the Arya Samaj – not from a primal people, but comparable in other ways.

633 Koppers, Wilhelm. "Birsa Bhagoan." In *Encyclopedia mundarica*, edited by J. Hoffmann and A. van Emelen. Vol. 2b. Patna: Government Printing Office, 1950, pp. 564-71.

634 Kurundamannil, Joseph Chakko. "Yuomayan: A messianic movement in Kerala, India." D. Missiology thesis, Fuller Theological Seminary School of World Mission, 1979, 174 pp.
   By a member of the Mar Thoma Church. Set in the context of the Kannett Revival Church (pp. 77-119); pp.120-66, Yuomayan Christianity and other religions. Founded by Justus Joseph (1835-87), who had Anglican training.

635 Latourette, Kenneth Scott. *A history of the expansion of Christianity.* Vol. 6, *The great century in northern Africa and Asia, 1800-A.D. 1914.* London: Eyre and Spottiswoode; New York: Harper & Brothers, 1944, 502 pp., maps.
   Pp. 181-82, Birsa movement and its background.

636 Lazarus, Henry. "Village religion in Tamilnad." *Religion and Society* (Bangalore) 8, no. 2 (1961): 57-60.
   Pp. 59-60, Dravida Kazhagam movements among the Tamils, led by Periyar E. V. Ramasamy, as religiopolitical reform movements, anti-Brahmin, seeking return rather ineffectually to pre-Brahmin Dravidian cults, and breaking idols; among outcastes in period before 1960s.

637 Lloyd, John Meirion. "The Mizo district." *Glad Tidings*, July 1961.
"A thousand tribal prophets" among the Mizo in the late 1950s – under Pentecostal preaching influence.

638 Lloyd, John Meirion. *On every high hill*. Liverpool: Foreign Mission Office, 1957, 84 pp., illus.
Pp. 54-57, a Welsh missionary on Puma Zai anti-Christian song movement among the Mizo, about 1908.

639 Longkumer, Akumla. "A study of the revival movement in Nagaland." Th.M. dissertation (missiology), Fuller Theological Seminary School of World Mission, 1981, 109 pp.

640 Low, Donald Anthony. *Lion rampant: Essays in the study of British imperialism*. Studies in Commonwealth politics and history, 1. London: Frank Cass & Co., 1973, 230 pp.
P. 123, the Church of Revealed Salvation, or Pratyaska Raksha Sabha, early 1920s, among outcastes in Travancore/Cochin.

641 Lusty, G. H. "The advent of Birsa." *Wide World Magazine*, October 1910, pp. 38-49, illus.

642 McCall, Anthony Gilchrist. *Lushai chrysalis*. London: Luzac & Co., 1949, 320 pp.
Pp. 219-25, native revivalism, 1898-1938, in Lushai, on the Burmese border; ecstatic indigenous developments within the Welsh Baptist mission.

643 MacDougall, John [Douglas]. "Agrarian reform vs. religious revitalization: Collective resistance to peasantization among the Mundas, Oraons, and Santals, 1858-95." *Contributions to Indian Sociology*, n.s. 11, no. 2 (1977): 295-327.
Pp. 303, 304, brief references to independent churches among Munda and Oraon Lutherans; pp. 306-11, revitalizing Santal religion, 1872-1890s, through the Kherwar movement (ancient term for Santals), which exhibited some Hindu borrowings; pp. 316-18, variations in peasantization explain why the Mundas and Oraons produced an agrarian, institutionalized movement, and the Santals a religious and noninstitutionalized movement.

644 MacDougall, John [Douglas]. "Agrarian reform vs. religious revitalization: The Sardar and Kherwar movements among tribals of

South: India

Bihar, India, 1858-95." Ph.D. dissertation (sociology), Harvard University, 1975, 452 pp.

645 MacDougall, John [Douglas]. "Participation in late nineteenth-century Adivasi movements." In *Aspects of tribal life in south Asia I: Strategy and suvival. Proceedings of an international seminar ... Berne 1977*, edited by R. R. Moser and M. K. Gautam. Studia Ethnologica Bernensia, 1. Berne: Institute of Ethnology, University of Berne, 1978, pp. 39-66.

646 MacDougall, John [Douglas]. "The role of religion in *adivasi* social movements: Two cases from late nineteenth century Bihar." In *Religion in modern India*, edited by G. R. Gupta. Main Currents in Indian sociology, 5. New Delhi: Vikas Publishing House; Durham: Carolina Academic Press, 1983, pp. 273-312.

Compares the Sardar movement (Ranchi) with political action, and the Kherwar movement (Santal Parganas) with religious revitalization – their relation to different situations.

647 McGavran, Donald A[nderson]. *Ethnic realities and the Church: Lessons from India*. South Pasadena, Calif.: William Carey Library, 1979, 262 pp.

Pp. 214-21, "indigenous churches" – mentions Jehovah Shammah, Gospel Association of India, Ceylon Pentecostals, Karta Bhoja (1830s) and Subba Rao movement; none of these from the scheduled tribes.

648 McLeod, W. H[ew]. "The Kukas: A millenarian sect in the Punjab." In *W. P. Morrell: A tribute*, edited by G. A. Wood and P. S. O'Connor. Dunedin: University of Otago Press, 1973, pp. 85-103 + notes, pp. 272-76.

Included for comparative purposes, although not of primal background. "A distinctively Sikh version of a common millenarian pattern," drawing on low socioeconomic groups in the mid-nineteenth century and seeking religious reform.

649 McPherson, William, ed. *Memorials of service in India from the correspondence of the late Major Samuel Charters McPherson, C.D.* London: John Murray, 1865, 400 pp., map, illus.

Contains a full account of McPherson's part in the Khonds abandoning human sacrifice to the earth goddess, and moving towards a single high God in the 1840s. The change was successful because it was basically their own decision; it was not related to Christian mission influence.

650 Mahapatra, L. K. "Social movements among the tribes of India." In *Tribal situation in India*, edited by K. S. Singh. Simla: Institute of Advanced Study, 1972, pp. 399-409, bib.

Pp. 399-402, definitions and classifications; pp. 402-7, survey of movements; pp. 408-9, conclusions.

651 Mahapatra, L. K. "Social movements among tribes in eastern India, with special reference to Orissa." *Sociologus*, n.s. 18, no. 1 (1968): 46-63.

652 Mahapatra, L. K., and Tripathy, Chandrabal. "Raj Mohini Devi: A social reformer among tribals of north central India." *Vanyajati* (Delhi) 4 (October 1956): 113-23.

On the woman leader of a socioreligious movement with Hindu and Gandhian influences among the Gond from 1951.

653 Majumdar, D[hirendra] N[ath]. "Acculturation among the Hajong of Meghalaya." *Man in India* (Ranchi) 52, no. 1 (1972): 46-63.

Includes religious syncretism and changes when a tribe is transformed into a Hindu caste, traditional religion being progressively abandoned as Hinduization occurs.

654 Majumdar, D[hirendra] N[ath]. "The light that failed?" *Journal of Social Research* (Ranchi) 21, nos. 1-2 (1959): 90-97. Also in *Anthropology and tribal warfare in India*, edited by L. P. Vidyarthi. Ranchi: [Bihar University?], 1959.

On Raj Mohini, Gond woman saint.

655 Majumdar, Ramesa-Chandra, ed. *The history and culture of the Indian people*. Vol. 9, *British paramountcy and Indian renaissance*. Bombay: Bhratiya Vidya Bhavan. 1st ed. 1963. 2d ed. 1970, 1205 pp., map. New York: Paragon Book Reprint Corp., 1963.

Pp. 456-57, Santal revolt; p. 467, Pagal Panthis semireligious revolt, 1825, by Hajongs and Garos in Bengal; pp. 904-6, Birsa movement; pp. 907-8, Naikas' tribal revolt led by Joria, 1867-68 – all by the editor.

656 Mandelbaum, David G. "Social trends and personal pressures: The growth of a culture pattern." In *Language, culture, and personality: Essays in memory of Edward Sapir*, edited by L. Spier. Menasha: Sapir Memorial Publication Fund, 1941, pp. 219-38.

A new trinity of gods among the Kota of south India after a 1924 fever epidemic.

South: India

657 Manhar, Namuram. *Satnam*. Bhilai: Laxmi Printing Press, 1986.
A booklet on the Satnami movement in Chhattisgarh.

658 Miller, Beatrice Diamond. "Revitalization movements: Theory and practice as evidenced among the Buddhists of Maharashtra, India." In *Anthropology and Archaeology*, edited by M. C. Pradhan, et al. Bombay: Oxford University Press, 1969, pp. 108-26.
An analysis of Dr. Ambedkar's conversion (into Buddhism) movement in terms of A. F. C. Wallace's revitalization theory and its six phases, with suggestions for modification of the theory to apply to more complex societies.

659 Minz, Nirmal. "Impact of traditional religions and modern secular ideologies on the tribal areas of Chotanagpur." *Religion and Society* (Bangalore) 9, no. 4 (1962): 46-56.
Pp. 48-50, Birsa, Parha, Tana Bhagat, and other Bhagat movements – some up-to-date information.

660 Minz, Nirmal. "Theology of *Janta* (the People): A tribal perspective." *Religion and Society* (Bangalore) 27, no. 4 (1980): 35-45.
The various freedom movements of tribals in Chotanagpur, including the revolts with religious leaders or aspects, 1860s-1920s, the subsequent "political messianism" and Jharkhand movement – by a bishop of the German Evangelical Lutheran Church.

661 Minz, Nirmal. "Tribal identity in India." *Religion and Society* (Bangalore) 25, no. 1 (1978): 70-79.
Central Belt tribes, chiefly Mundas, Oraons, Kharias, Hos, and Santals. Pp. 74-75, religious revitalization movements.

662 Misra, Kamal K. "From millenarianism to Jharkhand: The changing nature of social movements in tribal Chotanagpur." *Journal of Asian and African Studies* 21, nos. 3-4 (1986): 226-36.
Pp. 232-33, millenarian influences, especially from Christianity since 1945, on religious movements – the Santal revolt, Birsa Munda, and Bhagat; the shift from religious to tribal movements with almost the same objectives.

663 Moser, Rupert R. "Birsa Munda Bhagwan (1875-1900)." *Weiner Ethnohistorische Blatter*, no. 4 (1972), pp. 77-92.

664 Moser, Rupert R. "Movements versus rebellions: A contribution on criticism of ideology based on the example of tribal and peasant

movements in the tribal belt of Bihar." In *Aspects of tribal life in south Asia I: Strategy and survival. Proceedings of an international seminar . . . Berne 1977*, edited by R. R. Moser and M. K. Gautam. Studia Ethnologica Bernensia, 1. Berne: Institute of Ethnology, University of Berne, 1978, pp. 123-34.

A critique of the various terms used, especially those meaning "revolt"; classification as "defence," "revitalization" (case study of the Santals, 1855, pp. 128-30), and "political"; pp. 130-32, Jharkhand Mukti Morcha, 1972-, with religious dimensions.

665 Moser, Rupert R. "Das Sido-Kanhu 1855 bis 1856 und die Sido-Kanhu Baisi 1965 bis heute." *Mitteilungen der Antropologischen Gessellschaft in Wein* 103 (1973): 74-94?

Compares the "revitalization movement" of 1855 with social-reform activity among the Santal in recent times.

666 Moser, Rupert R., and Gautam, Mohan K., eds. *Aspects of tribal life in south Asia I: Strategy and survival. Proceedings of an international seminar . . . Berne 1977*. Studia Ethnologica Bernensia, 1. Berne: Institute of Ethnology, University of Berne, 1978, 233 pp.

See essays by J. MacDougall (entry 645), H.-G. Hrach (entry 619), M. K. Gautam (entry 601), R. R. Moser (664), B. M. Boal (entry 545).

667 Munda, Bharmi [Choreya Munda]. "Account of Birsa." Manuscript., 67 pp. (3 or 4 pages in Hindi, with Devanagari script; remainder in Mundari, with Kaithi script).

Discovered by K. S. Singh in May 1962. Dictated by a disciple of Birsa to his son; a first-hand account of Birsa's religion. See K. S. Singh (entry 733), p. 55 of notes.

668 Munda, Muchi Rai Tiru. *Shri Birsa Bhagwan*. Khunti: Adim Jati Sewa Mandal, 1949.

In Hindi. The first biography, which has served as a primary source for later writers. See K. S. Singh (entry 733), p. 56 of notes.

669 Munshi, Surendra. "Tribal absorption and Sanskritisation in Hindu society." *Contributions to Indian Sociology* (Delhi), n.s. 13, no. 2 (1979): 293-317.

Examines N. K. Bose's work on tribal absorption and M. N. Sriniras's work on Sanskritization, with special reference to the Coorgs (pp. 307-314).

South: India

670 Nagu, R. N. "Mahua Devi cult." *Bulletin, Tribal Research Institute* (Chhindwara) 2 (1962): 29-32.
    Among the Gond, 1946-.

671 Naik, T. B. *The Bhils: A study.* Delhi: Bharatiya Adimjati Sevak Sangh, 1956, xiv + 367 pp.
    Pp. 322-29, religious changes through the effect of Hindu, Muslim, and Christian influences, and changes in the reverse direction.

672 Naipul, V[idiadhar] S[urajprasad]. *India: A wounded civilization.* New York: Knopf; London: André Deutsch, 1977, 191 pp. Reprint. Harmondsworth: Penguin, 1979.
    Pp. 61-72 (1977 ed.), on Shiv Sena movement among the poorest people of Bombay; a cult of a now-deified guerrilla leader of the seventeenth century, and an important social and developmental force.

673 Navlakha, S. K. "Puritanistic cults: A brief study of causation, effects, and prospects in Bhil society." In *The changing tribes of Madhya Pradesh*, edited by T. B. Naik. Indore: Government Regional Press, 1961, pp. 32-43.
    Bhagat Hindu-syncretist movements (Lasodia, Govindgiri, Bisanami), with some account of Christian and primal Bhils.

674 Nayak, Bhagyabath. "The Church of the Kond Hills. Part 2: Growth of the church." *Light of Life* (Bombay) 16, no. 5 (1974): 10, 20, 21.
    P. 10, revivals of 1956 in two Kond village churches.

675 Neill, Stephen. *A history of Christianity in India: The beginnings to A.D. 1707.* Cambridge: Cambridge University Press, 1984, 583 pp.

676 Nelson, Amvitharaj. *A new day in Madras: A study of Protestant churches in Madras.* South Pasadena, Calif.: William Carey Library, 1974, 340 pp.
    Pp. 45-53, independent churches, some with tribal membership.

677 Newman, R. S. "Faith is all! Emotion and devotion in a Goan sect." *Numen* 28, no. 2 (1981): 216-46.
    "Christ Ashram" founded by Miguel Colaco (b. early 1930s?), an illiterate Catholic healer, perhaps in late 1960s.

678 "News from Murhu: A local prophet." *Quarterly Papers* (Ranchi, S.P.G. Mission), July-October 1895, p. 3.

On Birsa. Other issues between 1892 and 1920 have further material. See K. S. Singh (entry 733), p. 66 of notes.

679 O'Malley, L. S. S. *Bengal district gazetteer: Santal Parganas.* Vol. 22. Calcutta: Bengal Secretariat Book Depot, 1910, p. 146.
    On the Santals' leader of 1871, Bhegviath Manjhi.

680 Orans, Martin. *The Santals: A tribe in search of a Great Tradition.* Detroit: Wayne State University Press, 1965, 154 pp.
    Pp. 30-36, the Santal Rebellion, 1855-57; pp. 36-37, Kherwar (heroic term for Santal) movement; pp. 113-17, Sarna Dharam Samlet (Sacred Grove Religious Organization) – a neoprimal movement.

681 Orans, Martin. "A tribe in search of a Great Tradition: The emulation-solidarity conflict." *Man in India* (Ranchi) 39, no. 2 (1959): 108-14.
    The Santal Jharkhand or Sarna Dharam Samlet, a neoprimal movement under Hindu influence from the 1940s, reviving Santal culture and identity and stressing the religious basis of morality.

682 Orr, J[ames] Edwin. *The flaming tongue: The impact of twentieth century revival.* Chicago: Moody Press, 1973, 241 pp.
    Pp. 131-38, 220, revivals of Pandita Ramabai (1905-), among Khasi hills Presbyterians (1905-), among Baptist Garos, then the Nagas and the Mizos.

683 Pakem, B. "The Biates." In *The tribes of northeast India,* edited by S. Karotemprel. Shillong: Vendrame Missiological Institute, 1984, pp. 267-94.
    P. 288, briefly on Independent Church of India entering Biate country, on the borders of Assam and Meghalaya, in the 1970s.

684 Pangborn, Cyrus R. "The Ramakrishna Math and mission: A case study of a revitalization movement." In *Hinduism: New essays in the history of religions,* edited by B. L. Smith. Supplements to *Numen,* 33. Leiden: E. J. Brill, 1976, pp. 98-119.
    Uses A. F. C. Wallace's analysis (entry 263) to describe the Ramakrishna Order as a "revivalistic vitalistic, messianic revitalization movement," – but not as nativistic or millenarian; vitalistic because of the imported Western patterns of organization and structure (e.g., the Mission Association).

685 Parekh, B. M. C. *Sri Swami Narayan.* Rajkot, 1936.

South: India

On Sahajanand (later famous as Swami Narayan, d. 1830) and the movement he inspired among the Bhils, Kolis, etc., and low castes in Gujerat from 1800.

686 Parry, Nevill Edward. *The Lakhers*. London: Macmillan & Co., 1932, 640 pp., illus., map.
Pp. 19-24, Lushai revival movements; pp. 349-500, Lakher primal religion.

687 Pettitt, George. *The Tinnevelly Mission of the Church Missionary Society*. London: Seeleys, 1851, 574 pp.
Pp. 387-90, the anti-Christian reaction in Nalloor district; pp. 433-51, contains a memorandum sent to the press in Madras in 1846 in defense against the false public accusations by Alagappa Nadan (see entry 534), and others, of immoral influences and of government favoritism.

688 Pickett, J[arrell] W[askom]. "Possible Satnami people movements." In *Church growth and group conversion*, edited by J. W. Pickett, et al. South Pasadena, Calif.: William Carey Library, 1973, pp. 84-96. (First published as *Christian missions in mid-India*. Jubbulpore: Mission Press, 1938, 111 pp., map.)
Includes the Satnam reform movement of Ghasi Das, 1830-; against idolatry and Brahmanism.

689 Playne, Somerset, comp., and Wright, Arnold, ed. *Southern India: Its history, people, commerce, and industrial resources*. London: Foreign and Colonial Compiling and Publishing Co., 1914-15, 766 pp.
Pp. 484, 486, Indian Church of the Only Saviour, of Rabbi Chattampillai-Aiya (1823-), a Hindu-Hebraist movement founded in 1857.

690 Presler, Henry H. "Major reactions of tribals to civilization." *Indian Cultures Quarterly* (Jabalpur) 24 [i.e., 23], no. 2 (1966): 48-62.
Pp. 49-51, the Ramba (1879), Khond (1882), Gond and Kolan, Santal, and Bastar (1919) revolts with religious dimensions; pp. 59-60, Tana Bhagats. The whole article is relevant background.

691 Presler, Henry H. *Primitive religions in India: A textbook on the primitive religious type among India's tribals*. Indian Theological Library, 6. Madras: Christian Literature Society for Senate, Serampore College, 1971, 349 pp.

Pp. 186-89, new religious movements – Kherwar (based on Bodding [entry 546] and Tana Bhagat).

692 Pullapilly, Cyriac K. "The Izhavas of Kerala and their historic struggle for acceptance in the Hindu society." In *Religion and social conflict in south Asia*, edited by B. L. Smith. International Studies in Sociology and Social Anthropology, 22. Leiden: E. J. Brill, 1976, pp. 22-46.
    A low-class community with their own charismatic leader and new forms of religion.

693 Purti, Priya Nath James. *Shahid Birsa Munda*. Jugsalai, Tatanagar: Kishore Press, 1951.
    In Hindi. Cited by K. S. Singh (entry 733), p. 56 of notes, as sharing the same account of Birsa as M. R. Munda (entry 668), with further information not always accurate.

694 Raghavaiah, V[ennelakanti]. *Tribal revolts*. Nellore, Andhra Pradesh: Andhra Rashtra Adimajati Sevak Sangh, 1971, 269 pp.
    Pp. 118-35, 142, the more religious aspects of the Birsa movement; pp. 150-51, Santal rising; pp. 164-72, Tana Bhagats; pp. 182-84, Joria's Naik revolt, 1868 – all with some religious aspect. The main material is political and military, from a nationalist viewpoint.

695 Raj, Hilda. "Persistence of caste in south India – an analytic study of Hindu and Christian Nadars." Ph.D. dissertation (sociology), American University, 1958, 281 pp.
    P. 134, Hindu Church of the Lord Jesus, of Satampillai. On the Nadars converted to Protestant Christianity in the first part of the nineteenth century in Tinnevelly district.

696 Raj, P[ulidindi] Solomon. *A Christian folk religion in India ... with a special reference to the Bible Mission of Devadas*. Studies in the Intercultural History of Christianity, 40. Frankfurt: Peter Lang, 1986, 426 pp.
    On the Bible Mission, founded by Mungamwi Devadas, 1938, an independent church embracing many castes, with Lutheran background.

697 Raj, P[ulidindi] Solomon. "The influence of Pentecostal teaching on some folk Christian religions in India." *International Review of Mission*, no. 297 [75] (January 1986): 39-46.
    The Bible Mission independent church as the case study.

South: India

698 Rauschenbusch-Clough, E[mma]. *While serving sandals: Tales of a Jelugu pariah tribe*. London: Hodder & Stoughton; New York: Fleming H. Revell, 1899, 321 pp., illus.

Pp. 117-29, Rajayogi movement of Verabramham, with many Christian features, among villagers in the twentieth century.

699 Ray, Benoy Gopal. *Religious movements in modern Bengal*. Santinekatan: Visva-Bharti [University] Research Publications, 1965, 244 pp.

Chap. 6 (pp. 147-56), reform movements in aboriginal religions – Kwarkar, Singhrai, Birsa, Mahima Dharma.

700 Ray, P. C. "Socio-political and technological factors in transformation." In *The tribal world and its transformation*, edited by B. Singh and J. S. Bhandari. New Delhi: Concept Publishing Co., 1980, pp. 25-41.

Pp. 25-26, Santal rebellion; pp. 26, 33, Sapha Hor; pp. 29-30, 34, Birsa Munda; p. 40, Santals adopting Hindu gods.

701 Raychaudhuri, Bikash. "Social mobility among the Rabha of north Bengal. *Man in India* (Ranchi) 50, no. 1 (1970): 87-97.

Various tribal movements, some more religious in form, from 1930 to 1963, seeking to raise Rabha status in relation to Hinduism.

702 Reid, J[ohn C.I.E.]. *Final report on the survey and settlement operation in district of Ranchi (1902-10)*. Calcutta: Bengal Secretariat Book Depot, 1912, 144 pp.

P. 46, most Munda and Oraons as Birsaites, and Birsa's movements in 1897.

703 Rottger-Hogan, E. "Insurrection . . . or ostracism: A study of the Santal rebellion of 1855." *Contributions to Indian Sociology* (Bombay) 16, no. 1 (1982): 79-96.

704 Roy, N. B. "More light on the Santhal insurrection." *Indian Historical Records Commission Proceedings* (Chandigarh) 36, no. 2 (1961): 61-72.

Pp. 67-68, 70-71, the Santals, confused by being drawn into Hindu shrines and practices, responded to an alleged new revelation and miraculous events, including copies of St. John's Gospel in Hindi and Bengali regarded as descended from heaven – these were sacred, and read daily as being part of God's orders.

705 Roy, N. B. "New aspects of the Santhal insurrection of 1855-1856." *Indian Historical Records Commission Proceedings* (New Delhi) 35, no. 2 (1960): 172-91.

Refutes the economic explanations – stresses the threat of alien ways of life, and the dishonoring of their women and other offenses by European and other railway workers. Little on religion.

706 Roy, Sarat Chandra. "The effects on aborigines of Chotanagpur of their contact with Western civilization." *Journal of Bihar and Orissa Research Society* (Patna) 17, no. 4 (1931): 358-94. Reprinted in *Man in India* (Ranchi) 62, no. 1 (1982): 65-100.

Pp. 376-78, Birsa and Tana Bhagat movements, set in a discussion of the influence of the British administration and of Christian missions – both regarded favorably.

707 Roy, Sarat Chandra. *The Mundas and their country*. Ranchi: City Bar Library; Calcutta: City Book Society, 1912, x + 546 + xxxii pp., illus. Reprint. Bombay: Asia Publishing House, 1970.

Pp. 325-43, an account of the Birsa rising, needing modification in the light of of later information available from government and missionary records; pp. 284f., Sardar movement.

708 Roy, Sarat Chandra. "A new religious movement among the Oraons." *Man in India* (Ranchi) 1, no. 4 (1921): 267-324.

Almost identical with his later account (entry 709), chap. 6, with slightly different arrangement of materials, and introduction and conclusion. The later version is also updated in a few details.

709 Roy, Sarat Chandra. *Oraon religion and customs*. Ranchi and Calcutta: "Man in India" Office, 1928, 418 pp., illus.

Hinduized Bhagats, Kabirpanthi Bhagat, and especially Tana Bhagats (pp. 339-403); texts of catechism, hymns and songs, with English translation (pp. 353-93). A slightly enlarged reprint of his 1921 article (entry 708).

710 Roy-Burman, B. K. "Dynamics of persistence of tribal community in India." *Eastern Anthropologist* 31, no. 1 (1978): 93-99.

711 Russell, R[obert] V[ane], and Rai Bahadur, Hira Lal. *The castes and tribes of the central provinces of India*. Vol. 1. London: Macmillan & Co., 1916, 426 pp., maps, illus.

Pp. 307-16, Satnami movement among the Chamars.

South: India

712 Sa, Fidelis de. *Crises in Chotanagpur*. Bangalore: Redemptorist Publications, 1975.

P. 289, the Birsa movement, 1895-1900 – a short paragraph, by a Catholic priest: "For his purpose the Birsa movement had no relevance" (S. Fuchs, entry 590).

713 Sa, N. de. "The Tana Bhagats of Chotanagpur: Studies in sociopolitical movement and personality structure." Ph.D. dissertation, Patna, 1964.

714 Sachchidananda. "Birasa – an Adivasi fighter for freedom." *Vanyajati* (Delhi) 11, no. 4 (1954): 120-24.

A life of Birsa – a more popular treatment. Reprinted: entry 716, pp. 103-8.

715 Sachchidananda. "Influence of Hinduism on religious beliefs and practices of the Oraon." *Journal of Historical Research* (Ranchi) 3, no. 1 (1960).

Includes the Tana Bhagat and other Bhagat movements. Reprinted in entry 716, pp. 155-60.

716 Sachchidananda. *Profile of tribal cultures in Bihar*. Calcutta: Firma K. L. Mukhopadhyaya, 1965, 236 pp., illus.

Pp. 11, 208-99, useful overview of religious movements; pp. 103ff., reprint of entry 714; pp. 149-54, reprint of entry 717; pp. 155-60, reprint of entry 715.

717 Sachchidananda. "The study of culture change in tribal Bihar." *Adivasi* (Bulletin, Tribal Research Institute Bhubaneswar, Orissa) 3, no. 2 (1957-58).

Reprinted: entry 716, pp. 149-54.

718 Sachchidananda, ed. *Culture change in tribal Bihar: Munda and Oraon*. Calcutta: Bookland, 1964, 158 pp., illus.

Pp. 91-96, Birsa movement; pp. 99-104, 135, Tana Bhagats.

719 Sahay, Keshari N. "The impact of Christianity on the Oraon of the Chainpur belt in Chotanagpur: An analysis of its cultural processes." *American Anthropologist* 70, no. 5 (1968): 923-42.

No reference to independent movements, but a useful analysis in terms of five cultural processes: "oscillation, scrutinization, combination, indigenization, retroversion" – as between the old and the new.

720 Sahay, Keshari N. "Indigenization of Christianity in India." *Man in India* (Ranchi) 61, no. 1 (1981): 17-36, bib.

721 Sahay, Keshari N. "The study of culture change in tribal Bihar." *Journal of the Indian Anthropological Society* (Calcutta) 9, no. 1 (1974): 85-105.
Discusses the two processes of Christian and Hindu acculturation among the Oraon of Ranchi.

722 Sahay, Keshari N. "Tribal self-image and identity." In *Ethnicity, identity, and interaction*. Tribal Heritage of India, vol. 1, edited by S. C. Dube. New Delhi: Vikas Publishing House, 1977, pp. 8-57.
Especially pp. 47-57 on what "tribal" means, and the changes occurring in self-image when becoming a Hindu caste or a Christian community. Of theoretical value.

723 Sattampillai, A. N. [S. A. Nayaga Nadan, pseud.]. *A brief sketch of the Hindu Christian dogma*. Palamcotta, 1980.
By the founder of the Hindu Church of the Lord Jesus.

724 Schmitt, Erika. "'Sonat Santal Samaj': Eine soziale Bewegung der Santals im Dhanbad-Districkt, Bihar, India." *Sociologus* (Berlin) 23, no. 1 (1973): 3-21; no. 2 (1973): 97-115, English summary (p. 115).
A tribal association formed in 1970 by Santal elites, which sought internal Santal revival and reform to resist Hindu pressures, but collapsed after a few months; sociocultural rather than explicitly religious.

725 Sen, Jyoti. "Christianity and change among the Adivasis of Chotanagpur." *Bulletin, Anthropological Survey of India* 25, nos. 3-4 (1976): 9-12.

726 Sen, Jyoti. "The Jharkand movement." In *Tribal situation in India*, edited by K. S. Singh. Simla: Indian Institute of Advanced Study, 1972, pp. 432-37.

727 Sen, Jyoti. "Problems in tribal transformation." *Man in India* (Ranchi) 46, no. 4 (1966): 319-30.
On the scheduled tribes of Chotanagpur. P. 321, "reformatory sects" (millenarian, etc.) in the seventeenth to twentieth centuries; movement toward Hinduism or Christianity in first half of twentieth century; subsequent reassertions of tribal culture and identity in political forms.

South: India

728 Seunarine, J. F. *Reconversion to Hinduism through Suddhi*. Madras: Christian Literature Society, 1977, 105 pp.

Pp. 90-93, "revitalization process as a contribution to the understanding of Suddhi"–applied to the Hindu Arya Samaj movement.

729 Sevrin, Oscar. *The Bhagat movement in Chota Nagpur*. Kurseong: Indian Academy, 1917, pp. 273-335.

730 Shrivastava, L. N. R. "Munda eschatology." *Bulletin of Department of Anthropology of Bihar University* (Ranchi), 1957, pp. 66-70.

As background to Birsa Bhagwan movement of the 1980s.

731 Siddiqui, M. K. A. "Impact of Islam on some tribes of central and western India." *Man in India* (Ranchi) 59, no. 3 (1979): 193-96.

Superficial and transient Islamization of the aristocratic Raj Gonds; progress toward greater Islamization of the Tadvi Bhils, coincident with their search for tribal solidarity.

732 Singh, K[umar] Suresh. "Colonial transformation of tribal society in middle India." *Economic and Political Weekly* (Bombay), 29 July 1978, pp. 1221-32.

Pp. 1229-31, the different phases of tribal movements in the pre-independence period: 1. primary resistance (1795-1860); 2. agrarian revitalization (1860-1920), with religiopolitical aspects and charismatic leaders; 3. secular-political (1920-47), under Gandhi's influence. Emphasizes the need for research on the tribal peoples.

733 Singh, K[umar] Suresh. *The dust storm and the hanging mist: A study of Birsa Munda and his movement in Chotanagpur (1874-1901)*. Calcutta: K. L. Makhopadhyah, 1966, 208 pp. + 179 pp. of notes, references, and addenda, illus., maps, very full lists of sources (pp. 55-71 of notes).

Probably the most thorough study with the best range of sources, which are fully described in extensive notes and bibliography. See review by J. C. Jha (entry 624).

734 Singh, K[umar] Suresh, ed. *Tribal situation in India*. Transactions of the Indian Institute of Advanced Study, 13. Simla: Indian Institute of Advanced Study, 1972, 639 pp., map.

A valuable discussion in the form of the papers at a seminar, embracing most current issues and embracing new religious movements and the problems of acculturation, integration, etc. See P.

Ekka (entry 581), L. K. Mahaptra (entry 650), J. Sen (entry 726), S. C. Sinha (entry 739), and L. P. Vidyarthi (entry 771).

735 Singh, Roop [G.]. "Anatomy of three tribal movements in Rajasthan." *Eastern Anthropologist* 36, no. 2 (1983): 117-29.
Pp. 121-23, 127, the Bhils' Bhagat movement of the early twentieth century.

736 Singh, R[oop] G. "Neo-Buddhist movement among the Harijans of Ahmadpur: Search for new status and identity." *Journal of the Indian Anthropological Society* 16, no. 3 (1981): 203-8.

737 Singh, Roop [G.]. "The role of Bhagat movement in the inception of caste features in the Bhil tribe." *Eastern Anthropologist* 23, no. 2 (1970): 163-70.

738 Sinha, Surajit [Chandra]. "The media and nature of Hindu-Bhumij interactions." *Journal of Asiatic Society* (Letters and Science), no. 23 (1957), pp. 23-37.
On the various Bhagat movements and the Bhumij-Kshatriya movement.

739 Sinha, Surajit [Chandra]. "Solidarity movements in India: A review." In *Tribal situations in India*, edited by K. S. Singh. Simla: Indian Institute for Advanced Study, 1972, pp. 410-23.
Concentrates on sociopolitical movements aiming at solidarity as against nontribals, and the changing situations – pre-British period, British period, and independence era – with critical examination of the various models proposed for analysis, including Wallace's revitalization model (entry 263).

740 Sinha, Surajit [Chandra]. "Tribal solidarity and messianic movements." *Contributions to Indian Sociology* (Delhi), n.s. 2 (December 1968): 112-18.
A review article of *The Santals*, by M. Orans (entry 680) and *Rebellious prophets*, by S. Fuchs (entry 595); of theoretical value in examining acculturation.

741 Sinha, Surajit [Chandra]. "Tribes and Indian civilization: Transformation processes in modern India." *Man in India* (Ranchi) 61, no. 2 (1981): 105-42, bib.
The tribes are developing political solidarity movements, led by educated members, and so are emerging as self-conscious regional and

South: India

national minority groups; this differs from older methods of preserving identity and relating to other groups. Some religious and semireligious movements (Sacred Grove Religious Organization / Sarna Dharam Samlet, pp. 121-22); Jharkand Party, pp. 123-26; the Adis of East Siang district, revival of culture and universalizing of mythology, pp. 131-33, passim.

742 Sinha, Surajit [Chandra], ed. "Study of tribal solidarity movements: General propositions." *Research programmes on cultural anthropology and allied disciplines.* Anthropological Survey of India, no. 13. Calcutta: A.S. of I., 1970, 444 pp., illus.

743 Sinha, Surendra Prasad. "Birsa Dharam." *Journal of Historical Research* (Ranchi) 2 (1960): 32-42.

744 Sinha, Surendra Prasad. "The first Birsaite rising (1895)." *Journal of the Bihar Research Society* (Patna) (Altekar Memorial Volume) 45, nos. 1-4 (1959): 391-403.

745 Sinha, Surendra Prasad. "The genesis of the Birsa risings (1895-1900)." *Journal of Historical Research* (Ranchi) 3 (1961): 34-39.

746 Sinha, Surendra Prasad. *Life and times of Birsa Bhagwan.* Studies in Tribal Bihar, 1. Ranchi: Bihar Tribal Research Institute, 1964, 179 pp., illus., map, full bib. of unpublished and published materials (pp. 164-68).
    The religious stages and aspects are found especially at pp. 56, 72-79, 107-12, 120-21. Pp. 36-43, the Lutheran mission background; otherwise deals with the political aspects from a pro-Indian viewpoint. This was the first documented monograph on an important revitalization movement. For critical review, see K. S. Singh (entry 733), pp. 57-59 of notes.

747 Sinha, Surendra Prasad. "The nature of the religion of Birsa (1895-1900)." In *Aspects of religion in Indian society,* edited by L. P. Vidyarthi. Meerut City: Kedar Nath Ram Nath, [1961], pp. 316-22.
    A critical analysis of the teachings of Birsa Bhagwan, with an account of his personal development.

748 Sinha, Surendra Prasad. "Portrait of a Munda leader: Birsa Bhagwan (1895-1900)." In *Leadership in India,* edited by L. P. Vidyarthi. Bombay and London: Asia Publishing House, 1967, pp. 169-76.

749 Skrefsrud, L[ars] O[lsen]. "Christianity and Kherwarism." *Englishman* (Calcutta), 16 March 1881, p. 2.

A letter in reply to "Enquirer" in the previous issue, distinguishing between Christians, loyal to the government, and followers of Kherwarism, a "rabid socialistic agitation," seditious, using religion as a cloak for political ends.

750 Skrefsrud, L[ars] O[lsen]. [Letter to the editor]. *Statesman* (Calcutta), 8 November 1880.

On the Santals' Kherwar movements in their three divisions – Sapha Hors (purists), Babajaias (beggars), and Bhelwaragars (more syncretist, less Hindu).

751 Slaeter, I. *Lars Olsen Skrefsrud*. Stuttgart, 1928.

Pp. 101-2, Skrefsrud and the Kherwar movement among the Santals.

752 Soppit, C. A. *An historical and descriptive account of the Kachari tribes in the North Cachar hills*. Shillong: Assam Secretariat Press, 1885, 35 pp.

Pp. 6-7, Sombadan as a healer and his new movement and revolt, 1882.

753 Spencer, Dorothy M. "The hunt for Birsa: A fragment of history." *Bengal Past and Present* (Calcutta Historical Society), no. 155 [83, no. 1] (January-June 1964): 1-6.

Based on oral account of an eyewitness. Cited by K. S. Singh (entry 733), p. 34 of notes.

754 *Statesman*. Various editorials and letters sympathetic to the Birsa movement in Chota Nagpur in 1900, including, 14 January, 17 January, 25 March, 2 April, 3 April, 18 April, 22 April, 28 April (last two by A. Nottrot).

Cited by S. P. Sinha (entry 746), pp. 94-98.

755 Stevenson, H[enry] N[oel] C[ochrane]. "Religion and society among some tribes of Chota-Nagpur." B. Litt. thesis (social anthropology), University of Oxford, 1951.

756 Surendra, Lawrence. "Srikakulam tribal uprising." *Religion and Society* (Bangalore) 22, no. 2 (1975): 39-48.

South: India

On the Naxalite Marxist movement in Andhra Pradesh from the 1960s; pp. 46-47, on the neoprimal, anti-Hindu religious features, and similarities to millennialism.

757 Taylor, Richard W. "The Ambedkarite Buddhists." In *Ambedkar and the neo-Buddhist movements*, edited by T. S. Wilkinson and M. M. Thomas. Madras: Christian Literature Society, 1972, pp. 129-63.

758 Thurston, Edgar. *Omens and superstitions of southern India*. London: T. Fisher Unwin; New York: McBride, Nast, 1912, 320 pp., illus.
Pp. 265-66, the anti-British messiah, Korra Mallayya, of the Vizagapatam district in 1900, a neo-Hindu movement.

759 Tiru, Muchi Roy. *Sri Birsa Bhagwan*. Khunti: Bhaiya Ram Munda, Adimjati Sera Mandel, 1955.
In Hindi. Cited by S. P. Sinha (entry 747), p. 322. A small booklet based on information from old Mundas who had known Birsa intimately, and including some songs of the movement.

760 Troisi, Joseph. "Hindu-tribal religious interaction." *Indian Cultures* (Jabalpur) 37, no. 2 (1982): 1-33.
"An analysis of the influence of Hinduism on Santal beliefs and practices"–by a Santal scholar. Reciprocal borrowing has occurred throughout their contact. Pp. 29-31, the Kherwar movement from the 1870s–its various sections, including Bangham Manjhi's movement from 1930. The Hindu influence has been least in the sphere of religion.

761 Troisi, Joseph. "Hindu-tribal religious interaction." *Sevartham* (Ranchi) 5 (1980): 115-37.
See entry 760.

762 Troisi, Joseph. "Religious beliefs and practices among the Santals: A case study." Ph.D. thesis (sociology), University of Delhi, 1977.

763 Troisi, Joseph. "Social movements among the Santals." *Social Action* 26, no. 3 (1976): 253-66.
See a fuller version in entry 764.

764 Troisi, Joseph. "Social movements among the Santals." In *Social movements in India*, edited by M. S. A. Rao. Vol 2, *Sectarians, tribal, and women's movements*. New Delhi: Manohar Publications, 1979, pp. 123-48.

The 1855-57 rebellion; the Kherwar and the Jharkhand movements – viewed mainly as nativistic, with economic, political, and religious aspects. By a Jesuit.

765 Upadhyay, V. S. "[Combating] alien forces: A study of weaker ethnic groups in India." *Revue Ethnologique* 8:11, no. 19 (1982): 116-26.

766 Van der Schueren, T. *The Belgian mission of Bengal.* Calcutta: Thacker, Spink & Co., 1922-25.
  Pp. 10-13, "The Munda rising."

767 Van Exem, A. "Christian tribals and tribal community." *Indian Missiological Review* 8, no. 2 (1986): 91-101.

768 Van Exem, A. "Early evangelization in Chotanagpur." *Indian Missiological Review* 1, no. 4 (1979): 350-63.
  On Catholic missionary expansion; pp. 359, 363, "messianic movements" – Birsa and Tana Bhagat – in relation to tribal and Christian religions.

769 Van Exem, A. "Tribal religion at the crossroads." *Indian Missiological Review* 3, no. 2 (1981): 84-102.
  Deals with Munda religion, Hinduization, Christianity, and on p. 98, a passing reference to the Birsa movement.

770 Verma, K. K., and Sinha, Ramesh. "Socio-political movements among the Munda and the Oraon." In *The tribal world and its transformation*, edited by B. Singh and J. S. Bhandari. New Delhi: Concept Publishing Co., 1980, pp. 1-15.
  Pp. 4-11, Sardar, Birsa, Tana Bhagat, and Jharkand movements, with religious dimensions.

771 Vidyarthi, L[alita] P[rasad]. "An appraisal of the leadership pattern among the tribes of Bihar." In *Tribal situations in India*, edited by K. S. Singh. Simla: Indian Institute for Advanced Study, 1972, pp. 438-53.
  Surveys the changes in leadership over the nineteenth and twentieth centuries in the revolts and religious movements.

772 Vidyarthi, L[alita] P[rasad]. "Aspects of tribal leadership in Chota Nagpur." In *Leadership in India*, edited by L. P. Vidyarthi. Bombay and London: Asia Publishing House, 1967, pp. 127-44.

South: India

> Includes new movements led by Western-educated, urban-bred Christian tribals – Jharkhand Party, Chota Nagpur Samaj, Kisan Sasha, Chota Nagpur Catholic Sabha, Chota Nagpur Adivasi Maha Sabha.

773 Warren, Joseph. "India: Lodiana mission. Communication from Rev. Joseph Warren." *Home and Foreign Record* (Presbyterian Church in the U.S.A.), January 1854, p. 19. "India: Lodiana mission. Appeal for more workers." *Home and Foreign Record*, July 1854, p. 212.

> On the faqir-founded movement near Ludhiana, ca. 1853.

774 Webster, John C. B. *The Christian community and change: Nineteenth century north India*. Delhi: Macmillan, 1976, 293 pp.

> P. 122, a faqir-founded Christian movement south of Ludhiana, ca. 1853; pp. 122-23, Nishkalankis movement of Hakim Singh.

775 Weiner, Myron. *Sons of the soil: Migration and ethnic conflict in India*. Princeton: Princeton University Press, 1978, 383 pp.

> Pp. 151-56, description of the tribals of Ranchi; pp. 162-64, 178, the Birsa Munda rebellion of 1899, reformist, millenarian, and revivalist, under both Hindu and Christian influences; pp. 165, 202, Tana Bhagat movement (briefly). The main theme is the party political movements, which since the 1930s have replaced the earlier religious and millenarian movements among the tribal peoples.

776 Weisman, Steven R. "Aizawl journal: In a far corner of India a sect yearns for Israel." *New York Times*, 20 February 1987, illus., map.

> A Mizoram tribal group identifying from the 1960s with the "lost tribe" of Manasseh, after conversion by a Welsh Presbyterian mission from the 1890s.

777 Wherry, E. Morris. "Jottings by the way." *Foreign Missionary*, November 1874, p. 180.

> Hakim Singh and the Nishkalankis movement.

778 Wherry, E. Morris. "Lodiana Mission, North India: Letter of E. M. Wherry." *Foreign Missionary*, June 1871, pp. 9-11.

> "The best statement of Hakim Singh's beliefs" – founder of Nishkalankis movement.

779 Wherry, E. Morris. "Lodiana mission. North India: Lodiana. Letter of Rev. E. M. Wherry, May 1." *Foreign Missionary*, August 1872, pp. 88-91.

> Hakim Singh and the Nishkalankis movement.

780 Williams, Richard Aelwyn E[llis]. *Bihar and Orissa in 1931-32*. Bihar, Patna: Government Press, 1933.

    P. 7, Haribaba movement of 1931-32. Cited by K. S. Singh (entry 733), p. 49 of notes.

781 *Yug-Purush Guru Ghasi Das*. Raipur: Satnami Mitra Prakashan, n.d.

    A Jayanti Souvenit publication. Essays. Cited by A. Das (entry 563), p. 55, on the Satnami movement.

782 Zide, Norman H., and Munda, Ram Dayal. "Revolutionary Birsa and the songs related to him." *Journal of Social Research* (Ranchi) 12, no. 2 (1969): 37-60.

    An outline of the Birsa movement; pp. 49-59, texts of popular songs (focused on the military climax) mostly in Mundari, with English translations.

NEPAL

In this predominantly Hindu kingdom there is no great incentive for the kind of interaction movement with which we are concerned and almost no literature to be listed.

783 Caplan, Lionel. *Land and social change in east Nepal: A study of Hindu-tribal relations*. London: Routledge & Kegan Paul; Berkeley: University of California Press, 1970, xvi + 224 pp.

    In the Ilam district, 1964-65. Pp. 65-70, the Limbu tribal and Brahman religious traditions remaining distinct without Sanskritization of the Limbu. A "negative instance."

784 Jones, Rex L. "Sanskritization in eastern Nepal." *Ethnology* 15, no. 1 (1976): 63-75.

    The process of "Sanskritization" among the Limbu people in interaction with immigrant high-caste Hindus; pp. 69-70, on religious changes; p. 73, the Satya Hangma "revitalization cult" from the 1930s under a former Gurkha soldier calling himself Phalgunada (d. 1946) – a neoprimal movement.

SOUTHEAST

BURMA

New religious movements have arisen in Burma in the interaction between the primal religious traditions of the hill tribal peoples (such as the Karen and the Chin) and the invasive Buddhist and Christian (chiefly Baptist) faiths; sometimes all three contribute to the one movement. The Buddhist influence occurs largely through its own longstanding millennial tradition (see E. M. Mendelson's items, entries 805-808), which corresponds to the eschatological emphases common among many nineteenth-century Christian missionaries, and also contributes to political revolts, often with religious dimensions, such as the Saya San of 1930. Note the divergent British (C. Innes, entry 798) and Burmese (Cha Ne Cho-Ma Ma Lay, entry 790) interpretations.

Note also the tradition of a lost sacred book (especially, T. Stern, entry 816) and the revelation of new sacred scripts (G. Marin, entry 802). Some movements in Burma cannot be separated from their extension into Thailand, and further material (especially on Telakhon) will be found under Thailand. One unusual movement stems from an American woman missionary, Mrs. Mason. See *Baptist Missionary Magazine* (entry 786, especially the article by J. Clough), and R. G. Torbert (entry 821).

785 Banks, E. Pendleton. "Pau cin hau: A case of religious innovation among the northern Chin." In *American historical anthropology: Essays in honor of Leslie Spier*, edited by C. L. Riley and W. W. Taylor. London and Amsterdam: Feffer & Simons; Carbondale: Southern Illinois University Press, 1967, pp. 37-59.

A visionary movement, against old *nat* cults and keeping the dead in the house.

786 *Baptist Missionary Magazine* (Boston). Various relevant reports as follows:

45, no. 7 (1865): 221-27; 45, no. 9 (1865): 347, 408-11;

52, no. 7 (1872): 252-54 [A. Bunker and Anon. on Mrs. Mason's new movement];

53 (1873): 9-16 [C. H. Carpenter, "A tour among the Karens of Siam"; p. 14, Telakhon as "a peculiar sect" worshipping "Too-way"];

54, no. 6 (1874): 163 [article on Francis Mason, D.D.; summary report of his wife's new movement]; 54, no. 7 (1874): 233 [report by Rev. John Clough (Anglican) on Mrs. Mason's movement].

787 Benz, Ernst. *Buddhas Weiderkehr und die Zukunft Asiens*. Munich: Nymphenburger Verlags-Handlung, 1963, 274 pp.

P. 131, messianism of Buddhist Burma must necessarily have Christian sources. See E. Sarkisyanz's comment (entry 811), that these ideas appeared in Burma early in the nineteenth century, before Christian eschatology was influential.

788 Burma, Government of. "Report on the rebellion in Burma up to 3d May 1931, and communiqué issued by the government of Burma, 19th May 1931. Cmd. 3900." In *Parliamentary Papers*. Vol. 12. 1930-31.

On the Saya San revolt.

789 Cady, John F[rank]. *A history of modern Burma*. Ithaca, N.Y.: Cornell University Press, 1958, 682 pp., illus. map.

Pp. 309-21, on Saya San rebellion.

790 Cha Ne Cho-Ma Ma Lay. "A nationalist condemnation of British rule in Burma." In *The world of Southeast Asia*, edited by H. J. Benda and J. A. Larkin. New York: Harper & Row, 1967, pp. 160-64. Reprinted from "The real origin and causes of the Burma rebellion." In *Thu Lou Lu* [That kind of person]. Rangoon: Lok Kee Press, 1953, pp. 377-80, 387-89.

Rebuttal of the official British view of the Saya San revolt. See C. Innes (entry 798).

791 Childe, Donald B. *Asian survey*. London: Methodist Mission Society, 1958.

P. 49, "the independent fundamentalist Lushai church" under Rev. Lal Thanlaina.

792 Christian, John Leroy. *Modern Burma*. Berkeley: University of California Press, 1942, 381 pp.

P. 196, passing reference to Pau Cin Hau as animism plus Buddhism; p. 239, Saya San's revolt in 1930 as nationalist uprising led by a "charlatan," the only one versus the British in the twentieth century. No reference to any religious aspect.

793 Collins, Maurice S[tewart]. *Trials in Burma*. London: Faber & Faber, 1938, 294 pp.

Pp. 273-94, Saya San rebellion and its causes, by the Deputy Commissioner of Sagaing, Burma.

Southeast: Burma

794 Fürer-Haimendorf, Christoph von. "Die Stellung der Naturvölker in Indien und Südostasien." In *Die heutigen Naturvölker in Ausgleich mit der neuen zeit*, edited by D. Westermann. Stuttgart: F. Enke Verlag, 1940, pp. 126-97.
P. 187, Pau Cin Hau.

795 Furnivall, J. H. "Meitteya and Shinmale," and "Further notes on Shin-ma-le." *Journal of the Burma Research Society* 9 (December 1919): 158-59.
Two Buddhist cults among the Karen with similarities to Telakhon and Ywa cults. Shin-ma-le allegedly confused with John the Baptist.

796 Galusha, Elon. [Quotation from address at anniversary of American Tract Society.] *Missionary Register* (London), August 1831, p. 355.
A Burmese Karen cult (ca. 1828?) focused on a sacred book–a Church of England Prayer Book.

797 India, Government of. *Census of India, 1931*. Vol. 11, *Burma*, pt. 1, *Report*. Rangoon: Government Printing Office, 1933.
Pp. 214-15, "sects" peculiar to Burma; pp. 217-18, Pau Cin Hau movement, and pp. 194-95, his new script.

798 Innes, Charles. "An official view of the rebellion in Burma." In *The world of Southeast Asia*, edited by H. J. Benda and J. A. Larkin. New York: Harper & Row, 1967, pp. 141-44.
The colonial governor's approach to the Saya San rebellion, led by a former Buddhist monk. See Cha Ne Cho-Ma Ma Lay (entry 790).

799 Kuica, Rosiam. "Organization of the Presbyterian Church in Burma." Certificate in Church Management dissertation, Westhill College (Selly Oak, Birmingham), 1988.
Pp. 2, 3, 27, a Burmese Presbyterian minister on the Falam revival and secessions from 1945 to 1958.

800 Lewy, Guenter. *Religion and revolution*. New York: Oxford University Press, 1974, 674 pp.
Pp. 338-41, Saya San rebellion.

801 Lincoln, Jackson Stewart. *The dream in primitive culture*. London: Cresset Press, 1935, 359 pp.
P. 80, n. 2, on dreams as source of Pau Cin Hau's movement, including its revealed sacred script. Based on entry 797.

802 Marin, G. "An old Pwo-Karen alphabet." *Man*, article 5, 43 (January-February 1943): 17-19, illus.

On the Leke sect, 1860, named from their sacred book – founded near village of Hnikya, below Pa'an on the right bank of the Salween. Now there are a few thousand followers among Pwo-Karen, worshipping a single deity, *arija*. They use ancient Pwo-Karen script, reproduced on p. 18.

803 Marshall, Harry Ignatius. "The Karen people of Burma: A study in anthropology and ethnology." Contributions in History and Political Science, 8. *Ohio State University Bulletin* 26, no. 13 (29 April 1922): 1-329, illus., bib.

On various Karen millenarian and prophet movements: p. 123, influence of religious tracts; p. 264, Maw Lay cult; p. 264, Ko Pisan (Phu Pai San); p. 265, Hkli Bo Pa cult; p. 268, religious "prophets" and High God.

804 Mason, Francis. *The Karen apostle; or memoir of Ko Thah-Byu*. 1st American ed., revised by H. J. Ripley. Boston: Gould, Kendall & Lincoln, 1843, 153 pp.

Pp. 144-48, Judson's meeting with a Karen "prophet" in 1832, and Mason's in 1837; prophets in general. Ko Thah-Byu (ca. 1778-1840) was Judson's first convert, a bandit bought by him from slavery.

805 Mendelson, E. Michael. "The King of the Weaving Mountain." *Journal, Royal Central Asian Society* 48, nos. 3-4 (1961): 229-37.

A millenarian Buddhist movement in Burma in the 1950s.

806 Mendelson, E. [Michael]. "Messianic Buddhism and political behaviour in Burma." In *Abstracts of symposium papers, Tenth Pacific Science Congress*, by Pacific Science Association. Honolulu: Pacific Science Association, 1961, p. 109.

The "telescoping of the orthodox messianic process . . . is found again at the popular level in the nativistic movements which followed the collapse of the Burmese monarchy. The Saya San rebellion of the 1930s was inspired by such ideals . . . ," in the interaction between village "animism" and orthodox Buddhism.

807 Mendelson, E. Michael. "A messianic Buddhist Association in upper Burma." *Bulletin, School of Oriental and African Studies* 24, no. 3 (1961): 560-80, illus.

Southeast: **Burma**

A cult belonging neither to Theravada Buddhism nor to animism; a "messianic" or "charismatic" nativistic movement, connected with local royalty.

808 Mendelson, E. Michael. *Sangha and state in Burma: A study of monastic sectarianism and leadership*. Edited by J. P. Ferguson. Ithaca: Cornell University Press, 1975, 400 pp.
Pp. 205-9 on Saya San revolt.

809 North, Cornelius W. "Dr. H. W. Turner's PRINERM typology examined in the circumstances of upper Burma with particular reference to the cult of the 37 Royal Nats and the Pau Chin Hau movement." Diploma in New Religious Movements thesis, University of Birmingham, 1988, 48 pp., maps.
Buddhism and the primal nats cult coexist while the Pau Cin Hau movement in a Christian/primal context shows interaction and confirms the typology.

810 Richardson, Don. *Eternity in their hearts*. Ventura, Calif.: Regal Books, 1981. Reprint. 1983, 176 pp.
Chap. 2, "Peoples of the lost book" (pp. 73-102), on the traditions of a lost book of God among the Karen, Lahu, Wa, Shan, Kui, etc., of Burma, the Lisu of China, the Naga and Mizo of India. Nothing on Telakhon cult but useful background.

811 Sarkisyanz, Emanuel. *Buddhist backgrounds of the Burmese revolution*. The Hague: M. Nijhoff, 1965, xxix + 250 pp.
On Buddhist millenarianism (e.g., Burmese uprisings against British rule), chaps. 21-22 (pp. 149-65), messianism and Saya San revolt.

812 Sarkisyanz, Emanuel. "Messianic folk Buddhism as ideology of peasant revolts in nineteenth and early twentieth century Burma." *Review of Religious Research* (North Newton, Kan.) 10, no. 1 (1968): 32-38, bib.

813 Saw Kya Shinn; Kyaw Hpaung Yeh Kaw; Kyaw Taing Lone Gay; and Mahn Gyi Sein. "A brief outline on the traditional background of the Laikai (Ariya) religious sect." Translated from Burmese. N.p., [1982?], 31 pp. Mimeo.
Origin of Laikai script and scriptures; relations with Christian missionaries from 1834 and the new script for the Christian Bible; collection of written Laikai literature in 1861; rediscovery of the Laikai texts in 1921; translation into Burmese, 1981.

814 Smith, Donald Eugene. *Religion and politics in Burma*. Princeton, N.J.:
     Princeton University Press, 1965, 350 pp.
     Pp. 107-9, 121-22, Saya San revolt.

815 Solomon, Robert L. "Saya San and the Burmese rebellion." *Modern
     Asian Studies* (London) 3, no. 3 (1969): 209-23.

816 Stern, Theodore. "Ariya and the Golden Book: A millenarian Buddhist
     sect among the Karen." *Journal of Asian Studies 27,* no. 2 (1968): 297-
     328, bib.
     Very important article, especially for references, and for general
     survey of Buddhist millennial movements, as well as detailed study of
     Telakhon cult (1860-), pp. 314-27.

817 Stevenson, H[enry] N[oel] C[ochrane]. *The hill peoples of Burma*.
     Burma Pamphlets, no. 6. London: Longman's, 1944, 50 pp.
     P. 20, Hpo Pai San's new, independent, self-supporting cult in
     1866, combining Christian, Buddhist, and Karen elements; similarly in
     1933, Thompson Durnay's dispensed with the Bible.

818 Stoll, W. G. "Notes on the Yoon-tha-lin Karens, their history, manners,
     and customs." *Madras Journal of Literature and Science*, n.s. 6 (1861):
     52-67.
     Especially pp. 55-57, on millennial prophet-led revolt against the
     British in the 1850s in Burma.

819 Telford, J[ames] H[axton]. "Animism in Kengtung State." *Journal of the
     Burma Royal Society* 27, no. 2 (August 1937): 86-238.
     On the G'uisha ("Living Breath") cult: a full account by a
     missionary of the Lahu prophet Ma-Heh G'uisha in Kengtung in the
     late 1920s, and of his unsuccessful opposition to the British authorities.

820 Tien Ju-kang. "Religious cults and social structure of the Shan States of
     the Yunnan-Burma frontier." Ph.D. thesis, University of London, 1948.

821 Torbert, Robert G[eorge]. *Venture of faith: The story of the American
     Baptist Foreign Mission Society ... 1814-1954*. Philadelphia: Judson
     Press, 1955, 634 pp.
     Pp. 241-42, on the "original divine language cult" of Mrs. F.
     Mason, 1865-71.

822 Tun, M. C. W. "Dead on their feet." *Far Eastern Economic Review* 79,
     no. 7 (1973).

Southeast: **Burma**

P. 13, an elderly Lahu messiah in the Shan state, with followers resisting government troops in 1973.

823 Young, William Marcus. "Shan Mission, Kengtung." *News* (Rangoon) 18, no. 3 (1905): 11; 19, no. 5 (1906): 19.

American Baptist missionary's accounts of Shan and other peoples responding to Lahu prophets who opposed Christianity, predicted the coming of the whites, or became converted.

INDONESIA

This section covers Indonesia apart from Irian Jaya. Although this is clearly part of the Indonesian Republic, its geographical location and cultural affinities make it more convenient to place the literature on its new religious movements under Melanesia in Volume 3, as a cultural subregion. No political judgments – merely academic convenience and clarity – are implied.

The material presented here makes no claim to completeness, especially for Indonesian-language items, which are difficult of access. There are also problems in view of the complex religious history of some parts of Indonesia, with indigenous primal and invasive Hindu, Buddhist, Islamic, and Christian influences intermingling in various ways, so that some movements are polysyncretist. Only a few items (see R. S. Ellwood, entry 856, and A. Bright-Paul, entry 841) have been included on Subud, an "occult syncretism" lacking a primal religious component, although P. P. Sitompul's doctoral dissertation (entry 939) places Subud among the Kebatinan mystical societies, which are included (on these see J. A. N. Mulder, entries 908-910, and P. Stange, entries 944-947). These represent Javanese mysticism in an area where messianic ideas, Ratu Adil beliefs in a mythical "king of justice," and Islamic influences intermingle, both in folk religion and in more sophisticated movements.

Indonesia seems to be one of the very few areas with new religious movements related to Islam on the one hand, and a background of primal religion on the other; elsewhere these seem to occur only in black Africa. There are many reformist Islamic movements, but others are innovative and independent, rejecting Arabic Islam and the Meccan pilgrimage in favor of local prophets and rites. Other Islamic movements are primarily political or nationalist. Christian-related movements are represented by secessions and schisms, by indigenous revivals (as on Nias and Timor), and by charismatic founders (see A. G. Hoekema, entries 870-871, and L. M. Yoder, entries 983-985). Neoprimal movements have occurred (e.g., Mejapi, Samin, Njuli, Garing) and synthesist examples are found in Pormalin and Adat Bungan on Sarawak. V. Lanternari (entry 897) offers a quick overview; J. W. M. Bakker (entries 826 and 828) has more substantial surveys for after 1945; and J. van der Kroef's items (entries 966-974) lead further into the field.

824 Adriaanse, Laurens. *Sadrach's kring*. Leiden: D. Donner, 1899, 444 pp.
    On Sadrach Suropranato's development of Tunggulwulung's Kristen-Djowo independent church in central Java from the 1880s, by a Dutch Gereformierde Kerken missionary.

825 Adriaanse, Laurens. "Syncretisme in British-Indie em op Java." *De Macedonier* (Leiden), 1935, pp. 193-98, 225-30, 257-62, 293-98, 328-35, 360-68.
    On Sadrach's independent congregations.

826 Bakker, J[ohn] W. M. "Nieuwe godsdiensten in Indonesie." *Indische Missie Tijdschrift* (The Hague) 41 (1958): 46-53.
    A valuable survey of the contemporary causes, religious and social, and of the main features of new Islamic-related and Buddhist-related Javanese movements, and of others combining two or more imported traditions, including Christianity.

827 Bakker, J[ohn] W. M. "Perkembangan Agama dan Kapercayaan Di Indonesia Sekarang." *Umat Baru* (Jogyakarta), no. 63 [11] (1978): 153-74, 183-87.
    The development of religions and mysticism in Indonesia today; in a Catholic pastoral magazine.

828 Bakker, J[ohn] W. M. "Religious unrest in Java." *Worldmission* (New York) 14 (1963): 45-55.
    A Jesuit missionary on the discrepancy between Islamic apologetics and achievement leading to "hundreds of new sects," syncretizing indigenous, Islamic, Hindu, and Christian elements, in millennial expectation of the Ratu Adil.

829 Bartels, Dieter. "Guarding the invisible mountain: Intervillage alliances, religious syncretism, and ethnic identity among Ambonese Christians and Moslems in the Moluccas." Ph.D. dissertation (anthropology), Cornell University, 1977, 360 pp.
    "Vertical" syncretisms (Ambonese-Islamic, Ambonese-Christian) and "horizontal" syncretisms (Islamic-Christian) developed by Ambonese religion, transcending both invasive religions.

830 Bartels, Dieter. *Politicians and magicians: Power, adaptive strategies, and syncretism in the central Moluccas*. Papers in International Studies,

Southeast: Indonesia

Southeast Asia Series, no. 52. Athens, Ohio: Center for International Studies, Ohio University, 1979, pp. 282-99.

Power regarded as accumulated from diverse juxtaposed sources, old and new.

831 Benda, Harry J[indrich], and Castles, Lance. "The Samin movement." *Bijdragen tot de Taal-, Land- en Volkenkunde* 125, no. 2 (1969): 207-40, map.

A major article on the origins, under Samin ca. 1890, its persistence and economic basis; pp. 224-38, the "religion of Adam," a nonviolent, moral syncretism, different from both orthodox and folk Islam, and probably not messianic.

832 Bennett, John Godolphin. *Concerning Subud.* London: Hodder & Stoughton, 1958, illus. 2d ed. New York: University Books, 1959, 186 pp.

"A mixture of Coueism, Javanese mysticism and Moral Rearmament" founded by Pak Subuh, a spiritualist.

833 Berry, Robert C. "KGPI: The Kerapatan Protestant Church in Indonesia." *Enterprise* (Toronto, Canadian Baptist Overseas Mission Board), Spring 1977, p. 2.

The general secretary describes the independent church with which the board has been cooperating since 1973.

834 Berry, Robert C. "Pioneers of the 1980s." *Enterprise* (Toronto, Canadian Baptist Overseas Mission Board), no. 296 (Spring 1982), p. 23.

Joint mission with independent churches in Kalimantan.

835 Beyer, Ulrich. "Messianische Protestbewegung in Java-Indonisien." *Zeitschrift für Mission* 3, no. 4 (1977): 237-45.

Sawito Kartowibowo (1977) as example of naive mystical movement under charismatic leaders seeking relief from the stress in expected return of Ratu Adil, the mythical "king of justice."

836 Bijlevelt, J. "De Saminbeweging." *Kolonial Tijdschrift* (The Hague) 12 (1923): 10-24.

The Samin movement.

837 [Blumberger, P. J. T.] "Saminisme." In *Encyclopedie van Nederlandsch-Indie*, by D. G. Stibbe, et al. The Hague: M. Nijhoff, 1917-39, 3:683-84.

On the Samin movement.

838 Boland, B. J. *The struggle of Islam in modern Indonesia*. Institut voor Taal-, Land- en Volkenkunde Verhandelingen, 59. The Hague: M. Nijhoff, 1971, 283 pp.

P. 217, Kebatinan movements, Subud, and Javanese mysticism in general.

839 Bottomley, G. "Indonesian millennialism in comparative perspective." B.A. (Hons.) thesis (anthropology), University of Sydney, 1968.

840 Brandes, J. "Iets over een ouderen Dipanegara in vervand met een prototype van der voorspelling van Jayabaya." *Tijdschrift voor Indische Taal-, Land- en Volkenkunde* 32 (1989):268-430.

The "older" Dipanagara revolt of ca. 1720 – the oldest known messianic movement in Java.

841 Bright-Paul, Anthony. *Stairway to Subud*. New York: Dharma Book Co.; Kingston-on-Thames: Coombe Springs Press, 1965, 256 pp.

Autobiographical account.

842 Brookes, Graham F. "Spirit movements in Timor." In *Cargo cults and the quest for paradise: Transoceanic comparisons and connections . . .*, edited by G. W. Trompf. Religion and Society Series. Berlin and New York: Mouton de Gruyter, 1990, pp. 260-291.

Chap. 7, the Nunkolo spirit movement led by Mrs. J. Mnao in 1943; its passing over into a revival movement and continuing influence. The Timor Spirit movement, 1965-71 – with healings, exorcism, revelations, and attack on magic; millennial (return of Christ), but not cargoist.

843 Brookes, Graham F. "Spirit movements in Timor: A survey." Master's qualifying dissertation, Melbourne College of Divinity, 1977.

A missiological account.

844 Byrne, Frank. "The flood gates open: Expanding mission in West Kalimantan." *Enterprise* (Toronto, Canadian Baptist Overseas Mission Board), Winter 1979, pp. 6-9, 27, illus.

A report on the joint mission with a Protestant Fellowship Church of Indonesia.

845 Cachet, F[rans] Lion. *Een jaar op reis dienst der sending*. Amsterdam: J. A. Wormser, 1896, 879 pp.

Pp. 282-91, 491, 549-60, Sadrach and his independent congregations.

Southeast: Indonesia

846 Canadian Baptist Overseas Mission Board. "The Kerapatan Protestant Church." *Missionfax* (Toronto, The Board), [April 1981], p. 4.

On the partnership between church and board from 1973, and the joint mission planned to Kalimantan.

847 Carey, P. B. R. *Babad Dipanagara: An account of the outbreak of the Java war, 1825-1830*. Kuala Lumpur, 1981.

Cited by J. L. Peacock (entry 921), p. 529: "An outstanding account of religiously based revolts before the twentieth century."

848 Cooley, Frank L. *Indonesia, church, and society*. New York: Friendship Press, 1968, 128 pp., map.

Pp. 72-73, the 1916-25 Nias revival and continuing "spiritual movements"; pp. 87-88, Coolen's independent "Javanese Christianity" and the Christian villages movement on Java; pp. 90-91, briefly on Sadrach's Javanese Christian movement 1867-1930s; pp. 105-7, Pentecostal churches, especially the Church of the Messiah from 1945; p. 48, passing reference to syncretistic groups in Batakland and Nias.

849 Cooley, Frank L. "The revival in Timor." In *Gospel and frontier people*, edited by R. P. Beaver. Pasadena: William Carey Library, 1973, pp. 205-30.

Includes reference to earlier revivals, 1943-46 and 1963-64 (Ratu Alu), as well as that of 1965-70.

850 Coolsma, S[ierk]. *De zendingseeuw voor Nederlansch Oost-Indie*. Utrecht: C. H. E. Breijer, 1901, 892 pp.

Pp. 140-42, et passim, support by Judge Anthings for Tunggul Wuling in Semarang.

851 Coomans, M. "Sejarah Gereja Katoli di wilayah Keuskupan Banjarmasin dan Keuskupan Samarinda." In *Sejarah Gereja Katolik Indonesia*. Vol. 3A, *Wilayah-wilayah keuskapan dan Mejelis Agung Waligereja Indonesia abad ke-20*. Jakarta, 1974, pp. 399-442.

852 Danandjaja, James. "Acculturation in Tano Niha (the island of Nias)." *Kroeber Anthropological Society Papers* 44 (1971): 1-29.

Missions as agents of change, and (pp. 15-18, 25) the contribution of an indigenous religious movement, "the Great Repentance."

853 Digan, Parig. "Indonesia." *Pro Mundi Vita Bulletin* (Brussels), no. 64 (January-February 1977), 13 pp.

P. 13, tens of millions of people in the new religions, as "half-way houses" between tradition and modernization; the forms called *kebatinan* granted official recognition in 1973.

854 Drewes, G. W. J. "Drie Javaansche Goeroe's: Hun leven, onderricht en Messiasprediking." Dissertation, University of Leiden, 1925.

855 Du Bois, Cora. *The people of Alor: A social-psychological study of an East Indian island*. Minneapolis: University of Minnesota Press, 1944, 654 pp. Reprint. New York: Harper Torchbooks, 2 vols., 1961, with further introduction, "Two decades later," pp. xvi-xxx.
   1944, and 1961, vol. 1, pp. 165, 292-348, Malelaka's cult and his autobiography.

856 Ellwood, Robert S., Jr. *Religious and spiritual groups in modern North America*. Englewood Cliffs, N.J.: Prentice-Hall, 1973, 334 pp.
   Pp. 286-91, account of Subud and selected text: Indonesian movement from a Muslim background.

857 Epton, Nina C[onsuelo]. *Magic and mystics of Java*. London: Octagon Press, 1974. Rev. ed. 1975, 212 pp.
   Pp. 192-211, on Sumarah, in Jogjakarta – a mystic Javanese society founded by Sukino in 1937 to worship God constantly in *sujud*, i.e., submission. Pp. 173-212, on magic and mystics in general.

858 Feuillet de Bruyn, W. K. H. "De Njoelibeweging in der Zuider en Ooster afdeeling van Borneo." *Koloniaal Tijdschrift* (The Hague) 23 (1934): 41-65.

859 Field, Margaret J[oyce]. *Angels and ministers of grace: An ethnopsychiatrist's contribution to biblical criticism*. London: Longman, 1971, 135 pp.
   Pp. 123-25, Subud, and the values of its dissociational experiences.

860 Geertz, Clifford. *The interpretation of cultures*. New York: Basic Books, 1973, 470 pp. London: Hutchinson, 1975, 470 pp.
   Pp. 142-69, "Ritual and social change: A Javanese example – Slametan," and disruption of a Permai member's funeral; pp. 150-53 et seq., Permai cult as an anti-Islamic revival.

861 Geertz, Clifford. *The religion of Java*. Glencoe, Ill.: Free Press, 1960, 396 pp., maps.

Southeast: Indonesia

Chap. 9 and p. 364, Permai: a modern Abangan cult, anti-Islamic renewal of traditional religion, with a Marxist slant.

862 Geertz, Clifford. "Religious change and social order in Soeharto's Indonesia." *Asia* (New York) 27 (Winter 1972-73): 62-84.

The increasing "denominationalization" of religious traditions into a pluralistic society with Islam, *kebatinan* (Javanese mysticism in many cults), Christianity, and Bali-Hinduism as the main types; pp. 74-76, Pangestu as an example of *kebatinan* movements. Overall the tendency is towards mystical personal religious experience rather than ritual and doctrine.

863 Geertz, Clifford. "Ritual and social change: A Javanese example." *American Anthropologist* 59, no. 1 (1957): 32-54.

Anti-Muslim politico-religious healing cult – "a fusion of Marxism and local primal (abangan) religious patterns" (pp. 39-40); pp. 40-47, case study of a funeral and Permai (passim); pp. 47-53, analysis.

864 Golongan Siradjabatak Indonesia. *Ransangan ni undang-undang dohot aturan ripe di Golongan Siradjabatak Indonesia*.

An "elementary book of the movement," the nativistic revival GSI founded in 1942. Cited with extract by A. M. Lumbantobing (entry 898), pp. 203-4.

865 Graaf, H[ermanus] J[ohannes] de. *De moord op Kapitein François Tack, 8 Febr. 1686*. Amsterdam: H. J. Paris:, 1935, 169 pp., map.

Pp. 14-19 especially, on religious and popular movements in the Kartasura period (1677-1744).

866 Hadiwijono, Harun. *Kebatinam dan Indjil* [Mysticism and the gospel]. Jakarta: Baden Penerbit Kristen, 1970, 168 pp.

867 Hadiwijono, Harun. *Man in present Javanese mysticism*. Baarn, Netherlands: Bosch & Kenning N.V., 1967, 271 pp.

Doctoral dissertation (theology), Free University, Amsterdam. Surveys the historical roots (Javanese, Hindu, Islamic) and studies five current representatives: Pagujuban Sumarah (Society of Self-Surrenderers, 1950-), Sapta Darma (1952-), Bratakesawar's writings (1952-), Pangestu (1949-), and Paryana Suryadipura's writings (1950-).

868 Hanks, Lucien M., Jr. "The locus of individual differences in certain primitive cultures (with ensuing discussion)." In *Culture and personality*,

edited by S. S. Sargent and M. W. Smith. New York: Viking Fund, 1949, pp. 107-26.

The Malafela prophet movement on Alor as one source of individual biographies for comparison of interpretations by psychologists and anthropologists; the former bring out individuality, the latter socialization.

869 Helbig, Karl. "Der Singamangaradja und die Sekte der Pormalim bei den batak." *Zeitschrift für Ethnologie* 67 (1935): 88-104.

On the legendary priest-kings of the Batak, the last forms in the nineteenth century; pp. 98-102, Pormalin sect, which worships Si Singa Mangaradja still – from 1870s to 1960.

870 Hoekema, A[lle] G. "Kyai Ibrahim Tunggul Wulung (c. 1800-1885): 'Een Javaanse Apollos.'" *Nederlands Theologisch Tijdschrift* 33, no. 2 (1979): 89-110.

On the founder of indigenous Christian communities.

871 Hoekema, Alle G. "Recent church growth in Indonesia." In *Exploring church growth*, edited by W. R. Shenk. Grand Rapids: Eerdmans, 1983, pp. 24-36.

P. 27, mystical groups (Kebatinan, etc.); pp. 28-29, messianic movements (Ratu Adil elements); p. 29, charismatic or revival movements (Nias 1915-16, Java 1960-65, and Timor 1965-).

872 Hoogeveen, R. *Memorie van Overgave* [Memorandum of transfer]. Onderafdeling Sorong 1947. Bureau of Native Affairs, Hollandia.

Samin movement.

873 Howell, Julia Day. "Vehicles of the Kalki Avatar: The experiments of a Javanese guru in rationalizing ecstatic religion." Ph.D. dissertation (anthropology), Stanford University, 1977, 239 pp.

W. Hardjanto Pradjapangarsa's publications since 1953, seeking to revitalize Javanese religion by emphasizing mystical ecstatic experience of immanent divinity, distinct from Islamic legalism and derived from the Kalki Avatar of Vishnu, but less successful than devotional movements related to a transcendent Being.

874 Indonesian Ministry of Information. "Saminisme." In *Republik Indonesia: Propinsi Djawa-Tengah*. 1952, pp. 480-82.

Brief official report on Samin movement.

Southeast: Indonesia

875 Indrakusuma, Joh. "L'homme parfait selon l'école du Pangestu: Étude de la spiritualité javanaise et de sa rencontre avec le christianisme." Christianisme et Cultures 3. Doctoral thesis (theology), Institut Catholique de Paris, 1973, 336 pp.

876 Ingwersen, H. Ph. "Iets over Sadrach." *De Macedonier* (Leiden), 1915, pp. 225-32, 321-32.
On Sadrach's independent congregations.

877 [Items concerning Sadrach's independent congregations]. *De Macedonier: Algemeen Zendings-Tijdschrift* (Leiden) (e.g., 1st ed., 1883, pp. 56-58).
See also articles by L. Adriaanse (entry 825) and H. Ph. Ingwersen (entry 876).

878 Jasper, J. E. *Verslag betreffende het onderzoek inzake de Saminbeweging ingesteld ingevolge het Gouvernements Besluit van 1 juni 1917*. No. 20. Batavia: Landsdrukkerij, 1918, 92 pp.
On the Samin movement. Report by an assistant-resident. A major source.

879 Jay, Robert R[avenelle]. *Religion and politics in rural central Java*. Cultural report series, 12. New Haven: Yale University Southeast Asia Studies, 1963, 117 pp., maps, bib.
Pp. 77-89, 101-5, the history of schism between Islamic orthodoxy and Javanese syncretistic Islam in one area of rural Java – later allied to political secularism; pp. 77-89, the religious aspect of the syncretist community; pp. 101-5, conclusion.

880 Jay, Robert Ravenelle. "Santri and Abangan: Religious schism in rural central Java." Ph.D. dissertation (anthropology), Harvard University, 1957.

881 Jong, Suffridus de. *Eend Javaanse Levenshouding*. Wageningen, Netherlands: H. Veenman & Zonen B.V., 1973, 213 pp.
Free University of Amsterdam doctoral dissertation (theology), 1973; vol. 1, *Mystiek: Pangestu* (pp. 9-63).

882 Joustra, M. "De Singa Mangaradja-figuur." In *Gedenkschrift van het Koninklijk Instituut voor de Taal-, Land- en Volkenkunde van Nederlandsch-Indie*. The Hague, 1926, pp. 211-22.

883 Kals, Bernard. "Land of culture, mystics, and quacks." *New York Times,* 11 September 1960, pp. 37-38.

884 Kamma, F[reerk] C[hristaans]. *Koreri: Messianic movements in the Biak-Numfor culture area.* Koninklijk Instituut voor Taal-, Land- en Volkenkunde. Translation Series, 15. The Hague: M. Nijhoff, 1972, xii + 328 pp. , illus., folding maps, major bib. (pp. 301-19, with 350 items).
Pp. 121-23, the prophet of Kao (Halmahera, in the Moluccas), 1875-76; pp. 235ff., Islamic movements and bib. references. Note: Movements in the Irian Jaya part of Indonesia are included in the section on that area in vol. 3 in this series, *Oceania,* along with other movements in the Melanesian culture area.

885 Kartodirdjo, Sartono. "Agrarian radicalism in Java: Its setting and development." In *Culture and politics in Indonesia,* edited by C. Holt. Ithaca: Cornell University Press, 1972, pp. 71-125.
Pp. 90-91, characteristic features; pp. 92-93, millenarism; pp. 94-97, messianism (Dipanegara, ca. 1720 and ca. 1820; Mangkuwidjaja, 1865; Banten, 1888, and many others), nativism, the Holy War; pp. 102-18, historical examples – Bekasi and Tanggerang revolts, Rifangi, Djumadilkobra, Djasmani, Ahmad Suhada, Gedangan movements – combining Islamic and pre-Islamic elements; pp. 118-25, recent movements – Hidup Betul and Agama Adam Makrifat.

886 Kartodirdjo, Sartono. "Peasant insurgents revisited: A comparative study of nineteenth and twentieth century peasant movements in Indonesia." In *India and Indonesia from the 1830s to 1914: The heyday of colonial rule.* Comparative history of India and Indonesia, 2. Leiden: E. J. Brill, 1987, xvii + 297 pp.

887 Kartodirdjo, Sartono. *The peasants' revolt of Banten in 1888: Its conditions, course, and sequel. A case study of social movements in Indonesia.* Verhandelingen van het Kononklijk Instituut voor Taal-, Land- en Volkenkunde, 50. The Hague: M. Nijhoff, 1966, 379 pp., maps.
In the district of Anjer, extreme northwest of Java. Studied within the framework of the common form of rural religious movements in nineteenth-century Java, with charismatic leaders promising access to mystical power. The more religious aspects on pp. 1-25, 141-75, 314-26.

888 Kartodirdjo, Sartono. *Protest movements in rural Java: A study of agrarian unrest in the nineteenth and early twentieth centuries.* Jakarta

Southeast: Indonesia

and London: Oxford University Press, for Institute of South East Asian Studies, 1973, 229 pp., bib.

Chap. 3, messianic movements, with special studies of movements of Kasan Mukmin 1903-4, Dermadjaja 1907, and Dietz 1918; revivalism and sectarian movements, especially anti-Islamic examples – Igama Djawa-Pasundan, Mashadi, Islam-Abangan, and other more secular sects; pp. 8-12, 106-18, general comments.

889 Kayser, Helga. *Aspekte des sozio-kulturellen Wandels auf Nias: Schul- und Gesundheitswesen der Rheinische Mission 1865-1940*. Munich: Renner, 1976, 228 pp.

890 King, Victor T. "Some observations on the Samin movement of north central Java: Suggestions for theoretical analysis of the dynamics of rural unrest." *Bijdragen tot de Taal-, Land- en Volkenkunde* 129 (1973): 457-81.

A shortened version of his M.A. thesis, University of London, 1971.

891 Koch, Kurt E. *World without chance?* Grand Rapids, Mich.: Kregel Publications, 1974, 96 pp.

Pp. 95-96, criticism of G. W. Peters's account of the Timor revival (entry 923).

892 Koentjaraningrat. *Anthropology in Indonesia: A bibliographical review*. Koninklijk Instituut voor Taal-, Land- en Volkenkunde: Bibliographical series. The Hague: M. Nijhoff, 1975.

Pp. 170-79, bibliographic essay on acculturation in Indonesia.

893 Korver, A. Pieter E. "The Samin movement and millenarism." *Bijdragen tot de Taal-, Land- en Volkenkunde* 132, nos. 2-3 (1976): 249-66.

The comparative method is used to show that the Samin movement belongs to millenarian movements in general; this enables a better analysis of its causes.

894 Kruyt, A. C. "The influence of Western civilization on the inhabitants of Poso (central Celebes)." In *The effect of Western influence on native civilizations in the Malay Archipelago*, edited by B. Schreike. Batavia: G. Kolff & Co., 1929, pp. 1-9.

895 Kruyt, A. C., and Adriani, N. "De godsdienstig-politieke beweging 'Mejapi' op Celebes." *Bijdragen tot de Taal-, Land- en Volkenkunde van Nederlandsche-Indie* 67 (1913): 135-51.

896 Lalawar, H. "Sejarah Gereja Katolik di wilayah Keuskupan Atambua dan Keuskupan Kupang." In *Sejarah Gereja Katolik Indonesia*. Vol. 3B, *Wilayah-wilayah keuskupan dan Majelis Agung Waligereja Indonesia abad ke-20*. Jakarta, 1974, pp. 1286-1345.

897 Lanternari, Vittorio. *The religions of the oppressed: A study of modern messianic cults*. London: MacGibbon & Kee, 1963, xx + 343 + xiii pp. Toronto: New American Library of Canada, 1963. New York: Knopf, 1963. New York: Mentor Books, 1965, xvi + 286 pp.

Pp. 214 (London ed., p. 267), Samin movement; pp. 214-15 (pp. 267-68), Sumatra nativist robber bands; p. 215 (p. 269), Njuli movement; p. 216 (p. 269), Mejapi–all brief references. Pp. 211-16 (pp. 263-70), messianism.

898 Lumbantobing, Andar M. "The confession of the Batak Church: An introduction and explanation." In *The Church and the confessions*, edited by V. Vajta and H. Weissgerber. Philadelphia: Fortress Press, 1963, pp. 119-47 (pp. 203-6, notes).

Pp. 121-25 (and pp. 203-4, notes), church attitude toward Gologan Siradjabatak Indonesia, a nativistic revival movement; pp. 128-29, 137, independent churches by secessions; pp. 129-37, various pentecostal and other movements; pp. 139-47, the Huria Kristen Batak Protestant confession combatting these.

899 Mallinckrodt, J. "De Njoeli-beweging onder de Lawangan-Dajaks van de Zuider-en Ooster-afdeeling van Borneo." *Koloniale Studien* (Weltervreden) 9, no. 2 (1925): 396-424.

900 Mangoenkoesoemo, Tjipto. *Het Saminisme: Rapport uitgebracht aan de Vereeniging "Insulinde."* Semarang: Semarang Drukkery en Boekhandel H. A. Benjamin, 1918.

Important as a source on the Samin movement.

901 Michel, Th. "Religion in Indonesia today." *Bulletin Secretariatus pro non-Christianis* 15, no. 2 (1980): 213-20.

Pp. 213, 217, references to a "native religious movement, Kebatinan," and its nonrecognition as an "official religion."

Southeast: Indonesia

902 Middelkoop, Pieter. *Curse, retribution, enmity as data in natural religion, especially in Timor, confronted with the Scriptures*. Amsterdam: Jacob Van Kampen, 1960, 168 pp.

Includes extended study of the Nunkolo revival on Timor, 1942-45; p. 112, brief report of the 1921 revival on Kisar island (reprinted in G. W. Peters [entry 923], pp. 44-45).

903 Middelkoop, Pieter. "Een geestesbeweging in Nuenkolo op Timor." Parts 1-5. *De Heerbaan* (Amsterdam) 4, no. 9 (1951): 244-52; 4, no. 10 (1951): 272-76; 4, no. 11 (1951): 301-6; 5, no. 4 (1952): 172-77; 5, no. 6 (1952): 320-24.

A Dutch missionary report on Mrs. J. Mnao and the Nunkolo revival on Timor from 1943. See G. F. Brookes (entry 842) for account based on P. Middelkoop.

904 Modigliani, Elio. *Fra i Batacchi indipendenti*. Rome: Societa Geografica Italiano, 1892, 189 pp.

This Italian traveler's experiences with the Pormalin movement, ca. 1880; Catholic borrowing for which he was the source.

905 Mortimer, Rex. "Traditional modes and communist movements." In *Peasant rebellion and communist rebellion in Asia*, edited by J. W. Lewis. Stanford, Calif.: Stanford University Press, 1974, 364 pp.

Pp. 100-102, "magical-mystical movements of a messianic kind" as behind rebellions in Indonesia.

906 Mottram, V[ernon] H[enry]. *The physical basis of personality*. Harmondsworth: Penguin Books, 1944, 124 pp., illus. Reprint. 1949, 159 pp., illus. 2d ed. London: Penguin Books, 1952, 170 pp., illus.

1952 ed., Epilogue, pp. 164-65, enthusiastic personal endorsement of Subud as a way of awakening "the real self" rather than as a new religion.

907 Mühlmann, Wilhelm E. "Mouvements islamiques et hindous." In *Messianismes révolutionnaires du tiers monde*, edited by W. E. Mühlmann. Paris: Gallimard, 1968, pp. 152-71, bib.

Translated from the German original. Pp. 159-63, Samin movement.

908 Mulder, Jan Anton Niels. "Aliran Kebatinam as an expression of the Javanese worldview." *Journal of Southeast Asian Studies* 1, no. 2 (September 1970): 105-14.

909 Mulder, [Jan Anton] Niels. *Mysticism and daily life in contemporary Java: Cultural persistence and change.* Singapore: Singapore University Press, 1978, 250 pp.

A valuable survey, including the world view, ethic, and attitude toward life (pp. 1-46) of Kebatinan mysticism.

910 Mulder, [Jan Anton] Niels. "Samanism and Buddhism: A note on a field visit to a Samin community." *Asia Quarterly* (Brussels), no. 3 (1974), pp. 253-58.

On assimilation of Saminism to Buddhism, assisted by nontheistic beliefs and by the pressure to belong to one of the recognized religions.

911 Müller-Krüger, Theodor. "Das Christentum in Indonesien." In *Handbuch der Orientalistik: 3. Indonesien, Malaysia, und die Philippinen*, edited by H. Kahler. Vol. 2 (1), *Religionen.* Leiden: E. J. Brill, 1975.

Pp. 159-60, revival movements in and from the churches.

912 Müller-Krüger, Theodor. *Die "Grosse Reue" auf Nias: Geschichte und Gestalt einer Erweckung auf dem Missionsfelde.* Allgemeine Missions-Studien, 10. Gutersloh: C. Bertelsmann, 1931, 192 pp., map.

The "Great Repentance" of 1916-22, on Nias Island, Sumatra, with messianic overtones, and similar to millenarian movements such as Njuli, Mejapi, and Parhudamdam.

913 Müller-Krüger, Theodor. *Nach Zehn Jahren.* Barmen and Wuppertal: Verlag der Rheinischen Missionsgesellschaft, 1950.

Pp. 67-69, continuing phenomena from the Nias revival of 1916-22.

914 Müller-Krüger, Theodor. "Neue Erweckungsbewegungen in der Nias- und Batakkirche." *Evangelische Missions Zeitschrift* 7 (1950): 161-70.

Revival movements in Nias during and after World War II.

915 Müller-Krüger, Theodor. *Sedjarah geredja di Indonesia.* Jakarta: Badam Penerbit Kristen, 1959, 248 pp., maps. Rev. German translation. *Der Protestantismus in Indonesien.* Stuttgart: Evangelisches Verlagswerk, 1968, 388 pp.

German translation, pp. 193ff., C. L. Coolen's church, et passim.

916 Müller-Krüger, Theodor. [Article in] *Das Wort in der Welt* (Hamburg), December 1972.

Revival movements in Timor and other primal cultures.

Southeast: Indonesia

917 Muskens, P. M. P. *Partner in nation building: The Catholic church in Indonesia*. Aachen: Missio Aktuell Verlag, 1979, 339 pp.

Revised and extended English translation of a 1969 Dutch doctoral dissertation and its 1973 Indonesian version. Pp. 89-93, the Javanese messianic tradition, with the 1976 messiah-king, Kartowibowo, as latest example; pp. 128-32, messianism in Sarekat Islam.

918 Needleman, Jacob. *The new religions*. Garden City, N.Y.: Doubleday & Co., 1970. Reprint. London: Penguin Press, 1972, 245 pp.

Subud: pp. 103-28, 219-20, p. 233 (source references). Largely based on E. van Hien (entry 976) and J. G. Bennett (entry 832).

919 Neumann, J. H. "De Perhoedamdam in Deli." *Nededeelingen* ... *Nederlansch Zendelinggenootschap* 62, no. 3 (1918): 185-90.

920 "Overgang zonder katechismusles: Een bujzondere kerk op Java." *Bijeen* (Hertogenbosch), September 1971, pp. 22-23, illus.

On the relation established by the Java Sunda Religion (a Kebatinan group) with the Catholic Church in 1964, and the Catholic attitude toward subsequent problems; in the form of a series of questions to the Rev. F. Lubbers O.S.C., a Catholic official, who saw the J.S.R. contributing to the indigenization of Catholicism in Indonesia.

921 Peacock, J. L. "Southeast Asia religions: Modern movements in insular cultures." In *Encyclopedia of religion*, edited by M. Eliade. Vol. 13. New York: Macmillan, 1987, pp. 527-30.

P. 528, Javanese Kebatinan movements as twentieth-century developments with ancient roots.

922 Pedersen, Paul Bedholdt. *Batak blood and Protestant soul: The development of national Batak churches in north Sumatra*. Grand Rapids, Mich.: Eerdmans, 1970, 212 pp.

Pp. 148-55, Huria Kristen Indonesia, and other independent churches.

923 Peters, George W. *Indonesia revival: Focus on Timor*. Grand Rapids, Mich.: Zondervan, 1973, 120 pp.

Pp. 44-49, earlier revivals in Timor, including the Nias movement of 1916-22.

924 Pieper, A. *Die Auswirkung der Erweckung auf Nias*. Barmen: Verlag des Missionshauses, 1928, 23 pp.

925 Pigeaud, T[heodore] G[unther] T[homas]. "Aanteekeningen betreffende den Javaanschen Oosthoek." *Tijdschrift voor Indische Taal-, Land- en Volkenkunde* 72 (1932): 215-313.
Religious and popular movements in the Kartasura period, 1677-1744.

926 Pigeaud, T[heodore] G[unther] T[homas]. *Javaanse volksvertoningen*. Batavia: Volkslectuur; The Hague: Martinus Nijhoff, 1938, 545 pp., illus.
Cited in R. R. Jay (entry 879), pp. 108, 112, as describing syncretistic cults in central Java (e.g., pp. 314-18 on a village cult combining Near East Sufi elements with Javanese elements).

927 Pleyte, C. M. "Singa Mangaradja, de heili koning der Bataks: Zijne afkomst en de openbaring der eerste wetten." *Bijdragen tot de Taal-, Land- en Volkenkunde van Nederlandsche-Indie* 1 (1903): 1-17.
Based on ms. by "Dr. H. N. van der Tuuk."

928 Polak, A. "Some aspects of a process of change in an Indonesian community." *Tropical Man* (Yearbook, Department of Social Research, Royal Tropical Institute, Amsterdam) 4 (1971) [appeared 1973]: 108-16.
A north Lombok indigenous unorthodox Muslim community, *Wetu Telu*, under pressure to conform, and the political influence involved.

929 *Prisma* (Jakarta, Institute for Social and Economic Research and Study) [Special issue on the common people's aspirations and the social-religious movements], no. 1 (January 1977), 80 pp.
In Indonesian. Analyzes some *Ratu Adil* (Righteous King) and religious protest movements. See O. S. W. Wahono (entry 980).

930 Radja, Haba L. "Een verhaaal: De geestesbeweging in de Timor Kerk Leidschendam." November 1972.

931 "Religion and revolution in Indonesia." *Herder Correspondence* 3, no. 2 (1966): 55-61, map.
Pp. 57-59, "new religions" and eclectic syncretisms, with millenarian hopes, hostile to older religions (especially to Islam) and to material advancement; their transformation under government

Southeast: Indonesia

influence in the 1950s, their registration (360 movements) and the linking of over 100 in a Congress; their suppression in the 1960s.

932 Rinkes, D. A. [Essay in] *Tijdschrift voor Indische Taal-, Land- en Volkenkunde* 53 (1911): 435-581.
Religious and popular movements in the Kartasura period (1677-1744).

933 Rofe, H[useidn]. *The path of Subud*. 3d ed. London: Rider & Co., 1959, 191 pp.
On the teachings of Pak Subuh (with a portrait).

934 Sastrapratedja, M. "Popular religiosity as a basis for interreligious encounter: An Indonesian experience." *East Asian Pastoral Review* 22, no. 5 (1985): 362-67.

935 Schreiner, Lothar. *Das Bekenntnis der Batak-Kirche Enstehung, Gestalt, Bedeutung, und einer revidieste Ubersetzung*. Theologische Existenz Heute, n.s. 137. Munich: Kaiser Verlag, 1966, 72 pp.
Includes Batak secession churches (p. 39).

936 Schumann, Olaf. "Indonesischer Mystizismus und Islam." *Zeitschrift für Mission* 2, no. 2 (1976): 64-87.
Pp. 68-70, relations between Kebatinan and Islam; pp. 82-85, Kebatinan today; pp. 70-82, on Javanese mysticism as relevant background.

937 Selosoemardjan. "Social changes in Jogjakarta." Ph.D. dissertation (sociology), Cornell University, 1959, 552 pp.
Pp. 224-25, *Gerinda*, Javanese religio-political messianism.

938 Siregar, Basatua P. "Von einer innerkirchlichen Reformbewegung in der Batak-Kirche zur GKPI." *Evangelische Missions Zeitschrift* 29, no. 3 (1972): 110-25; 30, no. 1 (1973): 52-53.
The Geradja Kristen Protestant Indonesia, a protest movement within the largest Batak church (HKPB), which became an independent church in 1964.

939 Sitompul, Pangarisan Paul. "Susila Budhi Dharma Subud – international mystical movement of Indonesia." Ph.D. dissertation (religion), Claremont Graduate School, 1974, 239 pp.
Interprets Subud as part of the indigenous religion of Java, among other Kebatinan societies.

940 Snouck-Hurgronje, Christiaan. *Verspreide Geschriften* [Collected works]. Vol. 4, pt. 2. Bonn and Leipzig: K. Schroeder, 1923.

Pp. 409-10, on Sarekat Islam (a short article he wrote ca. 1916) as a movement of self-expression before the world, as response to European influence on the indigenous society–the first national mass movement. Also pp. 400-401, for earlier article on same subject.

941 Soedjito Sosrodihardjo. "A sectarian group in Java, with reference to a midland village: A study in the sociology of religion." M.A. thesis, University of London, 1959.

942 Soekotjo, Sisit Heru, and Yoder, Lawrence M[cCulloh]. *Sejarah Gereja Injili di Tana Jawa*. Jakarta: Badan Penerbit Kristen, 1980. English translation. "History of the Evangelical Church of Java," translated by L. M. Yoder. Unpublished manuscript, ca. 1980, 383 pp., held by Mennonite Central Committee, Akron, Ohio.

Includes account of Tunggul Wulung and his nineteenth-century independent Christian movement. Tunggul Wulung is one of the "fathers" of this church in Java–see chap. 2, section A, pp. 1-13.

943 Soetopo, C. "Sedjarah hidup Sadrach dan Kegiatannja." M.A. thesis, Sekolah Tinggi Theologia / Duta Wacana, Yogyakarta, 1971.

On Sadrach's independent church.

944 Stange, Paul. "Javanese mysticism in the revolutionary period." *Journal of Studies in Mysticism* 1, no. 2 (Spring 1978): 115-30. Reprinted from *Proceedings of the Conference on Modern Indonesian History*, Madison, Wis., 1975.

Discusses *kejawen* ("Javanism," or emphasis on traditional culture), and Kebatinan (the various new mystical movements).

945 Stange, Paul. "Revelation and derivation in Javanese cults." Paper presented at the 6th annual conference of the Australian Association for Study of Religions, Adelaide 1981, 26 pp.

On the problem of definition of religion by government, for the Kebatinan groups; pp. 10-13, Pangestu; pp. 13-14, Sapta Darma; pp. 15-17, Sumarah–all based on revelatory experiences in the mid-1930s, and all exhibiting the influence of the social situation in the forms that developed.

946 Stange, Paul. "The Sumarah movement in Javanese mysticism." Ph.D. dissertation (history: Asia), University of Wisconsin, 1980, 455 pp.

Southeast: Indonesia

947 Stange, Paul, comp. and trans. *Selected Sumarah teaching*. Perth: Department of Asian Studies, Western Australian Institute of Technology, 1977, 34 pp.

Introduction by Stange, to Paguyuban Sumarah, a form of Kebatinan; texts from its founder, the current leader, and others.

948 Stöhr, Waldemar. "Die Religionen der Altvölker Indonesiens und der Philippinen." In *Die Religionen Indonesiens*, edited by W. Stöhr and P. Zoetmulder. Die Religionen der Menschheit, 5, 1. Stuttgart: W. Kohlhammer, 1965, pp. 1-221.

Pp. 201-7, "Continuity and change"–includes new movements such as the Nias Revival, Singaman-garadja, Pormalin, Tungud (Philippines), Mejapi, Njuli, etc.

949 Straathof, W. "Java Soenda religie: Geschiedenis leer en denkwijze." *Wereld en Zending* (Amsterdam) 3, no. 1 (1974): 48-64.

History and beliefs of Agama Djawa Sunda religion from 1850 with Kebatinan characteristics.

950 Sumanto, Wp. I. *Kyai Sadrach: Seorang pencari kebenaran*. Jakarta: B. P. K. Gunung Mulia, 1974.

951 Sutarman Soediman Partonadi. *Sadrach's community and its contextual roots: A nineteenth century Javanese expression of Christianity*. Currents of Encounter Series. Amsterdam: Editions Rodopi; Grand Rapids, Mich.: W. B. Eerdmans, 1988, 317 pp.

952 Tari, Mel and Nona. *The gentle breeze of Jesus*. Carol Stream, Ill.: Creation House, 1974, 191 pp., illus.

An Indonesian pastor and his American wife on the Timor revival of 1965-.

953 The, Siauw Giap. "Het verzet van de bevolking tegen Nederlandse kestuursmaatregeben, 1870-1914." *Bijdragen en Mededelingen betreffende de geschiedenis der Nederlanden* 66 (1971): 70-78.

On the Samin movement.

954 The, Siauw Giap. "The Samin and Samat movements in Java: Two examples of peasant resistance." *Revue du Sud-Est Asiatique et de l'Extrême-Orient*, no. 2 (1967), pp. 303-10; no. 1 (1968), pp. 107-13.

955 The, Siauw Giap. "The Samin movement in Java: Complementary remarks." *Revue du Sud-Est Asiatique et de l'Extrème-Orient,* no. 1 (1969), pp. 73-77.

956 Tichelman G[erardus] L[auwrens]. [Article in] *Mededeelingen van de Vereeniging van Ambtenaren bij het Binnenlandsch Bestuur* (Batavia), no. 45 (1937).
   Parhu damdam movement of Bataks in Sumatra.

957 Tideman, J. "De Batara Gowa op Zuid-Celebes." *Bijdragen tot de Taal-, Land- en Volkenkunde* 7de Volgreeks, 7de D1., 61 (1908): 350-90.
   The Batara Gowa movement in Celebes.

958 Tideman, J. *Simeloengoen.* Leiden: Louis H. Becherer, 1922, 304 pp., maps, illus.
   Pp. 165-72, the Pormalin sect; pp. 172-77, Parhoedamdam Beweging.

959 United States Government, Department of the Army. *Area handbook for Indonesia,* edited by J. W. Henderson, et al. American University, Foreign Area Studies Division. DA Pam 550-178. Washington, D.C.: Government Printing Office, 1970, 569 pp.
   Pp. 230-31, Islamic movements – reforming modernist and popular syncretisms, all briefly treated; pp. 236-37, mysticism and animism, but no special movements named.

960 Utrecht, Ernst. "The Javanese dukun and his role in social unrest." *Cultures et Développement* 7, no. 2 (1975): 319-55.
   Millenarian movements as a persistent part of Indonesian culture; case study of Muljono, a *dukun* (diviner/magician, etc.) in one of the 300 or so rural mystical movements, in 1966-67, when his movement was eliminated by the army.

961 Utrecht, Ernst. "Religion and social protest in Indonesia." *Social Compass* 25, nos. 3-4 (1978): 395-418.
   Pp. 408-9, the Samin movement, using Siauw Gap The's works.

962 Van Akkeren, Philip. "A contemporary Indonesian messiah, a profile." *Journal, Oriental Society of Australia* (Sydney) 7 (1970): 134-46.
   Purwoko (b. 1932), a self-appointed Javanese Ratu Adil; expressed in a modern semi-intellectual setting, and devoted to world peace.

Southeast: Indonesia

963 Van Akkeren, Philip. *Sri and Christ: A study of the indigenous church in east Java*. World Studies of Churches in Mission. London: Lutterworth Press, 1970, 229 pp., maps.

Pp. 40-48, messianic expectations and Western spiritual influences; pp. 53-76, the semi-independent leader C. L. Coolen (d. 1873); pp. 154-57, the Kristen-Djowo movement, 1857-85.

964 Van den Berg, E. J. "De Parhoedamdambeweging." *Mededeelingen van Wege het Nederlandsch Zendelingenootschap* 64, no. 1 (1920): 22-38. Also in *Encyclopaedie van Nederlandsch-Indië*. Vol. 3. 2d ed. The Hague: M. Nijhoff, 1919, p. 343.

965 Van der Bent, Ans J., ed. *Handbook: Member churches*. Geneva: World Council of Churches, 1982, 283 pp.

P. 83, Indonesian Christian Church (Huria Kristen Indonesia); seceded in 1927 from Huria Kristen Batak on issues of independence and identity.

966 Van der Kroef, Justus M[aria]. *Indonesia in the modern world*. 2 vols. Bandung: Masa Baru, 1954.

Vol. 1, pp. 119-21 (notes, pp. 131-32), outline of messianic ideas and movements, including Njuli, Mejapi, and "Parhudamdam."

967 Van der Kroef, Justus M[aria]. "Javanese messianic expectations: Their origin and cultural context." *Comparative Studies in Society and History* 1, no. 4 (1958): 299-323.

968 Van der Kroef, Justus M[aria]. "The messiah in Indonesia and Melanesia." *Scientific Monthly* (Lancaster, Pa.) 75, no. 3 (1952): 161-65.
A survey with general theory.

969 Van der Kroef, Justus M[aria]. "Messianic movements in the Celebes, Sumatra, and Borneo." In *Millennial dreams in action*, edited by S. L. Thrupp. The Hague: Mouton & Co., 1962, pp. 80-121. Reprint. New York: Shocken Books, 1970.

970 Van der Kroef, Justus M[aria]. "Mouvements religieux modernes d'acculturation en Indonésie." In *Histoire des religions*, edited by H.-C. Puech. Vol. 3. Encyclopédie de la Pléiade. Paris: Gallimard, 1976, pp. 1110-41, bib.
A major survey.

971 Van der Kroef, Justus M[aria]. "Muslim movements in Indonesia." *Eastern World* (London), June 1954, pp. 18-20.

On the various Islamic movements – political, extremist bands, labor and service organizations, but not on new religious movements.

972 Van der Kroef, Justus M[aria]. "New religious sects in Java." *Far Eastern Survey* (New York) 30, no. 2 (1961): 18-25, bib.

Pro- and anti-Islamic, political, mystical, eclectic, urban, rural, syncretistic, and folk religion (i.e., a wider survey than of those with a primal or traditional Javanese element).

973 Van der Kroef, Justus M[aria]. "Racial messiahs." In *Race, individual, and collective behaviour*, edited by E. T. Thompson and E. C. Hughes. Glencoe: Free Press, 1958, pp. 357-74.

Extended and revised from entry 968.

974 Van der Kroef, Justus M[aria]. "Southeast Asia – some anthropological aspects." *Human Organization* 10, no. 1 (1951): 5-15.

Pp. 9-10, "robber-bands" with religious sanctions; messianism.

975 Van Duuren, David A. P. "Permalims en Parhudamdams: Twee profetische bewegingen bij de Bataks rond de eeuwwisseling." M.A. thesis, University of Utrecht, 1983.

Two prophetic movements at the turn of the century.

976 Van Hien, Edward [Gordon]. *What is Subud?* London: Rider & Co., 1963, 175 pp. New rev. ed. The author, 1968, 174 pp.

977 Van Naerssen, Fritz Herman. *Cultuurcontacten en sociale conflicten in Indonesië*. Amsterdam: J. M. Meulenhoff, 1946, 24 pp.

P. 24, notes, which amount to a survey of literature on prophetic movements in Indonesia.

978 Van Ufford, Ph. Quarles. "Why don't you sit down? Sadrach and the struggle for religious independence in the earliest phase of the Church of Central Java (1861-1899)." In *Man, meaning, and history: Essays in honour H. G. Schulte-Nordholt*, edited by R. Schefold, et al. The Hague: M. Nijhoff, 1980, pp. 204-29.

P. 209, Coolen's church; pp. 209-10, Tunggul Wulung's church; otherwise on Sadrach's Kring (or "circle") independent congregations.

Southeast: Indonesia

979 *Verslag betreffende het onderzoek in zake de Saminbeweging, ingesteld ingevolge het Gouvernements Besluit van 1 Januari 1917.* No. 20. Batavia, 1918.

An important source on the Samin movement.

980 Wahono, Oleh S. Wismoady. "Mesianisme dalam perjuangan petani: Tinjauan dari sisi kekristenan" [Messianism in peasant revolt: A reflection from the Christian side]. *Prisma* (Jakarta, Institute for Social and Economic Research and Study), no. 1 (January 1977), pp. 54-62.

With comparisons with similar movements in Latin America and the Philippines. By an Indonesian professor of Old Testament.

981 Wertheim, W[illem] F[rederik]. *Effects of Western civilization on Indonesian society.* Secretariat Paper 11. New York: International Secretariat, Institute of Pacific Relations, 1950, 83 pp.

Chap. 4 (pp. 50-67), Islamic reform – Islam as a modernizing, unifying, prenationalistic influence after World War II; p. 69 Samin movement as both an escape into an idealized past and a rural precursor of dynamic nationalism.

982 Wertheim, Willem Frederik. *Indonesian society in transition: A study in social change.* The Hague: W. van Haeve; Bandung: Sumur Bandung, 1956, 360 pp., maps. 2d rev. ed., 1959, 394 pp.

Chap. 8 (pp. 192-222), religious reform; chap. 10 (pp. 274-308), cultural dynamics; p. 318, the Samin movement.

983 Yoder, Lawrence McCulloh. "The Church of the Muria: A history of the Muria-Christian Church of Indonesia – GKMI." M.Th. dissertation (missiology), Fuller Theological Seminary, School of World Mission, 1981, 634 pp.

A Chinese church related to the Dutch Mennonite mission; pp. 78-90, assertion of independence without breaking fellowship.

984 Yoder, Lawrence McCulloh. "The introduction and expression of Islam and Christianity in the cultural context of north central Java." Ph.D. dissertation (missiology), Fuller Theological Seminary, School of World Mission, 1987, 545 pp., illus.

Pp. 281-345, Tunggul Wulung's semi-independent Christian movement in the nineteenth century in the Muria area of Java.

985 Yoder, Lawrence McCulloh. "Tunggul Wulung." *Wiyata Wacana* (Pati) 3, no. 2 (1974): 24-36.

On Tunggul Wulung and his nineteenth-century independent Christian movement in the Muria area, as one of the "fathers" of the Evangelical Church of Java.

986 Zoetmulder, P. J. "The Wayang as a philosophical theme." *Indonesia* (Jakarta), no. 12 (October 1971), pp. 85-96.
Includes Kebatinan and Kejawen as intertwined.

KAMPUCHEA

Formerly known as Cambodia, and as the Khmer Republic, Kampuchea has been predominantly Buddhist since the fourteenth century, with a more recent minority Christian community that includes some very small Chinese independent churches. The Vietnamese population brought the Cao Dai movement into Kampuchea, but most were expelled in 1970. Hill peoples in the northeast have much in common with the nearby peoples in Laos and Vietnam, but there does not appear to have been much religious interaction with the incoming Buddhist and Christian faiths. D. P. Chandler reports an earlier movement similar to some of those in the neighboring states – nationalistic and millennial in the Buddhist manner.

987 Chandler, David P. "An anti-Vietnamese rebellion in early nineteenth century Cambodia: Pre-colonial imperialism and a pre-nationalist response." *Journal of Southeast Asian Studies* 6, no. 1 (1975): 16-24.
A movement led by the "Holy Men," with Buddhist millennial aspects, in 1820 under a monk named Kai.

988 United States Government, Department of the Army. *Area handbook for the Khmer Republic (Cambodia)*, edited by D. P. Whitaker, et al. American University, Foreign Area Studies Division. Washington, D.C.: Government Printing Office, 1973, 387 pp.

LAOS

Little is known about the Khmu' and Hmong (Meo) peoples and their religious traditions in comparison with other tribal peoples of Southeast Asia. Their contacts with Buddhism have been limited, and those with Christian missions have taken place only since the turn of the twentieth century. The Khmu' have been subordinate to the coastal Lao, who are folk Buddhists, and their culture has been deteriorating. In their response to Christian missions, they have shown continuing dependency. Some scanty information is presented about their mythological culture-hero, the white king Djiung, or

Southeast: Laos

Cian; the revitalization or neoprimal movement that looks back to him reveals strong cargo-cult features. In contrast, the Hmong, a vigorous people but also under cultural stress, have produced first a mass movement into Christianity since 1949, followed by various small prophet movements of a messianic nature with some cargo aspects that we might designate as synthesist. Notable among these is that of Pa Chai Vue, a messiah whose followers fought the French, the Lao, and the Vietnamese for three years.

Among the Lao there has been a series of "nativistic-messianic" (E. Sarkisyanz's term) movements in the Buddhist millennial tradition and associated with the desire for independence from Thailand and restoration of the seventeenth-century Lao kingdom. These developments, however, are less clearly within the scope of this collection than are those among the upland Khmu' and Hmong.

989 Barney, G. Linwood. "The Meo–an incipient church?" *Practical Anthropology* 4, no. 2 (1957): 31-50. Reprinted in *Supplement 1960* (selected reprints . . .), pp. 41-52. Also in *Readings in missionary anthropology II*, compiled by W. A. Smalley. Enl. ed. South Pasadena, Calif.: William Carey Library, 1978, pp. 466-77.

P. 48 (1960 reprint), "Meo Trinity" movement on the fringe of the young church between 1950 and 1957.

990 Barney, G. L[inwood]. "The Meo of Xieng Khouang Province." In *Southeast Asian tribes, minorities, and nations*, edited by P. Kunstadter. Vol. 1. Princeton, N.J.: Princeton University Press, 1967, pp. 271-94.

Pp. 291-92, the possibility of seeing Meo changes as a revitalization movement.

991 Bessac, Susanne, and Bessac, Frank B. "American perceptions of Hmong ethnicity: A study of Hmong refugees in Missoula, Montana." *Contributions to Southeast Asia Ethnography* 1 (September 1982).

Pp. 69-70, brief references to Hmong messianic movements, including the Pa Chai movement, and a garbled account of Shong Lue Yang and his movement.

992 Chia Koua Vang; Gnia Yee Yang; and Smalley, William A. *Life of Shong Lue Yang*. Forthcoming.

English translation from Hmong original; on the Hmong messiah originally from Vietnam, who developed an alphabetic script and gathered a movement among the Hmong until it was suppressed and he was assassinated.

993 Halpern, Joel M. "Laos and her tribal problems." *Michigan Alumnus Quarterly Review* 67, no. 10 (1960): 59-67.
Pp. 63-64, Djiung (Cian) messianic cargo cult in Laos; the Khmu' in 1957.

994 Halpern, Joel M. *Laos profiles*. Laos Project Paper 18. Department of Anthropology, University of California, Los Angeles, 1 June 1961, pp. 144-45.
Khmu' messianic movement, 1957.

995 Halpern, Joel M., and Kunstadter, Peter. "Laos: Introduction." In *Southeast Asian tribes, minorities, and nations*, edited by P. Kunstadter. Vol. 1. Princeton, N.J.: Princeton University Press, 1967, pp. 233-58.
P. 242, comparison of messianic cults among the Khmu' and the Meo.

996 Lemoine, Jacques. "Les écritures Hmong." *Bulletin des Amis du Royaume Lao* 7-8 (1972).
Pp. 142-46 contain the first published mention of Shong Lue Yang and his writing system.

997 Mottin, Jean. *Contes et légendes Hmong Blanc*. Bangkok: Don Bosco Press, 1980.
Contains a translation into French of one of the variants of the story of Pa Chai Vue.

998 Mottin, Jean. *History of the Hmong (Meo)*. Bangkok: Odeon Store, 1980, 63 pp., illus., maps.
P. 43, mentions the "war of the insane," and earlier pages sketch causal factors.

999 Sarkisyanz, Emanuel. "De Religionen Kambodschas, Birmas, Laos. . . ." In *De Religionen Südostasiens*, edited by A. Hofer, et al. Stuttgart: W. Kohlhammer, 1975.
Pp. 490-92, Phu-mi-Bun (or Phi Bun), a revolt of 1902 in Thailand; other "nativistic" independence movements led by Buddhist monks in the millennial tradition, seeking freedom from Thailand.

1000 Smalley, William A[llen]. "Cian: Khmu? culture hero." *Felicitation volumes of Southeast Asian studies presented to His Highness Prince Dhaninivat Kromamun Bidyalabh Bridhyakorn*. 2 vols. Bangkok: Siam Society, 1965, 349 pp.
Pp. 41-54, a "recent cargo cult" among the Khmu' of Laos.

Southeast: Laos

1001 Smalley, William A[llen]. "The gospel and the cultures of Laos."
Practical Anthropology 3, no. 3 (1956): 47-57. Reprinted in *Supplement
1960* (selected reprints . . .), pp. 63-69.
Pp. 66-67, incipient Meo prophets of "Jesuses" but with
revitalization processes within the Christian Church rather than in
"nativistic" movements.

1002 Smalley, William A[llen]; Chia Koua Vang; and Gnia Yee Yang.
*Mother of writing: The origin and development of a Hmong messianic
script.* Chicago: University of Chicago Press, forthcoming.

1003 Tapp, Nicholas. "The relevance of telephone directories to a lineage-
based society: A consideration of some messianic myths among the
Hmong." *Journal of the Siam Society* 70 (1982): 114-27.
The frequent messianic appearances among the Hmong in China
and Southeast Asia are attributed to the tension between their own
statelessness and a powerful surrounding state.

MALAYSIA

Malaysia includes eleven states in predominantly Islamic West, or peninsular,
Malaysia, and two states, Sarawak and Sabah (formerly North Borneo), that
make up East Malaysia and contain most of the aboriginal population; after
the Muslim Malays, the Chinese are the largest group. There are no items for
the Muslim population; the items by Ackerman and Lee refer to other
elements – Chinese, Indian, Eurasian, etc., and include influence from
Western pentecostalism as well as a new monotheistic religion. While not
within our definitions of new religious movements, they have been included
for comparative purposes and because more primal elements may yet be
detected. One item (P. D. R. Williams-Hunt, entry 1018) reveals an
individual practitioner rather than a movement. In East Malaysia clear
examples are the Bungan movement in Sarawak and the Garing movement in
Sabah.

1004 Ackerman, S. E. "The language of religious innovation: Spirit
possession, exorcism in a Malaysian Catholic Pentecostal movement."
Journal of Anthropological Research 37, no. 1 (1981): 90-100, bib.
"A traditional idiom of power" is transformed into a charter for
religious change as an alternative to folk occultism.

1005 Ackerman, S. E., and Lee, Raymond L. M. "Pray to the Heavenly Father: A Chinese new religion in Malaysia." *Numen* 29, no. 1 (1982): 62-74.

Baitiangong ("Pray to the Heavenly Father") founded 1976 as rescuing polytheists for monotheism.

1006 Aichner, P. "Adat Bungan." *Sarawak Museum Journal* (Kuching), n.s. 7, no. 8 (1956): 476-77.

The Bungan movement.

1007 Bray, Jenny. *Longhouse of faith.* Lawas, Sarawak, Malaysia: Borneo Evangelical Mission, 1971, 135 pp., illus.

Pp. 15, 17-18, 21, 45, 47-48, 51, 73, 76, 94-95, 101-2, 118, Bungan – passing vague references in a missionary story.

1008 Conley, William W[allace]. *The Kalimantan Kenyah: A study of tribal conversion in terms of dynamic cultural themes.* Nutley, N.J.: Presbyterian and Reformed Publishing Co., 1976, 458 pp.

Pp. 46-53, Kenyah primal religion and Bungan Malan, the creator spirit; pp. 309-11, Bungan movement from 1947; pp. 326-27, 351-53, Bungan Malan cult.

1009 Lee, Raymond L. M. "Dancing with the gods: a spirit medium festival in urban Malaysia." *Anthropos* 78, nos. 3-4 (1983): 355-68.

A Sino-Malay spirit festival in 1980 as a syncretist movement.

1010 Lee, Raymond L. M. "Sai Baba, salvation, and syncretism: Religious change in a Hindu movement in urban Malaysia." *Contributions to Indian Sociology*, n.s. 16, no. 1 (1982): 125-40.

A Hindu movement. In spite of devotees' openness to religious innovation, any syncretism is superficial.

1011 Lee, Raymond L. M., and Ackerman, S. E. "Conflict and solidarity in a Pentecostal group in urban Malaysia." *Sociological Review*, n.s. 28, no. 4 (1980): 809-27.

A Catholic group of Eurasians, Chinese, etc., in Bandar Baru, near Kuala Lumpur, seceding about 1976 from a larger group.

1012 O'Hanlon, Redmond. *Into the heart of Borneo ... a journey made in 1983 to the mountains of Batu Tiban.* Edinburgh: Salamander Press, 1984, 192 pp., illus., map.

Southeast: Malaysia

> Pp. 101-2, an English traveler's brief, garbled, and flippant account of the Bungan cult; p. 161, Kayan longhouse with rows of egg-holding offering sticks to Bungan on the landing.

1013 Prattis, Ian. "The Kayan-Kenyah 'Bungan cult' in Sarawak." *Sarawak Museum Journal*, n.s., nos. 21-22 [11] (1963), pp. 64-87.

1014 Rousseau, Jérôme. "Transformations religieuses dans le centre de Borneo." *Anthropologie et Sociétés* (Université Laval) 3, no. 3 (1979): 127-40, 162, bib.

> On the Bungan cult among the Kayan and the Kenyah, mainly in Sarawak but also in Indonesian Kalimantan.

1015 Singaravelu, S. "Some aspects of syncretism between Hindu religious beliefs and the indigenous Malay folk-belief in peninsular Malaysia." *Adyar Library Bulletin*, Golden Jubilee volume, 1986, pp. 535-40.

> The Hindu god Siva as equivalent to the Malay high deity, Bataru Guru.

1016 White, E. "Bungan: A new Kayan belief." *Sarawak Museum Journal* (Kuching, Sarawak), n.s. 7, no. 8 (1956): 472-75.

> "Badly informed" (according to J. Rousseau, entry 1014).

1017 Williams, Thomas Rhys. "The form of a north Borneo nativistic behaviour." *American Anthropologist* 65, no. 31 (June 1963): 543-51.

> The Garing movement among the Muruts in 1948; religious but few explicitly religious factors; moral and social reforms that upset the community and led to suppression by the government.

1018 Williams-Hunt, P. D. R. "An up-to-date shaman." *Man*, article 196, 50 (1950): 116, illus.

> Healer who uses a model airplane with submachine gun to "shoot" evil spirits.

THE PHILIPPINES

There is no part of the world with a greater variety of new religious movements than the Philippines. Spanish Catholicism dominated much of the country from the sixteenth to the end of the nineteenth century, and from the seventeenth century on there were many neoprimal movements associated with political and cultural revolts.

Southeast: The Philippines

In the present century Catholicism has become less imperial, much more variegated, and has been joined by a massive American Protestant missionary presence. Beneath both Christian traditions there lies a folk form of Christianity that reflects the long Catholic influence and also continues much of the original primal religious world. The term *Filipino indigenes* has been suggested for those who have retained their ancestral ways and have resisted Western or Islamic acculturation. These would be mostly the tribal peoples in the mountain provinces of northern Luzon, and have been estimated to comprise about ten percent of the population; but there are senses in which this term could apply to most of the population. *Filipino* is the term that has mostly replaced *Tagalog* for the national language, which is based on that of the ancient Tagalog tribes.

While Spanish and American colonialism provoked independent religious reactions, these have not ceased with the coming of independence in 1946. Their extent and complexity is revealed in Covar's list (entry 1061), although this includes many imported religious bodies among the 586 he has named. The Philippines press is the only source for some movements, especially those mystical bodies and sodalities that gravitate toward Mt. Banahaw. Samples of feature articles are included here; much other similar material, albeit somewhat repetitive, may be found in the extensive indexes to the Manila press maintained in the National Library of the Philippines. Unfortunately, owing to the destruction of libraries in the battle for Manila in World War II, there is a paucity of back numbers of serials and of much Filipiana, so that documentation is much better after about 1950.

There has been a special relation between nationalism and religious movements, seen in three main forms: first, in a large range of movements called "Rizalist" after Jose Rizal, scholar, patriot, and martyr (d. 1896), who has been deified by some; second, in the Philippine Independent Church, to which a separate collection is devoted (including items on Aglipay), as a "particular movement"; and third, in the very large Iglesia ni Cristo, with yet another form of nationalism – as the chosen nation, and also treated as a "particular movement" in a separate section.

1019 Abesamis, Gil. *The pastoral ministry in the IEMELIF Church*. B.D. thesis, Union Theological Seminary (Dasmarinas, Cavite), [1969 or 1965?], 122 pp.
Zamora's Methodist secession.

1020 Achutegui, P[edro] S. de. Review of *Churches and sects in the Philippines: A descriptive study of contemporary religious movements*, by D. J. Elwood (entry 1085). *Philippine Studies* 16, no. 3 (1968): 577-86.
Critique of some of Elwood's data.

Southeast: The Philippines

1021 Adalba-Lim, Estefania, et al. "A cursory study of the Laipiang Malaya–its membership, organization, and implications to present Philippine society." *Philippine Sociological Review* 15, nos. 3-4 (July-October 1967): 151-62.

The uprising of 1967, led by faith-healer Valentin de los Santos, misjudged as political and suppressed with much loss of life.

1022 Agoncillo, Teodoro A. "The revolt of the masses: The story of Bonifacio and the Katipunan." Philippine study series. *Philippine's Social Sciences and Humanites Review* (Quezon City) 21 (1956).

Pp. 43-44, Katipunan; pp. 195-96, Colorum under Juan Magdala. Publication of this item was suspended for eight years by President Quirino as being a Marxist interpretation of the 1896 revolution.

1023 Alejandro, D. D. Review of *The story of Methodism in the Philippines*, by R. L. Deats (entry 1073). *Silliman Journal* (Dumaguete City) 12, no. 2 (1965): 230-33.

P. 233, Methodist independent church origins.

1024 Alip, Eufronio M. "The mystic lure of Mount Banahao." *Philippine Magazine*, no. 356 [34, no. 12] (1937): 542-43, 561-62, illus.

The cult and pilgrimage center for various independent movements.

1025 Allison, Stephen H., and Malony, H. Newton. "Filipino psychic surgery: Myth, magic, or miracle." *Journal of Religion and Health* 20, no. 1 (1981): 48-62.

Not on religious movements, but relevant to the attitude toward healing in these.

1026 Alonso, Isidoro. "National churches." In *The Catholic Church in the Philippines today*, edited by I. Alonso, et al. Historical Conservation Society, 13. Manila: The Society (distributed by Bookmark Inc.), 1968, pp. 38-41.

Pp. 38-39, Philippine Independent Church; p. 40, Iglesia ni Cristo and Watawat Ng Lahi–outline accounts.

1027 Anderson, Gerald H[arry], ed. *Studies in Philippine church history*. Ithaca, N.Y.: Cornell University Press, 1969, 421 pp.

See essays by D. J. Elwood (entry 1087); in Iglesia ni Cristo section, by A. J. Sanders (entry 1479); in Philippine Independent Church section, by H. E. Chandlee (entry 1553) and by M. D. Clifford (entry 1559).

1028 Apolinario, Eulalio S. *Balitaktakan Katoliko vs. Manolotes*. Manila: Aklatang Lunas, 1955, 160 pp.
A Catholic polemic against the Iglesia ni Cristo.

1029 Aranas, Simeon. *Kaligaligayang Bundok ng Banahaw* ... [Delightful mountain of Banahaw]. 2 vols. Manila: P. Sayo, 1927.
In Tagalog and in verse, on the sacred mountain of pilgrimage and cult center of the Cofradia de San Jose. Cited and quoted by R. C. Ileto (entry 1140), pp. 84-91.

1030 Araneta-Gonzalez, Patricia. "Banashaw: Per omnia saecula saeculorum." *Diliman Review* (Diliman, Quezon City) 28, no. 3 (May-June 1980): 52-54.
On Mt. Banahaw and its religious communities, especially Iglesia del Ciudad Mistica de Dios, founded by Maria Bernarda Balitaan (1876-1925).

1031 Arens, Richard. "The early Pulahan movement in Samar and Leyte." *Journal of History* (Philippines National Historical Society) 7, no. 4 (1959): 303-71.
The "red turban" neoprimal religio-political movements of the mountain people from 1894-1905, and again in the 1920s and 1940s.

1032 Arens, Richard. "Religious rituals and their economic implications in Philippine society." *Philippine Sociological Review* 7, nos. 1-2 (1959): 34-45.
P. 40, "oraciones," or mutilated Latin prayers; p. 40, Anting-anting; p. 44, Pulahan and Watawat ng Lahi, also Colorum movements.

1033 Artigas y Cuerva, Manuel. *Galeria de Filipinos ilustres*. ... 2 vols. Histografia filipina. Vol. 1, Manila: "El Renaciamiento," 1917, 663 pp.; vol. 2, Manila: A. Pobre, 1918, 528 pp.
Vol. 1, pp. 86-98, Gregorio Aglipay y Labayan; vol. 2, pp. 395-97, Apolinario de la Cruz.

1034 Atienza, Max. "Mamma Toy." *Philippine Weekly Examiner*, no. 45 (22 April 1963), pp. 5, 21, 25, 28, illus.
On H. C. Moncado (entries 1190-1193).

1035 Avila, Charles R. *Peasant theology: Reflections by Filipino peasants on their process of social revolution*. W.S.C.F. Asia Books, 1. Bangkok: World Student Christian Federation Asia Office, n.d., 71 pp.

Southeast: The Philippines

A moving presentation of the peasant situations that have led to over two hundred revolts, often sustained by religious convictions, since the arrival of the Spanish.

1036 Bacdayan, Albert S. "Religious conversion and social change: A northern Luzon case." *Practical Anthropology* 17, no. 3 (1970): 119-27. Revised from version in entry 1037.
　　　Prophetess Ina ("Mother") 1942–in Lacma, a village in north Luzon; a "biblical revitalization movement" within the church community.

1037 Bacdayan, Albert S. "Religious conversion and social reintegration in a western Bontoc village complex." *St. Louis Quarterly* 5, nos. 1-2 (1967): 27-40.
　　　P. 30, illiterate prophetess Ina's movement in 1942; pp. 35-36, her sabbath and new villages.

1038 Banguis, Fabian L., comp. *General Hilario Camino Moncado*. Los Angeles: Filipino Federation of America, 1946, 35 pp., photo.

1039 Baricanosa, Jose B. *Ang Sampung Utos ni Dr. Jose Rizal*. Calamba, Laguna: Tanggapang Pangkalahatan, Iglesia Watawat ng Lahi, 1958.
　　　The ten commandments of Dr. Jose Rizal.

1040 Bautista, Jose P. *Manila Tribune*, 13 January 1931.
　　　A contemporary feature article on the Tayug Colorum.

1041 Bayot, Felix. "The life story of Nicholas Zamora." Translated into English and condensed by Juan Nabong. *Philippine Christian Advance* (Manila), April 1950, pp. 5-7.
　　　The founder of Iglesia Evangelica Metodista in 1909.

1042 Bentley, Barbara. [Letter to President F. Marcos.] *Survival International Review*, no. 39 [7, no. 1] (1982), p. 23.
　　　Concerning the atrocities perpetrated by the "fanatical Rock Christ sect ... against the tribal Surbanon," Malindang area of Zamboanga on Mindanao.

1043 Blair, E[mma] H[elen], and Robertson, J[ames] A[lexander], eds. "Insurrections by Filipinos in the seventeenth century." In *The Philippine islands, 1493-1898*. Vol. 38, *1674-1683*. Manila and Cleveland: A. H. Clark, 1903-9, pp. 87-240.

Southeast: The Philippines

Excerpts from colonial chronicles of some twenty revolts against missions and forced labor. Pp. 87-94, Bohol and Leyte revolts, 1622; pp. 92-96, Apolinario de la Cruz and the 1840-41 revolt – a reprint of J. M. de la Matta's report (entry 1180), with editorial note. See also entry 1179, vol. 52.

1044 Brent, Charles H. "The joy of pioneering." *Spirit of Missions* (New York) 70 (1905): 838-47, illus.

P. 845, Guardia de Honor and Sapilada members among the Igorot, showing response to the Protestant Episcopal mission, of which Brent was the bishop.

1045 Bulatao, Jaime. "Altered states of consciousness in Philippine religion." In *Filipino religious psychology*, edited by L. N. Mercado. Tacloban City: Divine Word University Publications, 1977, pp. x-xxi.

A Jesuit's keynote speech at a colloquium. Alludes to healers, mediums, visions, etc.

1046 Bulosan, Carlos. *America is in the heart: A personal history*. New York: Harcourt Brace, 1946. Reprint. Seattle: University of Washington Press, 1973, xxiv + 327 pp.

Pp. 58-62, "a graphic if inaccurate account" of the Tayug Colorum groups, as witnessed by the author in his youth.

1047 Caddawan, Pablito P. "Isneg patterns of decision-making and social structure." *Bulletin, Christian Institute for Ethnic Studies in Asia* (Manila) 4, nos. 1-2 (1970): 26-32.

Pp. 31-32, the Crusaders, indigenous healing by a "magic" syncretist group, among the author's Isneg people.

1048 Calang, Juan. "Librito sa orasyones (1900)." Translated and annotated by F. R. Demetrio, S.J. Museum and Archives Publication 7. Cayagan de Oro City: Folklore Department, Xavier University, 1972, ca. 120 pp. Mimeo.

See entry 1075 for analysis and comments; included as indicative of much folk Catholicism and peasant religion.

1049 Chesis, Gert. *Geistheiler auf den Philippinen*. Perlinger: Worgl-Osterreich, 1981, 255 pp., illus.

1050 Chio, Julita M. "A historical study of the Filipino Crusaders World Army, Inc., in Sudlon Cebu." M.A. thesis, De la Salle College (Manila), 1973.

Southeast: The Philippines

1051 Clymer, Kenton J. *Protestant missionaries in the Philippines 1898-1916: An enquiry into the American colonial mentality.* Urbana: University of Illinois Press, 1986, 267 pp., illus., map.

Pp. 127-29, Iglesia ni Cristo; pp. 116-23, 194-95, 230 n. 6, Philippine Independent Church; pp. 123-26, Aurora's Cristianos Vivos Metodistas schism, 1905; pp. 125-27, Iglesia Metodista en las Islas Filipinas of Zamora; p. 131, Presbyterian schism in 1913 – Cristianos Filipinos, joining with others in 1919 to form the Iglesia Evangelica Unido de Cristo.

1052 Coats, George Yarrington. "Philippine constabulary 1901-1957." Ph.D. thesis, Ohio State University (Columbus), 1968, 416 pp.

Chap. 13, on the Dios-Dios movement.

1053 Concepcion, Juan de la. *Historia general de Philipinas.* Sampaloc, 1768. Reprint. Manila: A. de la Rosa y Balagatas, 14 vols., 1788-92.

Vol. 5, pp. 20-25, Tamblot's revolt on Bohol and Leyte, and Banka's revolt, 1621 – from "the outstanding example of a synthetic historiography produced in the islands," by a Recollect missionary.

1054 Constantino, Renato. *The Philippines: A past revisited.* Quezon City: Tala Publishing Services, 1975, 457 pp.

Pp. 135-37, Cofradia de San Jose and Colorums; pp. 246-49, Aglipayanism; pp. 264-71, "nativistic revival" (Ruperto Rio, Apo Ipe and Felipe Salvador, Papa Isio); pp. 276-79, Dios-Dios; pp. 349-56, "minor messiahs" and Colorums; p. 427, notes. Useful surveys.

1055 Covar, P[rospero] R[eyes]. "Brief communication and research notes: A perspective on revitalization." *Philippine Sociological Review* 21, nos. 3-4 (1973): 283-87.

A perspective on revitalization.

1056 Covar, Prospero R[eyes]. "Congregation as a social process in the Watawat ng Lahi." *Philippine Sociological Review* 8, nos. 3-4 (1960): 1-16, diagrams.

Includes appendices in Tagalog containing the Ten Guideposts and the Ten Commandments of Rizal.

1057 Covar, Prospero R[eyes]. "General characterization of contemporary religious movements in the Philippines." *Asian Studies* (Quezon City) 13, no. 2 (1975): 79-92.

Characteristics of popular folk movements, including Sapilada, Balangay, Sagrada Famila de Rizal, Bathalismo, Union Cristiana

Espiritista, Kapatirang Pag-ibig sa Dios, etc, all with Filipino *anitism* as the base culture.

1058 Covar, Prospero R[eyes]. "The Iglesia Watawat ng Lahi: An anthropological study of a social movement in the Philippines." Dissertation (anthropology), University of Arizona, 1975, 174 pp., illus. Reprint of parts of abstract and chap. 5 as "Rizal's second coming," in *Ermita* 1, no. 1 (1976): 26-28.

Uses H. G. Barnett's model of innovative movements for analysis of this Rizalist millennial cult – its history, ideology, and social structure, with elements from traditional, Catholic, and Protestant sources; see especially chap. 5 (pp. 68-94), on the world view, with Rizal as the third person of the Trinity in an articulated theology.

1059 Covar, Prospero R[eyes]. "The Iglesia Watawat ng Lahi: A sociological study of a social movement." M.A. dissertation, University of the Philippines, 1961, 110 pp. Typescript.

The "Banner of the Race" Rizalist cult.

1060 Covar, Prospero R[eyes]. "Mananalangin sa Bundok Banahaw: Ang relihiyon at ang Pagkataong Pilinino." *Ulat ng Ikalawang Pambansang Kumperensya sa Sikolohiyang Pilipino* [Proceedings of the National Association for Filipino Psychology], edited by L. F. Antonio, et al., no. 2 (1977), pp. 84-92.

"People who pray in Mt. Banahaw: Religion and Filipino personality."

1061 Covar, Prospero R[eyes]. "Philippine folk Christianity." Submitted to the Modern History Program Committee, Philippine Social Science Council, Quezon City, 1975, 228 pp. (bib., pp. 160-99). Mimeo.

An unpublished research report. Pt. 2, pp. 36-152 (pp. 149-52, references cited), on Iglesia Watawat ng Lahi, drawn from his 1975 dissertation. Appendix A, pp. 202-17, master list of 586 religious organizations in the Philippines; Appendix B, pp. 218-27, Papers of Incorporation, Banner of the Race.

1062 Covar, Prospero R[eyes]. "Potensiya, bisa at anting-anting." *Sagisag* (Quezon City) 4, no. 4 (1979): 50, illus.

"Potency, efficacy, and talisman."

1063 Covar, Prospero R[eyes]. "Religious leadership in the Iglesia Watawat ng Lahi." In *Filipino religious psychology*, edited by L. N. Mercado. Tacloban City: Divine Word University Publications, 1977, pp. 109-26.

Southeast: The Philippines

1064 Crippen, Harlan R. "Philippine agararian unrest: Historical backgrounds." *Science and society* (Chelmsford, Essex) 10, no. 4 (1946): 337-60.

1065 Cruikshank, Robert Bruce. "A history of Samar Island, the Philippines, 1768-1898." Ph.D. dissertation (modern history), University of Wisconsin-Madison, 1975, 364 pp.
Includes chap. 6 (pp. 181-200) on the cult of Bonga, which emerged from pilgrimages to Catholic shrines after the cholera epidemic of 1882-83. It was a neoprimal or syncretist millennial movement with prophets and healing, suppressed by the government by 1887.

1066 Cruz, Apolinario de la. "Declaracion de Apolinario de la Cruz." *La Politica de Espana en Filipinas* (Madrid) 2, no. 32 (1891): 113-14; 2, no. 33 (1891): 130-31; 2, no. 35 (1891): 155.
The official version of Apolinario's testimony between his capture and his summary execution in 1841, in Tayabas.

1067 Cullamar, Evelyn Tan. *Babaylanism in Negros: 1896-1907*. Quezon City: New Day Philippines, 1896, 119 pp., illus., map, bib.
The evolution of a religio-political protest movement by the peasantry during the late Spanish and early American period; seen as a revitalization movement.

1068 Cullen, Vincent C. "Bukidnon animism and Christianity." In *Bukidnon: Politics and religion*, edited by A. de Gusman II and E. M. Pacheco. Institute of Philippine Culture papers, no. 11. Quezon City: Ateneo de Manila for the Institute, 1973, pp. 1-13.
Catholic and Protestant influence compared with indigenous millennial prophet movements ("baylan") and with Colorum and Rizalist secret societies on Mindanao since 1900.

1069 Cullen, Vincent G. "Social change and religion among the Bukidnon." *Philippine Studies* (Quezon City) 27, no. 2 (1978): 160-75.

1070 Dansalan Research Center. Dansalan Junior College, Marawi City, holds the collected resources of Victoria V. Flores-Tolentino (1952-79) on the Equifrilibricum World Religion, Inc. (Moncadistas) – documents, books, periodicals, notes, taped interviews, etc.

1071 Deats, Richard L[ouis]. "Nationalism and the churches in the Philippines." *Silliman Journal* 12, no. 2 (1965): 152-67.
Pp. 159-62, Philippine Independent Church, an outline; as one way of dealing with nationalism, compared to the Roman Catholic method, and the solution found in two Methodist secessions to form independent churches.

1072 Deats, Richard L[ouis]. "Nicolas Zamora: Religious nationalist." In *Studies in Philippine church history*, edited by G. H. Anderson. Ithaca, N.Y.: Cornell University Press, 1969, pp. 325-36.
On Iglesia Evangelica Metodista, founded in 1909.

1073 Deats, Richard L[ouis]. *The story of Methodism in the Philippines.* Manila: National Council of Churches in the Philippines for United Theological Seminary, 1964, 131 pp., illus.
Pp. 4-6, Zamora's family and early history; pp. 26-27, 34-36, Philippine Independent Church; pp. 37, 39-45, Zamora and Iglesia Evangelica Methodista en las Islas Filapinas, founded in 1909.

1074 Del Rosario, Romeo [Laus]. "The schism in the Methodist Episcopal Church in the Philippines in 1933." Ph.D. dissertation (church history), Boston University, 1981, 756 pp.

1075 Demetrio, Francisco R. "On Orasyones: Or magical power and living Christianity." *Silliman Journal* 19, no. 3 (1972): 355-63.
On a popular booklet of magical prayers (orasyones), reverenced in the rural Philippines and here analyzed by a Catholic priest-folklorist as being a mixture of sense and nonsense.

1076 Devins, John Bancroft. *An observer in the Philippines or life in our possessions.* New York: American Tract Society, 1905, 416 pp., illus.
A Protestant minister with a favorable view of Aglipayanism.

1077 Diaz, Casimoro. *Conquistas de las islas filipinas.* . . . Madrid: Ruiz de Morga, 1698. Manila and Valladolid: L. N. de Gaviria, 1890, 854 pp.
Pp. 132-36, the nativistic rising under Tamblot in 1620 on Bohol and Leyte; also Bankaw's revolt, 1621; pp. 640-44, Tapar's revolt.

1078 Dizon, Nicolas C. *The "Master" vs. Juan de la Cruz.* Honolulu: Mercantile Press, 1931, 118 pp., illus.
The "Master" is the founder of the Filipino Federation of America, H. C. Moncado (see entries 1190-1193). A critical survey of

Southeast: The Philippines

Moncado and the Federation by the pastor of the Filipino Community Church in Honolulu; pp. 42-47, pictures of Moncado.

1079 Doeppers, Daniel F. "The evolution of the geography of religious adherence in the Philippines before 1898." *Journal of Historical Geography* 2, no. 2 (1976): 95-110.

Historical geography of religions – local ethnic, Catholic, and Islamic, related to different strategies of conversion, as background to independent movements.

1080 Eastwood, Tristram. "Notes on the Ciudad Mistica." *Ermita* (Manila) 1, no. 3 (20 March-19 April 1976): 26-27, illus.

1081 Eggan, Fred. "Some aspects of culture change in the northern Philippines." *American Anthropologist*, n.s., 43 (1941): 11-18.

Pp. 17-18, the Tinguian in 1934-35, who had few signs of Christian influence and no nativistic movements, compared with the latter among the Ilocano, Christianized in the sixteenth through seventeenth centuries.

1082 Eggan, Fred, and Pacyaya, Alfredo. "The Sapilada religion: Reformation and accommodation among the Igorots of Northern Luzon." *Southwestern Journal of Anthropology* 18, no. 2 (1962): 95-113, bib.

Founded by Pedro Degan in 1898, and still existing in the 1960s.

1083 Eleazor, Eulogio V. "The Colorum uprising in Surigao del Norte." *Philippines Free Press* 55, no. 19 (12 May 1962): 20-21, illus.

A general article on the 1922-24 movement.

1084 Elesterio, Fernando G. *Three essays on Philippine religious culture.* Monograph Series, 7. Manila: De La Salle University Press, 1989, 82 pp., illus.

Three lectures at Wasada University, Japan, 1987. Pp. 1-16, "Pre-Magellanic elements in contemporary Filipino culture"; pp. 17-29, "The Filipino 'Angel' and his church" (Iglesia ni Cristo) and pp. 57-78, Appendix – its official Constitution, as deposited with the government; pp. 40-56, "Ultra-nationalist [Rizalist] Filipino religions" – Watawat ng Lahi and Samahan ng Tatlong Persona Solo Dios.

1085 Elwood, Douglas J. *Churches and sects in the Philippines: A descriptive study of contemporary religious movements.* Silliman University

Monographs, Series A, Religious Studies, 1. Dumaguete City: Silliman University Press, 1968, 213 pp.

A first report on over 350 distinct bodies, excluding Roman Catholic ones: over two-thirds of the 350 originated since World War II, many through schisms; over 80% of evangelical Protestant Christians are in independent groups.

1086 Elwood, Douglas J. "Contemporary churches and sects in the Philippines." *South East Asia Journal of Theology* (Singapore) 9, no. 2 (1967): 56-78.

A summary of the first stages of his research.

1087 Elwood, Douglas J. "Varieties of Christianity." Extract in *Studies in Philippine church history*. Ithaca, N.Y.: Cornell University Press, 1969, pp. 370-86.

1088 Elwood, Douglas J., and Magdamo, Patricia Ling. *Christ in Philippine context*. Quezon City: New Day Publishers, 1971, 373 pp., maps.

Pp. 202-3, "Folk healing movements such as the Espiritistas," representing syncretism of Christian and indigenous beliefs.

1089 Enverga, Tobias Y. "Annual pilgrimage to Mt. Banihaw." *Sunday Times Magazine* (Manila) 16, no. 33 (26 March 1961): 10-12, illus.

The sacred mountain, and its many communities.

1090 Fabian, Mac A. "Leader of the Colorum uprising." *Philippines Free Press* 47, no. 18 (5 May 1956): 26-27.

The 1931 revolt under Pedro Calusa, involving only 31 rebels; he escaped unhurt "because he had an anting-anting," and later became a peaceful farmer.

1091 Falcon, Floro [*sic.*] R. "The Philippine Benevolent Missionaries Association." *Diwa: Studies in Philosophy and Theology* (Graduate School, Divine Word Seminary, Tagaytay City, Philippines) 4, no. 1 (1979): 54-86.

Activities and teaching of an independent church.

1092 Falcon, Floro [*sic.*] R. "Religious leadership in the Philippine Benevolent Missionaries Association." In *Filipino religious psychology*, edited by L. N. Mercado. Tacloban City: Divine Word University Publications, 1977, pp. 141-48, and discussion, pp. 166-72.

Southeast: The Philippines

1093 "'Fanatics' in the Philippines." *China Weekly Review* (Shanghai) 56 (11 April 1931): 216.
On the Tayug Colorum rising of 1931.

1094 Fernandez, Pablo, and Kobak, Cantius J., eds. "Piratical raids and native uprisings in 17th century Samar and Leyte." *Philippiniana Sacra* (Manila) 14, no. 41 (1979): 351-414; 14, no. 42 (1979): 411-568.
English translation with portions of the manuscripts of Fr. Francisco Ignacio Alcina (seventeenth-century Jesuit scholar), *Historia de las islas e indios de Bisayas* . . . , 1668, pt. 1, pp. 397-405, the Bohol revolt on Samar; pt. 2, pp. 519-26, revolt on Leyte.

1095 Fey, H. E. "Farmer's revolt in the Philippines." *Christian Century* (Chicago) 48 (1931): 1004.
The religious revolt at Tayug, Pangasinan, 1931.

1096 Finegan, Philip M. "Philippine Islands." In *The Catholic Encyclopedia*. Vol. 12. New York: Encyclopedia Press, 1911, pp. 10-17.
P. 13a, Apolinario de la Cruz and his "deluded fanatics"; pp. 15b-16a, Aglipayanism.

1097 Flores, Ernesto A., Jr. "This sect celebrates Christmas in September." *Weekly Graphic* 33, no. 25 (14 December 1966): 18, illus.
Crusaders of the Divine Church of Christ in Pangasinan at their "New Jerusalem"; founder R. S. Magliba as a "second Messiah" and healer, exhorting to plain living.

1098 Flores-Tolentino, Victoria V. "The Moncado believers: A case study in religious typology." *PSSC Social Science Information* 7, no. 2 (1979): 3-14, 36.
See also entry 1070.

1099 Forbes, William Forbes. *The Philippines Islands*. Boston: Houghton Mifflin Co., 1928.
Pp. 228-29, F. Salvador and Santa Yglesia or "Holy Church."

1100 Foronda, Marcelino A., [Jr.]. "The canonization of Rizal." *Journal of History* (Philippine National Historical Society) 8, no. 2 (1960): 93-140. Adapted as "How Rizal became a saint," *Sunday Chronicle Magazine* 16, no. 25 (18 June 1961): 10-12.

1101 Foronda, Marcelino A., [Jr.]. *Cults honoring Rizal.* Introduction by Rev. Brother C. Peter. Manila: R. P. Garcia Publishing Co., 1961, 98 pp., illus.

Pp. 45-98, appendix including prayers and hymns, constitutions, etc., in Tagalog with English translation; bib., pp. 43-44. Also in *Historical Bulletin* (special Rizal number), 1961.

1102 Foronda, Marcelino A., [Jr.]. "National churches." *Unitas* (Manila) 36, no. 3 (1963): 357-65.

Pp. 358-59, Philippine Independent Church; pp. 359-60, Iglesia ni Cristo; p. 360, Watawat ng Lahi; pp. 360-65, discussion of these movements.

1103 Francisco, Gabriel Beato. *Kasaysayan ni Apolinario de la Cruz na may pamagat na Hermano Pule* [Story of Apolinario de la Cruz who was addressed as Brother Pule]. N.p., 1915, 136 pp.

An account, in Tagalog, of his life at the Hospital of San Juan de Dios, by an educated Tagalog writer, based on contemporary popular accounts – cited and used by R. C. Ileto (entry 1140), pp. 56ff.

1104 Frankland, M. "Healers or cruel hoaxers?" *Observer Magazine* (London), 25 August 1974, pp. 10-12, 15, illus.

"Spiritualist" healers in Manila and the province of Pangasinan, akin to the "psychic surgery" in Brazil.

1105 Galang, Joaquin Ser. *Si Kristo at si Rizal sa harap ng Iglesia Romana.* Manila: Minerva Associated Enterprises, 1956.

Includes Iglesia ni Cristo.

1106 Galen, Tor L. "A new religious sect." *Philippine Free Press* 46, no. 36 (3 September 1955): 20-21, illus.

The "Catholic Apostles Initiated by the Holy Spirit," founded in 1951 by Felix M. Misamis Occidental.

1107 Garcia, Dolores G. "Felix Manalo: The man and his mission." *Pasugo* (Manila), 27 July 1964, pp. 179-83.

An Iglesia ni Cristo view of its founder.

1108 Garvan, John M. *The Manobos of Mindanao.* Memoirs, National Academy of Sciences, 23, no. 1. Washington, D.C.: Government Printing Office, 1941, pp. 1-265, illus.

Pp. 229-40, the Tungud neoprimal movement of 1908-10 under prophet Meskinan (here regarded as a fraud) – animals destroyed and

Southeast: The Philippines

no farming while awaiting destruction of the world by the single god Magbabaya as a prelude to renewal (in the Ghost Dance manner); summarized in "Religious acculturation in the Philippines," by J. M. Rich. *Practical Anthropology* 17, no. 5 (1970): 205.

1109 Gatbonton. [Editorials.] *Sentinel* (Manila), 9 February 1957; 2 March 1957.
By the editor of this Catholic weekly.

1110 Gavina, Napoleon R. "Nueva Ecija's religious Adarnistas." *Kislap-Graphic* [later (Weekly) *Graphic*] 26, no. 45 (4 May 1960): 16.
Candida Balantac's Adarnista sect, or *Iglesiang Pilapina*, a Rizalist movement.

1111 Giron, Eric S. "The miserable rebels." *Mirror*, 10 June 1967.
Lapiang Malaya.

1112 Go, Fe Susan. "Mothers, maids, and the creatures of night: Persistence of Philippine folk religion." *Philippine Quarterly of Culture and Society* (Cebu City) 7, no. 3 (1979): 186-203.
Filipino folk-Christianity: pp. 195-99, appendix of stories told her from faithful Catholics about "animistic," etc., experiences; pp. 186-87, surveys the literature on new religious movements from the nineteenth century on.

1113 Gonzalez, Enrique. "The baptismal rites in Filipino Christian churches." *Loyola Studies* (Loyola House of Studies, Ateneo University, Quezon City) 1, no. 2 (1967): 36-42. Reprinted in *Philippine Studies* 16, no. 1 (1968): 160-68.
Pp. 160-66, Aglipayan churches (based on P. S. de Achutegui and M. A. Bernad [entry 1519]), vol. 2; pp. 166-67, Iglesia ni Cristo; p. 164, n. 1, list of ten Aglipayan churches. Aglipayan and I.N.C. baptisms regarded as valid.

1114 Govantes, Felipe Maria de. *Compendio de la historia de Filipinas.* Manila: Colegio de Santo Tomas, 1877, xviii + 534 + 198 pp., illus.
Pp. 378-80, Apolinario de la Cruz.

1115 Gowing, Peter G[ordon]. "Christianity in the Philippines yesterday and today. II: Non-Roman Catholicism." *Silliman Journal* (Dumaguete City) 12, no. 2 (1965): 109-51.
Pp. 121-36, Philippine Independent Church; p. 146, other independents; p. 150, Iglesia ni Cristo.

1116 Gowing, Peter G[ordon]. *Islands under the cross: The story of the church in the Philippines*. Manila: National Council of Churches in the Philippines, 1967, 286 pp., maps, illus. Rev. ed. Grand Rapids, Mich.: W. B. Eerdmann, [1967].

Pp. 51-53, early revolts; pp. 76-77, Apolinario de la Cruz; pp. 96-99, Katipunan; p. 132, Zamora's Methodist secession; pp. 133-42, 145, 200-211, Philippine Independent Church (also bib., pp. 267-70); pp. 211-14, various "sects" including Iglesia ni Cristo.

1117 Gowing, Peter G[ordon]. Review of *The religious thought of Jose Rizal*, by E. A. Hessel (entry 1132). *Silliman Journal* (Dumaguete City) 10, no. 4 (October-December 1963): 421-23.

1118 Guansing, Benjamin I., and Luat, Ernesto P., eds. *1962-63 Philippines Christian Yearbook*. Manila: Printers Art, [ca. 1962], xvi + 161 pp.

Pp. 1-12, 159-61, for lists of indigenous religious movements; 90 separate organizations listed, with membership estimates for 72. Superseded by D. J. Elwood's survey (entry 1085).

1119 Guariglia, Guglielmo. *Prophetismus und Heilserwartungs-Bewegungen als völkerkundliches und religionsgeshichtliches Problem*. Vienna: F. Berger, 1959, xvi + 332 pp., maps, bib.

Pp. 244-45, Manobos of Mindanao with their Tungud movement, 1908-10. Based on Garvan (entry 1108), and wrongly described as Indonesian.

1120 Guerrero, Amadia Ma. "An elegy for the colorums." *Graphic* 37, no. 34 (27 January 1971): 12-13.

A retelling of the rising of 1931 in eastern Pangasinan under Pedro Calosa.

1121 Guerrero, Amadia Ma. "Justice and the Lapiang Malaya." *Graphic 38*, no. 26 (1 December 1971): 10-11, illus.

Exposure of the injustices associated with the Lapiang Malaya massacre of 18 May 1967 and subsequent incarceration of members for four years.

1122 Guerrero, Leon Maria. *The first Filipino – a biography of Jose Rizal*. National Heroes Commission Publications. Manila: National Heroes Commission, 1963, xxiii + 549 pp.

The author is one of the great Philippine literary figures. A prize biography.

Southeast: The Philippines

1123 Guerrero, Milagros C[amayon]. "The Colorum uprisings: 1924-1931." *Asian Studies* (Quezon City) 5 (April 1967): 65-78.

1124 Guerrero, Milagros Camayon. "Luzon at war: Contradictions in Philippine society, 1898-1902." Ph.D. dissertation (Asian history), University of Michigan, 1977, 261 pp., maps.
     Pp. 164-229, "Peasants in the revolution": pp. 168-75, Pansacula movement; pp. 175-85, Santa Iglesia; pp. 185-212, Guardia de Honor; pp. 212-17, Colorum movements.

1125 Gumabong, Rodolfo P. "The Alaphs of Iloilo." *Philippines Free Press* 53, no. 35 (August 1960): 20-22, illus.
     On the Alaph ("Mighty Above Power Heaven") Divine Temple, founded ca. 1945 by "Pope" Roberto Mahilom, Jr. in Fabrica, Negros Occidental as a peasant protest and healing movement, which was in conflict with government forces.

1126 Gutierrez, Marcelino. "The IEMELIF–first indigenous church in the Philippines." *Philippine Christian Advance* (Manila, National Council of Churches) 2, no. 4 (1950): 3-5.
     On Zamora's Iglesia Evangelica Metodista, en las Islas Filipinas, 1909-.

1127 Guzman, Alfonso de II, and Pacheco, Esther M., eds. *Bukidnon: Politics and religion*. I.P.C. Papers, 11. Quezon City: Ateneo de Manila for Institute of Philippine Culture, 1973, 114 pp., bib.
     Pp. 7-13, Baylan (prophet) movements, nativistic and utopian-colorum, etc.

1128 Hall, Anne T. "The Entrencherado revolt." *Asian Studies* (Quezon City), 19 April 1975, p. 292.
     A Panay island millennial movement from the 1920s, led by Florencio Entrencherado (b. 1871).

1129 Hart, Donn V[orhis]. "Buhawi of the Bisayas: The revitalization process and legend-making in the Philippines." In *Studies in Philippine Anthropology (in honor of H. O. Bever)*, edited by M. D. Zamora. Quezon City: Alemar-Phoenix, 1967, pp. 366-96.

1130 Hart, Donn V[orhis]. *Compradinazgo: Ritual kinship in the Philippines*. DeKalb: Northern Illinois University Press, 1977, 256 pp., illus.
     P. 118, brief reference to Aglipayans having preserved compadrinazgo rites; pp. 120-21, Iglesia ni Cristo beginnings in Sato in

1956; not needing baptismal sponsors nor sharing in the compadrinazgo system.

1131 Hayden, Joseph Ralston. *The Philippines: A study in national development*. New York: Macmillan Co., 1945, 984 pp., illus.
Pp. 378-81, Colorums, anting-anting, "Christs," etc.; pp. 382-400, good account of Sakdalism; pp. 57-74, Philippine Independent Church; pp. 915-17, notes.

1132 Hessel, Eugene A. *The religious thought of Jose Rizal: Its context and theological significance*. Manila: Philippine Education Co., 1961, 289 pp. Rev. ed. Manila: New Day Publishers, 1983, 344 pp.
An American theologian who is a Rizal enthusiast. A comprehensive study based on thorough documentation.

1133 Hessel, Eugene A. "Rizal's retraction: A note on the debate." *Silliman Journal* 12, no. 2 (1965): 168-83, bib. in notes.
On the question of whether Rizal returned to the Catholic faith and repudiated Freemasonry on the eve of his execution.

1134 Horn, Florence. *Orphans of the Pacific: The Philippines*. New York: Reynal & Hitchcock, 1941, 316 pp., illus.
Pp. 117-20, Aglipay and his church; pp. 258-59, H. C. Moncado; pp. 259-63, Sakdalism or Ganap–a journalistic account, "sometimes flippant, sometimes shrewd," but nothing on any religious dimension.

1135 Hurley, [Gerald] Vic[tor]. *Jungle patrol: The story of the Philippine constabulary*. New York: E. P. Dutton & Co., 1938, 399 pp., illus.
Chap. 5 (pp. 117-28), the "Popes"; chap. 6 (pp. 129-35), the Pulajans; chap. 7 (pp. 136-40), banditry; pp. 359-63, Colorums; pp. 364-69, Moros and the Alangkat movement. By an American officer who served several decades among the Moros.

1136 Iglesia Evangelica Metodista en Las Islas Filipinas [IEMELIF]. *Aklat Pang-alaala sa ika–50 anipersario ng Iglesia Evangelica Metodista en las Islas Filipinas, 1909-1959*. Tondo: Golden Jubilee Executive Committee IEMELIF, 1959, 165 pp. illus. English translation. *Fiftieth anniversary issue of the IEMELIF Church, 1909-1959*, translated by R. Santos. Manila: The Church.
Zamora's secession's fiftieth anniversary record.

1137 Iglesia Watawat ng Lahi. *Dasalan*. Calamba, Laguna: Tanggapang Pangkalahatan.

Southeast: The Philippines

A book of ritual of this Iglesia.

1138 Iglesia Watawat ng Lahi. *Sunday Times Magazine* (Manila) 11 (8 January 1956): 20-23.

1139 Ikehata, S. "Popular Catholicism in the 19th century Philippines: Focus on the Cofradia de San Jose movement." *Journal of Asian and African Studies* 30 (1985): 1-77.

1140 Ileto, Reynaldo Clemena. "*Pasion* and the interpretation of change in Tagalog society (ca. 1840-1912)." Ph.D. dissertation (history), Cornell University, 1975, 261 pp.
    Pp. 20-91, the Cofradia de San Jose from 1840; pp. 92-138, the Colorum society of 1897 and Katipunan; pp. 232-37, religio-political movement under "prophet" Rios in 1902, and p. 253, its revival in 1907; pp. 237-38, Solo Dios society of 1904, under Francisco; pp. 252-56, Rizalist movements and Watawat ng Lahi; pp. 257-313, Santa Iglesia, a religio-political movement 1902-10 in Luzon under F. Salvador; Katipunan, passim.

1141 Ileto, Reynaldo Clemena. *Pasyon and revolution: Popular movements in the Philippines, 1840-1910.* Manila: Ateneo de Manila University Press, 1979, 352 pp.
    Places the Philippine revolution in the context of native traditions and explains the persistence of radical peasant brotherhoods.

1142 J. M. P. "Ruins from a magnificent reign." *Sunday Times Magazine* (Manila), 19 January 1964, pp. 28-29, illus.
    On the Moncado colony in Marawi City, now in ruins.

1143 J. [M.] P. "Watawat ng Lahi." *Sunday Chronicle Magazine* 16, no. 25 (13 August 1961): 34-39.
    Pictorial coverage, with short historical account.

1144 Jenks, Albert Ernest. *The Bontoc Igorot.* Ethnological Survey Publications, 1. Manila: Bureau of Public Printing, 1905, 266 pp., illus., maps. Reprint. New York: Johnson Reprint Corp., 1970.
    Pp. 204-5, messianic movement, with return of culture-hero Lumawig, with new sources of strength; Sapilada and O-lot.

1145 Joaquin, Nick. "Guardia de Honor." *Philippines Free Press reader.* Manila: Philippines Free Press, 1968, pp. 54-55.
    Fiction, reprinted from the weekly.

1146 Jocano, F. Landa. "Filipino Catholicism: A case study in religious change." *Asian Studies* (Quezon City) 5, no. 1 (1967): 42-64.

A vivid, well-documented, and detailed account of folk Catholicism by an anthropologist; no "new movements," but reveals a popular alternative to such developments.

1147 Jocano, F. Landa. "Ideology and radical movements in the Philippines." In *Modernization in south-east Asia*, edited by H. D. Evers. Singapore: Oxford University Press, 1973, pp. 199-222.

1148 Jose, F. Sionil. "The betrayal of the masses." *Solidarity* (Manila) 1, no. 4 (1966): 1-10.

P. 6, on Pedro Calosa, leader of the Colorum rising at Tayug in Pangasinan.

1149 Kavanagh, Joseph J. "Hilario Camino Moncado." *Philippine Studies Quarterly* 4, no. 3 (1956): 433-40.

An obituary article, with history of his periodicals, and much useful information.

1150 Keesing, Felix Maxwell, and Keesing, Marie. *Taming Philippine headhunters: A study of government and culture change in northern Luzon*. London: George Allen & Unwin; Stanford: Stanford University Press, 1934, 288 pp., illus., maps.

Pp. 231-32, Sapilada belief in new indigenous movements in north Luzon. Cited in F. Eggan, et al. (entry 1082), p. 97.

1151 King, Victor T. Review of *Popular uprisings in the Philippines*, by D. R. Sturtevant (entry 1263). *Modern Asian Studies* 12, no. 1 (1978): 168-72.

Critical of the explanation in terms of cultural alienation, and conflicts between Little and Great Traditions, as ignoring sociological factors such as class, status, distribution of political power, and economic deprivation.

1152 *K. M. P. Tidings* (Journal of the Iglesia ni Cristo youth organization, Kapisanang Maligayang Pagtatagumpay ["Happy Triumph Association"]).

The youth organization functions similarly to the Y.M.C.A. and Y.W.C.A.

1153 Lanternari, Vittorio. *The religions of the oppressed: A study of modern messianic cults*. London: MacGibbon & Kee, 1963, xx + 343 + xiii pp.

Southeast: The Philippines

Toronto: New American Library of Canada, 1963. New York: Knopf, 1963. New York: Mentor Books, 1965, xvi + 286 pp.

Pp. 221-23 (Mentor ed.; pp. 277-80 in MacGibbon & Kee ed.), brief survey from Apolinario de la Cruz to the Philippine Independent Church and Colorums.

1154 Larkin, John A. *The Pampangans: Colonial society in a Philippine province*. Berkeley: University of California Press, 1972, xvii + 340 pp., illus.

Pp. 234-39, brief but good treatment of Salvador's Santa Iglesia, 1902-10; pp. 180-81, 223, Philippine Independent Church.

1155 Latourette, Kenneth Scott. *A history of the expansion of Christianity.* Vol. 5, *The great century in the Americas, Australasia, and Africa, A.D. 1800-A.D. 1914.* New York: Harper & Brothers; London: Eyre & Spottiswoode, 1943, 470 pp., bib.

Pp. 267-68, Philippine Independent Church; p. 268, Colorum movements; p. 269, Guardia de Honor and Tungud.

1156 Lava, Jesus, and Araneta, Antonio. *Faith healing and psychic surgery in the Philippines*. Manila: Philippine Society for Psychical Research, 1982.

1157 Lee, David C. "Some reflections about the Cofradia de San Jose as a Philippine religious uprising." *Asian Studies* (Quezon City) 9, no. 2 (1971): 126-43.

1158 Lema, Lerma S. de. "The Pantay-Pantay community of Baraguis, Legaspi City: A study of a messianic movement." Research paper (for Anthropology 151, Dr. G. Oosterwal), Andrews University (Berrien Springs, Mich.), 28 March 1968, 13 pp. Typescript.
Within the Watawat ng Lahi, or "Banner of the Race Church."

1159 Leon, Anna Leah S. de. "The mystical city in Mt Banahaw: The Gospel, according to Maria Bernarda Balitan, is that since God became woman in 1876, we are now living in the Age of Woman." *Philippine Panorama* (Manila), 8 August 1982, pp. 14, 16-21, illus.

1160 Le Roy, James Alfred. *Philippine life in town and country: Our Asiatic neighbours*. New York: G. P. Putnam's Sons, 1905, 311 pp., illus., maps.
Pp. 120-36, "fanatical, superstitious and criminal elements" in such movements as Guardia de Honor, Colorums, etc.; pp. 161-68, hostile account of the Philippine Independent Church, but see P. S. de

Achutegui and M. A. Bernad (entry 1519) vol. 1, pp. 232-33, on his later changed views on Aglipayanism.

1161 Locsin, Teodoro M. "Felix Manalo – or one foot in heaven." *Philippines Free Press* 41, no. 6 (11 February 1950): 2-3, illus.
An interview with the founder of Iglesia ni Cristo.

1162 Lopez, Salvatore P.; Lansang, Jose A.; and Intengan, Jesus Ma. "From farce to tragedy: A history of the rise and fall of Sakdalism." *Philippines Herald Magazine*, 11 May 1935.

1163 Love, Robert S. "The Samahan of Papa God: Tradition and conversion in a Tagalog peasant religious movement." Ph.D. dissertation (anthropology), Cornell University, 1977, 356 pp.
Besides Samahan of Papa God, passim, see pp. 45, 46-49, 52, Iglesia ni Cristo; p. 46, long n. 20, Philippine Independent Church as still appealing to peasants; p. 41ff., Ma Dimas, reviver of Adoracion Nocturna Filipina in 1954 as pious association; p. 60, Lapiang Malaya revolt, 1967; p. 61, Samahan movements (true indigenous religion) as including Rizalists; pp. 62, 67-69, Inang Mahiwaga, a branch of Bathalismo; p. 64 a Samahan called Iglesia Bundok ng Kabanalan (Church of the Mountain of Holiness); chap. 4 (pp. 215-66), the search for secret truth.

1164 Lynch, Frank. "Organized religion in the Philippines." In *Area handbook on the Philippines*, edited by F. Eggan. University of Chicago Human Relations Area Files, preliminary ed., 4 vols., 1955.
Vol. 2, chap. 9 (pp. 471-744), "Organized religion"; pp. 476-686, Catholicism; pp. 687-717, Aglipayanism; pp. 718-29, Iglesia ni Cristo; pp. 730-44, Protestantism.

1165 Macaraig, Serafin Egmidio. *Social problems*. Manila: Educational Supply Co., 1929, 431 pp.
Chap. 30 (pp. 407-21), secret societies; p. 409, Pulajanes and their Iglesia Catolica Indepencia Romana; pp. 409-10, Colorums.

1166 McCoy, Alfred W[illiam]. "Ylo-Ilo: Factional conflict in a colonial economy, Iloilo Province, Philippines, 1937-1955." 2 vols. Ph.D. dissertation (Asian history), Yale University, 1977, 829 pp.

1167 Malay, Paulina Carolina. "Filipiniana: Rizal as a saint." *Weekly Women's Magazine* 3, no. 44 (5 March 1954): 33.

Southeast: The Philippines

Many towns have "Banal sects" that venerate Rizal. Lespagi City
has "Pantay-Pantay society" ("Rizalinos") with anniversary procession
and a kind of mass at Rizal's monument. Some "colorum sects" also
venerate Rizal (e.g., Tabayas, Quezon, at the foot of Mt. Banashaw,
has a Rizal chapel; and the "Rizalina" sect in Barrio Caluluan,
Concepcion, Tarlac, has a "nunnery" for its priestesses, who are first
trained in rituals.

1168 Manila, Quijano de. "Apocalypse in Cabuan." *Philippines Free Press* 62,
no. 51 (20 December 1969): 6-7, 64-66, illus.
Guardia de Honor in the 1890s.

1169 Manila, Quijano de. "When God built Zion in Pangasinan Hills."
Philippines Free Press 62, no. 50 (13 December 1969): 2-3, 84, 86-88,
illus.

1170 Mantubia, Eribato. "Preliminary studies on the Lola Maria and her
mission." *Philippine Priests' Forum* (Manila) 8, no. 2 (1976): 39-43.
In Barrio Pantao, Libon, Albay. Lola ("Grandmother") [Elena
Omelin, b. 1951] was cured by the Virgin Mary and since 1973 has
healed others (while she is possessed by the Virgin Mary) and
composed native hymns. She is accepted by Fr. Mantubia (her parish
priest) and so represents a movement not separated from the Church.

1171 Maquiso, Elena G. "The Langkat: Its relationship to the Ulahingan."
Silliman Journal 17, no. 4 (1970).
A religious healing movement among the Manobos in Cotabato,
founded by Mampurok in 1928. He claimed to fulfill the Manobo epic,
Ulahingan. Some Muslim members.

1172 Marasigan, Vicente. *A Banahaw guru: Symbolic deeds of Agapito
Illustrisimo.* Quezon City: Ateneo de Manila University Press, 1985,
190 pp., illus.
On the teachings of Illustrisimo, founder of the Samahan ng
Tatlong Persona Solo Dios in 1936, based on sacred Mt. Banahaw; pp.
47-58, illustrations; pp. 59-129 (in Tagalog) and pp. 129-90 (in English),
the movement's own account of the history of its founder. By a Jesuit
scholar who lived with the movement.

1173 Marasigan, Vicente. "Grass roots pentecostalism." *Philippine Priests'
Forum* (Manila) 7, no. 3 (1975): 61-65.
On Mang Bernabe, a "Catholic shaman" (so described by the
author, a priest)—a "dissolute womaniser" becomes healer and loyal

Catholic shoemaker, accepted within his local Catholic parish. Theoretical discussion of possession, etc. An example of a movement remaining within the church in an ancillary way.

1174 Marasigan, Vicente. *Paglalakbay sa Banahaw* [Pilgrim's guidelines].
In Tagalog and English. A booklet by a Jesuit scholar of the Loyola School of Theology, Ateneo de Manila University. A guide to the shrines and movements.

1175 Marasigan, Vicente. "Southeast Asian shamanism: Liturgical dramatization." *East Asian Pastoral Review* 20, no. 4 (1983): 353-56.
A case study of Tatlong Persona Solo Dios (Three Persons One God) on Mt. Banahaw–a spirit-possession movement founded by Agapito Illustrisismo.

1176 Marche, Alfred. *Lucon et Palaouan: Six années de voyages aux Philippines*. Paris: Librairie Hachette et Cie., 1887. English translation. *Luzon and Palawan*. Manila: Filipiniana Book Guild, 1970, 296 pp., illus.
A French explorer of the 1880s, cited and used by R. C. Ileto (entry 1140), Pp. 78-87 on Apolinario de la Cruz and the Mt. Banahaw pilgrimages; pp. 111-13 of the French original on Apolinario de la Cruz and Mt. Banahaw.

1177 Marquez, Socorro. "The mysteries of Banahaw." *College Folio* (University of the Philippines) 3, no. 1 (1912): 2-4.

1178 Martinez, Gloria Sales. "A strange and awesome Christian movement." *Weekly Graphic* (Manila) 32, no. 25 (15 December 1965): 137.
The Cursillo movement within the Roman Catholic Church, introduced from Spain by two American members; personal testimonies useful for comparative purposes between internal revival and independent movements.

1179 Mas y Sans, Sinobaldo de. *Informe sobre el estudo de las Islas Filipinas en 1842*. Vols. 1 and 2. Madrid: N.p., 1843. Vol. 3, *Politica interior*. Unpublished and restricted circulation. Reprint of vol. 3 (with English translation, pp. 111-215, by C. Botor). Manila: Historical Conservation Society, 1963, 215 pp. Also in *The Philippine islands 1493-1898*, edited by E. H. Blair and J. A. Robertson. Vol. 52. Cleveland: A. H. Clark, 1963.
Vol. 1, pp. 59-64 in second set of pagination–the best contemporary account of the original Colorum movement in the 1815

Southeast: The Philippines

rising; vol. 3, a secret report on social ills in 1842, with the Tayabas revolt as one symptom – pp. 114-15 and note on pp. 134-35, Apolinario de la Cruz (in Blair and Robertson, pp. 92-93 and note 37).

1180 Matta, Juan Manuel de la. "Apolinario de la Cruz: Relacion en que se da cuenta de haber estallado la conspiracion en Tayabas." 16 November 1841. Chicago, Newberry Library, Ayer Collection (Shelf 1373). Manuscript.
The official government report on the Tayabas revolt.

1181 Mayo, Katherine. *The isles of fear: The truth about the Philippines*. New York: Harcourt Brace & Co., 1925, 372 pp., illus., map.
Pp. 181-83, Cabruan town and Guardia de Honor; pp. 188ff., 194, a Rizalist cult in 1924 among the self-styled "colorums sect" of Surigao, led by Lantayag, with Sococo village as the "Holy City," and suppressed by military action.

1182 Medina, Juan de. *Historia de los sucesos de la Orden de n. gran. P. S. Augustin de estas islas filipinas. . . .* Vol. 1. Manila: Chofre y comp., 1893, 489 pp. (Originally written in 1630).
An Augustinian missionary in the Philippines, 1610-35. Pp. 226-28 (original), the nativistic revolt of 1620 on Bohol and Leyte, under Tamblot.

1183 Meek, George W., et al. "Paranormal healing in the Philippines." In *Healers and the healing process*, edited by G. W. Meek. Wheaton, Ill., London, and Madras: Theosophical Publishing House, 1977, pp. 59-127.
Features Josefine Sison (N. Luzon); Felisa Macanas (N. Luzon); a team of Romy and Joe Bugarin, Jose Mercado, and Marcelo Jainer treating a party of 39 New Zealanders in Manila; Tony Agpaoa of Baguio City.

1184 Meek, George W., ed. "A study of psychic surgery and spiritual healing in the Philippines." Part 1 of a projected 3-part study. Fort Meyers, Fla.: George W. Meek & Associates, July 1973, no pagination, many color photographs. Limited photocopied issue.
A report by a team of Western scholars or professional people, assisted by nine Filipino healers and the (spiritist?) Churches with which they are associated, mostly within Kardecist influence, since the Union Spiritista Cristina Filipinas of 1905. Intended as one part of a doctoral dissertation. Copy held in the Centre, Selly Oak Colleges.

1185 Mendoza, Conrado. "Ex-Colorum becomes charcoal dealer." *Philippines Free Press*, 20 September 1958, p. 46, illus.
"General" Pedro Calosa as peaceful farmer and charcoal dealer in Tayug, still waiting for his land-tenure papers.

1186 Mercado, Leonardo N. "Notes on Christ and local community in Philippine context." *Verbum (SVD)* 21, nos. 3-4 (1980): 303-15.
Pp. 305-9, Christology in Iglesia Watawat ng Lahi, the Moncadistas (of Hilario Moncado), and the Philippine Benevolent Missionaries Association, Inc.; pp. 309-11, folk Christianity.

1187 Mercado, Leonardo N., ed. *Filipino religious psychology*. Tacloban City: Divine Word University Publications, 1977, xxi + 224 pp.
See A. L. Velez (entry 1285), P. R. Covar (entry 1063), M. A. C. Guanzon (entry 1431), F. R. Falcon (entry 1092), E. A. Pastores (entry 1211). See also the articles contributed by the editor, and pp. 173-79, conclusions; pp. 192-207, Philippine Benevolent Missionary Association's "Mission Laws" (in Tagalog).

1188 Mercado, Monina Allarey. "The little religions." *Graphic* 33, no. 39 (22 March 1967): 21-23.
Cults in the Philippines.

1189 Methodist Episcopal Church. *Annual report of the Board of Foreign Missions of the Methodist Episcopal Church*. New York: Board of Foreign Missions of the Methodist Episcopal Church, 1909.
P. 67, report of the effects of the Zamora secession.

1190 Moncado, Hilario Camino. *Divinity of woman, her superiority over man*. Los Angeles: Filipino Federation of America, 1927, 76 pp., illus.
Pp. 8-14, biographical sketch of the author, by W. J. Schaefle.

1191 Moncado, Hilario Camino. *Moncado speaks*. Rosarito, Mexico: The author, 1955, 34 pp.
A chronological autobiography in outline; pp. 11-20 cover his relations with the Filipino Federation of America.

1192 Moncado, Hilaro Camino. [Various listings of publications on political issues, travel, etc.]. In *National Union Catalog of Pre-1956 Imprints*, vol. 390. London and Chicago: Mansell; American Library Association, 1975, p. 493.

Southeast: The Philippines

1193 Moncado, Hilario Camino, ed. *Filipino Nation* (Los Angeles, Filipino Publishing Co.), 1924-33.
A journal of the Filipino Federation of America, formerly called *Equifrilibricum* and later the *Modernist*.

1194 *Moncado Mission Bulletin*.
A small monthly, 1955-, related to Hilario Camino Moncado, published in Hawaii. Discussed and used in J. J. Kavanagh (entry 1149).

1195 Montero y Vidal, Jose. *Historia general de Filipinas, desde el descubrimiento de dichas islas hasta nuestros dias*. 3 vols. Madrid: M. Tello, 1887-95.
Vol. 3, pp. 37-55, Apolinario de la Cruz. A basic historical work.

1196 Montgomery, James H., and McGavran, Donald A. *The discipling of a nation*. Santa Clara, Calif.: Global Church Growth Bulletin, 1980, 175 pp.
Pp. 117-19, Iglesia Evangelica Metodista en las Islas Filipinas – outline of its growth.

1197 Motoyama, Hiroshi. *Psychic surgery in the Philippines*. Tokyo: Institute of Religious Psychology.
Emphasizes the religious element.

1198 Munger, Henry W. *Christ and the Filipino soul*. Bowling Green, Mo., 1967.
Pp. 28-31, on Juan Perfecto's and subsequent Pulahan movement from the 1870s to 1901; by an American Baptist missionary.

1199 Murillo Velarde, Pedro. *Historia general de la provincia de Philipinas de la compania de Jesus: Segunda parte desde el ano de 1616, hasta el de 1716*. Manila: N. de la Cruz Bagay, 1749, 419 pp., illus., map.
Pp. 17-18, fol. 17, the nativistic revolt under Tamblot in 1620 on the islands of Bohol and Leyte. A Jesuit historian's account; fol. 18, Bankaw's revolt, 1621.

1200 Nayas, Ramon. "The strength of the poor." *Philippines Free Press*, 21 April 1923, pp. 4-5.
Various peasant religious movements of the time.

1201 Ofrenia, R. E. "On folk Christianity." *U. P. Newsletter* (University of the Philippines) 3, no. 12 (March 1975): 2, 7.

Review article on P. R. Covar's unpublished "Philippine folk Christianity" (entry 1061).

1202 Olaes, Rodolfo O. "A critical study of Rizal's early religious thought: From his early years until the end of his period of study in Madrid." B.D. thesis, Union Theological Seminary (Dasmarinas, Cavite, Philippines), 1966, 80 pp.

Stresses that Rizal's religious ideas "were not really corrupted by European influences," but that he had criticised Roman Catholicism before he left for Europe.

1203 Oldham, William F. "The Zamora defection." *Philippine Christian Advocate* (Manila) 8, no. 3 (March 1909): 3-5.

A contemporary comment on the first Methodist secession, founding the IEMELIF church.

1204 Olson, William H. *Beyond the plains: A sudy of the northern Cotabato Manobos*. Manila: Christian Institute for Ethnic Studies, 1967, 49 pp., illus.

Pp. 12-13, the *langkat* (convert) sect, founded by Manporok in the 1920s; revived in the 1960s with Kerenan as the Supreme Being.

1205 Oosterwal, Gottfried. "Messianic movements." *Philippine Sociological Review* 16, nos. 1-2 (1968): 40-50.

1206 Pacis, Vicente A. "A key to Rizal cult revival." *Graphic* 31 (16 June 1961): 9-10.

1207 Pal, Agaton P. "The people's conception of the world." *University of Manila Journal of East Asian Studies*, 5 October 1960, pp. 390-98. Reprinted in *Social foundations of community development*, edited by S. C. Espiritu and C. L. Hunt. Manila: R. M. Garcia Publishing House, 1964, 684 pp.

1208 Palazon, Juan. *Majayjay: How a town came into being*. Manila: Historical Conservation Society, 1964, 216 pp. (pp. 27-110 in Tagalog, pp. 113-84 in Spanish; pp. 9-24, English summary), illus.

Pp. 18-19, Apolinario de la Cruz (in English), with pp. 81-84, full text (in Tagalog), and also pp. 159-62 (in Spanish).

1209 Pascricha, Josephine A. "Jose Rival as Filipino Christ and messenger of God." *Sports-TV-Movies Parade*, 30 December 1979, pp. 10-11.

Southeast: The Philippines

1210 Pascual, Ricardo R[oque]. "The religion of Rizal." *Historical Bulletin* (Philippine Historical Association) 3, no. 4 (1959): 1-22.

Neither Catholic nor Protestant, nor identified with any indigenous religion; he was a free-thinking, rationalist believer in God.

1211 Pastores, Elizabeth A. "Religious leadership in the Lapiang Malaya: A historical note." In *Filipino religious psychology*, edited by L. N. Mercado. Tacloban City: Divine Word University Publications, 1977, pp. 149-65, and discussion, pp. 166-72.

1212 Patanne, E. P. "A round-up of religious rebels." *Sunday Times Magazine* (Manila), 18 June 1967, pp. 20-21.

Lapiang Malaya uprisings of 1966-67, as a current example of ancient peasant revolts.

1213 Phelan, John Leddy. *The hispanization of the Philippines: Spanish aims and Filipino responses, 1565-1700*. Madison: University of Wisconsin Press, 1959, 218 pp. (pp. 199-206, bibliographical essay), illus., maps.

Pp. 78-84, syncretism; chap. 10, "patterns of resistance" – pp. 147-48 on seventeenth-century risings (Pangasinan, Bohol, and Leyte), and p. 198, n. 16, four sources (in Spanish).

1214 "The Philippines." *Pro Mundi Vita* (Brussels) 30 (1970): 40 pp. Reprinted in the Philippines as *The Philippines: The church in an unfinished society*. N.p., n.d., 69 pp.

Pp. 20-21 (pp. 31-33 in reprint), "other religious groups and sects" – a survey.

1215 Pimental, Margot. "Unveiling the mysteries of the holy mountain." *Sunburst* (Manila) 4, no. 10 (1976): 30-33, illus.

On a documentary film on Mt. Banahaw featuring Tres Personas Solo Dios (1936-) and Ciudad Mistica de Dios (1911-).

1216 Pimentel, Narciso, Jr. "Behind the Lapiang Malaya massacre." *Graphic*, 20 June 1967.

1217 Polotan, Kerinia. "The other Christians." *Philippines Free Press* 58, no. 18 (1965): 5, 87-93, illus.

Pp. 89-92, Philippine Independent Church; pp. 92-93, Iglesia ni Cristo.

1218 Polotan, Kerinia. "Tatang and the Lapiang Malaya." *Philippines Free Press* 60, no. 22 (1967): 2-3, 66-67, illus.

1219 Pope, Jean. "Tatangs unhappy end." *Sunday Times Magazine* (Manila), 10 September 1967, pp. 26-29.

1220 Punongbayan, M. R. "Si Kristo sa Judea, Dito'y Sina Rizal." *Asia-Philippine Leader* 1, no. 2 (1971): 33-35, 46, illus.

1221 Raterta, Pedro. "A critical evaluation of the religious ideas of Jose Rizal as found in the English translation of his works." B.D. thesis, Union Theological Seminary (Dasmarinas, Cavite), 1957.

1222 Regaldo, Felix B., and Franco, Quintan B. *History of Panay*. Jaro, Iloilo City: Central Philippine University, 1973, 593 pp., illus., bib.
        Pp. 118-20, Tapara's new religion and revolt, 1633; pp. 316-20, Philippine Independent Church, especially since 1945; pp. 320-23, Iglesia ni Cristo, and its move into Panay.

1223 Reilly, Henry. "Filipino bandit terror in Luzon – career of Felipe Salvador shows danger of such uprisings in Islands – tools for native boss." *Chicago Tribune*, 2 August 1914.
        A feature article on the founder of Santa Iglesia – cited and used by R. C. Ileto (entry 1140), pp. 259ff.

1224 Requiza, Moreno C. "A preliminary report of the Katatiran ng Mga Maka-Apo." Research paper for Dr. G. Oosterval, Andrews University (Berrien Springs, Mich.), [late 1960s], 39 pp. Typescript.
        On the "Brotherhood of Believers of the Apo" or "Brotherhood of the Love of God." Copy in the Centre, Selly Oak Colleges.

1225 Rewick, Kenneth O. "Moncado: A study in charismatic leadership." N.p., [1964], 32 + 3 pp., illus. with newspaper cuttings and other items (7 pp.), and Moncado commemoration banquet (3 May 1962) program (15 pp.), photocopy of typescript, tipped in.
        A scholarly account of the founder of the Filipino Federation of America. Copy in University of Hawaii Asia collection.

1226 Reyes, Lorenzo Delos. *Every day new and wonder*. Los Angeles: Filipino Nation Magazine Press, 1931, illus.
        A mystical exposition of the Filipino Federation of America, emphasizing judgment and eschatology and the five essential doctrines.

1227 Reyes [y Florentino], Isabelo de los, [Sr.]. *Apuntes para un ensayo de teodicea filipina: La religión del "Katipúnan," o sea la antigua de los Filipinos*. Madrid: J. Corrales, 1899, 39 pp. 2d ed. 1900, 64 pp., illus.

Southeast: The Philippines

English translation. *Religion of the Katipunan*, translated by J. Revilla. Manila, 1953.

On the "liberal (new) religion based on ancient Filipino worship of the god Bathala," and incorporating an array of nineteenth-century liberal ideas.

1228 Reyes [y Florentino], Isabelo de los, [Sr.]. *El folk-lore Filipino*. 2 vols. Biblioteca La España oriental. Vol. 1, Manila: Chofrey y Cia, 1889, 345 pp.; vol. 2, Manila: Impr. de Santa Cruz, 1890, 300 pp.

Vol. 1, pp. 258-66, "Dios Diosan"–summaries of movements, especially in his own time: p. 260, Dupungay (1559), Tapar (1673), a "babalayan," and Apolinario de la Cruz, pp. 266ff., Lungao (1811), "Ludovic I" (1881), Maria Santissima (1886), etc.

1229 Ricarte, Artemio. *Memoirs of General Artemio Ricarte*. Manila: National Heroes Commission, 1963, 242 pp., illus.

Translated from the Tagalog original by a Katipunero. Pp. 82-84, on the Colorums. Cited by R. C. Ileto (entry 1140), p. 92; see also p. 252, n. 67 on significance of Ricarte.

1230 Rich, John A. "Pinatikan: Religious tattoos in a Davao sect." *Philippine Sociological Review* 16, nos. 3-4 (1968): 196.

Tattoos in many parts of body, each associated with Latin prayer phrases as sources of power in the Holy Stone of the Catholic Apostolic Church of Holy Spirit in Mati, Davao Oriental.

1231 Rich, John A. "Religious acculturation in the Philippines." *Political Anthropology* 17, no. 5 (1970): 196-209.

P. 205, Tungud movement of Meskinan, based on J. M. Garvan (entry 1108).

1232 Robb, Walter. "What ho, the Guard!" *American Chamber of Commerce Journal* (Manila) 11 (February 1931): 3, 18, 25-26.

Strong comment by the journal's editor on the performance of the constabulary in relation to peace and order and to the Tayug Colorums.

1233 Roces, Alejandro R. "I write as I write: 'Iglesia' support grossly overestimated." *Manila Chronicle* 23, no. 213 (20 November 1967): 5.

Iglesia ni Cristo's political strength.

1234 Rodgers, James [Burton]. *Forty years in the Philippines: A history of the Philippine mission of the Presbyterian Church of the United States of*

America. New York: Board of Foreign Missions of the Presbyterian Church in the United States of America, 1940, 205 pp.

By the head of the first Presbyterian mission, friendly to the early Aglipayans – see pp. 19-23, 25, Aglipay's assistance to Rodgers; p. 33, Zamora's independent Methodist church; p. 176, ex-Presbyterian Iglesia de los Cristianos Filipinos; chap. 22 (pp. 176-80), the independent churches and a union among them; pp. 179-80, 183-84, Iglesia ni Cristo; p. 184, Mt. San Cristobal "Holy Voices" gathering.

1235 Romero, Ma. Fe Hernaez. *Negros Occidental between two foreign powers (1888-1909).* Bacolod: Enterprise Publications for the Negros Occidental Historical Commission, 1974, 336 pp., illus., maps.

Pp. 168-72, Babaylanes under Papa Isio (the more religious aspects); pp. 219-35, Aglipayanism.

1236 Sancho, Manuel. *Relacion expresiva de los principales acontecimientos de la titulada Cofradia del Senor San Jose.* First published in *La politica de Espana en Filipines,* by W. E. Retana, 2, no. 21 (1892): 250-51; no. 23 (1892): 289-91; no. 25 (1892): 18-19; no. 26 (1892): 30-32; no. 29 (1892): 74-75; no. 31 (1892): 99-101.

Apolinario's Confraternity of San Jose. The most detailed information available, although biased.

1237 San Juan, Epifanio, Jr. "Towards Rizal – an interpretation of Noli me tangere and El Filibusterismo." *Solidarity* (Manila) 5, no. 12 (1970): 8-28.

1238 S[an]ta-Romana, Mariano. "The Lapiang Malaya and Philippine independence." *Far Eastern Freemason* 48 (1967): 30-33.

1239 Santos, A. B. "Why they rampaged: Peasants in arms." *Asia Magazine* (Hong Kong) 7, no. 35 (1967): 7-10.

A millennial peasant synthesist movement among Tagalog led by Valentin de los Santos, clashing with the Marcos government in 1967.

1240 Santos, Ben, photographer. "What's left of the Moncado colony in Marawi City." *Sunday Times Magazine* (Manila) 18, no. 10 (14 October 1962): 18-19, illus.

1241 Santos, Jose Paez. *A ng tatlong na "tulisan" sa Pilipinas.* Gerona: Tarlak [?], 1936, 79 pp., illus.

Southeast: The Philippines

Includes J. Hernandez (d. 1877), Tangkad Filipe Salvador (1870-1912); pp. 9-27, Apo Ipe and his Santa Iglesia – and M. L. Sakay (1870-1907).

1242 Santos, Ramon P. "The ritual music of the Iglesia del Ciudad Mistica de Dios: A preliminary report." *Asian Studies* (Quezon City) 13, no. 2 (1975): 93-117.

A movement with headquarters on Mt. Banahaw.

1243 Sarkisyanz, Emanuel. "Longing for lost primeval bliss as revolutionary expectation on both sides of the Pacific: Millennialism in crisis in Peru and the Philippines." Paper presented at European Regional Conference, New Ecumenical Research Association, June 1984, Waggis, Switzerland, 16 pp. Computer printout.

Pp. 9-13, the Philippines: Bonifacio, Rizalistas, Colorums and Katipunan, folk-Marxists. Peru section published separately. Copy in the Centre, Selly Oak Colleges.

1244 Schaefle, William J. *Moncado and his mission*. Los Angeles: Filipino Federation of America Press, 1928.

An apologia by Moncado's press agent.

1245 Schlegel, Stuart L. "The Upi Espiristas: A case study in cultural adjustment." *Journal for the Scientific Study of Religion* 4, no. 2 (1965): 198-212, bib.

A special cult group within the Episcopal (Anglican) Church in Upi valley, Mindanao; the inadequacy of sociological explanations.

1246 Scott, William Henry. "The *Apo Dios* concept in northern Luzon." *Philippine Studies* (Manila) 8, no. 4 (1960: 772-88. Reprinted in *On the Cordillera*. Manila: M. C. S. Enterprises, pp. 123-43. Reprinted in *Practical Anthropology* 8, no. 5 (1961): 207-16. Also in *Acculturation in the Philippines*, edited by P. Gowing and W. H. Scott. Quezon City: New Day Press, 1971, pp. 117-27.

The relation between the primal and the Christian conceptions of God; the Supreme God, Apo-Dios, has taken the culture hero and the divinities as subjects.

1247 Sherman, Harold. *"Wonder" healers of the Philippines*. Los Angeles and London: Psychic Press, 1966. Reprint. California: DeVorss, [1967], 1974, 339 pp.

Pp. 168-231, includes Tony Agpaoa.

1248 Shoesmith, Dennis. "The glorious religion of Jose Rizal: Radical consciousness in a contemporary folk religious movement in the southern Philippines." In *Peasants and politics: Grass roots reaction to change in Asia*, edited by D. B. Miller. London: Edward Arnold, 1979, pp. 149-79; also p. 5, editorial comment.
　　　Politico-social ideas, internal tensions, and religious content.

1249 Sitoy, T. Valentino, Jr. "The search for unity among non-Roman Christians in the Philippines." *Silliman Journal* (Dumaguete City) 12, no. 2 (1965): 196-210.
　　　P. 196 lists "queer-sounding sects"; pp. 199-200, Iglesia ni Cristo; pp. 205-6, Philippine independent Church. By a Protestant theologian.

1250 Smart, John E. "The Manolay cult: The genesis and dissolution of millenarian sentiments among the Isneg of northern Luzon." *Asian Studies* (Quezon City) 8, no. 1 (1970): 53-93.
　　　Neoprimal movement, flourishing 1937-39, contrasted with the Sapilada and Guardia de Honor movements.

1251 Sobrepena, Enrique C. *That they may be one*. Manila: United Church of Christ, [1954], 140 pp.
　　　Pp. 23-27, Philippine Independent Church and seven secessions from it; pp. 27-29, Zamora's secession and later divisions; pp. 29-30, Presbyterian division; pp. 30-31, further Methodist divisions; pp. 31-38, other new groups and locally founded churches.

1252 [Society of Jesus.] *Cartas de los Padres de la Compagnia de Jesus de la Mision de Filipinas*. Vols. 2-10. Manila: Colegio de Santo Tomas, 1877-95.
　　　Vol. 9 (1891), pp. 533, etc., letters from Fr. Pastels (1877) and Fr. Urios (1879) reporting apocalyptic movements with neglect of farming among the Manobo on Mindanao. Extracts in J. M. Garvan (entry 1108), pp. 239-40.

1253 Somera, Rene D. "Pamumuwesto of Mount Banahaw." *Philippine Studies* 34 (1986): 436-51.

1254 Steinberg, David Joel. "An ambiguous legacy: Years of war in the Philippines." *Pacific Affairs* 45, no. 2 (1972): 165-90.

1255 Steinberg, David Joel. *The Philippines: A singular and a plural place*. Boulder, Colo.: Westview Press, 1982, 160 pp.

Southeast: The Philippines

Pp. 63-78, historical outline of religion and recent visit of the Pope – the Independent Church, millennial and Rizalist movements.

1256 Stevenson, Dwight E[shelman]. *Christianity in the Philippines: A report on the only Christian nation of the Orient*. Lexington, Ky.: College of the Bible, 1955, 48 pp.
Pp. 15-18, the Aglipay movement; pp. 30-31, Methodist and Presbyterian schisms; pp. 31-33, Iglesia ni Cristo.

1257 Stubbs, Roy Manning. "Philippine radicalism: The central Luzon uprisings, 1925-1935." Ph.D. dissertation (history), University of California at Berkeley, 1951, 225 pp.
Four peasant uprisings: pp. 24-53, Pedro Kabola's Kapisanan Makabola Makasinag, secret society, 1925; pp. 54-93, Pedro Calosa's Colorum sect at Tayung, 1931 – semireligious; pp. 94-125, P. Dionisio and V. Almazar's secret society, the Tangulan, with 40,000 members in 1941; pp. 126-200, B. Ramos's Sakdalism, with 150,000 members, 1933-35. The Colorum study is a valuable account, using archival sources.

1258 Stuntz, Homer C[lyde]. *The Philippines and the Far East*. Cincinnati: Jennings & Pye; New York: Easton & Mains, 1904, 514 pp., illus.
Pp. 342, 392, and chap. 29 (pp. 488-96), the Aglipayan movement; p. 381, on the Anting-Anting shirt as impervious to bullets. By a Methodist bishop.

1259 Sturtevant, David R[eeves]. *Agrarian unrest in the Philippines: Guardia de Honor and Rizalistas*. Papers in International Studies, Southern Asia Series, 8. Athens: Ohio University Center for International Studies, South East Asia Program, 1969, vi + 30 pp.
Pp. v-vi, preface by N. J. D. Versluys. Pp. 1-4, Guardia de Honor (for earlier, longer form see entry 1261). Pp. 18-30, revitalization movements, the millennial tradition and Rizalista sects (Lapiang Malaya, millennial movements from 1894, the "endless variations" of Rizalism); reprinted in *Society, culture, and the Filipino*, ed. M. R. Hollsteiner, et al. vol. 3 (Quezon City: Institute of Philippine Culture, Ateneo de Manila, 1973), pp. 478-83.

1260 Sturtevant, David Reeves. "Epilog for an old Colorum." *Solidarity* (Manila) 3 (1968): 10-18.

1261 Sturtevant, David R[eeves]. "Guardia de Honor: Revitalization within the revolution." *Asian Studies* (Quezon City) 4, no. 2 (1966): 342-52.
See entry 1259.

1262 Sturtevant, David R[eeves]. "Peasant unrest in the Philippines." In *The world of Southeast Asia*, edited by H. J. Benda and J. A. Larkin. New York: Harper & Row, 1967, pp. 164-69.
Interviews with captured adherents of the Sakdal movement.

1263 Sturtevant, David R[eeves]. *Popular uprisings in the Philippines*. Ithaca: Cornell University Press, 1976, 317 pp., maps, bib.
Chap. 4 (pp. 77-95), religious rebellions in the Philippines; chap. 5 (pp. 96-114), Guardia de Honor; chap. 6 (pp. 115-38), bandits and popes; chap. 7 (pp. 141-57), Colorumism; chap. 8 (pp. 158-74), millennial empire of Florencio I.

1264 Sturtevant, David R[eeves]. "Rural discord: The peasantry and nationalism." *Solidarity* (Manila) 7, no. 2 (1972): 27-41.
Pp. 30-36, movements with religious aspects; supernatural aspects faded after 1931 (failed revolt) but reappeared from the late 1950s.

1265 Sturtevant, David R[eeves]. "Sakdalism and Philippine radicalism." *Journal of Asian Studies* (Ann Arbor) 21 (1961-62): 199-213.

1266 Sweet, David. "A proto-political peasant movement in the Spanish Philippines: The Cofradia de San Jose and the Tayabas rebellion of 1841." *Asian Studies* (Quezon City) 8, no. 1 (1970): 94-119, map.

1267 "A sympathetic look at a zealous group." *Sunday Times Magazine* (Manila) 11 (8 January 1956): 20-23.
The Lapiang Malaya clashed with the government – thirty-four died in 1967 – the leader had taught them "a beautiful way to pray"; critical of Roman Catholic institution.

1268 Tabios, Aurora D. "The Watawat ng Lahi or Pantay-patay community of Buraguis, Legazpi City." M.A. thesis, Legazpi College, 1962.

1269 Thompson, David. "The Filipino Federation of America, Incorporated: A study in the natural history of an institution." *Social Process in Hawaii* (Honolulu) 7 (1941): 24-35.
Comprehensive account of the religio-political movement founded by Hilario Camino Moncado (b. 1893) among demoralized immigrants.

1270 Toliver, Ralph. "A preliminary inquiry into the history and growth of the church in the Philippines." Research project, School of World Mission, Fuller Theological Seminary (Pasadena), n.d., 185 pp.

Southeast: The Philippines

1271 Trivino, J. F. "Lessons from Cagbunga incident." *This Week: Magazine of the Sunday Chronicle* (Manila) 11 (15 January 1956): 5.
On Iglesia Watawat ng Lahi.

1272 Tuggy, Arthur [Leonard]. "I didn't ask you." *Conservative Baptist* (Wheaton, Ill.), Spring 1971, pp. 4-5.

1273 Tuggy, Arthur Leonard. *The Philippine church: Growth in a changing society.* Church Growth Series. Grand Rapids: Eerdmans, 1971, 191 pp.
Pp. 115-21, 143-45, Philippine Independent Church; pp. 145-47, 159, 166, 168, Iglesia ni Cristo; pp. 98-99, 105, Nicolas Zamora's schism.

1274 Tuggy, A[rthur] Leonard, and Toliver, Ralph. *Seeing the church in the Philippines.* Manila: O.M.F. Publishers, 1972, 172 + 19 pp.
Pp. 42-43, Philippine Independent Church; pp. 140-41, Iglesia ni Cristo; pp. D and E, Appendix B, 1960 census figures for these bodies by local areas.

1275 Tupas, Rodolfo G. "Don't go over to the LM side : Poverty and depression drive people to 'messiahs.'" *Sunday Times Magazine* (Manila), 18 June 1967, pp. 18-19.
Imaginary conversation between an intellectual and a peasant in the Lapiang Malaya movement.

1276 Tutay, Filemon V. "The 'Colorums' today." *Philippines Free Press* (Manila) 47, no. 49 (1956): 6-7, 179, illus.
A contemporary Colorum settlement of over two hundred members in a common "barracks," rejecting church buildings and living "for world peace," in Barrio San Isidro, San Luis, Pampanga, and recognizing Apo Asiong of Calamba, Laguna, as supreme head of all Colorums, with supernatural powers.

1277 Tutay, Filemon V. "From 'Papa' to 'Tatang.'" *Philippines Free Press* 60, no. 23 (10 June 1967): 4, 95-99, illus. Reprinted in *A Free Press reader,* 1968, pp. 30-39.
Self-appointed leaders claiming supernatural powers, in Colorum and similar movements – pope Rios; the 1924 Surigao movement; Pedro Cabula, 1925-31; Sakdalistas, 1930s-1945; Pulehans and pope Faustino on Leyte, 1902-7; pope Pabla on Samar, 1903-6; "Emperor" Entrecherado on Iloilo, 1906-27; Lapiang Malaya of Tatung Valentin, 1950s-1964.

1278 United States Government, Department of the Army. *Area handbook for the Philippines*, edited by N. Vreeland. Foreign Area Studies, American University. DA Pam 550-72. 2d ed. Washington, D.C.: Government Printing Office, 1976, 455 pp.

Pp. 179-85, "indigenous Christian cults" (Aglipayanism, pp. 180-83; Iglesia ni Cristo, pp. 183-84); pp. 185-87, Islam; pp. 188-89, Protestant schisms.

1279 United States Government, Department of the Army. *Reports of the Philippine Commission to the Secretary of War.* [Report year irregular and title varies.] 32 vols. Washington, D.C.: Government Printing Office, 1901-16.

Various information (e.g., 1902, vol. 2, pp. 71f., the Colorums at Mt. Cristobal; 1905, vol. 1, pp. 19-20, 1906, vol. 1, pp. 66-67, 1907, vol. 1, p. 58, on the litigation, 1902-8, between Catholic and Independent churches over property – resolved in favor of the former.

1280 Urgena, Cynthia B. "The Colorum uprising of Pangasinan." M.A. thesis (history), University of the Philippines, 1960, 102 pp., illus.

Under Pedro Calosa, an Ilocano, in 1931.

1281 Uyan, Vezancio. "The Espiritista movement in Mayayao, Ifugao Mountain Province." *Proceedings of the Baguio Religious Acculturation Conference, January 1958.* Baguio, 1958, pp. 3-5.

Also includes an account of a conversion of a municipality from tribal religion to Union Espiritista Christiana Filipinos.

1282 Valentine, Tom. *Psychic surgery*. Chicago: Henry Regenery [*sic.*] Co., 1973, 157 pp.

Includes full account of Tony Agpaoa of the Philippines.

1283 Van der Bent, Ans J., ed. *Handbook: Member churches*. Geneva: World Council of Churches, 1982, 283 pp.

P. 95, Iglesia Evangelica Metodista en Las Islas Filipinas [Evangelical Methodist Church in the Philippines, IEMELIF], formed in 1909 by Nicholas Zamora; pp. 95-96, Philippine Independent Church.

1284 Vano, Monolo. *Light in Rizal's death cell*. Quezon City: New Day Publications, 1985, 79 pp.

The last twenty-four hours of Rizal.

Southeast: The Philippines

1285 Velez, Amosa L. "Faith-healing among Cebuano Espiritistas." In *Filipino religious psychology*, edited by L. N. Mercado. Tacloban City: Divine Word University Publications, 1977, pp. 41-50, and comment and synthesis, pp. 51-58.

1286 Vera, José de. "The story behind Bloody Sunday in Pasa." *Manila Daily Bulletin*, 26 May 1967.

1287 Von der Mehden, Fred R. *Religion and nationalism in Southeast Asia*. Madison: University of Wisconsin Press, 1963, 253 pp., bib.

Background material on Burma, Indonesia, and the Philippines. P. 25, the Colorums, summarizing R. M. Stubbs (entry 1257); p. 143, Aglipayan Church.

1288 Wagan, Venancio P. *Bathalismo, Inc (Inang Mahiwaga)*. Mambangan, San Leonardo, Nueva Ecija: Tanggapang Pangbansa, n.d., 120 pp., illus.

In Tagalog. Documents, hymns, rituals, etc. of Bathalismo cult; as found by M. A. Foronda in 1960.

1289 Watson, Lyall. "Challenges and opportunities: Medical science." In *Healers and the healing process*, edited by G. W. Meek. Wheaton, Ill., London, and Madras: Theosophical Publishing House, 1977, pp. 238-47.

Pp. 239-42, reports by an English scholar of healing by Jose Mercado and others.

1290 White, John Roberts. *Bullets and bolos: Fifteen years in the Philippine Islands*. New York and London: Century Co., 1928, 348 pp., illus., map.

Pp. 33, 81-107, Isio and Babaylanes (see also index); p. 163, Aglipay receiving secret service funds. By an American officer in the Philippine constabulary.

1291 Woods, Robert G. "Origin of the Colorum." *Philippine Magazine* 26, no. 7 (1929): 428-29; no. 8 (1930): 506, 512, 514, 516-17.

Journalistic treatment by the chief clerk of the Philippine constabulary.

1292 Woods, Robert G. "The strange story of the Colorum sect." *Asia* (Concord, N.H.) 32, no. 7 (1932): 450-54, 459-60, illus.

A detailed history, with a number of different movements of the 1920s traced without any apparent reason to the Luzon Colorums.

1293 Worcester, Dean C. *The Philippines, past and present.* 2 vols. New York: Macmillan, 1914, 1003 pp., plates, maps. New 1-vol. abridged ed., with 4 extra chapters by J. R. Hayden, 1930.

Vol. 1, pp. 437-39, Aglipay blessing a healing spring, and miracle healers; vol. 2, p. 944, Colorum at Mt. San Cristobal; vol. 2, pp. 944-45, "Pope" Isio in Negros, Cabaruan cult in Pangasinan with own new town, and other healers. By a zoologist who became the first American secretary of the interior in the Philippines.

1294 Worm, Alfred. "The fairies of Mt. Banahaw." *American Chamber of Commerce Journal*, 9 September 1929, p. 18.

1295 Yuson, Alfred A. "Holying in Banahaw." *Ermita* (Manila) 1, no. 3 (20 March-19 April 1976): 21-23, illus., map.

Mt. Banahaw as a mystic, holy mountain, and some of the spiritual activities it attracts. A journalistic article.

1296 Zafra, Nicolas. "Readings in Philippine history." Manila: University of the Philippines, 1947. New ed. 1953, 631 pp. New ed. 1956, 681 pp. Mimeo.

Pp. 378-79 (1956 ed.), the new religion of the god Lungao undergirding the Ilocos revolt of 1911. Not found in his later version, "Philippine history through selected sources," 1967.

1297 Zaide, Gregorio F. *History of the Filipino people.* Revised from typescript. Manila: N.p., 1950, 311 pp. Reprint. Manila: Modern Book, 1969.

P. 85, Tamblot's revolt, Bohol, 1621-22, and Bankaw's revolt, Limasawa, 1622, as neoprimal movements; p. 87, new religion, Panay, 1663; p. 89, Apolinario de la Cruz, 1840-41; pp. 164-73, Katipunan secret society, 1892-96; p. 230, briefly discusses the Aglipayan schism. By an author loyal to Catholicism.

1298 Zaide, Gregorio F. *History of the Katipunan.* Manila: Loyal Press, 1939, xiii + 206 pp., illus.

Pp. 12-13, teachings summarized; an introductory history of the secret society and of Bonifacio.

1299 Zaide, Gregorio F. *Philippine history and civilization.* Manila: Philippine Educational Co., 1939, 755 pp., illus., maps, bib.

Pp. 257-58, 328-30, Apolinario de la Cruz and the Katipunan.

Southeast: The Philippines

1300 Zaide, Gregorio F. *Philippine political and cultural history.* 2 vols.
Manila: Philippine Education Co., 1949, 403 pp. and 407 pp.
Vol. 1, pp. 364-66, Apolinario de la Cruz; vol. 2, chap. 12, pp.
152-62, the Katipunan.

1301 Zapanta, P. A. "The Lapiang Malaya story: Tragedy of the deluded."
Sunday Times Magazine (Manila), 4 June 1967, pp. 12-16, 18-23, illus.
Retelling the story of the massacre of the Lapiang Malaya, with
vivid photographs.

SINGAPORE

New religious movements have not played a significant role in the recent
history of this modernized, sophisticated, pluralist society–except for
Chinese spirit-cults, which do not belong to our category, but which do
represent a cognate form of folk religion. A few items are therefore listed
here for comparative purposes.

1302 Elliot, Alan John Anthony. *Chinese spirit-medium cults in Singapore.*
London School of Economics, Monographs in Social Anthropology,
n.s. 14. London: London School of Economics & Political Science,
Department of Anthropology, 1955, 179 pp.
On "Shenism" (i.e., spirit-medium cults invoking the gods in
popular religion).

1303 Topley, Marjorie. "The emergence and social function of Chinese
religious associations in Singapore." *Comparative Studies in Society and
History* 3, no. 3 (1961): 289-314.

1304 Wilson, Bryan R[onald]. *Magic and the millennium: A sociological study
of religious movements of protest among tribal and third-world peoples.*
London: Heinemann Educational Books; New York: Harper & Row,
1973, 547 pp.
Pp. 126-29, Chinese spirit-medium cults or "Shenism." Based
mainly on A. J. A. Elliot (entry 1302) and M. Topley (entry 1303).

THAILAND

Movements among the tribal peoples in the more northern areas of this
predominantly Buddhist country are difficult to separate from those in
Burma and in Laos, since tribal cultures and histories do not lie confined
within political boundaries. Thus, material on the Telakhon and the Leke

movements will also be found in the section on Burma, and items on the Phu Mi Bun and the Khmu' movements are mainly under Laos. The most important article dealing with this whole area is probably that of T. Stern in 1968 (entry 816), and this is to be found in the Burma collection. Important in other ways are the direct reports of E. Ballard and A. Eubank (entry 1306) and the relevant parts of J. E. Hudspith's dissertation (entry 1313); both are by missionaries and are included under Thailand because that is the location to which they primarily refer. As the item of F. Cripps (entry 1309) shows, even remnants of the great Taiping movement in China turned up in Thailand and in other countries to the south.

Much of the Buddhism of Thailand is of the folk variety embodying some synthesis with local primal religious forms, and this is aided by millennial strands native to both traditions. This has led to a range of movements including the Phu Mi Bun type and others led by a white-robed monk or other charismatic figure (see C. F. Keyes's items, entries 1315-1316), which are mildly millennial, sometimes heterodox in relation to Buddhism, and often reforming in relation to the tribal spirit or *nat* religions. These independent versions of localized Buddhism may correspond in some ways to the prophet-healing types of African independent churches.

1305 Anderson, Kirsten Ewers. "Two indigenous Karen religious denominations." *Folk* (Copenhagen) 23 (1981): 251-61, illus.

Among the Pwo Karen of western central Thailand: Lu Baung ("Yellow Thread") and Wi Maung as two new "sects" deriving from a nineteenth-century holy man, rejecting sacrifice to spirits, and incorporating Buddhist precepts and symbols.

1306 Ballard, Emilie, and Eubank, Allan. "A call to prayer for the Telakhons." *Thailand Tattler* (American Baptist Mission) 14, no. 5 (1969): 1, 7. Also other articles in 15, no. 1 (1970): 3; no. 2 (1970): 1, 7.

1307 Bennett, Cephas. "Tavoy mission – journal of Mr. Bennett." *Baptist Missionary Magazine*, 28 August 1848, pp. 316-23.

Pp. 318-20, a Sgaw-Karen cult of Buddhist features found in 1848 by missionaries, east of Tavoy.

1308 Bunnag, Tej. "The 1901-1902 Holy Man's Rebellion in northeast Thailand." *Social Science Review* 5, no. 1 (1967): 78-86.

In Thai.

1309 Cripps, Francis. *The far province*. London: Hutchinson, 1965, 206 pp.

Southeast: Thailand

> P. 190, Taiping remnant entry into Thailand in the 1860s to 1872; p. 191, false prophets in 1902 in the northeast predicted a cataclysm – and were suppressed by the army.

1310 Dodge, Paul S. *Two weeks on an elephant: Diary of the first visit to the Telakhon of Thailand, November-December 1962*. Bangkok: Church of Christ in Thailand, n.d.
> Quoted in J. E. Hudspith (entry 1313), p. 274, etc.

1311 Filbeck, David [Lee]. "T'in culture: An ethnography of the T'in tribe of northern Thailand." Chiang Mai: Department of Anthropology and Sociology, Chiang Mai University, 1973. Mimeo.
> Chap. 8 (pp. 14-27) describes an abortive messianic movement among the Mal and Pray (T'in) people.

1312 Hinton, Peter. "The Karen, millennialism, and the politics of accommodation to the lowland states." In *Ethnic adaptation and identity: The Karen on the Thai frontier with Burma*, edited by C. F. Keyes. Philadelphia: Institute for the Study of Human Issues, 1979, 81-94.
> Pp. 84-85, 92, the "White Monk," Khae Chae Uae, in 1968-69; pp. 90-92, Ywa and Telakhon sects interpreted as "groping towards pan-Karen solidarity" – a different interpretation from that of T. Stern (entry 816) on Burma.

1313 Hudspith, J. Edwin. "Tribal highways and byways: A church growth study in north Thailand." M.A. dissertation (missions), Fuller Theological Seminary, School of World Mission, 1969, 320 pp.
> Pp. 234, 271, 274-97, Telakhon movement; pp. 234, 275, 282f., Leke movement; pp. 264-66, Karen myth of lost book. By a Baptist missionary.

1314 Ishii, Yoneo. "A note on Buddhist millenarian revolts in northeastern Siam." *Journal of Southeast Asian Studies* 6, no. 2 (1975): 121-26.
> On underlying cultural ideas beneath "holy man" or "man of merit" movements, especially in 1699, 1902, and 1924 – all looking to a "magical saviour," the *phu mi kun.*

1315 Keyes, Charles F[enton]. "Millennialism, Theravada Buddhism, and Thai society." *Journal of Asian Studies* 6, no. 2 (1977): 283-302.
> Millennialism as a religious phenomenon, and the possibility of a Buddhist millennialism; millenarian movements as ideological responses to crises of power, and not in themselves new religions but

transitory phenomena. Case study, pp. 291-301, the 1899-1902 uprising in northeast Thailand (and more recent minor movements); extensive bibliography of Thai and other sources.

1316 Keyes, Charles F[enton], ed. *Ethnic adaptation and identity: The Karen on the Thai frontier with Burma*. Philadelphia: Institute for the Study of Human Issues, 1979, 278 pp., illus.

See P. Hinton (entry 1312), and also pp. 12, 20-22, 35, 50-51, 112-13, 132-33, on various Karen millennialisms, Telakhon, Cekosi, Khruba Khao, and other cults.

1317 Kirsch, A. Thomas. "Complexity in the Thai religious system: An interpretation." *Journal of Asian Studies* 36, no. 2 (1977): 241-66.

Background information, valuable for all Thailand movements.

1318 Lewis, Paul [White], and Lewis, Elaine. *Peoples of the Golden Triangle: Six tribes in Thailand*. London and New York: Thames & Hudson, 1984, 300 pp., illus.

P. 197, brief account of messianic movements among the Lahu in Thailand and Burma.

1319 Lomax, Louis E[mmanuel]. *Thailand: The war that is, the war that will be*. New York: Random House, Vintage Books, 1967, 175 pp.

Pp. 65-76, "waiting for the messiah," Lunk Phaw Yi, a Buddhist miracle-worker in 1966.

1320 McKinnon, John, and Bhruksasri, Wanat, eds. *Highlanders of Thailand*. Kuala Lumpur and New York: Oxford University Press, 1983, 358 pp., illus., map.

P. 52, unifying effect of Karen and Lahu messianic movements from the late nineteenth century; pp. 161-64, Karen as religiously eclectic, the Ywa and Telakhon cults (based on T. Stern, entry 816), the White Monk; pp. 229, 231, 236, Lahu revitalization movements.

1321 Marlowe, David H. "Upland-lowland relationships: The case of the S'kaw Karen of central upland western Chiang Mai." In *Tribesmen and peasants in northern Thailand*, edited by P. Hinton. Chiang Mai: Tribal Research Centre, 1969, pp. 53-68.

1322 Mikusol, Paitoon. "Social and cultural history of northwestern Thailand from 1868-1910: A case study of the Huamuang Khamen Padong (Surin, Shanghka, and Khukhan)." Ph.D. dissertation (cultural anthropology), University of Washington, 1984, 273 pp.

Southeast: Thailand

Includes messianic figures and their impact; suppression of the Holy Men's Rebellion in 1902.

1323 Murdoch, John B. "The 1901-1902 'Holy Man's Rebellion.'" *Journal of the Siam Society* 62 (January 1976): 47-67.
Based on T. Bunnag (entry 1308) and C. F. Keyes (entry 1315) and treated as occurring in both Laos and Thailand.

1324 Nartsupha, C. "The ideology of holy men revolts in north east Thailand." *Senri Ethnological Studies* 13 (1984): 111-34.

1325 Sarkisyanz, Emanuel. "Die Religionen Kambodschas, Birmas, Laos. . . ." In *Die Religionen Südostasiens*, edited by A. Hofer, et al. Die Religionen der Menschheit, 23. Stuttgart: W. Kohlhammer, 1975.
Pp. 523-24, on "separatist" movements in northern Thailand.

1326 Skrobanek, Walter. *Buddhistische Politik in Thailand: Mit besonderer Berucksichtigung des heterodoxen Messianismus*. Weisbaden: F. Steiner, 1976, 315 pp.
Pp. 78-103, Phi-Bun revolt of 1902, messianic and nativistic.

1327 Tambiah, S[tanley] J[eyaraja]. *Buddhism and the spirit cults in northeast Thailand*. Cambridge Studies in Social Anthropology, 2. London: Cambridge University Press, 1970. Reprint. 1977, 388 pp.
Pp. 300-304, an example of contrasting Buddhist and primal festivals celebrated by the same village; pp. 337-50, a syncretized worldview; pp. 367-77, the false disjunction between primal and universal (or literate) religious traditions.

1328 Tanabe, S. "Ideological practice in peasant rebellions: Siam at the turn of the twentieth century." *Senri Ethnological Studies* 13 (1984): 75-110.

1329 [Turner, Harold Walter.] "Telakhon." In *Encyclopaedia Britannica*, 15th ed., 1974. Vol. 9, Micropaedia, p. 867b-c.

1330 United States Government, Department of the Army. *Area handbook for Thailand*, edited by John W. Henderson, et al. Foreign Area Studies, American University. DA Pam 550-553. Washington, D.C.: Government Printing Office, 1971, 413 pp.
Pp. 163-65, religious minorities, but nothing on new primal movements.

1331 Walker, Anthony R. "Messianic movements among the Lahu of the Yunnan-Indochina borderlands." *South-East Asia* (Carbondale, Ill.) 3 (1974): 699-712, French summary (p. 698).

Periodic messianic prophets and supernatural healers as a source of translocal renewal movements, which then oppose government authorities; includes Ma Heh G'uisha, Paw hku Yi, and Paw khu Lon. A useful survey, with sources.

1332 Young, [Oliver] Gordon. *The hill tribes of northern Thailand.* Siam Society, Monograph 1. 2d ed. Bangkok: Siam Society, 1962, 92 pp., illus.

Pp. 10f., 19, on recent "man-gods" or prophets of the cult of G'uisha ("Living breath") among the Lahu of eastern Burma and northern Thailand, similar to the Ywa cult of the Karen.

VIETNAM

The movements in Vietnam belonging to our categories are, like others in Southeast Asia, less clearly defined as compared with other parts of the world, and yet reveal some important common features, such as millennial hopes that issue in cargo-cult conduct – ceasing to farm or work, anti-Western and nationalistic or indigenizing features, and syntheses between one or more of the universal religions present in Vietnam (chiefly Buddhism) and tribal forms. Thus the Ma Wih movement (see G. C. Hickey, entry 1350) and the Sam Bram activities (see G. H. Smith, entry 1387) might be regarded as neoprimal types, albeit somewhat incipient. The Hung Giao Van Dong movement was a sophisticated nationalistic endeavor among intellectuals seeking to restore traditional values and embracing both Catholics and Buddhists.

The "Coconut Monk" movement also sought a synthesis of Christian, Buddhist, and ancient Vietnamese elements (see Lejuge, entry 1369). Little is known about a number of small independent churches formed from the 1960s, such as Vietnam Christ's Church, which would appear to resemble African examples.

The two most important movements have been Cao Dai and Hoa Hao. The former began in the Mekong Delta in 1919, synthesizing Buddhist, Christian, and Confucian elements, together with Taoist spirit mediumship. Like Hoa Hao, it is a social and religious movement that became involved with the political and military history of Vietnam, an inevitable result of a large membership of perhaps half a million followers, if we discount its own claims of several million adherents. Phat Giao Hoa Hao (normally called Hoa Hao) also came from a founder in the Mekong Delta, in 1939, as a

Southeast: Vietnam

Vietnamese reform movement within Hinayana Buddhism, strongly against foreign domination and claiming one and a half million adherents. R. L. Mole (entry 1373) provides extensive texts from the founder's writings, in translation.

1333 Benz, Ernst. *Neue religionen*. Stuttgart: Ernst Klett Verlag, 1971, 179 pp.
> Chap. 2 (pp. 25-43), Cao Dai.

1334 Bezacier, Louis. "Die Religionen Viet-Nams." In *Die Religionen Südostasiens*, edited by A. Hofer, et al. Die Religionen der Menschheit, 23. Stuttgart: W. Kohlhammer, 1975, pp. 293-357.
> Pp. 349-56, Cao Dai.

1335 Blandre, Bernard. "Viet Nam: Exécution de Ho Thai Bach." *Mouvements Religieux* (Sarreguemines), no. 58 (February 1985), pp. 3-4, bib.
> Cao Dai was suppressed by the Vietnam government in 1977; Ho Thai Bach, a leader, was executed in January 1985.

1336 Boal, Barbara [Mather]. "Cao Dai and Hoa Hao." In *A Lion handbook of the world's religions*. Tring, Hertfordshire: Lion Publishing, 1982, pp. 243-44.
> A summary outline set in the context of political developments.

1337 *Cao-Dai: Giao-Ly*.
> A magazine of the Cao Dai religion published in the late 1940s in Saigon by Tuan Bao. Cited by K. P. Landon (entry 1367), p. 202.

1338 "Cinéma et Caodaïsme en conflict au Vietnam." *La Presse*, no. 590 (26 February-4 March 1957).
> Cited by N. T. Huân (entry 1357), p. 280.

1339 Coulet, George[s]. *Cultes et religions de l'Indochine annamite*. Saigon: Imprimerie Commerciale C. Ardin, 1929, 241 pp., illus.

1340 Coulet, George[s]. *Les sociétés secretes en Terre d'Annam*. Saigon: Imprimerie Commerciale C. Ardin, 1926, 452 pp.

1341 Dournes, Jacques. "Sam Bram, le mage, et le Blanc dans l'Indochine centrale des années trente." *Ethnographie*, n.s., no. 76 [119, no. 1] (1978): 85-108, maps, bib., English summary.

A kind of prophet among the Torai who supported local cultural identity against the threats of European culture, and who was misunderstood as a Communist revolutionary.

1342 Dufeil, Michel-M[arie]. "Les sectes du Sud Viet-Nam." *La Vie Intellectuelle* (Paris) 28 (December 1956): 61-92.
Pp. 69-75, Hoa Hao; pp. 75-91, Cao Dai and its five branches (pp. 85-86), each focused on different major traditions of this syncretic religion.

1343 Dunstheimer, G. G. H. "Une étude sur la religion vietnamienne (technique et panthéon des médiums vietnamiens [Dong] de Maurice Durand)." *Archives de Sociologie des Religions*, no. 11 [6] (January-June 1961), pp. 141-45.

1344 Ellwood, Robert S., Jr. "Cao Dai." In *Encyclopedia of religion*, edited by M. Eliade. Vol. 3. New York: Macmillan, 1987, pp. 72-73.

1345 Fall, Bernard B. "The political-religious sects of Vietnam." *Pacific Affairs* (New York) 28, no. 3 (1955): 235-53, map.
Cao Dai, Hoa Hao, Binh-Xuyen (the latter being more of a criminal racket) – their history until overcome by Premier Diem in 1955.

1346 Gobron, Gabriel ["Frère Gago" among Caodaïsts]. *Histoire du Caodaïsme: Bouddhisme rénové, spiritisme annamite, religion nouvelle in Eurasie*. Paris: Éditions Dervy, 1948, 196 pp. illus.
Materials and documents collected 1937-39, before the death of the author. Includes origins of Annamite spiritualism, and other principles and beliefs, the "Popes" of Cao Dai, relation to oriental wisdom and Islam, temples at Pnom Penh and Long-Thanh. Dervy is a publisher of the occult.

1347 Gobron, Gabriel. "Les origines du spiritisme vietnamien." In *Histoire et philosophie du Caodaïsme*. Paris: Éditions Dervy, 1949, 215 pp., illus.
By a French member of Cao Dai, with official approval by the movement.

1348 Greene, Graham. *The quiet American*. London: William Heinemann, 1955, 247 pp.
A novel. Pp. 85-93, popular description of a Cao Dai festival ca. 1952; stresses the political nature of Cao Dai. Passing mention of Hoa Hao as a rival movement.

Southeast: Vietnam

1349 Hickey, Gerald Cannon. *Preliminary research report on the PMS (Saigon).* Lansing: Michigan State University Vietnam Advisory Group, Field Administration Division, 1957.
Pp. 9-10, revolt among the Jarai connected with a messianic movement, until the late 1930s.

1350 Hickey, Gerald Cannon. "Some aspects of hill tribe life in Vietnam." In *South East Asian tribes, minorities, and nations,* edited by P. Kunstadter. Vol. 2. Princeton: Princeton University Press, 1967, pp. 745-69.
Vol. 2, p. 753, millennial "age of gold" movement among the Bahnar, Sedang, and Jerai, 1935-38.

1351 Hickey, Gerald Cannon. *Village in Vietnam.* New Haven and London: Yale University Press, 1964, 325 pp.
Pp. 66-73, 290-94, Cao Dai sects and history; pp. 218-32, shrine and rituals.

1352 Hill, Frances R. "Millenarian machines in South Vietnam." *Comparative Studies in Society and History* 13, no. 3 (1971): 325-50.
On the Cao Dai example.

1353 Höltker, Georg. "Caodismus: Ein religiöser Synkretismus in Süd-Vietnam." *Neue Zeitschrift für Missionswissenschaft* 24, no. 3 (1968): 211.

1354 Ho-Phap. *Le Caodaïsme, 3e amnistie de Dieu en Orient: La constitution religieuse du Caodaïsme expliquées et commentées par Sa Sainteté Ho-Phap.* Paris: Éditions Dervy, 1953, 194 pp., illus.
A form of official catechism.

1355 Hou Su Shuang. *Important points of Tao Yuan at a glance.* Singapore, 1932.
Tao Yuan (also known as Red Swastika Society), in 1921 at Tsin-an; claimed to unite five religions – similar to Cao Dai.

1356 Huân Nguyên Tran. "Histoire d'une secte religieuse au Viet-Nam: Le Caodaïsme." *Revue de Synthèse* (Paris) 28 (1958): 265-81. Reprinted in *Tradition et révolution au Vietnam,* edited by J. Chesneaux. Paris: Éditions Anthropos, n.d., chap. 7.

1357 Huân Nguyên Tran [Nguyên Trung Hâu, pseud.]. *Lu' o'c-su Dao Cao Dai*. Tourane, 1956. French version. *Histoire sommaire du Caodaïsme*. Saigon: Pham Van Son, 1956.
A short history of Cao Dai.

1358 Huân Nguyên Tran [Traân Huân Nguyên, pseud.]. "Les sectes religieuses au Viet-Nam." In *Histoire des religions*, edited by H. C. Puech. Encyclopédie de la Pléiade. Vol. 3. Paris: Gallimard, 1976, pp. 449-73, bib.
Pp. 451-61, Cao Dai (history and beliefs); pp. 461-68, Hoa Hao; pp. 468-70, sects' interference in politics; pp. 470f., Noi-Dao, more Taoist than Buddhist.

1359 Hunger, Wilhelm. "Neue 'Menscheitsreligion' in Vietnam." *Die Katholischen Missionen* (Freiburg) 71, no. 1 (1952): 44-47, illus.
On Cao Dai; interpreted as a twentieth-century Manichaeism. A popular survey.

1360 Huỳnh Phu So. *Sâm-gi'ang Thi-văn Toàn Bô* [The complete collection of the prophetic essays and poems of the venerable founder Huỳnh.] Phât Giáo Hòa H'ao, 1966.
An official collection of the writings of the founder of Hoa Hao. For free translations of some sections, see R. L. Mole (entry 1373), pp. 24-26, 35-57.

1361 Huynh-Van-Nhiêm. [Address of the Vice-President of Buddhism Hoa Hao.] *Bulletin, Secretariatus Pro Non-Christianis*, no. 25 [9, no. 1] (1974): 62-64.
In French. See pp. 51-54, report by P. Rossano on meeting with the Premier V.-P. of the Central Council of "Église Bouddhiste Phat-Giao-Hoa-Hao."

1362 Jumper, Roy. "The Cao Dai of Tay Ninh: The politics of a political-religious sect in South Vietnam." In *Asian Studies, I*, edited by B. G. Gokhale. Bombay: Popular Prakashan, 1966, pp. 142-54. New York: Humanities Press, 1967.
Examines politcal evolution of Cao Dai and its political role until its status of acceptance by the military junta after the coup of 1963.

1363 Jumper, Roy. "Sects and communism in South Vietnam." *Orbis* 3, no. 1 (1959): 85-96.

Southeast: Vietnam

1364 Kaszuba, F. [The social and political significance of religious sects in South Viet Nam.] *Euhemer* 19, no. 1 (1975): 63-74.
   In Polish. Cao Dai and Hoa Hao as syncretist movements.

1365 Kōichiro, Unō. [The South Kingdom seen from the South: Study of Vietnamese religious movements (2).] *Japanese Journal of Ethnology* (Tokyo) 45, no. 2 (1980): 111-33, illus., maps, bib., English summary (pp. 111-12).
   In Japanese.

1366 Lai, Joseph Nguyen Huy. *La tradition religieuse, spirituelle, et sociale au Vietnam: Sa confrontation avec le christianisme.* Paris: Beauchesne Éditeur, 1981, 525 pp.
   Chap. 5, Cao Dai and Hoa Hao. See review by "J. D." in *Anthropologie* 77, no. 2 (1981): 209-13.

1367 Landon, Kenneth Perry. *Southeast Asia: Crossroads of religion.* Haskell Lectures in Comparative Religion, 1947. Chicago and London: Chicago University Press, 1949, 215 pp.
   Pp. 200-202, Cao Dai as a Westernized development of Annamese spiritism, founded by an ardent Taoist to unite the best in Buddhism, Confucianism, Taoism, and Christianity with Annamese spirit and ancestor cults.

1368 Lanternari, Vittorio. *The religions of the oppressed: A study of modern messianic cults.* London: MacGibbon & Kee, 1963, xx + 343 + xiii pp. Toronto: New American Library of Canada, 1963. New York: Knopf, 1963. New York: Mentor Books, 1965, xvi + 286 pp.
   Pp. 216-21 (pp. 270-77, London ed.), Cao Dai and Hoa Hao movements.

1369 Lejuge, Fr. "La secte religieuse du moine de cocotier dans le delta de Mekong." *Cultures et Développement* (Louvain, Belgium) 4, no. 4 (1972): 827-43, graph, illus.
   On Nguyen Thanh Nam (b. 1910) and his syncretist movement (1952-59), which became more political from 1960. Vietnamese, Christian, and Buddhist elements.

1370 Lemaitre. *Religions, cultes, rites, et superstitions en terre d'Annam: Influence de l'idée philosophique sur la vie politique et sociale du peuple annamite. Conférence faite aux officiers de la garnison de Saigon le 16 Septembre 1932.* Saigon: Imprimerie de l'Union, 1932.

1371 Lestrac, G[abriel] Abadie de. "Une nouvelle religion: Le Caodaïsme." *Vu* (Paris), no. 234 (7 September 1932), pp. 1424-26, illus.

1372 McLane, John R. "Archaic movements and revolution in southern Vietnam." In *National liberation: Revolution in the third world*, edited by N. Miller and R. Aya. New York: Free Press, 1971, pp. 68-101.
    The decay of traditional rural society giving rise to "archaic religious movements"–Cao Dai and Hoa Hao; the evolution of these into political-military forces; their postwar struggle with one another, the Viet Minh, and the French. Also on Binh Xuyen, a secular movement.

1373 Mole, Robert L. *A brief survey of the Phât-Giáo Hòa-H'ao*. Bethesda, Md.: Naval Medical School, National Naval Medical Center, 1969, 98 pp., bib.
    By a U.S. navy chaplain; reproduced for orientation of naval medical personnel. Pp. 24-26, extract from the collected poems and essays of Huynh Phu So, freely translated; pp. 35-57, free translation from same source, on theology and practices.

1374 *National Geographic Magazine* 120, no. 4 (1961): 464-65, illus.
    One of the few published color photographs of a Cao Dai ceremony, at Tay-Ninh, ca. 1961.

1375 Oliver, Victor L[loyd]. *Caodai spiritism: A study of religion in Vietnamese society*. Studies in the History of Religions, 34. Leiden: Brill, 1976, xi + 145 pp., bib.
    A comprehensive study–history, holy cities, sectarian divisions, seances and mediums, social role.

1376 Oliver, Victor L[loyd]. "Caodaism: A Vietnamese example of sectarian development." Ph.D. dissertation (religion), Syracuse University, 1972, 239 pp.
    A comprehensive study–history, holy cities, sectarian divisions, seances and mediums, social role.

1377 Oliver, Victor L[loyd]. "Caodaism: A Vietnamese socio-religious movement." In *Dynamic religious movements*, edited by D. J. Hesselgrave. Grand Rapids, Mich.: Baker Book House, 1978, pp. 273-96.

1378 Oliver, Victor L[loyd]. "The development of Caodai sectarianism." *Religion: Journal of Religion and Religions* 4, no. 1 (1974): 1-25.

Southeast: Vietnam

1379 Passano, P. "Dialogue in Thailand, South Vietnam, Sri Lanka, southern India." *Bulletin, Secretariatus Pro Non-Christianis*, no. 25 [9, no. 1] (1974): 50-61.
Pp. 51-54, Viet Nam: Hoa Hao, Buddhism, Cao Dai, Baha'i.

1380 Phan Truong Manh. *Résumé sur le Caodisme*. Saigon: Cao Dai Institute.
Typical of many leaflets in French published by the head of the Institute about the 1940s. Cited by K. P. Landon (entry 1367), p. 202.

1381 Rambo, A. Terry. "Vietnam: Searching for integration." In *Religions and societies: Asia and the Middle East*, edited by C. Caldarola. Berlin and New York: Mouton Publishers, 1982, pp. 407-44.
Pp. 428-35, Cao Dai and Hoa Hao as "millenarian movements."

1382 Rondot, Pierre. "Der Caodaismus." *Kairos* (Salzburg) 7, no. 2 (1965): 157-58.
With reference to article by G. Lanczkowski in *Kairos* 6, nos. 3-4 (entry 319).

1383 Sacks, I. Milton. "Some religious components in Vietnamese politics." In *Religion and change in contemporary Asia*, edited by R. F. Spencer. Minneapolis: University of Minnesota Press, 1971, pp. 44-66.
On Cao Dai and Hoa Hao.

1384 "Service de Propagande du Caodaïsme." *Revue Caodaïque*, 1948.
In French and Vietnamese. Cited by Nguyen Tran Huan (entry 1357), p. 280.

1385 Simon, Pierre J., and Barouh-Simon, Ida. "Les génies de Quatre Palais: Contribution à l'étude du culte vietnamien des Ba-Dong." *L'Homme* 10, no. 4 (1970): 81-101.
A spirit-possession therapeutic cult in a Vietnamese refugee community in France, which differs from similar cults in Vietnam and may be a syncretism arising in the refugee situation.

1386 Simon, Pierre J., and Barouh-Simon, Ida. *Hâù Bóng: Un culte vietnamien de possession transplanté en France*. Cahiers de l'Homme, n.s. 13. École Pratique des Hautes Études: VIe section: Sciences Économiques et Sociales. Paris: Mouton & Co., 1973, 87 pp., illus.

1387 Smith, Gordon Hedderly. *The blood hunters, a narrative of pioneer missionary work among the savages of French Indo-China.* Chicago: World Wide Prayer and Missionary Union, 1942. 3d ed. 1945, 140 pp.

By a Christian and Missionary Alliance missionary in Indochina. P. 89, Sam Bram's movement–sold bottles of magic water and encouraged an early rising against the French. Tribute was paid to him and rice was pulled up since the spirits were going to feed his adherents.

1388 Smith, R. B. "An introduction to Caodaism." Pt. 1, "Origins and early history"; Pt. 2, "Beliefs and organization." *Bulletin, School of Oriental and African Studies* 33, nos. 2-3 (1970): 335-49; 33, no. 3 (1970): 573-89.

Unites Taoist spirit-mediumship and a "reformed" Buddhism.

1389 Tac Pham Cong. *Le Caodaïsme – Phap-Chanh-Truyen.* Paris: Éditions Dervy, 1953.

1390 Tran Van Tuyen. "Cao Daism." *Viet-My: Journal of the Vietnamese American Association* 2, no. 4 (December 1957).

1391 United States Government, Department of the Army. *Area handbook for Vietnam,* edited by G. L. Harris, et al. American University, Foreign Area Studies Dividion. DA Pam 550-178. Washington, D.C.: Government Printing Office, 1962, 513 pp.

Pp. 127-37, religion, including pp. 133-36, convenient outlines of Cao Dai and Hoa Hao. This replaced an earlier edition (1967) edited by H. H. Smith.

1392 United States Government, Department of the Navy. *The religions of Vietnam.* Command Information Pamphlet ET 11-67. Washington, D.C.: Government Printing Office, April 1968, 16 pp., illus.

Pp. 11-14, Cao Dai and Hoa Hao.

1393 United States Government, Department of the Navy, Bureau of Naval Personnel. *The religions of South Vietnam in faith and fact.* NAVPERS 15991. [Washington, D.C.]: Government Printing Office, 1967, 97 pp., map, illus.

Pp. 47-52, Cao Dai; pp. 53-58, Hoa Hao.

1394 Vinginiano, G. "V. Hugo e i Caodaisti." *Religio: Revista di Studi Religiosi* 11, no. 5 (1935): 478-80.

Southeast: Vietnam

1395 Werner, Jayne Susan. "The Cao Dài: The politics of a Vietnamese syncretic religious movement." Ph.D. dissertation (government), Cornell University, 1976, 741 pp.

The largest mass-based religious movement in modern times in Vietnam – represents reaction of animisms to superimposed universal religions.

1396 Werner, Jayne Susan. *Peasant politics and religious sectarianism: Peasant and priest in the Cao Dai in Vietnam*. New Haven: Yale University Southeast Asian Studies, 1981, 123 pp.

See entry 1395.

1397 White, Peter T., and Garrett, W. E. (photographer). "South Vietnam fights the Red tide." *National Geographic Magazine* 120, no. 4 (1961): 445-89, illus.

P. 452, brief account of Cao Dai; pp. 464-65, splendid double-page photograph of interior of Tay ninh temple, and p. 467, Tay ninh exterior; p. 466, photo of some women worshippers.

Particular Movements

Iglesia ni Cristo (The Philippines)

In Tagalog as Iglesia ni Kristo (Church of Christ), but with "Cristo" in Spanish or English, this is one of the two largest new religious movements in the Philippines, the other being the Philippine Independent Church (see next section). The INC or INK, as it is often called, was founded in 1914 by Felix Manalo (1886-1963), who was born a Roman Catholic and traversed Methodism, Presbyterianism, the Disciples of Christ, and the Seventh Day Adventists before founding his own church. This claims to be the true Church of Christ, refounded through Manalo, the "angel of the East" mentioned in Revelation 7:1. The "East" refers to the Philippines, and Filipinos are therefore the elect people. This interpretation of nationalism is found in other Philippine movements, and elsewhere, as in various Korean new religions, and in the Israelitas del Nuevo Pacto Universal in Peru. The theology of the Iglesia is unitarian, based on a biblical literalism.

1398 Alejandro, Rufino. *Ignorance or bad faith: Manalo and Co. and the art of misrepresentation*. Malabon: N.p., 1984.

1399 Alonzo, Manuel P., Jr. *A historical-critical study of the Iglesia ni Kristo*. Manila: University of Santo Tomas Press, 1959, 95 pp. Also in *Boletin Ecclesiastico de Filipinas*, no. 361 [22] (July 1958), pp. 426-33; no. 362 [22] (August 1958), pp. 491-504; no. 363 [22] (September 1958), pp. 554-56; no. 364 [22] (October 1958), pp. 636-43; no. 365 [22] (November 1958), pp. 700-705; no. 366 [22] (December 1958), pp. 766-71; no. 367 [23] (January 1959), pp. 28-38; no. 368 [23] (February 1959),

Iglesia Ni Cristo

pp. 102-5; no. 369 [23] (March 1959), pp. 170-76; no. 371 [23] (May 1959), pp. 286-98.

History, organization, biblical exegesis, doctrines, and moral teaching; criticism of the last three, and practical recommendations to the Catholic Church.

1400 Alvior, Efren. *Manalo and his Iglesia*. Manila: G. T. Printers, 1971.
Hostile to the Iglesia. See also entry 1413.

1401 Ando, Hirofumi. "The altar and the ballot-box: The Iglesia ni Kristo in the 1965 Philippine elections." *Philippine Journal of Public Adninistration* (Manila) 10, no. 4 (1966): 359-66.

1402 Ando, Hirofumi. "A study of the Iglesia ni Cristo: A politico-religious sect in the Philippines." *Pacific Affairs* 42, no. 3 (1969): 334-45.
Sociological analysis of the relation to the social setting.

1403 "Anti-INC rally planned." *Manila Times* 23, no. 40 (1969): 24-A.
Opposition to the Iglesia in politics.

1404 Apolinario, Eulalio S. *Anghel nga ba si Manalo. . . ?* Manila: Aklatang Lunas, 1956, 68 pp.
A Catholic critique of the Iglesia ni Cristo.

1405 Araneta, Francisco. "The reason why: The eglesia [*sic*] and our non-parties." *Manila Chronicle* 23, no. 208 (1967): 5.
A Jesuit on the Iglesia and its place in politics.

1406 Asis, R. V. "Felix Manalo religious leader passes." *Chronicle Magazine* 18, no. 17 (1963): 20-22.

1407 Ayers, Alexander P. *Tunay nga bang "Sugo ng Diyos" si G. Felix Y. Manalo?* Caloocan City: Berean Research Publication, 1985.

1408 Baldemor, Rogelio, and Tuggy, [Arthur] Leonard. "I debated the Iglesia ni Cristo." *Conservative Baptist* (U.S.), Summer 1972, pp. 6-7.
By Baptist pastors; report of a debate between a Filipino Baptist (Baldemor) and a senior leader of the Iglesia.

1409 Beech, Ronald Ward. "An introductory survey of the Iglesia ni Cristo." M.Div. thesis, Philippine Baptist Theological Seminary (Baguio City), 1972.

1410 *Bombshell.*
A weekly published in Manila in Tagalog and English from 26 August 1954. For articles attacking Manalo and the INC, see J. R. Santa-Romana (entry 1485), pp. 410-11.

1411 "Brotherhood of believers." *Asia Magazine* (Hong Kong) 5, no. 28 (1965): 4, 6, 8, illus.
On the Iglesia.

1412 Caliwag, F. M. "New Iglesia ni Kristo leader defines church's status." *Sunday Times Magazine* (Manila) 18, no. 38 (1963): 22-23, illus.

1413 Catañgay, Tomas C. "Response to Efren Alvior's pamphlet: 'Present day objection to Christ's deity answered.'" *Pasugo* (Quezon City, Iglesia ni Cristo) 31, no. 3 (1979): 16-17, 28; 31, no. 5 (1979): 25-27; 32, no. 4 (1980): 18-20, 26.
An example of the Iglesia's doctrinal methods and position, in reply to entry 1400.

1414 Catholic Laymen's Organization of Volunteers. "The INK issue in this election. Confidential: For Christian and Catholic lay leaders only." Manila: Catholic Laymen's Organization of Volunteers, [late 1960s?], 8 + 2 pp. Mimeo.
Mustering Catholic voters against the Iglesia ni Cristo block vote. Copy in Ateneo de Manila University vertical files.

1415 "Catholics mad about Iglesia meet." *News Behind the News* 1, no. 38 (1954), pp. 2, 7.
See J. R. Santa-Romana (entry 1485), pp. 410-11, for further items.

1416 Constantino, J. de. "En [*sic*] faith and freedom: Enconsistencies [*sic*] of INK figures." *Manila Chronicle* 23, no. 236 (1967): 5.
The Iglesia's voting strength.

1417 "Consular invoice for INC shipment issued on palace orders." *Manila Chronicle* 25, no. 283 (30 January 1970): 1.
Iglesia ni Cristo favors from President Marcos.

1418 "Counter-rally poised by INK in Manila." *Manila Times* 23, no. 39 (1969): 1-A.
The Iglesia in political action.

Iglesia Ni Cristo

1419 Cruz, Paschalis. *Nueva Ecija* (San Fernando, Pampanga), 11 July 1952, 182 pp.
An approved Roman Catholic account of the Iglesia.

1420 Deats, Richard L[ouis]. "Iglesia ni Cristo: Pioneers in church-sponsored land reform." *Church and Community* (Manila, United Church of Christ) 7, no. 5 (1967): 26-28.

1421 Elesterio, Fernando G. *The Iglesia ni Cristo: Its Christology and ecclesiology*. Cardinal Bea studies, Ateneo University Publications, 5. Quezon City: Cardinal Bea Institute, Loyola School of Theology, Ateneo de Manila University, 1977, 217 pp.

1422 Faustino, Renato G. "Iglesia power." *Philippines Free Press* 62, no. 41 (1969): 2-3, 55-56, illus.
The estimated 400,000 votes of Iglesia ni Cristo members, who supported Marcos in 1965 and other "just and humane" candidates.

1423 "F. M. sees INC rice harvest." *Manila Daily Bulletin* 232, no. 7 (1967): 12.
President Ferdinand Marcos and the Iglesia.

1424 Gabriel, Melanio P., Jr. *Ang Mga Lihim at Mga Kabulaanan ng Iglesia ni Kristo (Manalo)*. Republic of the Philippines: N.p., 1981.

1425 Galang, Zoilo M. "Iglesia ni Kristo." In *The encyclopedia of the Philippines*. Vol. 10. Manila: Vera & Sons Co., 1935-36, pp. 432-34.

1426 Galang, Zoilo M. "Manalo, Felix Isagun." In *The encyclopedia of the Philippines*. Vol. 9, *Builders of the new Philippines*. Manila: Philippines Education Co., 1936, pp. 392-94.

1427 Garcia, Dolores G. "Felix Manalo: The man and his mission." *Pasugo* (Manila, INC), 27 July 1964, pp. 179-83.
An official church account.

1428 Gatbonton, Mario T. "Aglipayan confusion," and an editorial. *Sentinel* (Manila), February 1957, and further comment, 2 March 1957, p. 5.
Relation between the Independent Church and the Protestant Episcopal Church – see reply by T. E. Pasco, "An Aglipayan replies," *Christian Register* (Sta. Cruz, Manila) 5, no. 10 (1957).

1429 "Gen. Padilla raps INC on elections." *Manila Times* 25, no. 26 (1970): 22.

A senator's opposition to the Iglesia in politics.

1430 Greschat, Hans-Jürgen. "Die philippinische Iglesia Cristo." In *Religionen, Geschichte, Ökumene,* edited by R. Flasche and E. Geldbach. Leiden: E. J. Brill, 1981, pp. 216-24.

1431 Guanzon, M. A. C. "An analysis of religious leadership in the Iglesia ni Kristo." In *Filipino religious psychology,* edited by L. N. Mercado. Tacloban: Divine Word University, 1977, pp. 127-40.

1432 Gumban, Johnny V. "The Christian Churches' encounter with the *Iglesia ni Cristo* in the Philippines." *South East Asia Journal of Theology* 10, no. 1 (1968): 39-46.

A simple general survey.

1433 "Iglesia is backing Marcos–Osmiña." *Manila Times* 24, no. 242 (1969): 1-A.

The Iglesia's support for President Ferdinand Marcos.

1434 Iglesia ni Cristo. *Articles of incorporation.* Manila: Securities and Exchange Commission, 1914.

1435 Iglesia ni Cristo. *Himnario Ilocano Cancanta a nasantoan a pagdayawtay iti Dios.* Bigan: Burgos Press, 1938, 220 pp.

1436 Iglesia ni Cristo. *Isang Pagbubunyag sa Iglesia ni Cristo.* Manila: The Church, 1964.

An exposition of the teachings of the Iglesia. See A. L. Tuggy (entry 1503) for a detailed study of the doctrinal content.

1437 Iglesia ni Cristo. *This is the Iglesia ni Cristo: "Church of Christ."* Quezon City: Iglesia ni Cristo, n.d., 96 pp., illus.

An account of the history, beliefs, and worship, with color photos of many striking, large churches, and addresses in other countries.

1438 "Iglesia ni Kristo calumniates translators of the Catholic Tagalog New Testament." *Sentinel* (Manila) 4, no. 45 (1952).

For other items in the *Sentinel,* a Catholic weekly, see J. R. Santa Romana (entry 1485), pp. 410-11.

Iglesia Ni Cristo

1439 "Iglesia ni Kristo members lose suit on unionism issue." *Manila Chronicle* 20, no. 118 (1964): 1, 11.

1440 "The Iglesia ni Kristo vote." *Sentinel* (Manila) 4 (4 October 1952).

1441 "Iglesia workers set strike on hacienda." *Manila Chronicle* 20, no. 44 (1964): 1, 13.
     The Iglesia in industrial trouble.

1442 "INC distributes free land titles." *Manila Daily Bulletin* 273, no. 2 (1971): 2.
     The Iglesia's contribution to development.

1443 "INC is put to the test in S. Juan." *Manila Daily Bulletin* 233, no. 11 (1967): 2.

1444 "INC justifies exempt imports." *Manila Chronicle* 25, no. 284 (1970): 7.
     The Iglesia on customs dues.

1445 "INC opposes priests' entry to charter meet." *Manila Times* 25, no. 43 (1970): 18.
     The Iglesia's opposition to Catholicism.

1446 "INC warns on poseurs." *Manila Chronicle* 26, no. 160 (1970): 3.

1447 "INK exemption from unions hit." *Daily Mirror* (Manila) 14, no. 224 (1963): 30.

1448 "INK stand on labor backed." *Evening News* (Manila) 18, no. 99 (1963): 10.

1449 Javier, Antonio B. *Pagsusuri sa mga aral ng Iglesia ni Cristo (Manalo)*. Manila, 1965.

1450 Kavanagh, Joseph J. "The 'Iglesia ni Kristo.'" *Philippine Studies* 3, no. 1 (1955): 19-42.
     On the Iglesia's founder, history, membership, worship, beliefs, and publications.

1451 Kavanagh, Joseph J. "Voice of the Iglesia ni Cristo, 1951-1961." *Philippine Studies* (Manila) 9, no. 4 (1961): 651-65.

Iglesia Ni Cristo

A survey of the contents of *Pasugo* (official organ of Iglesia ni Cristo) from 1951-61, with a critique; a valuable means of access to this journal.

1452 Kiunisala, Edward R. "Iglesia' turns from Osmona Jr. to Marcos." *Philippines Free Press* 62, no. 44 (1969): 7, 69, illus.
The Iglesia's political allegiance.

1453 Lynch, Frank. "Iglesia ni Kristo." In *Area handbook of the Philippines*. Vol. 2. Chicago: University of Chicago Press, Philippine Studies Program, 1955, pp. 718-29.

1454 Makabenta, F. P. "Faith, ambiguity, and the Iglesia ni Kristo." *Chronicle Magazine* (Manila) 19, no. 3 (1964): 4-9, illus.

1455 Manalo, Eduardo V. "Verses in the Bible that are misinterpreted to prove that Jesus Christ is God." *Pasugo* (Manila, Iglesia ni Cristo), February 1973, pp. 16-17.

1456 Manalo, Eraño G., and Castro, Cesar. *Christ God investigated–false*. No imprint, n.d., 64 pp.
In English and Tagalog.

1457 Manalo, Felix. *Ang sulo sa ikatitiyak sa Iglesia Katolika Apostolika Romano*. Quezon City: Ipinalimbag ng Pangawasiwaan ng "Ang Pasugo," 1940, 122 pp.

1458 "Manalo's basic lie uncovered." *Sentinel* (Manila) 4 (4 October 1952).
On the founder of the Iglesia.

1459 Manila, Quijano de. "The empire of the Iglesia." *Philippines Free Press* 56, no. 17 (1963): 44-48, illus.
A feature article by a staff writer.

1460 Marfil, F. P. "INK head's birthday turns out to be reunion of politicians." *Chronicle Magazine* (Manila) 20 (23 January 1965): 10-15, illus.
Mainly photographs of anniversary celebrations at Cathedral in San Juan.

1461 Mijarez, P. "1m. [one million] INC radio-TV parts exempted from duties." *Manila Chronicle* 25, no. 282 (1970): 1.

Iglesia Ni Cristo

Customs charges of one million pesos escaped by presidential patronage.

1462 "Minor sect makes deep imprint on RP politics." *New Philippines* (Manila), no. 12 (May 1974), pp. 22-24.
The Iglesia in relation to national politics.

1463 Modesto, Salvador Trani. "The Iglesia ni Kristo." *Unitas* (Manila) 31, no. 4 (1958): 627-718.

1464 Nalus, Victor M. *The Roman Catholic Church*. Manila: Afan Publishing House, 1953, 82 pp.
A doctrinal work from the Iglesia highly critical of Catholicism.

1465 "Origins and beliefs of other sects: Topic no. 2–Iglesia ni Kristo." *Filipino Christian Youth* (Manila, Philippine Federation of Christian Churches) 3, no. 4 (1950): 22-24.

1466 Pacis, V[icente] A. "Thinking full circle: En eglesia [*sic*] religious or political grouping." *Manila Chronicle* 23, no. 208 (1967): 5.
The Iglesia in politics.

1467 "Padilla denounces INC importation." *Philippines Free Press* (Manila) 63, no. 6 (7 February 1970): 45.
On the Iglesia's exemption from customs duties. For other articles in this weekly see J. R. Santa Romana (entry 1485), pp. 410-11.

1468 "Padilla hits INC importation." *Manila Times* 24, no. 338 (30 January 1970): 1-4.
The Iglesia's customs exemption.

1469 *Pasugo* (Manila, Afan Publishing House).
Monthly, 1951-. Official voice of Iglesia ni Kristo. Some articles in English. See J. J. Kavanagh (entry 1451) for critical survey of contents, 1951-61. See *Index to Philippine Periodicals* 19, no. 1 (1974): 491-93 for list of contents of seven issues of vol. 26 (1974).

1470 "Paying IOU? Rep. Romnaldez on INC imports." *Manila Daily Bulletin* 30, no. 259 (30 January 1970): 1, 2, 3.

1471 Plopino Luz. *The literature of the Iglesia ni Cristo*. M.L.S. thesis (library science), University of the Philippines, 1981.

Iglesia Ni Cristo

1472 Querol, N. M. "Death comes for the 'angel from the east.'" *Philippines Herald Magazine* (Manila), 20 April 1963, pp. 8-9, illus.
An obituary on Felix Manalo, founder of Iglesia.

1473 Querol, N. M. "The other side: INC support not always godsend thing." *Manila Times* 24, no. 244 (28 October 1969): 5-A.
On the Iglesia's support for President Marcos.

1474 Rama, N. G. "The religious vote: The combination of politics and religion can make a mess of democratic elections." *Philippines Free Press* 58, no. 18 (1 May 1965): 12.

1475 Roces, Alejandro [R.]. "Nixon and Manalo." *Panorama* 21 (July 1969).
On the Iglesia's founder and President Nixon.

1476 Roperos, G. M. "Iglesia ni Kristo." *Sunday Times Magazine* (Manila) 16, no. 22 (11 January 1959): 20-29.

1477 Rosquites, Brandon V. "Barrio Maligaya: A sanctuary in the wilderness." In *55th anniversary of the Iglesia ni Cristo*. Quezon City: The Church, 1969, pp. 30-39.
A very well-illustrated account of the notable land reclamation and development settlement from 1964; "Maligaya" (happiness) as equivalent to Felix (Latin for "happy"), Manalo's name.

1478 Salava, Federico C. "On 'Iglesia power.'" *Philippines Free Press* 62, no. 45 (8 November 1969): 41.
A drastic critique of a number of members and voters claimed for Iglesia ni Cristo, reducing these to under 400,000 and 100,000 respectively.

1479 Sanders, Albert J[ames]. "An appraisal of the Iglesia ni Cristo." In *Studies in Philippine church history*, edited by G. H. Anderson. Ithaca, N.Y.: Cornell University Press, 1969, pp. 350-65.

1480 Sanders, Albert J[ames]. "Iglesia ni Cristo: Factors contributing to its growth and its future." *Southeast Asia Journal of Theology* 4, no. 1 (1962): 43-56.
Similar to entries 1481 and 1482.

1481 Sanders, Albert J[ames]. *A Protestant view of the Iglesia ni Cristo.* Quezon City: Philippine Federation of Christian Churches, 1962, 77 pp.

Iglesia Ni Cristo

Revised and enlarged from his 1952 article (entry 1482). As completely indigenous in organization and support, with a unitarian theology and a peculiar form of biblical criticism; its history and growth factors.

1482 Sanders, Albert J[ames]. "A Protestant view of the Iglesia ni Cristo." *Union Voice* (Manila, Union Theological Seminary) 9, no. 2 (1952): 8-12, 28.
By a senior Presbyterian seminary professor of theology.

1483 Sandoval, C. P. "Distorted sense of judgment." *Pasugo* (Manila, Iglesia ni Cristo), December 1963, pp. 34-37.

1484 S[an]ta-Romana, Julita R[eyes]. "The Iglesia ni Kristo." *Sower* (Makati, San Carlos Seminary) 1 (April 1959): 36-42.
A summary version of entry 1485.

1485 S[an]ta-Romana, Julita R[eyes]. "The Iglesia ni Kristo: A study." *Journal of East Asiatic Studies* (University of Manila) 4, no. 3 (July 1955): 329-437.
The published version of her M.A. thesis (history), University of Manila Graduate School, College of Liberal Arts, March 1955.

1486 S[an]ta-Romana, Julita R[eyes]. "The Iglesia ni Kristo: Its rise to a progressive militant minority." *Graphic* (Manila) 33, no. 39 (22 March 1967): 14-15, illus.

1487 S[an]ta-Romana, Julita R[eyes]. "Membership and the norm of discipline in the Iglesia ni Kristo." *Philippine Sociological Review* 3, no. 1 (1955): 4-14.
An edited version of two sections of her 1955 M.A. thesis; see entry 1485.

1488 Santiago, Benjamin. *Ang aral ng Dios at and aral ng diablo.* N.p., n.d., 110 pp.
By a member of the Iglesia.

1489 Santiago, Benjamin. *Ang Iglesia Katolika Apostolika Romana.* N.p., n.d., 41 pp.
On the Iglesia, by a member.

1490 Santiago, Benjamin. *Bakit kaya napopoot ang mga tao sa Iglesia ni Cristo? Mababasa minyo ang katugunan sa babasahing ito*. N.p., n.d., 14 pp.

By a member of the Iglesia.

1491 Soliongo, L.P. "Seriously speaking–the Eglesia [*sic*] vote as the vote of sheep." *Manila Chronicle* 23, no. 215 (22 November 1967): 9.

The Iglesia in politics.

1492 Solwen, M. V. "By the way: INC supremo's birthday fete had same touches." *Manila Times* 24, no. 312 (4 January 1920): 5-A.

On Felix Manalo.

1493 Stackhouse, Max L. "The Philippine tinderbox." Part 1. *Christian Century* (Chicago) 99, no. 16 (5 May 1982): 538-42.

Pp. 541-42, the Iglesia as "the largest and fastest growing . . . of any organization outside the army"–a good contemporary survey.

1494 "Students rap Erano Manalo." *Manila Chronicle* 24, no. 362 (18 April 1969): 20.

Opposition to the son of the founder of the Iglesia, by now head of the church.

1495 "Student unrest: Rallies against INC, F. M." *Manila Times* 23, no. 48 (15 August 1969): 1-A.

Opposition to the Iglesia and to President Ferdinand Marcos.

1496 Sumcad, Edwin A. "About the Cebuano and Iglesia ni Kristo votes–is [*sic*] there any?" *Weekly Graphic* (Manila) 31, no. 34 (17 February 1965): 12, 86.

1497 "3 INK ministers slain." *Daily Mirror* (Manila) 22, no. 234 (1 February 1972): 18.

1498 Tipon, Emmanuel S. "Iglesia politics revealed: The Iglesia vote, democracy, and the Philippines." *Philippines Free Press* 62, no. 46 (15 November 1969): 8-9, 58.

A new estimate of numbers based on forty "cathedral-sized" and 3,000 "chapel-sized" churches; maximum of 1,800,000 members and between 585,000 and 1,170,000 voters.

1499 "Today's mail: Debunking the INC myth." *Philippines Herald* (Manila) 49, no. 87 (4 November 1969): 8.

Iglesia Ni Cristo

The Iglesia's alleged political power.

1500 Trinidad, Juan. *Ang Iglesia ni Kristo at iba't ibang sektang protestante.* . . . Manila: Catholic Trade School, 1947. Reprint. 1958, 110 pp.
In Tagalog. A Catholic critique.

1501 Trinidad, R. "From the Iglesia ni Cristo: The biblical truth." *Sunday Times Magazine* (Manila) 25 (15 November 1970).

1502 Tuggy, A[rthur] L[eonard]. "An angel and his church." In *Dynamic religious movements*, edited by D. J. Hesselgrave. Grand Rapids, Mich.: Baker Book House, 1978, pp. 85-101.
On Manalo, "Angel of the East," and his Iglesia.

1503 Tuggy, Arthur Leonard. *Iglesia ni Cristo: A study in independent church dynamics.* Quezon City: Conservative Baptist Publishing, 1976, 272 pp., graphs, maps, figures, illus.
Based on study of the church's documents and personal contact. Includes, pp. 22-24, the author's visit to the various movements on Mt. Banahaw (Colorums, etc.). A comprehensive study made in an eirenic spirit.

1504 Tuggy, Arthur [Leonard]. *The Philippine church: Growth in a changing society.* Grand Rapids, Mich.: William B. Eerdmans, 1971, 191 pp.
Pp. 145-47, growth of Iglesia ni Cristo.

1505 Tumangday, Nick G. "The divinity of Christ: The biblical doctrine of the divinity of Christ compared with the Christology of the Iglesia ni Kristo." M.A. thesis, Philippine Union College, School of Graduate Studies, 1965, 259 pp. Typescript.

1506 Unisala, E. R. "'Iglesia' turns from Osmena Jr. to Marcos." *Philippines Free Press* 62, no. 44 (1 November 1969): 7, 69.
Nationwide Iglesia ni Cristo intelligence network sees irreversible Marcos victory trend. Can a "Catholic backlash" be squeezed out of Sarging's "sour grapes"?

1507 Vengco, Sabino, Jr. "The validity of the Iglesia ni Kristo baptism." *Loyola Studies* (Loyola House of Studies, Ateneo de Manila University, Quezon City), prefatory issue, 2d semester 1965-66, pp. 50-57.

1508 Vinluan, Victor. *A critical analysis of the Christology of the Iglesia ni Cristo, Manalo*. B.D. thesis, Union Theological Seminary (Dasmarinas, Cavite), 1957.

1509 "We the people: INC political strength a myth, reader claims." *Manila Times* 22, no. 194 (6 September 1967): 7-A.

Philippine Independent Church (The Philippines)

The Iglesia Filipina Independente (or P.I.C.) is the best-known body of Philippine origin, as well as one of the two largest, with a membership that has seen early growth to perhaps several million sympathizers, followed by a substantial decline and more recent stabilization at something over a million adherents. Its origin is interwoven with the revolt against Spain in 1896, and against the Catholic Church's failure to indigenize its clergy. The founder, Gregorio Aglipay (1860-1940), was a Filipino priest who became its Supreme Bishop when Isabelo de los Reyes organized the P.I.C. in 1902. Both are represented in the items included here. The P.I.C.'s main concerns were independence and national responsibility, and its religious practices remained the same as those of Rome, from which it had broken. A drift into Unitarianism produced litigation within the church and splits in the 1940s (see S. A. Fonacier, entry 1580), but a return to orthodoxy led to alliance with the Philippine Episcopal Church (American Protestant Episcopal Church in origin) for consecration of bishops and then for intercommunion, in 1961, and for joint ministerial training at St. Andrew's Seminary, Manila.

E. C. Sobrepena (entry 1251 in the Philippines section), surveys the various splits in the P.I.C., and two members of St. Andrew's Seminary have written about its liturgy (E. H. Chandlee) and made available early documents and history (W. H. Scott's many items). Some of the key documents will be found under the name of the Church itself, and also extracts from its journal, *Christian Register*. Catholic examinations were polemical at first, but latterly more scholarly, such as those of P. S. de Achutegui and M. A. Bernad (but see P. G. Gowing's critical review, entry 1588). There have been recent signs of desire for a more Filipino ethos and training than that developed in alliance with the American-related Episcopalians. This church is so different from most of the other movements dealt with in the Philippines that it might well have been left to the bibliographers of Christian church history. Its expression, however, of the revitalization urge among an oppressed people in a colonial situation offers much in common with our other movements, and at the popular level of its membership the interaction of the primal religious inheritance with both the

Philippine Independent Church

Catholic and the Protestant traditions may be more extensive than the official positions of the Church reveal.

In view of the hundreds of items in the bibliographies of the four volumes on the Philippine Independent Church by P. S. de Achutegui and M. A. Bernad (entry 1519), with special strength in Aglipayan sources, the material on this subject given here is confined to a small selection from these sources and a larger selection from other materials, especially those published since the above bibliographies.

1510 Achutegui, Pedro S. de. "Bishop Isabelo de los Reyes Jr.: An ecumenical tribute." *Philippine Studies* (Manila) 19, no. 4 (October 1971): 557-72.

1511 Achutegui, Pedro S. de. Review of *Churches and sects in the Philippines: A descriptive study of contemporary religious movements*, by D. J. Elwood (entry 1085). *Philippine Studies* 16, no. 3 (1968): 577-86.
Critique of some data.

1512 Achutegui, Pedro S. de, and Bernad, Miguel A[nselmo]. "The Aglipayan Churches and the census of 1960." *Philippine Studies* (Manila) 12 (July 1964): 446-59.
Introduction to most Aglipayan offshoots.

1513 Achutegui, Pedro S. de, and Bernad, Miguel A[nselmo]. "Aglipay as ecclesiastical governor of Nuevo Segovia: His circular letters." *Philippine Studies* (Manila) 7, no. 2 (1959): 135-61.

1514 Achutegui, Pedro S. de, and Bernad, Miguel A[nselmo]. "Bishop Whittemore's 'History.'" *Philippine Studies* 10, no. 4 (1962): 684-705.
A highly critical response to L. B. Whittemore's *Struggle for freedom* (entry 1706).

1515 Achutegui, Pedro S. de, and Bernad, Miguel A[nselmo]. "Brent, Herzog, Morayta, and Aglipay." *Philippine Studies* (Manila) 8, no. 3 (1960): 568-83.
Aglipay's correspondence with Bishop C. H. Brent, Bishop E. Herzog (Swiss national Church), and Don M. Morayta (deputy in Spanish Cortes) seeking recognition for himself and his independent church. Digest in *Historical Abstracts* 7 (1961): no. 2556.

1516 Achutegui, Pedro S. de, and Bernad, Miguel A[nselmo]. "The examination papers of Gregorio Aglipay in the Manila Archdiocesan archives." *Philippine Studies* (Manila) 6, no. 4 (1958): 437-53.

Philippine Independent Church

1517 Achutegui, Pedro S. de, and Bernad, Miguel A[nselmo]. "New light on Gregorio Aglipay from unpublished documents in the Manila Archdiocesan archives." *Philippine Studies* (Manila) 6, no. 2 (1958): 174-209.

An important article correcting misinformation in many earlier accounts.

1518 Achutegui, Pedro S. de, and Bernad, Miguel A[nselmo]. "Philippine Independent Church." In *New Catholic encyclopedia*. Vol. 11. New York: McGraw-Hill Book Co., 1967, p. 279.

1519 Achutegui, Pedro S. de, and Bernad, Miguel A[nselmo]. *Religious revolution in the Philippines: The life and church of Gregorio Aglipay, 1860-1960*. Vol. 1, *From Aglipay's birth to his death: 1860-1940*. Manila: Ateneo de Manila, 1960, 579 pp., illus. 2d rev. ed. 1961. Vol. 2, *The life and church of Gregorio Aglipay*. Manila: Ateneo de Manila, 1966, 501 pp., illus. 2d rev. ed. 1968. Vol. 3, *A documentary history. Parts 1 and 2: The religious coup d'état, 1989-1901*. Manila: Ateneo de Manila, 1971, xxxii + 384 pp., illus. Vol. 4, *Documents relevant to the religious revolution in the Philippines. Part 3: The schism of 1902*. Manila: Ateneo de Manila, 1972, xv + 379 pp., illus.

Vol. 2, a history of the Church from 1940 until its merger with the Protestant Episcopal Church (U.S.) in 1961; with documentary appendix 2, new constitution and canons (pp. 443-50). Vol. 3, includes additional biographical material on Aglipay. Vol. 4, 96 documents, mainly in Spanish, from the period 1897-1904, each with an English review of its content; includes beginnings of the Church, and the Jaro schism.

1520 Achutegui, Pedro S. de, and Bernad, Miguel A[nselmo]. "The true birth date of Gregorio Aglipay." *Philippine Studies* (Manila) 5, no. 4 (1957): 370-87.

1521 Aglipay, Gregorio. *Catequesis de la Iglesia Filipina Independiente por el Emmo, Sr.* Edited by Isabelo de los Reyes, Sr. Manila: The Church, 1912, xxvi + 102 pp.

Pp. v-xxvi, Prologo by Jose Ferrandiz; a comprehensive account of the beliefs and practices of the Church.

1522 Aglipay, Gregorio. "The Filipino National Church." *Manila Times*, 25 December 1902. Reprinted in P. S. de Achutegui and M. A. Bernad (entry 1519), vol. 3, pp. 365-67.

Philippine Independent Church

1523 Aglipay, Gregorio. "The Independent Catholic Church in the Philippines." *Independent* (New York), no. 2865 [55] (29 October 1903), pp. 2571-75.

1524 Aglipay, Gregorio. *Sensacionales discurso's y escritos sobre los grandes principios de la Iglesia Filipina Independiente, y varias oraciones de dicha Iglesia.* Manila: [The Church], 1924, 30 pp.
    A collection of speeches, with 3 pp. of prayers.

1525 Aglipay, Gregorio. *Tres discursos notables ... exponiendo les enseñangas de la Iglesia Filipina Independiente.* Manila: Social and Commercial Press, 1935, 25 pp.
    Addresses at the Unitarian Assembly in the U.S. and the International Conference of Liberal Churches, Copenhagen, 1934; a third address on "El sublime misterio y la gloria final."

1526 Aglipay, Gregorio, and Reyes y Lopez, Isabelo de los, Sr. *Evoluciones y estado actual de la Iglesia Filipina Independiente. La Iglesia Independiente y la Romana comparadas.* Manila, 1928, 19 pp.
    Pp. 1-6, under first title, by Aglipay; pp. 6-9, under second title, by de los Reyes, comparing the creeds, the Commandments (the Roman "variations" on them), and the prayers of the two churches.

1527 Aglipayan Church. "An evolving monument to Filipino nationalism." *New Philippines* (Manila), no. 12 (May 1974), p. 4, illus.

1528 *Aglipayan Review.*
    Beginning with the July-August 1980 issue, replaced the *Christian Register* as the organ of the Philippine Independent Church.

1529 Alcantara, Cristan L. "The Philippine Independent Church." M.A. thesis, National University (Manila), 1951, 108 pp. Mimeo.

1530 Alip, Eufronio M. "Aglipayanism: A critical exposition." *Unitas* (Manila) 20 (October 1941).

1531 Alipit, Ramon A. "The position of the Philippine Independent Church." *South East Asia Journal of Theology* 4, no. 1 (1962): 32-36.
    The Episcopal Priest; on history, the concordat with the Episcopal Church, internal reforms, and future prospects.

1532 Alonso, Isidoro C. E. E., et al. *The Catholic Church in the Philippines today.* Manila: Historical Conservation Society, 1968, 131 pp.

Philippine Independent Church

Pp. 38-39, Philippine Independent Church; p. 40, Iglesia ni Cristo and Watawat ng Lahi.

1533 Anderson, Gerald H., and Gowing, Peter G. "The Philippines: Bulwark of the Church in Asia." In *Christ and crisis in Southeast Asia*, edited by G. H. Anderson. New York: Friendship Press, 1968, pp. 143-48. Reprinted as "The Philippine Independent Church–yesterday and today" in *66th foundation anniversary: Philippine Independent Church*. Sta. Cruz, Manila: Executive Committee, National Cathedral Commission, 1968, pp. 61-62.

1534 Apon, Ross. *The union of the Aglipayan Church and the Protestant Episcopal Church*. N.p., [1948], pp. 15-22. Apparently reprinted from *Philippine Evangel*.
    Seen in Missionary Research Library, New York.

1535 Artigas y Cuerva, Manuel. *Galeria de filipinos ilustres*. Manila: El Renacimiento, 1917.
    Pp. 86-98, biography of Aglipay.

1536 Baldemeca, Donato Y. "Reflections of a parish priest." *Diocesan Chronicle* (Manila, Philippine Episcopal Church) 38, no. 4 (1960): 9-11, illus.
    A member on his church as national, free, and Catholic, but welcoming help with training priests from the Episcopal Church.

1537 Belen de Lara, Gavino. *Mpa banal na katwiam nang Iglesia Filipina Independiente*. Manila: General Printing Press, 1935, 50 pp.

1538 Berbano, Teodoro C. "The Philippine Independent Church: A date with history." *Graphic* (Manila) 33, no. 39 (22 March 1967): 26-27, 70, illus.
    Tells the story once again.

1539 Binsted, [Norman Spencer]. "Bishop Binsted's convocation address: Excerpts." *Christian Register* (Sta. Cruz, Manila) 3, no. 10 (1955): 8.
    Included as a sample of the Protestant Episcopal Church attitude expressed in an address to the Philippine Independent Church before relations were formalized.

1540 Binsted, Norman [Spencer]. "The Philippine Independent Church." *Historical Magazine of the Protestant Episcopal Church* 27, no. 3 (1958): 209-46.

Philippine Independent Church

History of the Church's efforts to secure recognition and consecration for its bishops, its relations with Unitarians, and its final acceptance by the American Protestant Episcopal Church; by a bishop of the latter.

1541 Binstead [*sic*], Norman S[pencer]. "Statement concerning the Philippine Independent Church." *Historical Magazine of the Protestant Episcopal Church* 17, no. 2 (1948): 138-39.
Incorporated in the order of service for the consecration of the three bishops in 1948.

1542 Boonen, Mathias. "Le schisme Aglipayen." In *Obstacles à l'Apostolat: Compte-rendu de la septième Semaine Missiologique de Louvain (1929)*. Louvain: Éditions du Muséum Lessianum; Éditions de l'Aucam, 1929, pp. 104-30.

1543 Brand, Donald Vincent. "The Philippine Independent Church: A social movement." Ph.D. dissertation (sociology), Cornell University, 1980, 140 pp.

1544 Briggs, C[harles] W. "Report" [in the ninetieth annual report]. *Baptist Missionary Magazine*, July 1904, pp. 223-26.
Pp. 224-25, on the Aglipay movement and its possibilities if given Protestant help. By a pioneer Baptist missionary.

1545 Briggs, C[harles] W. *The progressing Philippines*. Philadelphia: Griffith & Rowland Press, 1913, 174 pp., illus.
Pp. 67-68, brief summary of Rizal's career; pp. 113-21, Philippine Independent Church – a sympathetic account.

1546 Buttenbruch, Theodor. "Die Kampfesart des Aglipayanismus." *Die Katholischen Missionen* (Freiburg) 42, no. 4 (1914): 93-95.
As cited by P. S. de Achutegui and M. A. Bernad (entry 1519), vol. 1, p. 211. By a Catholic missionary.

1547 Canlas, Querubin D. "The Philippine Independent and Episcopal Churches: A study of their histories and the factors that led them to a concordat relationship." *South East Asia Journal of Theology* 20, no. 2 (1979): 65-67.
A digest of his dissertation, 1976.

1548 Canlas, Querubin D. "A tale of two churches: A study of the concordat relations between the Philippine Independent Church and the

Philippine Episcopal Church." D.Th. dissertation, South East Asia Graduate School of Theology, 1976.

Without use of the P.I.C. archives at St. Andrew's Theological Seminary, Manila.

1549 Canterbury, Archbishop of. *The faith and order of the Philippine Independent Church*. Report of the commission appointed by the Archbishop of Canterbury. ... London: Church Information Office, 1963, 24 pp.

1550 Castillo, Jose Lopez del. *Ley de matrimonio, comentada*. Manila, 1930.
Pp. 315-22, list of Aglipayan ministers at that time.

1551 Chandlee, H[arry] Ellsworth. *De los Reyes: Supreme Bishop in the Philippines*. Pioneer Builders for Christ Series. New York: National Council of the Protestant Episcopal Church, 1962, 21 pp.

Drawing on personal interviews with the head of the Philippine Independent Church.

1552 Chandlee, H[arry] Ellsworth. "The last sixty years." *Diocesan Chronicle* (Manila, Philippine Episcopal Church) 38, no. 4 (1960): 5-6, 13.
On the Philippine Independent Church.

1553 Chandlee, H[arry] Ellsworth. "The liturgy of the Philippine Independent Church." *Studia Liturgica* 3, no. 2 (1964): 88-106. Reprinted in *Studies in Philippine church history*, edited by G. H. Anderson. Ithaca, N.Y.: Cornell University Press, 1969, pp. 256-76.

Brief historical introduction as background for the origins and development of liturgy and customs. The first Independent Church Service-Book described and evaluated; also the methods and process of liturgical revision and reform culminating in the official liturgical books. Their contents are described; also the contemporary liturgical situation.

1554 Chandlee, H[arry] Ellsworth. "The Philippine Independent Church." *Christian Register* (Sta. Cruz, Manila, Philippine Independent Church) 3, no. 10 (1955): 7-8.

A sympathetic survey of the origins, history, and features, with special attention to its relations with the Protestant Episcopal Church of the U.S.; in the P.I.C.'s own journal.

1555 Chandlee, H[arry] Ellsworth. "The Philippine Independent Church." *Pan-Anglican* (Hartford, Conn.) 5, no. 2 (1954): 22-26.

Philippine Independent Church

1556 Chandlee, H[arry] Ellsworth. "The Philippine missal." *Living Church* (Milwaukee) 143 (27 August 1961): 9, 13.
Explains how it was drawn up; fuller account in entry 1553.

1557 "The church in the Philippines." *Church and Community* (Christchurch, N.Z.), November 1964, p. 4.
News reports on the relations between the Philippine Independent and the Anglican Churches, and the former's admission to the National Council of Churches in the Philippines.

1558 Clifford, Mary Dorita. "Aglipayanism as a political movement." Ph.D. dissertation (modern history), St. Louis (Missouri) University, 1960, 593 pp.

1559 Clifford, Mary Dorita. "Iglesia Filipina Independiente: The revolutionary church." In *Studies in Philippine church history*, edited by G. H. Anderson. Ithaca, N.Y.: Cornell University Press, 1969, pp. 223-55.

1560 Coleman, Ambrose. "The inside of the Aglipayan Church." *American Catholic Quarterly Review* 30 (April 1905): 368-81.
Philippine Independent Church interpreted as political, not religious, as a patriotic revolt including atheists and rationalists among its leaders; contains some detailed information, but all from a hostile early Catholic viewpoint.

1561 Cornish, Louis C[raig]. *The Philippines calling*. Philadelphia, Pa.: Dorrance & Co., 1942. Reprint. 1946, 313 pp.
Report of a visit by an American Unitarian leader; on the situation before 1940 and the P.I.C.'s relation to Unitarianism. Pp. 46-134, 194-98, more especially on Philippine Independent Church; p. 80, Isabelo de los Reyes on the church and its seven sacraments.

1562 Cornish, Louis C[raig]. "A visit to the independent church of the Philippines." *Christian Register* (Sta. Cruz, Manila), 23 February; 2, 9, 16, 30 March; 6 April 1939.
The P.I.C.'s own journal.

1563 Cornish, Louis C[raig]. *Work and dreams and the wide horizon*. Boston: Beacon Press, 1937, 403 pp.
Pp. 355-80, "The Independent Church of the Philippines."

1564 Costa, H[oracio] de la, and Schumacher, John N. *Church and state: The Philippine experience.* Loyola Papers, 3. Quezon City: Loyola School of Theology, Ateneo de Manila University, 1978, 65 pp.

Pp. 28-34, Aglipay in the revolution, 1898-99; pp. 39-41, 44, the Aglipayan schism; pp. 48, 53, 63, Aglipayanism; the whole essay is valuable as background.

1565 Cruz, Romero V[ictorino]. "The founding of the Aglipayan Church: An appraisal." *Philippine Social Sciences and Humanities Review* (Quezon City) 26 no. 2 (1961): 187-212.

The factors operating in the founding of the church, including emphasis on Jesuit aggravations as felt by Aglipay.

1566 David, Jose Gutierrez. "Court of Appeals dooms Fonacier: Decision of the special division, by Judge J. G. David." *Christian Register* (Sta. Cruz, Manila, Philippine Independent Church) 1, no. 2 (1952): 1-2.

Successful defense by Isabelo de los Reyes, Jr., against Santiago A. Fonacier's appeal from a trial court judgment against him.

1567 Deats, Richard L[ouis]. *Nationalism and Christianity in the Philippines.* Dallas: Southern Methodist University Press, 1967, 207 pp., bib.

P. 40, Katipunan; chap. 3 (pp. 63-87, 170-73), Philippine Independent Church, now merged with U.S. Episcopalians. By a Protestant missionary.

1568 Deats, Richard Louis. "The universal gospel and modern nationalism: The Philippines as a case study." Ph.D. dissertation (religion), Boston University, 1964, 267 pp.

Chap. 3, Philippine Independent Church. For revised form, see entry 1567.

1569 *Democracia* (Manila).

The daily newspaper of the former Federal Party, with material on the early Aglipayan movement, especially in the issues of 27, 28, and 29 January, 29 and 30 March, 9, 11, and 20 August 1903.

1570 Desmedt, R. J. "Iglesia Filipina Independiente." In *Devant les sectes non-chrétiennes,* by Muséum Lessianum. Louvain: Desclée de Brouwer, [1962], pp. 183-95.

1571 *Diocesan Chronicle* (Manila, Philippine Episcopal Church), Philippine Independent Church issue, 38, no. 4 (August 1960).

Philippine Independent Church

See also D. Y. Baldemega (entry 1536), H. E. Chandlee (entry 1552), A. Pisig (entry 1651), W. S. Mandell (entry 1617), and I. de los Reyes, Jr. (entry 1664).

1572 Doeppers, Daniel F. "Changing patterns of Aglipayan adherence in the Philippines, 1918-1970." *Philippine Studies* 25, no. 3 (1977): 265-77, graphs, maps.
Refers to all churches descended from the original Independent Church. There is an "inexorable but not precipitous decline" in adherents to the Philippine Independent Church.

1573 Doeppers, Daniel F. "The Philippine revolution and the geography of schism." *Geographical Review* 66, no. 2 (1976): 158-77.
Pp. 162-73, the complex distribution of early allegiance to the Philippine Independent Church.

1574 Dreese, Velva A. "The Aglipayan movement in the Philippine Islands." M.A. thesis, College of Missions (Indianapolis), 1927.

1575 Eggan, F[rederick Russell]. "Aglipayanism." In *Area handbook of the Philippines*. Vol. 2. Chicago: University of Chicago Press, Philippine Studies Program, 1955, pp. 687-717.

1576 "El Sr. Gregorio Aglipay, Governador eclesiastico de la Diocesis de Nueva Segovia." *La Republica Filipina*, 15 December 1898, pp. 1-2. Reprinted in *Religious revolution in the Philippines: The life and church of Gregorio Aglipay 1860-1960*, by P. S. de Achutegui and M. A. Bernad. Vol. 3, *A documentary history. Parts 1 and 2: The religious coup d'état, 1989-1901*. Manila: Ateneo de Manila, 1971, pp. 139-41.
The first biographical sketch of Aglipay.

1577 Evangelista, Gregorio C. "Aglipay: A religious and revolutionary leader." *Philippine Panorama* (Manila), n.s. 4, no. 14 (6 April 1975): 8.
Familiar material.

1578 Fernandez, Perfecto V. "The legal status of the churches of the Philippines." *Diliman Review* (Quezon City) 8, nos. 1-3 (1960): 23-120.
Pp. 97-99, summary of the dispute between S. A. Fonacier and other bishops in the Philippine Independent Church in 1946.

1579 Ferrer, Cornelio M. "The Philippine Independent Church." *Philippine Christian Advance and Rural Fellowship Bulletin* 14, no. 4 (1964): 14.

Philippine Independent Church

1580 Fonacier, S[antiago] A. "The Philippine Independent Church story." *This Week: Magazine of the Sunday Chronicle* 13, no. 48 (1958): 7-9.
By the leader of the Unitarian splinter group in the late 1940s – a letter commenting on the article by I. T. Runes (entry 1673).

1581 Fonacier, Tomas S. *Gregorio Aglipay y Labayan: A short biography.* Manila: McCullough Print, 1954, 49 pp.
By an Aglipayan.

1582 Galang, Zoilo M. "The Aglipayan Church." In *The encyclopedia of the Philippines.* Vol. 5. Manila: P. Vera & Sons Co., 1935, pp. 610-26, illus. 2d and 3d eds. Manila: Exequiel Floro, 1950, pp. 143-57.

1583 Galang, Zoilo M. "Aglipay, Gregorio." In *The encyclopedia of the Philippines.* Vol. 9, *Builders of the new Philippines.* Manila: Philippine Education Co., 1936, pp. 27-28.

1584 Garces, Adriano. "Sermon." *La Iglesia Filipina Independiente: Revista Catolica,* 10 and 17 March 1904. English translation by E. A. Bonoan and H. W. Scott, in *Christian Register* (Sta. Cruz, Manila) 24, no. 5 (1979): 13-15.

1585 Garcia, Candido Fernández. *La doctrina de la Iglesia Filipina Independiente – exposicion y critica.* Manila: University of Santo Tomas Press, 1924, 542 pp.
A definitive study from the Roman Catholic viewpoint. See review in *Boletin Eclesiastico* (Manila), 1925, pp. 476-77.

1586 Garcia, Q. M. Review of *Religious revolution in the Philippines . . .* , vol. 4, *Documents relevant to the religious revolution . . . , Part 3: The schism of 1902,* by P. S. de Achutegui and M. A. Bernad (entry 1519). *Philippiniana Sacra* (Manila) 9, (January-April 1974): 177-79.
Critical of the authors' treatment of the friars.

1587 Go, Fe Susan. "The Philippine Independent Church: Religious conversion and the spread of Aglipayanism in Cebu province." *Philippine Quarterly of Culture and Society* 8, nos. 2-3 (1980): 150-67, map, bib.

1588 Gowing, Peter G. "An anti-Independiente tract." *Silliman Journal* 15, no. 2 (1968): 304-8.
Critical review of vol. 2 of P. S. de Achetegui and M. A. Bernad (entry 1519).

Philippine Independent Church

1589 Gowing, Peter G. "The proclamation of the Iglesia Filipina Independiente." *Christian Register* (Sta. Cruz, Manila) 24, no. 4 (1979): 10.

    The circumstances of the proclamation by I. de los Reyes, unexpectedly and without the knowledge of Aglipay.

1590 Gracia, Manuel A. "Aglipayaismo, su fundador y su padrino." *Seminarium* (Singapore, Malayian Seminary) 3, no. 6 (1938): 352-53.

1591 Greschat, Hans-Jürgen. "Religioser Nationalismus auf der Philippinen." In *Humanitas Religiosa: Festschrift fur Haralds Biezais*. Stockholm: Almqvist & Wiksell International, 1979, pp. 242-51.

    On the Philippine Independent Church.

1592 Hayden, Joseph Ralston. *The Philippines: A study in national development*. New York: Macmillan, 1942, xxvi + 984 pp.

    Pp. 572, 573, Philippine Independent Church.

1593 *Iglesia Filipina Independiente: Revista Catolica* (Manila), 11 October 1903-15 December 1904.

    Weekly, edited by Isabelo de los Reyes, Sr., on the activities of the Philippine Independent Church; in Spanish, with sections in Tagalog, Ilocano, and Pangasinan.

1594 International Research Associates. "Project concordat: An opinion research study conducted by the International Research Associates in the Philippines for the Joint Council of the Episcopal Church and the Philippine Independent Church from May through September 1963." [Manila]: The Research Group INRA, [1965?], 314 pp., graphs. Mimeo.

    Copy in St. Andrew's Theological Seminary Library. As sample pages, see pp. 54-57, 60-61, 64-66, 74-75.

1595 Joy, C. R. Letter. *Christian Century* (Chicago) 48, no. 31 (1931): 100, 1002.

    Correcting D. A. McCarthy's letter (entry 1611) – an American Unitarian in defense of Aglipay and his church.

1596 Lagasca, Manuel. *The Philippine Independent Church: Its origin, significance, and importance. A reply to Rev. Godofredo Albano*. Manila: N.p., 1939, 44 pp., illus.

    Some imaginative material; by an Aglipayan priest who was a close friend of Aglipay's.

Philippine Independent Church

1597 Lagunzad, Linda Abarquez. "The organization, administration, and development of the Iglesia Filipina Independiente archives." M.L.S. thesis (library science), University of the Philippines, 1971, 99 pp.

1598 Laubach, Frank C[harles]. "The missionary significance of the last ten years. 4: In the Philippines." *International Review of Missions*, no. 43 [11] (July 1922): 361-76.
Pp. 361-63, Philippine Independent Church as serving to purge Catholicism of abuses.

1599 Laubach, Frank Charles. *The people of the Philippines, their religious progress and preparation for spiritual leadership in the Far East.* New York: George H. Doran Co., 1925, xxi + 23-515 pp., illus., maps.
Pp. 137-57, Aglipayan Church and its loss of property to the Catholic Church in 1906. A Protestant criticism of the movement.

1600 Le Fierro, Vincente L. "The first three decades of the Independent Church." *Philippines Herald Mid-Week Magazine*, 27 September 1933.

1601 Leo XIII (Pope). "The Church in the Philippines: Leo XIII–for a perpetual remembrance." *American Catholic Quarterly Review*, April 1903, pp. xxviii, 372-79.
Full text of Encyclical Letter to the Philippines, September 1902, "Quae mare sinico," in response to the Aglipayan schism.

1602 Le Roy, James A[lfred]. "The Aglipay schism in the Philippines." *Independent* (New York), no. 2891 [66] (28 April 1904), pp. 953-57.

1603 Lerrigo, P. H. J. "The Filipino National Church." *Baptist Missionary Magazine*, September 1903, pp. 642-43.
A brief critical survey.

1604 Letters on Aglipayanism. *Sentinel* (Manila) 9, no. 13 (30 March 1957): 5.

1605 Llamoso, Emiliano L. "Education of Philippine Independent Church clergy." M.Ed. thesis, University of the Philippines, 1968, 118 pp.

1606 Llanes, Jose L. *Father of Philippines socialism: The life of Senator Isabelo de los Reyes.* Manila, 1960. Reprinted from *This Week: Magazine of the Manila Chronicle*, 24 July 1949, pp. 16-17, 20; 31 July 1949, pp. 16, 22, 25-26, 28; 7 August 1949.

Philippine Independent Church

1607 Llanes, Jose L. "The life and labors of Isabelo de los Reyes." *Comment: The Filipino Journal of Ideas, Discussion, and the Arts* (Manila), no. 11 (1960), pp. 62-81.
Based on primary sources – his letters, memoirs, etc.

1608 Lopez, Santiago. *Mons Aglipay y la religion de porvenir (cronica una historica reunion). Mons. Aglipay and religion of the future (chronicle of a historic reunion)*. Manila: N.p., 13 + 13 pp.
Spanish and English versions on facing pages. An apologist for Aglipay sets forth and defends his Unitarian view of Jesus and the biblical materials as a modern rational theology.

1609 Lynch, D. "A defunct religion." *America* 8, no. 14 (11 January 1913): 319-20.
Agllipayanism, with roots in the Katipunan secret society. By a Jesuit.

1610 McAllister, Edward Albert, Jr. "Christianity and the Aglipayan movement – a study of missionary activity in the Philippines with special reference to nationalistic influence." Th.M. dissertation, Eastern Baptist Seminary (Philadelphia), 1970.

1611 McCarthy, Denis A. "That Independent Filipino Church." *Christian Century* (Chicago) 48, no. 28 (15 July 1931): 930.
A letter commenting on W. A. Vrooman's letter (entry 1703).

1612 McGavran, Donald Anderson. "The Independent Church in the Philippines: The story of a spiritual quest." *Encounter* (Indianapolis) 19, no. 3 (1958): 299-321.
A good historical account; support on pp. 319, 321 for assistance to the Iglesia ni Cristo and similar movements in Africa – quite an advanced opinion for this period.

1613 Majul, Cesar Adib. *Apolinario Mabini, revolutionary*. Manila: National Heroes Commission, 1964, 223 pp., illus.
A prize essay. Chap. 14 (pp. 154-76), church, state, and politics: pp. 154-56, 171-76, support of this anticlerical Masonic sympathizer for Aglipay and the Filipino National Church, 1898-99.

1614 Majul, Cesar Adib. "Mabini and the revolution." *Diliman Review* (Quezon City) 5, nos. 1-4 (1957): 1-477. Reprinted as *Mabini and the Philippine revolution*. Philippine Studies, 4. Quezon City: University of the Philippines, 1960, xxi + 477 pp.

Philippine Independent Church

Pp. 408-30 (1957), the National Church of 1899 (in distinction from its "offshoot," the Philippine Independent Church of 1902) still loyal to Rome.

1615 Manaligod, Ambrosio M. *Gregorio Aglipay: Hero or villain*. Sta. Mesa, Manila: Communication Foundation for Asia, 1977, 180 pp.

His first forty years as a prophetic leader concerned with reform within the Catholic Church; by a Filipino Catholic priest who uses the documents in P. S. de Achutegui and M. A. Bernad (entry 1519), vols. 3 and 4, to reach different conclusions.

1616 Mandac, Simeon. "Gregorio Aglipay (1860-1940)." *Historical Bulletin* (Manila, Philippine Historical Association) 12, nos. 1-4 (1968): 234-50.

By a former secretary of Aglipay, 1901-7. Reconstructed from his *Mons. Gregorio Aglipay and his valiant combatants*, and includes Aglipay's answer to his excommunication (pp. 243-49).

1617 Mandell, Wayland S. "Building for the future: Clergy training in the Independent Church." *Diocesan Chronicle* (Manila, Philippine Episcopal Church) 38, no. 4 (1960): 7-8.

1618 Masa, Jorge O. "That Filipino Independent Church." *Christian Century* (Chicago) 48, no. 31 (5 August 1931): 1000, 1002.

Letter favorable to the Church and in answer to previous letters by W. A. Vrooman (entry 1703) and D. A. McCarthy (entry 1611).

1619 Mercader, Cesar, and Mercader Felix. "The church schism in the Philippines." *Weekly Graphic* (Manila) 33, no. 15 (5 October 1966): 22-23; no. 16 (12 October 1966): 30.

1620 Moore, Joseph G., et al. "A study of the Philippine Independent Church." New York: General Division of Research and Field Study, National Council of the Protestant Episcopal Church, U.S.A., [ca. 1964], 4 + 16 + 18 + 5 + 165 + 3 pp. Mimeo.

Made in 1962, with detailed study of and recommendations for each building and parish of the Philippine Independent Church in relation to its local situation (pp. 1-165). Copy at St. Andrew's Theological Seminary, Manila.

1621 Myrick, Conrad. Review of *Religious revolution in the Philippines*, by P. S. de Achutegui and M. A. Bernad (entry 1519), vol. 1. *Southeast Asia Journal of Theology* 4, no. 1 (July 1962): 75-76.

Philippine Independent Church

1622 O'Connor, Patrick. "Aglipayan-Church aligns with U.S. Protestants." *Sentinel* (Manila) 11, no. 24 (1959): 6.

1623 O'Connor, Patrick. "Papers give insight on Aglipayan schism." *Sentinel* (Manila) 11, no. 23 (1959): 1, 6.

1624 O'Connor, Patrick. "Unpublished papers throw new light on the beginnings of the Aglipay heresy." *Sentinel* (Manila) 11, no. 22 (1959): 1, 6.

1625 Oosthuizen, G[erhardus] C[ornelis]. *Theological battleground in Asia and Africa*. London: C. Hurst & Co., 1972, 444 pp.
 Pp. 271-82, the Philippine Independent Church; pp. 282-83, separation in the Philippines (especially Iglesia ni Cristo), and relevant footnotes.

1626 Ortega, Juan. "El bautismo en la secta aglipayana." *Boletin Eclesiastico* 21 (October 1947).

1627 Osias, Camilo, and Lorenzana, Avelina. *Evangelical Christianity in the Philippines*. Dayton, Ohio: United Bretheren Publishing House, [ca. 1931], xx + 240 pp.
 Pp. 128-30, Aglipayan Church and its contributions; summary is reprinted in Z. M. Galang (entry 1583), pp. 624-25.

1628 Parker, Donald Dean. "Church and state in the Philippines, 1896-1906." Ph.D. dissertation (religion), University of Chicago, 1936, 469 pp., map, bib. (pp. 459-68).
 Chap. 7 on the Philippine Independent Church.

1629 Pasco, Tito E. "An Anglipayan replies." *Christian Register* (Sta. Cruz, Manila) 5, no. 10 (1957): 3-4.
 Defending the autonomy of the Philippine Independent Church against confusion with the Protestant Episcopal Church.

1630 Philippine Episcopal Church. "Correspondence and other papers relating to the Petition of the Philippine Independent Church to the Protestant Episcopal Church in the U.S.A. for Episcopal consecration of its bishops." *Diocesan Chronicle* (Manila, Philippine Episcopal Church) 24, no. 6 (September 1947), supplement, 39 pp.

Philippine Independent Church

1631 Philippine Independent Church. "Amended constitution of the Iglesia Filipina Independiente." *Christian Register* (Sta. Cruz, Manila), November 1953, pp. 3, 5.

1632 Philippine Independent Church. *Catecismo de la Iglesia Filipina Independiente*. Manila: Imprenta de Fajardo y Compania, 1905, 48 pp.
   Largely written by Isabelo de los Reyes, as representing official doctrine even if differing from the position of most Church members; much reconciliation with current science.

1633 Philippine Independent Church. *Christian Register* (Sta. Cruz, Manila) 1, no. 1- (1952-).
   The official monthly journal, replaced by the *Aglipayan Review*. See P. S. de Achutegui and M. A. Bernad (entry 1519), vol. 2, pp. 451-52, on the history of the *Christian Register*.

1634 Philippine Independent Church. "Constitucion de la Iglesia Filipina Independiente." *La Verdad* (Manila) 1, no. 1 (21 January 1903): 5. Reprinted in P. S. de Achutegui and M. A. Bernad (entry 1519), vol. 4, pp. 130-41. English translation by W. H. Scott, "First constitution of the Philippine Independent Church – 1902," in *Christian Register* (Manila) 24, no. 2 (1979): 6-9, 13.

1635 Philippine [Independent] Church. "Constituciones provisionales de la Iglesia Filipina." *La Iglesia Independiente: Revista Catolica*, 5 June 1904. Reprinted in P. S. de Achutegui and M. A. Bernad (entry 1519), vol. 3, pp. 113-17. English translation by W. H. Scott, "Provisional ordinances of the Philippine Church 1899," *Christian Register* 24, no. 1 (1979): 8-11.
   The ordinances adopted at Paniqui, 23 October 1899, known as the "Paniqui Constituciones," and endorsed by Aglipay.

1636 Philippine Independent Church. "The creed from the *Oficio divino* (Barcelona 1906), and *The creed from the catequesis de la Iglesia Filipina Independiente* (Manila 1912)." *Christian Register* (Sta. Cruz, Manila), March-April 1980, pp. 9, 12.

1637 Philippine Independent Church. *Doctrina y reglas constitutionales de la Iglesia Filipina Independiente*. Manila: Modest Reyes y Co., 1904, 87 + 4 pp. (including the Six Epistles, pp. 49-87). Also as *Constitutions and canons of the Philippine Independent Church*. Rev. ed. Manila: The Church, 1961, 40 pp.

Philippine Independent Church

1638 Philippine Independent Church. *The Filipino missal: The liturgy for the holy mass according to the use of the Iglesia Filipina Independiente, including the pontifical, ordinal, and articles of religion.* Manila: Supreme Council of Bishops, 1961, xxiv + 280 pp., illus.
See also entry 1639.

1639 Philippine Independent Church. *The Filipino ritual: The administration of the sacrament and other rites and ceremonies of the Church according to the use of the Philippine Independent Church, together with the morning and evening prayer and psalter.* Manila: Supreme Council of Bishops, 1961, xxiii + 341 pp.
In English, combining Roman Catholic, American Episcopal prayer book, and their own rites. See H. E. Chandlee (entry 1552).

1640 Philippine Independent Church. *The national directory of the Philippine Independent Church.* Manila: National Directory Committee of the Philippine Independent Church, 1963, 130 pp., illus.
Also various other years.

1641 Philippine Independent Church. "The ordinary of the mass." *Studia Liturgica* 5, no. 4 (Winter 1966): 20 pp. [not serial in this item.]
Replacing *Oficio divino*, the former service book, since 1961.

1642 Philippine Independent Church. "Proclamation of the Philippine Independent Church, 2 August 1902." English translation by W. H. Scott in the *Christian Register* (Manila) 24, no. 4 (1979): 11-13, from the *Revista Catolica* (Manila, Philippine Independent Church) 1, no. 2 (18 October 1902): 6-7.
Contains Isabelo de los Reyes Sr.'s dramatic speech in the General Council of the Democratic Labor Union, 3 August 1902.

1643 Philippine Independent Church. *66th. foundation anniversary.* Sta. Cruz, Manila: Executive Committee of National Cathedral Commission, Philippine Independent Church, 1968, 80 pp., illus.

1644 Philippine Independent Church. *La Verdad* (Manila), 20 January 1903 to 5 August 1903.
In Spanish, English, and Tagalog; official weekly organ.

1645 "The Philippine Independent Church." *Studia Liturgica* 1, no. 3 (1962): 208.

Philippine Independent Church

Reports of publication of the *Filipino missal* (entry 1638) and *Filipino ritual* (entry 1639), and of establishment of full intercommunion with the Protestant Episcopal Church in the U.S.A.

1646 Philippines, Republic of. Court of Appeals, Manila. Special Division. "Iglesia Filipina Independiente, Gerardo M. Bacaya and Isabelo de los Reyes, Jr., Plaintiff – Appellees, versus Santiago A. Fonacier, Defendant – Apellant. CA-G, R.No. 6371-R. Decision ... June 27, 1952, Jose Gutierrez David." *Christian Register* (Manila) 1, no. 2 (July 1952): 1-2.

A judgment supporting the plaintiffs as legitimate leaders of the Church, and rejecting Fonacier's challenge to the legality of their acts and their position.

1647 Philippines, Republic of. Court of First Instance of Manila, Branch I. "Iglesia Filipina Independiente and Isabelo de los Reyes, Jr., Plaintiffs, versus – Civil Case No. 72138 Santiago Fonacier, Defendant. Resolution ... 25 October, 1957, by Froilan Bayona, Judge." *Christian Register* (Manila) 6, nos. 6-7 (November-December 1957): 7.

Establishing ownership of the church at Cabatuan, which the local priest had claimed belonged to the Fonacier secession group.

1648 Philippines, Republic of. Supreme Court. "Decision of the Supreme Court. [No. L-5917, January 28, 1955]: Santiago A. Fonacier, petitioner versus Court of Appeals, and Isabelo de los Reyes, Jr., respondents." *Official Gazette* 51, no. 3 (March 1955): 1332-53. Reprint. Manila: The Supreme Court, 1955, 36 pp.

1649 Philippines, Republic of. Supreme Court. *Santiago A. Fonacier versus the Court of Appeals and Isabelo de los Reyes, Jr.: Reply brief for the respondent-appellee Isabelo de los Reyes, Jr.*, by Claro M. Recto. Manila, 1952, 164 pp.

1650 Piepkorn, Arthur Carl. *Profiles in belief*. Vol. 2, *Protestant denominations*. San Francisco: Harper & Row, 1978, 721 pp.

Pp. 252-53, Philippine Independent Church: an outline, included in view of its United States connections.

1651 Pisig, Apolonio. "Organizing the laymen." *Diocesan Chronicle* (Manila, Philippine Episcopal Church) 38, no. 4 (August 1960): 12.

On the Philippine Independent Church.

Philippine Independent Church

1652 Poblete, Pascual Hicaro. *Pasiong Mahal ng Ating Panginoong Jesucristo*. Prepared for the Philippine Independent Church. Manila: Limbagan ng Dia Filipino Press, 1935, 178 pp., illus.
On the Philippine Independent Church.

1653 Poethig, Richard P. "Philippine Independent Church, the agony of Philippine nationalism." *Silliman Journal* (Dumaguete City) 14 (1967): 27-54.

1654 Ramirez, Sixto. "Catholic approach to Aglipayans." *Sower* (Makati, San Carlos Seminary) 3 (1st quarter 1961): 41-52.
An eirenic attitude, exploring how to improve relationships.

1655 Remollino, A. "Replica a la obra del P. Fray Candido Garcia Fernandez titulada '*La doctrina de la Iglesia Filipina Independiente, exposicion y critica.*'" Manila: Fajardo, 1926, 39 pp.

1656 Retana [y Gamboa], Wenceslao Emilio. *La Iglesia Filipina Independiente: Sin nuevo cisma religioso*. Madrid, 1901, 33 pp.

1657 Reyes, Jose Sevilla de los. *Biography of Senator Isabelo de los Reyes, father of labor and proclaimer of the Philippine Independent Church*. Manila: Nueva Era Press, 1947, viii + 33 pp., portraits.

1658 Reyes [y Florentino], Isabelo de los, Jr. "Excerpts from a sermon by the Supreme Bishop of the Philippine Independent Church ... February 11, 1962 at the Cathedral of St. Mary and St. John, Quezon City." *Philippine Chronicle* (Manila, Philippine Episcopal Church) 42, no. 2 (1962): 7, 21.

1659 Reyes [y Florentino], Isabelo de los, Jr. "Historical statement." *Christian Register* (Manila, Philippine Independent Church), 2 August 1952.

1660 Reyes [y Florentino], Isabelo de los, Jr. "The Iglesia Filipina Independiente: The Philippine Independent Church." *Historical Magazine of the Protestant Episcopal Church* 17, no. 2 (June 1948): 132-37. Reprinted in *Fifty years of Protestantism in the Philippines*, edited by R. Apon, et al. Manila: Manila Times, n.d., pp. 47-50. Also reprinted in *The three pillars of the Philippine Independent Church*, by J. M. Ruiz. Manila: Villamor Publishing Co., 1950, pp. 20-26.
By the Supreme Bishop of the Church, responsible for major reforms from 1946.

1661 Reyes [y Florentino], Isabelo de los, Jr. "Independent Church passes milestone: New church is offshoot of desire for reforms." *Manila Chronicle*, 2 August 1952.

1662 Reyes [y Florentino], Isabelo de los, Jr. "The Philippine Independent Church today." *Diocesan Chronicle* (Manila, Philippine Episcopal Church) 38, no. 4 (August 1960): 3-4.

1663 Reyes [y Florentino], Isabelo de los, Sr., ed. *La libre razon descubre les grandes absurdes del catolicismo (controversis religiosa entre Aglipayanos y catolicos) por los obispos de la Iglesia Filipina Independiente*. Manila: [Philippine Independent Church?], 1930, 111 pp.

1664 Reyes [y Florentino], Isabelo de los, Sr., ed. *Oficio divino de la Iglesia Filipina Independiente*. Barcelona, 1906.
      Adopted as official book in 1906: "a reformed liturgy, strongly Unitarian in tone, denying several important Catholic teachings, while adhering closely to the external forms of Catholic services" (H. E. Chandlee [entry 1552], p. 5).

1665 Reyes [y Florentino], Isabelo de los, Sr. "Proclamation of the Philippine Independent Church." English translation by W. H. Scott from *La Iglesia Filipina Independiente: Revista Catolica* 2 (October 1902): 6-7, in *Christian Register* (Manila) 24, no. 4 (July-August 1979): 11-13.

1666 Reyes [y Florentino], Isabelo de los, Sr. *La religion Katipunan*. 2d ed. Madrid: Tip. de J. Corrales, 1900.
      Useful as showing the origins of Aglipayan beliefs.

1667 Rivera, Juan A. *The Aglipayan movement*. M.A. dissertation, University of the Philippines, 1932, 33 pp., published in the *Philippine Social Science Review* (Manila) 9, no. 4 (December 1937): 301-28; 10, no. 1 (January 1938): 9-34, bib.
      By an *Independiente* who actually interviewed Aglipay.

1668 Robertson, James A[lexander]. "The Aglipay schism in the Philippine Isalnds." *Catholic Historical Review* (Washington, D.C.) 4, no. 3 (October 1918): 315-44.

1669 Rodriguez, Isacio Rodriguez. *Gregorio Aglipay y los origenes de la Iglesia Filipina Independiente (1898-1917)*. Biblioteca "Missionalia Hispanica," 13. 2 vols. Madrid: Consejo Superior de Investigaciones

Philippine Independent Church

Cientificas, Departmento de Misionologia Espanola, 1960, 597 pp. and 399 pp., including 371 pp. of documents.

A critical Roman Catholic account; see review by C. Myrick in *South East Asia Journal of Theology* 4, no. 1 (July 1962): 77.

1670 Roperos, G. M. "The Aglipayans." *Sunday Times Magazine* (Manila), 2 August 1959, pp. 32-39, illus.

A comprehensive article surveying contemporary activities of the Philippine Independent Church; many good illustrations.

1671 Rosal, Nicolas Ll. *Aglipayanism, yesterday and today: A Catholic study.* Manila: University of Santo Tomas Press, 1959, 46 pp.

A history and critique to show Catholics the differences – Aglipayanism rejects papal authority, exalts nationalism, was founded by a man, and lacked valid sacraments; a plea to "return to the fold."

1672 Ruiz, Juan M. *The three pillars of the Philippine Independent Church.* Manila: Villamor Publishing Co., 1950, 27 pp. Reprinted from *The Philippine Liberal*; with reprint of Isabelo de los Reyes, Jr., "The Philippine Independent Church," from *Fifty years of Protestantism in the Philippines*, edited by R. Abon. Manila: Manila Times, n.d., pp. 47-50, illus.

Bibliographies of Isabelo de los Reyes, Felipe Buencamino, Sr., and Gregorio Aglipay.

1673 Runes, Ildefonso T. "The birth of a new church." *This Week: Magazine of the Sunday Chronicle* 13, no. 44 (2 November 1958): 29-31, illus.

On the Philippine Independent Church. See criticism by S. A. Fonacier (entry 1580), as containing serious factual inaccuracies.

1674 Salanga, Alfredo Navarro. *The Aglipay question: Literary and historical studies on Gregorio Aglipay.* A Crisis Book. Quezon City: Communications Research Institute for Social and Ideological Studies, 1982, 130 pp.

1675 Schmitz, Josef. *The Abra mission in northern Luzon, Philippines, 1598-1955: An historical study.* San Carlos Publications. Series D. Occasional Monographs, 2. Cebu City: University of San Carlos, 1971, 240 pp., illus., maps.

Pp. 131-33, 141-42, Philippine Independent Church, effects on one area, from a Catholic missions viewpoint; also Katipunan secret society of 100,000 members.

Philippine Independent Church

1676 Schumacher, John [N.]. *Readings in Philippine church history*. Quezon City: Loyola School of Theology, Ateneo de Manila University, 1979. Reprint, 1987, 428 pp., maps.

Pp. 317-33, 402 (with references, pp. 398-99), Aglipayan schism. By a Jesuit.

1677 Schumacher, John N. *Revolutionary clergy: The Filipino clergy and national movement, 1850-1903*. Quezon City: Ateneo de Manila Press, 1981, 298 pp.

1678 Scott, W[illiam] H[enry]. "Aglipay and Henry VIII." *N.P.O. Bulletin* (National Priests' Organization, Philippine Independent Church) 2, no. 1 (June 1980): 3-4.

A detailed account of Henry VIII's marriage affairs and of two popes in explanation of Aglipay's comments in his manifesto of 1898.

1679 Scott, W[illiam] H[enry]. "Aglipay as patriot and prophet." *Christian Register* (Sta. Cruz, Manila) 24, no. 5 (September-October 1979): 7-8.

Favorable review of A. M. Manaligod's biography (entry 1615), which treats Aglipay's first forty years as a Catholic.

1680 Scott, William Henry. "Biblia y ciencia, amor y libertad." *Christian Register* (Manila, Philippine Independent Church) 13, no. 9 (October 1964): 9-10.

In English: a eulogy of Aglipay and his Church, by an American Episcopal Church missionary serving as director of the Aglipay Institute – a school of the Independent Church.

1681 Scott, William Henry. "Don Belong translates Scripture." *Aglipayan Review* (Manila) 1, no. 1 (July-August 1980): 6.

On Isabelo de los Reyes, Sr., as translator of the New Testament into Ilocano between 1898 and 1905 – a little known activity.

1682 Scott, William H[enry]. "Gregorio Aglipay as Katipunero." *N.P.O. Bulletin* (National Priests' Organization, Philippine Independent Church) 2, no. 2 (1980): 4 pp.

Aglipay's political outlook and founding of a local Katipunero in 1897.

1683 Scott, W[illiam] H[enry]. "Gregorio Aglipay in U.S.T." *N.P.O. Bulletin* (National Priests' Organization, Philippine Independent Church) 1, no. 2 (November 1979): 3-4.

Philippine Independent Church

Details of his education, culminating in a B.A. at the University of San Tomas in 1888 with Jose Rizal, and latter's influence.

1684 Scott, W[illiam] H[enry]. "Gregorio Aglipay's schooldays." *Aglipayan Review* (Manila, Philippine Independent Church) 1, no. 2 (September-October 1980): 5, 12.
Details of his education, late development, alienation from the outdated system, and association with Jose Rizal.

1685 Scott, W[illiam] H[enry]. "Gregorio Aglipay's youth." *Christian Register* (Sta. Cruz, Manila) 25, no. 3 (May-June 1980): 4-7.
His family, and the social situation in Ilocos Norte, where he grew up.

1686 Scott, W[illiam] H[enry]. "The Philippine Independent Church in history." *East and West Review* 28, no. 1 (January 1962): 3-13. Reprinted in *Silliman Journal* (Dumaguete City) 10, no. 3 (1963): 298-310.

1687 Scott, W[illiam] H[enry]. "The proper use of documents." *Philippine Studies* 11, no. 2 (1963): 328-35.
A criticism of P. S. de Achutegui and M. A. Bernad's study of the Philippine Independent Church (entry 1519), and see their reply, pp. 335-41.

1688 Scott, W[illiam] H[enry]. "The spirit of Gregorio Aglipay." *Christian Register* (Manila, Philippine Independent Church), no. 1 (1975), pp. 3, 6. Reprinted in *Who are you Filipino youth?* Quezon City: Tala Publishing Corp., 1976, pp. 38-40.
Address during the 34th Aglipay annual death anniversary celebration, Cultural Center, Batac Municipality, Ilocos Norte, 17 September 1974.

1689 Scott, W[illiam] H[enry]. "Theological education in the I.F.T. 75 years ago." *N.P.O. Newsletter* (National Priests' Organization, Philippine Independent Church) 1, no. 1 (September 1979): 5-6.
Details of early minor and major seminaries from 1903 to 1905.

1690 Scott, William Henry. "Today Don Belong would be joining a civil liberties group championing human rights." *Who* 2, no. 33 (17 November 1979): 11-13.
On Isabelo de los Reyes, Sr.

1691 Scott, W[illiam] H[enry]. "Young Aglipay's Ilocos Norte." *Christian Register* (Sta. Cruz, Manila) 25, no. 1 (January-February 1980): 13, 15.
The underdeveloped, disturbed, and remote region where he spent his first sixteen years.

1692 Seylers, Franz. "'Aus der eignene Quelle trinken.' Über den Aufbruch in der Philippinischen Unabhängigen Kirche und die Herausforderungen für die Utrechter Union." *Internationale Kirchliche Zeitschrift* 3 (1988): 129-69.

1693 Seylers, Franz. "Die Philippinischen Unabhängige Kirche." *Ökumenische Rundschau* 3 (1988): 352-62.

1694 Sison, Juan C. "Critica de la validez de los sacramentos en la Iglesia Aglipayana." Doctoral dissertation, University of Santo Tomas (Manila), 1941, 155 pp.
See review in *Boletin Eclesiastico* (Manila) 21 (1947): 316-19. A thorough study from a Roman Catholic viewpoint.

1695 Taft, Mrs. William Howard [Helen Herron]. *Recollections of full years.* New York: Dodd Mead & Co., 1914, 395 pp., illus.
Pp. 258-62, Aglipayanism, and the social encounter with Aglipay avoided by the Catholic Apostolic Delegate.

1696 Taft, William Howard. "[Civil Governor's report on the Aglipayan schism] November 10, 1902." *Reports of the Philippine Commission* (1900-1903), pp. 319-20. Reprinted in P. S. de Achutegui and M. A. Bernad (entry 1519), vol. 4, pp. 184-86.

1697 Tuggy, Arthur [Leonard]. *The Philippine Church: Growth in a changing society.* Grand Rapids: William B. Eerdmans, 1971, 191 pp.
Pp. 115-22, Philippine Independent Church; pp. 143-45, its decline.

1698 Vacas, Felix. "Aglipayanism unmasked: The doctrine of Aglipayanism compared with the Protestant-Episcopalian and Catholic." *Unitas* (Manila) 34, no. 2 (April-June 1961): 227-63.
By a Dominican monk.

1699 Vacas, Felix. "Exposicion y critica del bautismo Aglipayano." *Unitas* (Manila) 30, no. 2 (April-June 1957): 227-301; 30, no. 3 (July-September 1957): 463-534; 30, no. 4 (October-December 1957): 687-

Philippine Independent Church

737; 31, no. 1 (January 1958): 5-76. Reprint. Manila: University of Santo Tomas Press, 1958, 259 pp.

In Spanish; a Dominican critique of baptism in the Philippine Independent Church.

1700 Valleser, Sebastian. *Ang Iglesia Filipina Independiente sa kahayag sa Biblia ug katarungan Ikaduhang patik*. Cebu: Independent Press, 1932, 24 pp.

1701 Victoriano, Enrique L. "What Aglipayans believe." *Philippine Studies* (Manila) 8 (1960): 292-99.

A Jesuit on the Aglipayan doctrines of the Trinity and of Christ, expounded by quotations from the church's official documents and the speeches of Aglipay and Isabelo de los Reyes.

1702 Von der Mehden, Fred R. *Religion and nationalism in south east Asia*. Madison: University of Wisconsin Press, 1963.

P. 143, the Aglipayan schism as a nationalist expression.

1703 Vrooman, W. A. "Protestants in the Philippines." *Christian Century* (Chicago) 48, no. 25 (24 June 1931): 843.

A letter in favor of the Philippine Independent Church as a "liberal Protestant" movement.

1704 Wentzel, Constance White. *A half century in the Philippines*. New York: National Council [of the Protestant Episcopal Church], 1952, 64 pp.

Pp. 12-14, Philippine Independent Church and the consecration of its bishops in 1948 – a very brief outline.

1705 Whitney, John R. "Philippine national religion and Philippine Independent Church." *Anglican Theological Review* 53, no. 2 (1971): 86-103.

The relations of ethnicity (with a Sagado Episcopalian as an example) and nationalism, with the Independent Church as a development both indigenous and ecumenical.

1706 Whittemore, L[ewis] B[liss]. *Struggle for freedom: History of the Philippine Independent Church*. Greenwich, Conn.: Seabury Press; London: S.P.C.K., 1961, 228 pp.

By a sympathetic American Episcopalian, and used as a source book (although factually careless) at the U.S. Episcopalian convention of 1961, which accepted the P.I.C. into full intercommunion. Pp. 92-103, Aglipay makes a decision; pp. 104-24, religious reformation.

Philippine Independent Church

1707 Wise, F. H. "The history of the Philippine Independent Church (Iglesia Filipina Independiente)." M.A. dissertation, University of the Philippines, 1954, 272 pp., bib. (pp. 267-72). Mimeographed in 1965 by Silliman University College of Theology, St. Andrew's Theological Seminary and Union Theological Seminary.
    A not very accurate account by a Protestant minister.

1708 Zaide, Gregorio F. *Philippine history and civilization.* Manila: Philippine Associated Publishers, 1939, 755 pp., illus.
    Pp. 257-58, Apolinario de la Cruz revolt; pp. 328-30, Aglipay; pp. 330-31, Filipino Christian Church, by secession from Aglipayanism in 1928.

Unification Church (Korea)

This new religious movement, known in Korea as T'ongil-gyo, was founded by Mun Sŏn-myŏng, or Sun Myung Moon as he is known elsewhere. Since it is somewhat marginal to our category, especially in its history and forms outside Korea, where its main expansion has occurred, we include only a selection of items, mainly in European languages, which refer to its origins and history in Korea and to its presence in Japan. The indigenous religion in Korea could be called shamanism (although in an unusual form more like spirit possession) and has never died out despite the massive influence of the invasive religions of Confucianism, of Buddhism, and of Christianity. The rapid and extensive growth of the latter in Korea has provided one of the factors for the rise of a movement that may be seen as an interaction among the primal religious tradition of Korea, Confucianism, and Christianity.

1709 Boettcher, Robert B. *Gifts of deceit: Moon, Park, and the Korean scandal.* New York: Holt, Rinehart, and Winston, 1980.

1710 Catholic Bishops' Conference (Japan). "Statement of the Catholic Bishops' Conference of Japan on the Holy Spirit Association for the Unification of World Christianity (22 June 1985)." *Japan Missionary Bulletin* 39, no. 3 (1985): 58-59.

1711 Ch'oi Syn-duk. "Korea's Tong-il movement." In *Transactions of the Korea Branch, Royal Asiatic Society: The new religions in Korea,* edited by S. F. Palmer (Seoul) 43 (1967): 167-80.
    By a former active member of the Unification Church.

Unification Church

1712 Chong Sun Kim. *Rev. Sun Myung Moon*. Washington, D.C.: University Press of America, 1978.

1713 "A Christian 'new religion.'" *Japanese Religions* 9, no. 1 (1976): 68-71.
On the Unification Church of Sun Myung Moon.

1714 Chryssides, George D[avid]. *The advent of Sun Myung Moon: The origins, beliefs, and practices of the Unification Church*. London: Macmillan, 1990, 210 pp.
A fair and systematic phenomenological study, with emphasis on the Korean background; probably the most initimate account by a nonmember. Pp. 89-103, five "new Christian" groups as precursors; pp. 175-86, "Personal reflections."

1715 Chryssides, George D[avid]. "The four position foundations." *Religion Today* (London) 2, no. 3 (1985): 7-8.
In searching for the origins of this basic doctrine, rejects Confucianism (suggested by W. Lewis) and Taoism as developed within Ch'ŏndo-gyo (suggested by R. Flasche), explores possible Marxist influence, and recognizes the Christian contribution of a personal deity.

1716 Chryssides, George D[avid]. "The Welsh connection: Pentecostalism and the Unification Church." *Religion Today* (London) 5, no. 3 (1990): 6-8.

1717 Chun Young Bok. "The Korean background of the Unification Church." *Japanese Religions* (Kyoto) 9, no. 2 (1976): 14-18.
By the Secretary, Evangelical Department of the General Assembly of the Korean Church in Japan.

1718 Cozin, Mark. "A millenarian movement in Korea and Great Britain." *A sociological yearbook of religion in Britain*, edited by M. Hill, no. 6 (1973), pp. 100-121.

1719 Dayton, Donald W. "Protestant Christian missions in Korea as a source of Unification thought." In *Religion in the Pacific era*. New York: Paragon Press, 1985, pp. 78-92.

1720 Edwards, Cliff. "Sun Myung Moon and the scholars." *Dialog: A Journal of Theology* 21 (Winter 1982): 56-59
An important report and reflection on the Unification Church seminar in Tenerife in 1982, showing the uniqueness of such methods,

with scholarly critiques of the Unification theology, and analysis of its roots.

1721 Eu Hyo Won. *Divine principle*. English translation from Korean original in 2 vols., 1957 and 1966. Washington, D.C.: (H.S.A.U.W.C.), 1973. 5th ed. New York: H.S.A.U.W.C., 1977, 536 pp., photo.
The Holy Spirit Association for Unification of World Christianity – its teaching, based on the revelation to S. M. Moon.

1722 Flasche, Rainer. "Die Lehren de Vereinigungskirche." In *Neue Religionen – Heil oder unheil? Beispiel Vereinigungskirche Sun Myung Moon*, edited by K. E. Becher and H.-P. Schreiner. Landau and Pfalz: Pfalzische Verlagsanstalt, 1982, pp. 97-148.
Especially pp. 101-13, on the roots of the beliefs in the Chinese-Korean mind.

1723 Flasche, Rainer. "Religiöse Neugründungen: Ihre Entwickslungsstrukturen und Entstehungsbedingungen am Beispiel des Vereinigungskirche (T'ong'ilgyo)." *Zeitschrift für Missionswissenschaft und Religionswissenschaft* 68, no. 1 (1984): 24-51, English summary.
Especially section 3, on the origins of Unification beliefs in Korean history, and in Taoist and Ch'ŏndo-gyo teachings.

1724 Flasche, Rainer. "The Unification Church in the context of East Asian religious traditions." *Acta Comparanda II*. Antwerp: Faculteit voor Vergleijkende Godsdienstwetenschappen, 1987, pp. 25-48.
Paper presented at a New ERA Conference, Puerto Rico, 1984, interpreting the four-position theology as a development from Taoism.

1725 Hunt, Everett N., Jr. "Moon Sun Myung and the Tong-il (Unification Church)." In *Dynamic religious movements*, edited by D. J. Hesselgrave. Grand Rapids: Baker Book House, 1978, pp. 103-27.
Primarily on the Korean history and the *Divine principle*'s teachings, by a long-serving American missionary in Korea.

1726 "Japanese Christian concerns about Unification Church." *Ecumenical Press Service* 55, no. 15 (1988): 88.04.109.

1727 Kim, David S. C. "MTS President David S. C. Kim speaks to church members on anniversary celebration." *Cornerstone* (Barrytown, N.Y., Unification Theological Seminary) 8, no. 5 (1984): 1-3, 4, 6, illus.

Unification Church

His experience in the Church from 1954, a vauable Korean account, including the Church's version (with photos) of Pastor McCabe's visit in 1956 – see J. McCabe (entry 1733).

1728 Leaman, See. "The Unification Church – blessing or monster?" *Japan Missionary Bulletin* 29, no. 9 (1975): 513-20. Reprinted from *Japan Christian Activity News*, 14 March, 18 April, 9 May, 23 May 1975.
In Japanese.

1729 [Lee Hang Nyong, ed.]. *Research on the Unification Principle: Seminars of Korean Scholars on Unification Ideology.* Seoul: Song Hwa Press, 1981, 304 pp.

1730 Lee Sang Hun. *Explaining Unification thought.* English translation from Japanese. New York: Unification Thought Institute, 1982, 357 pp.
A philosophical exposition and apologia.

1731 Lee Sang Hun. *The new cultural revolution and Unification thought.* New York: Unification Thought Institute, 1973, xvi + 300 pp., illus.
An English translation of *T'ong-il sasang*, based on the teachings of S. M. Moon.

1732 Lewis, Warren. "Hero with the thousand-and-first face." In *A time for consideration: A scholarly appraisal of the Unification Church*, edited by M. D. Bryant and H. W. Richardson. Symposium Series. New York and Toronto: Edwin Mellon Press, 1978, pp. 275-89.
S. M. Moon interpreted as a shaman in the north Korean tradition, with *The nine songs* of Chinese shamanism as "the tap root of Moon's spirituality"; by a nonmember professor at the Unification Seminary in Barrytown, N.Y.

1733 McCabe, J[oshua]. "Korean report." *Apostolic Herald* (Bradford, U.K.), November 1956, pp. 163-64, and cover photo.
An early Christian contact and report on the Unification Church in 1956, by a pastor of the Apotolic Church sent from Australia to explore relationships with this seemingly Pentecostal movement.

1734 Mignot, Ed. "The cult of Heung Jin and the New Pentecost." *Areopagus* (Hong Kong) 1, nos. 3-4 (1988): 52.

1735 Mignot, Ed. "Marriage rituals in Tongil." *Areopagus* (Hong Kong) 2, no. 4 (1989): 36-37.

1736 Nemeshegyi, Peter. "Unification Church and Christianity." *Japan Missionary Bulletin* (Tokyo) 39, no. 3 (1985): 60-63.

1737 Sohn Kyoo Tae. "Kirche in der Koreanischen Kultur und Gesellschaft." *Informationsbrief: Korea* (Stuttgart, Evangelisches Missionwerk in Südwestdeutschland), no. 9 (1985), 7 pp.
Pp. 6-8, on the Pentecostal churches (including the "Moon-Sekte") as Christianized versions of shamanism.

1738 Thelle, Notto R. "The Unification Church: A new religion." *Japanese Religions* (Kyoto) 9, no. 2 (1976): 2-13.

1739 Tillet, Gregory T. "Sources of doctrine in the Unification Church." *Update* (Aarhus) 8, no. 1 (1984): 3-8.

1740 [T'ongil-gyo.] "Holy Spirit Association for the Unification of World Christianity." *Korean Religions* (Seoul) 2, no. 2 (1970): 53-57.
A historical and doctrinal outline supplied by the headquarters of T'ong-il-gyo on its position.

1741 [Unification Church.] *The path of a pioneer: The early days of Reverend Sun Myung Moon and the Unification Church*, edited by J. Gullery. New York: HSA Publications, 1986, 69 pp., illus.
An official, popular biography.

Index of Authors and Sources

Note: References are to entry numbers, not pages.

Aberle, David F., 1-3, 211
Abesamis, Gil, 1019
Achutegui, Pedro S. de, 1020, 1085, 1510-1520
Ackerblom, B. *See* B. A.
Ackerman, S. E., 1004-1005, 1011
Adalba-Lim, Estefania, 1021
Adas, Michael, 289
Adelman, Fred, 419
Adriaanse, Laurens, 824-825
Adriani, N., 895
Aglipay, Gregorio, 1521-1526
Aglipayan Church, 1527
Aglipayan Review, 1528
Agoncillo, Teodoro A., 1022
Ahmed, Akbar S., 533
Aichner, P., 1006
Alcantara, Cristan L., 1529
Alejandro, D. D., 1023, 1398
Alip, Eufronio M., 1024, 1530
Alipit, Ramon A., 1531
Allison, Stephen H., 1025
Alonso, Isidoro C. E. E., 1026, 1532
Alonzo, Manuel P., Jr., 1399

Alvior, Efren, 1400
Ames, Michael M., 4
Amstutz, Josef, 290
Anderson, Gerald H., 1027, 1533
Anderson, Kirsten E., 1305
Ando, Hirofumi, 1401-1402
Anokhin, A. V., 420
Anthropological Quarterly, 291
Apolinario, Eulalio S., 1028, 1404
Apon, Ross, 1534
Appasamy, Paul, 534
Aquili, Eugene G. d', 144
Aranas, Simeon, 1029
Araneta, Antonio, 1156
Araneta, Francisco, 1405
Araneta-Gonzalez, Patricia, 1030
Archer, W. G., 535
Archives de Sociologie des Religions, 5
Arens, Richard, 1031-1032
Artigas y Cuerva, Manuel, 1033, 1535
Asis, R. V., 1406
Atienza, Max, 1034
Avila, Charles R., 1035

Ayers, Alexander P., 1407

B. A., 418
Baago, Kaj, 536
Baal, Jan van, 6, 7
Bacdayan, Albert S., 1036-1037
Bainbridge, William S., 220
Bakai, N., 421
Bakker, J. W. M., 826-828
Balandier, Georges, 8
Baldemeca, Donato Y., 1536
Baldemor, Rogelio, 1408
Ballard, Emilie, 1306
Banerji, M. G., 537
Banguis, Fabian L., 1038
Banks, E. Pendleton, 785
Banton, Michael, 9
Baptist Missionary Magazine, 786
Barber, Bernard, 10
Baricanosa, Jose B., 1039
Barker, Eileen, 11-12
Barkun, Michael, 13-14, 292
Barnett, H. G., 15
Barney, G. Linwood, 989-990
Barouh-Simon, Ida, 1385-1386
Barrett, David B., 293
Bartels, Dieter, 829-830
Bartlett, F. C., 16
Bastide, Roger, 17-20
Bates, E. S., 21, 294
Bateson, Gregory, 22
Bautista, Jose P., 1040
Bayot, Felix, 1041
Beckford, James A., 23-24
Beech, Ronald W., 1409
Belen de Lara, Gavino, 1537
Benda, Harry J., 831
Bengalee, 538
Bennett, Cephas, 1307
Bennett, John G., 832
Bentley, Barbara, 1042
Benz, Ernst, 25, 295, 787, 1333
Berbano, Teodoro C., 1538

Bernad, Miguel A., 1512-1520
Berndt, Manfred H., 435
Berquist, James A., 539
Berry, Robert C., 833-834
Bessac, Frank B., 991
Bessac, Susanne, 991
Beyer, Ulrich, 835
Bezacier, Louis, 1334
Bhadra, Ranajit K., 540
Bhandari, J. S., 541
Bhardwaj, Gopal, 542
Bhatt, Gavri S., 402
Bhruksasri, Wanat, 1320
Bieder, Werner, 453
Bihar, Government of, 543
Bijlevelt, J., 836
Binstead, Norman S. *See* Binsted, Norman S.
Binsted, Norman S., 1539-1541
Biswas, Prophilla C., 544
Blair, E. H., 1043
Blandre, Bernard, 1335
Blumberger, P. J. T., 837
Boal, Barbara M., 545, 1336
Bodding, P. O., 546-548
Boettcher, Robert B., 1709
Boland, B. J., 838
Bolton, Robert, 436
Bombshell, 1410
Boonen, Mathias, 1542
Boreman, Per, 357, 358
Bottomley, G., 839
Bourguignon, Erika, 26-29
Bower, Ursula G., 549
Bradley-Birt, F. B., 550-551
Brand, Donald V., 1543
Brandes, J., 840
Brännström, Olaus, 359
Bray, Jenny, 1007
Brent, Charles H., 1044
Brézault, Alain, 296
Briggs, C. W., 1544-1545
Briggs, George W., 552

Bright-Paul, Anthony, 841
Brookes, Graham F., 842-843
Brown, Peter, 30
Budd, Susan, 31
Bulatao, Jaime, 1045
Bulosan, Carlos, 1046
Bunnag, Tej, 1308
Burger, Henry G., 32
Bürkle, Horst, 33
Burma, Government of, 788
Burridge, Kenelm O. L., 34-37
Butler, John F., 297
Buttenbruch, Theodor, 1546
Byrne, Frank, 844

Cachet, F. Lion, 845
Caddawan, Pablito P., 1047
Cady, John F., 789
Calang, Juan, 1048
Caliwag, F. M., 1410
Campbell, A., 553
Campbell, J. M., 554
Camps, Arnulf, 298
Canadian Baptist Overseas
    Mission Board, 846
Canlas, Querubin D., 1547-1548
Canterbury, Archbishop of, 1549
Cao-Dai: Giao-Ly, 1337
Caplan, Lionel, 783
Carey, P. B. R., 847
Carstairs, R., 555
Carter, H. W., 556
Castillo, Jose L. del, 1550
Castles, Lance, 831
Castrén, Kaarlo, 360
Castren, Matthias A., 422
Castro, Cesar, 1456
Catañgay, Tomas C., 1413
Catholic Laymen's Organisation
    of Volunteers, 1414
Cha Ne Cho-Ma Ma Lay, 790
Chandlee, H. Ellsworth, 1551-
    1556

Chandler, David P., 987
Chang Byung-il, 454
Chang, Tom, 445
Chatterji, Saral K., 557
Chattopadhayaya, K. P., 558
Chaudhuri, Sashi B., 559
Chenu, Marie-Dominique, 38
Chéry, H.-Ch., 39, 299
Chesis, Gert, 1049
Chesneaux, Jean, 300-301
Chia Koua Vang, 992
Childe, Donald B., 791
Chio, Julita M., 1050
Ch'oe Chae-sok, 456
Ch'oe Sin-dok, 457-460
Ch'oi Syn-duk, 1711
Chong Sun Kim, 1712
Choudhury, Nirendra C., 560
Cho Yong-il, 455
Christian, John L., 792
Chryssides, George D., 1714-1716
Chun Young Bok, 1717
Chung Chai Sik, 461, 462
Clark, Charles A., 463
Clavreuil, Gérard, 296
Clemhout, Simone, 40, 41
Clemmer, Richard O., 42
Clifford, Mary D., 1558-1559
Clymer, Kenton J., 1051
Coats, George Y., 1052
Coleman, Ambrose, 1560
Colless, Brian, 43
Collet, Giancarlo, 290
Collis, Maurice S., 793
Colpe, Carsten, 44-46
Comhaire, Jean L., 302
Concepcion, Juan de la, 1053
Conley, William W., 1008
Constantino, J. de, 1416
Constantino, Renato, 1054
Cooley, Frank L., 848-849
Coolsma, S., 850
Coomans, M., 851

Cornish, Louis C., 1561-1563
Costa, H. de la, 1564
Coulet, George, 1339-1340
Covar, Prospero R., 47, 1055-1063
Cozin, Mark, 1718
Crespy, Georges, 48
Crippen, Harlan R., 1064
Cripps, Francis, 1309
Cruikshank, Robert B., 1065
Crumrine, N. Ross, 303
Cruz, Apolinario de la, 1066
Cruz, Paschalis, 1419
Cruz, Romeo V., 1565
Cullamar, Evelyn T., 1067
Cullen, Vincent G., 1068-1069
Culshaw, W. J., 561

Dahlback, Gustav, 358
Dammann, Ernst, 304
Danandjaja, James, 852
Dansalan Research Center, 1070
Dardess, John W., 437
Das, Amal K., 562
Das, Anthony, 563
Das, N. K., 564
Das, T. C., 565
Datta, Kalikinkar, 566-568
Datta-Majumder, Nabendu, 569-570
David, Jose G., 1566
Dayton, Donald W., 1719
Deats, Richard L., 1071-1073, 1420, 1567-1568
Del Rosario, Romeo, 1074
Deltgen, Florian, 49
Demetrio, Francisco R., 1075
Democracia, 1569
Derne, S., 571
Desmedt, R. J., 1570
Desroche, Henri, 50-54, 305
Devanandan, P. D., 572
Devins, John B., 1076
Dhan, Rekha O., 573

Diâkonova, V. P., 423
Diaz, Casimoro, 1077
Dietrich, Gabriele, 574
Digan, Parig, 853
Diocesan Chronicle (Philippine Episcopal Church), 1630
Diwakar, R. R., 575
Dizon, Nicolas C., 1078
Dodge, Paul S., 1310
Doeppers, Daniel F., 1079, 1572-1573
Dokhuma, James, 576
Dorsinfang-Smets, Annie, 306
Doshi, S. L., 577
Douglas, Mary, 55
Dournes, Jacques, 1341
Downs, Frederick S., 578
Dozon, Jean-Pierre, 56
Dreese, Velva A., 1574
Drewes, G. W. J., 854
Du Bois, Cora, 855
Du Toit, B. M., 57
Dube, S. C., 579
Dufeil, Michel-M., 1342
Dunstheimer, G. G. H., 1343

Earhart, H. Byron, 465
Eastwood, Tristram, 1080
Eckert, Georg, 58, 307
Edmonson, Munro S., 59
Edwards, Cliff, 1720
Eggan, Fred, 1081-1082, 1575
Eister, Allan W., 60-61
Ekka, Philip, 580-582
Eleazor, Eulogio V., 1083
Elesterio, Fernando G., 1084, 1421
Eliade, Mircea, 62
Elkin, A. P., 63
Ellenberger, Henri F., 308
Elliot, Alan J. A., 1302
Ellwood, Robert S., Jr., 856, 1344
Elmore, Wilber T., 583

Elwin, Verrier, 585
Elwood, Douglas J., 1085-1088
Emmet, Dorothy, 64
Enchakkalody, Th., 586
Engh, Arne, 361
England, John C., 403
Englishman, 587
Enverga, Tobias Y., 1089
Epton, Nina C., 857
Ertle, Brigitte, 65
Espinaola, Julio C., *See* Espínola, Julio C.
Espínola, Julio C., 66
Estruch, Juan, 67
Eu Hyo Won, 1721
Eubank, Allan, 1306
Evangelista, Gregorio C., 1577

Fabian, Johannes, 68-73
Fabian, Mac A., 1090
Falcon, Floro R., 1091-1092
Fall, Bernard B., 1345
Fallaize, E. N., 74
Farb, Peter, 75, 76
Faustino, Renato G., 1422
Fernandez, Pablo, 1094
Fernandez, Perfecto V., 1578
Ferrer, Cornelio M., 1579
Feuillet De Bruyn, W. K. H., 858
Fey, H. E., 1095
Feys, J., 588
Field, Margaret J., 859
Filbeck, David, 1311
Finegan, Philip M., 1096
Flanagan, Thomas, 77
Flasche, Rainer, 78, 1722-1724
Flores, Ernesto A., Jr., 1097
Flores-Tolentino, Victoria V., 1098
Flusser, David, 79
Fonacier, S. A., 1580
Fonacier, Tomas S., 1581
Forbes, Andrew D. W., 438

Forbes, William F., 1099
Ford, J. Massingberd, 80
Foronda, Marcelino A., Jr., 1100-1102
Fourquin, Guy, 81
Francisco, Gabriel B., 1103
Franco, Quintin B., 1222
Frankland, M., 1104
"Frère Gago." *See* Gobron, Gabriel
Friesen, J. Stanley, 82
Fuchs, Stephen, 83, 404-405, 589-599
Fürer-Haimendorf, Christoph von, 598-599, 794
Furnivall, J. H., 795

Gabriel, Melanio P., Jr., 1424
Galang, Joaquin S., 1105
Galang, Zoilo M., 1425-1426, 1582-1583
Galen, Tor L., 1106
Galusha, Elon, 796
Ganguly, P. G., 600
Garces, Adriano, 1584
Garcia, Candido F., 1585
Garcia, Dolores G., 1107, 1427
Garcia, Q. M., 1586
Garrett, W. E., 1397
Garvan, John M., 1108
Gatbonton, Mario T., 1109, 1428
Gautam, Mohan K., 601
Gavina, Napoleon R., 1110
Geertz, Clifford, 860-863
Geisendorfer, James V., 165
Gensichen, Hans-Werner, 84
Gerlach, Luther P., 85
Ghar Bandhu, 602
Ghurye, Govind S., 603
Gill, Sam D., 309
Giron, Eric S., 1111
Gjessing, Gutorm, 362-363
Glüer, Winfried, 439

Gnia Yee Yang, 992
Go, Fe S., 1126, 1587
Gobron, Gabriel, 1346-1347
Golongan Siradjabatak Indonesia, 864
Gonzalez, Enrique, 1112
Goodman, Felicitas D., 86
Goody, Jack, 87
Goswami, B. B., 604-607
Gough, Kathleen, 608
Govantes, Felipe M. de, 1114
Gowing, Peter G., 1115-1117, 1533, 1588-1589
Graaf, H. J. de, 865
Gracia, Manuel A., 1590
Gratus, Jack, 310
Greene, Graham, 1352
Greschat, Hans-Jürgen, 1430, 1591
Griswold, Hervey D., 609
Grootaers, Willem A., 440-441
Grotanelli, Christiano, 88
Guansing, Benjamin I., 1118
Guanzon, M. A. C., 1431
Guariglia, Guglielmo, 89-93, 311-312, 424, 610, 1119
Guerrero, Amadia M., 1120-1121
Guerrero, Leon M., 1122
Guerrero, Milagros C., 1123-1124
Gumabong, Rodolfo P., 1125
Gumban, Johnny V., 1432
Gupta, A. K. Sen, 611
Guptia, Pabitra, 564
Gusfield, Joseph R., 94
Gutierrez, Marcelino, 1126
Guzman, Alfonso de II, 1127

Hadaway, Christopher K., 95
Hadiwijono, Harun, 866-867
Haetta, Lars J., 364
Hall, Anne T., 1128
Halpern, Joel M., 993-995
Halsey, John J., 313

Hanks, Lucien M., Jr., 868
Hardgrave, Robert L., Jr., 612
Harrison, Michael I., 96
Hart, Donn V., 1129-1130
Hassan, Riffat, 97
Hayden, Joseph R., 1131, 1592
Heberle, Rudolf, 98
Heissig, Walter, 425
Helbig, Karl, 869
Herron, Helen. *See* Taft, William H.
Henderson, Gregory, 466
Herskovits, Melville J., 99-100, 219
Hessel, Eugene A., 1132-1133
Hesselgrave, David J., 101, 314
Hewitt, Gordon, 613
Hickey, Gerald C., 1349-1351
Hill, Frances R., 102, 1352
Hine, Virginia H., 85, 103
Hinton, Peter, 1312
Hminga, Changte L., 614
Hodne, Olaf, 615
Hodson, T. C., 616
Hoeckman, Remi, 104-105
Hoekema, Alle G., 870-871
Hoerschelmann, Werner, 617
Hoffmann, Johannes B., 618
Hollenweger, Walter J., 106, 315
Holmio, Armas K. E., 365
Höltker, Georg, 1353
Hong Son-gyong, 467
Hoogeveen, R., 872
Ho-Phap, 1354
Hopper, Rex. D., 107
Horn, Florence, 1134
Horton, Robin, 108
Hou Su Shuang, 1356
Houtart, François, 316, 406
Howell, Julia D., 873
Hrach, Hans-Georg, 619
Hsiao, Ching-fen, 442
Huân Nguyên T., 1356-1358

Hudspith, J. Edwin, 1313
Hulbert, Homer B., 468
Hultkrantz, Åke, 109
Hunger, Wilhelm, 1359
Hunt, Everett N., Jr., 1725
Hunt, W. S., 620
Hunter, W. W., 621
Hurley, Vic, 1135
Huynh Phu So, 1360
Huynh-Van-Nhièm, 1361
Hyon Sidong, 469

Iglesia Evangelica Metodista, 1136
Iglesia Filipina Independiente Revista Catolica, 1593
Iglesia Ni Cristo, 1434-1435
Ihrman, Claire, 317
Ikche, O., 470
Ikehata, S., 1139
Ileto, Reynaldo C., 1140-1141
India, Government of, 797
Indonesian Ministry of Information, 874
Indrakusuma, Joh, 875
Ingemann, Frances J., 394-395
Ingwersen, H. Ph., 876
Innes, Charles, 798
International Research Associates, 1594
Isenberg, Sheldon R., 110, 434
Ishii, Yoneo, 1317

J. M. P., 1142-1143
Jasper, J. E., 878
Javier, Antonio B., 1449
Jay, Edward J., 407, 622
Jay, Robert R., 879-880
Jeffreys, M. D. W., 111
Jenks, Albert E., 1144
Jha, Aditya P., 623
Jha, Jagdish C., 624
Ji Won-yong, 471

Joaquin, Nick, 1145
Jocano, F. Landa, 1146-1147
Jones, A. H. M., 112
Jones, Rex L., 784
Jones, Rufus M., 113
Jong, Suffridus de, 881
Jose, F. Sionil, 1148
Josson, H., 625
Joustra, M., 882
Joy, C. R., 1595
Jules-Rosette, Bennetta, 114
Juliusson, Per, 626
Jumper, Roy, 1362-1363
Junkin, William N., 472
Justinger, Judith M., 115

Kalia, S. L., 627
Kals, Bernard, 883
Kamma, F. C., 884
Kandulna, Anselm, 628-629
Kang Wi Jo, 473
Kantonen, Taito A., 366
Kartodirdjo, Sartono, 885-888
Kaszuba, F., 1364
Kaufmann, Robert, 116
Kavanagh, Joseph J., 1149, 1450-1451
Kayser, Helga, 889
Keesing, Felix M., 1150
Keesing, Marie, 1151
Kehoe, Alice B., 117
Keskitalo, Alf I., 118
Keyes, Charles F., 1315-1316
Khurana, B. K., 630-631
Kim, David S. C., 1727
Kim Han-gu, 474-475
Kim Myung H., 476
Kim Ui-hwan, 477
Kim Yong-bock, 478-479
Kim Yong-choon, 480-489
King, Victor T., 890, 1151
Kirsch, A. Thomas, 1317
Kiunisala, Edward R., 1452

Klimkeit, Hans-Joachim, 408-409, 425, 632
K. M. P. Tidings, 1152
Kobak, Cantius J., 1094
Köbben, A. J. F., 119
Koch, Kurt E., 891
Koentjaraningrat, 892
Koichiro, Uno, 1365
Koppers, Wilhelm, 120, 633
Kopytoff, Igor, 121
Korea Christian Academy, 491
Korea Study Committee, 492-493
Korean Overseas Information Service, 494
Korver, A. Pieter E., 893
Kostet, Oskar, 367
Krader, Lawrence, 426
Kraeling, Carl H., 122
Kruyt, A. C., 894-895
Kuby, David J., 123
Kuica, Rosiam, 799
Kunstadter, Peter, 998
Kurundamannil, Joseph C., 634
Kuznetsov, S. K., 387
Kyaw Hpaung Yeh Kaw, 813
Kyaw Taing Lone Gay, 813

La Barre, Weston, 124-125, 318, 427
Lagasca, Manuel, 1596
Lagunzad, Linda A., 1597
Lai, Joseph N. H., 1366
Lalawar, H., 896
Lanczkowski, Günther, 319
Landon, Kenneth P., 1367
Lanternari, Vittorio, 126-142, 320, 388, 428, 897, 1153, 1368
Laplantine, François, 143
Larkin, John A., 1154
Larsen, Egon, 321
Latourette, Kenneth S., 322, 635, 1155
Laubach, Frank C., 1598-1599

Laufer, Berthold, 429
Laugeson, Helen, 323
Laughlin, Charles D., Jr., 144
Lava, Jesus, 1156
Lazarus, Henry, 636
Leach, Edmund, 145
Leaman. *See* 1728
Leavitt, John, 146
Lebra, Takie S., 147
Lee, David C., 1157
Lee, Raymond L. M., 1005, 1009-1011
Lee Sang Hun, 1730-1731
Le Fierro, Vincente L., 1600
Lejuge, Fr., 1369
Lema, Lerma S. de, 1158
Lemaitre, 1370
Lemercinier, Genevieve, 406
Lemoine, Jacques, 996
Leon, Anna L. S. de, 1159
Leo XIII (Pope), 1601
Le Roy, James A., 1160, 1602
Lerrigo, P. H. J., 1603
Lestrac, G. Abadie de, 1371
Leverrier, Roger, 496
Lewis, Elaine, 1318
Lewis, I. M., 148-150
Lewis, Paul, 1318
Lewis, Warren, 1732
Lewy, Guenter, 151, 324, 800
Lex, Barbara W., 152
Lincoln, Jackson S., 801
Lindgren, Ethel J., 368, 410
Linton, Ralph, 100, 153
Ljungdahl, Axel, 154
Llamoso, Emiliano L., 1605
Llanes, Jose L., 1606-1607
Lloyd, John M., 637-638
Locsin, Teodoro M., 1161
Lomax, Louis E., 1319
Longkumer, Akumla, 639
Lopez, Salvatore P., 1162
Lopez, Santiago, 1608

Lorenzana, Avelina, 1627
Love, Robert S., 1163
Low, Donald A., 640
Lowie, Robert H., 155
Luat, Ernesto P., 1156
Lumbantobing, Andar M., 898
Lusty, G. H., 641
Luzbetak, Louis J., 156, 325
Lynch, D., 1609
Lynch, Frank, 1164, 1453

McAllister, Edward A., Jr., 1610
Macaraig, Serafin E., 1165
McAyley, J., 157
McCabe, J., 1733
McCall, Anthony G., 642
McCarthy, Denis A., 1611
McCoy, Alfred W., 1166
McCully, Elizabeth A., 497
MacDougall, John D., 643-646
McGavran, Donald A., 647, 1196, 1612
McKinnon, John, 1320
McLane, John R., 1372
McLeod, W. H., 648
MacPherson, William, 649
Magdamo, Patricia L., 1088
Mahapatra, L. K., 650-652
Mahn Gyi Sein, 813
Maier, Norman R. F., 158
Mair, Lucy P., 159, 326
Majul, Cesar A., 1613-1614
Majumdar, D. N., 653-654
Majumdar, Ramesa-Chandra, 655
Makabenta, F. P., 1454
Malay, Paulina C., 1167
Mallinckrodt, J., 899
Malony, H. Newton, 1025
Manaligod, Ambrosio M., 1615
Manalo, Eraño G., 1456
Manalo, Felix, 1457
Mänchen-Helfen, Otto, 430
Mandac, Simeon, 1616

Mandelbaum, David G., 656
Mandell, Wayland S., 1617
Mangoenkoesoemo, Tjipto, 900
Manhar, Namuram, 657
Manickam, P. Kambar, 539
Manila, Quijano de, 1168-1169, 1459
Manker, Ernst M., 369, 383
Mantubia, Eribato, 1170
Maquiso, Elena G., 1171
Marasigan, Vicente, 1172-1175
Marche, Alfred, 1176
Marfil, F. P., 1460
Marin, G., 802
Marinich, Vladimir G., 389
Marlowe, David H., 1321
Marquez, Socorro, 1177
Marshall, Harry I., 803
Martinez, Gloria S., 1178
Masa, Jorge O., 1618
Mason, Francis, 804
Masson, Joseph, 160-161
Mas y Sans, Sinobaldo de, 1179
Matta, Juan M. de la, 1180
Maurier, H., 162
Mayo, Katherine, 1181
Mbon, Friday, 163
Medina, Juan de, 1082
Meek, George W., 327, 1183-1184
Megged, Nahum, 164
Melton, J. Gordon, 165
Mendelson, E. Michael, 805-808
Mendoza, Conrado, 1185
Mercader, Cesar, 1619
Mercader, Felix, 1619
Mercado, Leonardo N., 1186-1187
Mercado, Monina A., 1188
Merton, Robert K., 166
Methodist Episcopal Church, 1189
Michel, Th., 901
Middelkoop, Pieter, 902-903
Mignot, Ed, 1734-1735

Mijarez, P., 1461
Mikusol, Paitoon, 1322
Miller, Beatrice D., 658
Miller, D. E., 167
Minz, Nirmal, 659-661
Misra, Kamal K., 662
Mitterhöfer, Jakob, 328
Modesto, Salvador T., 1463
Modigliani, Elio, 904
Mok Chong-gyun, 498
Mole, Robert L., 1373
Moncado, Hilario C., 1190-1193
Moncado Mission Bulletin, 1194
Monge, F., 329
Montero Y Vidal, Jose, 1195
Montgomery, James H., 1196
Montgomery, Robert L., 168
Moore, Joseph G., 1620
Moos, Felix, 499-500
Moreau, A. Scott, 169
Moritzen, Niels-Peter, 417
Mortimer, Rex, 905
Moser, Rupert R., 663-666
Moses, 330
Motoyama, Hiroshi, 1197
Mottin, Jean, 997-998
Mottram, V. H., 906
Mühlmann, Wilhelm E., 170-172,
    370, 431, 907
Mulder, Jan A. Niels, 908-910
Müller-Krüger, Theodor, 911-916
Mun Sang-hi, 501-504
Munda, Bharmi, 667
Munda, Choreya. *See* Munda,
    Bharmi
Munda, Muchi R. T., 668
Munda, Ram D., 782
Munger, Henry W., 1198
Munshi, Surendra, 669
Murdoch, John B., 1323
Murillo Velarde, Pedro, 1199
Muskens, P. M. P., 917
Myrick, Conrad, 1621

Na, John D. K., 505
Nagu, R. N., 670
Naik, T. B., 671
Naipaul, V. S., 672
Nalus, Victor M., 1464
Naquin, Susan, 443
Nartsupha, C., 1324
Navlakha, S. K., 673
Nayaga Nadan, S. A. *See*
    Sattampillai, A. N.
Nayak, Bhagyabath, 674
Nayas, Ramon, 1200
Needleman, Jacob, 918
Neill, Stephen, 675
Nelson, Amvitharaj, 676
Nemeshegyi, Peter, 1736
Neumann, J. H., 919
Newman, R. S., 677
Nguyên Trung Hâu. *See* Huân
    Nguyên T.
Nicholas, Ralph W., 173
Nida, Eugene A., 174, 331
North, Cornelius W., 809
Nottrott, A. *See Ghar Bandhu*
Nussbaum, Stan, 175

Obeyesekere, Gananath, 176
O'Connor, Patrick, 1622-1624
Ofrenia, R. E., 1201
Ogg, Li, 506
O'Hanlon, Redmond, 1012
Olaes, Rodolfo O., 1202
Oldham, William F., 1203
Oliver, Victor L., 1375-1378
Olson, William H., 1204
O'Malley, L. S. S., 679
Onghokham, 922
Oosterwal, Gottfried, 177, 332-
    333, 1205
Oosthuizen, G. C., 1625
Orans, Martin, 680-681
Orr, J. Edwin, 682

Ortega, Juan, 1626
Osias, Camilo, 1627
Overmyer, Daniel L., 444

Pacheco, Esther M., 1073
Pacis, Vicente A., 1206, 1466
Pacyaya, Alfredo, 1082
Paek Nak-chun. *See* Paik, L.
    George
Paik, L. George, 507
Paine, Robert, 371
Pakem, B., 683
Pal, Agaton P., 1207
Palazon, Juan, 1208
Palmer, S. J., 508-509
Pangborn, Cyrus R., 684
Parekh, B. M. C., 685
Park, Paul, 510
Park Pong Bae, 511
Parker, Donald D., 1628
Parry, Nevill E., 686
Pasco, Tito E., 1629
Pascricha, Josephine A., 1209
Pascual, Ricardo R., 1210
Passano, P., 1379
Pastores, Elizabeth A., 1211
Pasugo, 1469
Patanne, E. P., 1212
Pattisson, Peter R. M., 512
Peacock, J. L., 921
Pedersen, Paul B., 922
Peel, J. D. Y., 178
Perry, Elizabeth J., 445
Peters, George W., 923
Pettitt, George, 687
Phan Truong Manh, 1380
Phelan, John L., 1213
Philippine Episcopal Church, 1630
Philippine Independent Church,
    1631-1645
The Philippines, 1214
Philippines, Republic of, 1646-
    1649

Pickett, J. W., 688
Piddington, Ralph, 179
Pieper, A., 924
Piepkorn, Arthur C., 1650
Pigeaud, T. G. T., 925-926
Pillay, Gerald J., 180
Pimental, Margot, 1215
Pimental, Narciso, Jr., 1216
Pisig, Apolonio, 1651
Playne, Somerset, 689
Pleyte, C. M., 927
Plopino, Luz, 1471
Poblete, Pascual H., 1652
Poethig, Richard P., 1653
Poggi, Vincenzo, 334
Polak, A., 928
Pollak-Eltz, Angelina, 335
Polotan, Kerinia, 1217-1218
Pope, Jean, 1219
Posern-Zielinska, Miroslawa, 336
Posern-Zielinski, Aleksander, 181,
    336
Poulat, Emile, 182
Prattis, Ian, 1013
Presler, Henry H., 690-691
Prisma, 929
Prunner, Gernot, 513-516
Puech, Henri-Charles, 337
Pullapilly, Cyriac K., 692
Punongbayan, M. R., 1220
Purti, Priya N. J., 693
Pye, E. Michael, 183

Queiroz, Maria I. P. de, 184-190
Querol, N. M., 1472-1473

Radja, Haba L., 930
Ragavaiah, V., 694
Rai Bahadur, Hira L., 711
Raittila, Pekka, 372
Raj, Hilda, 695
Raj, P. Solomon, 696-697
Rama, N. G., 1474

Rambo, A. Terry, 1381
Ramirez, Sixto, 1654
Ranger, T. O., 191
Raterta, Pedro, 1221
Raun, Alo, 396
Rauschenbusch-Clough, E., 698
Ray, Benoy G., 699
Ray, P. C., 700
Raychaudhuri, Bikash, 701
Redfield, Robert, 100, 411
Regalado, Felix B., 1222
Reich, Wendy, 192
Reid, J., 702
Reilly, Henry, 1223
Remollino, A., 1655
Requiza, Moreno C., 1224
Retana, Wenceslao E., 1656
Rewick, Kenneth O., 1225
Reyes, Isabelo de los, Jr., 1226, 1658-1662
Reyes, Isabelo de los, Sr., 1227-1228, 1663-1666
Reyes, Jose S. de los, 1657
Reyes, Lorenzo D., 1226
Rha Young Bok, 518
Ricarte, Artemio, 1229
Rich, John A., 1230-1231
Richardson, Don, 810
Rinkes, D. A., 932
Rivera, Juan A., 1667
Robb, Walter, 1232
Robertson, James A., 1668
Robertson, Roland, 193
Roces, Alejandro R., 1233, 1475
Rodgers, James, 1234
Rodriguez, Isacio R., 1669
Rofe, H., 933
Romero, Ma. F. H., 1235
Rondot, Pierre, 1382
Roperos, G. M., 1476, 1670
Rosal, Nicolas L., 1671
Rosen, George, 194
Rosquites, Brandon V., 1477

Roszak, Theodore, 195
Rottger-Hogan, E., 703
Rousseau, Jérôme, 1014
Roy, N. B., 704-705
Roy, Sarat C., 706-709
Roy-Burman, B. K., 710
Ruiz, Juan M., 1672
Runes, Ildefonso T., 1673
Russell, R. V., 711
Russo, Antonio, 196
Ryan, Bryce, 197
Ryan, Michael T., 198
Ryu Tong-shik, 519-521

Sa, Fidelis de, 712
Sa, N. de, 713
Saarnivaara, Uuras, 373-374
Sachchidananda, 412, 714-718
Sacks, I. Milton, 1383
Sahay, Keshari N., 719-722
Salanga, Alfredo N., 1674
Salava, Federico C., 1478
San Juan, Epifanio, Jr., 1237
Sancho, Manuel, 1236
Sanders, Albert J., 1479-1482
Sandewall, Allan, 375
Sandoval, C. P., 1483
Sanford, Margaret, 199
Santa-Romana, J. R., 1484-1487
Santa-Romana, Mariano, 1238
Santiago, Benjamin, 1488-1490
Santos, A. B., 1239
Santos, Ben, 1240
Santos, Jose P., 1241
Santos, Ramon P., 1242
Sarkisyanz, Emanuel, 811-812, 999, 1243, 1325
Sastrapratedja, M., 934
Sattampillai, A. N., 723
Saw Kya Shinn, 813
Sawatsky, Rod, 200
Schaefle, William J., 1244
Schapera, I., 201

Scheiner, Irwin, 413
Schlegel, Stuart A., 1245
Schlosser, Katesa, 202, 338
Schmidt, Wilhelm, 432
Schmitt, Erika, 724
Schmitz, Josef, 1675
Schreike, B., 203, 414
Schreiner, Lothar, 935
Schreiter, Robert J., 204
Schrenk, A. G., 433
Schumacher, John N., 1676-1677
Schumann, Olaf, 936
Schwarz, Hillel, 205
Scott, James C., 415
Scott, William H., 1246, 1678-1691
Seaman, Gary N., 447
Sebeok, Thomas A., 390-396
Segal, Robert A., 206
Seiwert, Hubert, 448
Selosoemardjan, 937
Sen, Jyoti, 725-727
Seumois, André, 207
Seunarine, J. F., 208, 416, 728
Sevrin, Oscar, 729
Seylers, Franz, 1692-1693
Shambaugh, Cynthia L., 355
Shank, David A., 209, 339
Sharma, Arvind, 210
Shek, Richard, 449, 450
Shepperson, George, 211
Sherman, Harold, 1247
Shim Il-sup, 522
Shoesmith, Dennis, 1248
Shrivastava, L. N. R., 730
Siddiqui, M. K. A., 731
Sierksma, Fokke, 212-213, 340
Silvertsen, Dagmar, 376
Simon, Pierre J., 1385-1386
Simpson, George E., 214
Singaravelu, S., 1015
Singh, K. Suresh, 732-734
Singh, Roop G., 735-737
Sinha, Ramesh, 769

Sinha, Surajit, 738-742
Sinha, Surendra P., 743-748
Siregar, Basatua P., 938
Sison, Juan C., 1694
Sitompul, Pangarisan P., 939
Sitoy, T. Valentino, Jr., 1249
Skrefsrud, L. O., 749-750
Skrobanek, Walter, 1326
Slaeter, I., 751
Smalley, William A., 341, 992, 1000-1002
Smart, John E., 1250
Smart, Ninian, 342
Smith, Donald E., 814
Smith, Gordon H., 1387
Smith, Marian W., 215, 267
Smith, R. B., 1388
Smith, Wilfred C., 216
Snouck-Hurgronje, Christiaan, 940
Sobrepena, Enrique C., 1251
Social Science Research Council, 217
Society of Jesus, 1252
Soedjito Sosrodihardjo, 941
Soekotjo, Sisit H., 942
Soetopo, C., 943
Sohn Kyoo Tae, 1737
Soliongo, L. P., 1491
Solomon, Robert L., 815
Solwen, M. V., 1492
Somera, Rene D., 1253
Soppit, C. A., 752
Speer, Robert E., 524
Spencer, Arthur, 377
Spencer, Dorothy M., 753
Spencer, R. F., 218
Spier, Leslie, 219
Stackhouse, Max L., 1493
Stange, Paul, 944-947
Stark, Rodney, 220
Santa-Romana, Julita R., 1484-1487

Santa-Romana, Mariano, 1238
Statesman, 754
Steinberg, David J., 1254-1255
Stern, Theodore, 816
Stevenson, Dwight E., 1256
Stevenson, H. N. C., 755, 817
Stipe, Claude E., 221-222
Stöhr, Waldemar, 948
Stoll, W. G., 818
Straathof, W., 949
Ström, Åke V. O., 378
Stubbs, Roy M., 1257
Stuntz, Homer C., 1258
Sturtevant, David R., 1259-1265
Sumanto, Wp. I., 950
Sumcad, Edwin A., 1496
Suolinna, Kirsti, 379-381
Surendra, Lawrence, 756
Sutarman Soediman Partonadi, 951
Suttles, Wayne, 219
Sweet, David, 1266
Symmons-Symonolewicz, Konstantin, 223

Tabios, Aurora D., 1268
Tac Pham Cong, 1389
Taft, William H., 1696
Taft, Mrs. William Howard, 1695
T'ak Myong-hwan, 525, 526
Talmon, Yonina, 224, 225
Tambiah, S. J., 1327
Tanabe, S., 1328
Tapp, Nicholas, 1003
Tari, Mel, 952
Tari, Nona, 952
Taylor, Richard W., 757
Telford, J. H., 819
Thaxton, Ralph, 451
The, Siauw G., 953-955
Thelle, Notto R., 1738
Theobald, Robin, 226
Thomas, M. M., 227

Thompson, David, 1269
Thompson, Jack, 343
Thrupp, Sylvia L., 228
Thulin, Henning, 382
Thurston, Edgar, 758
Tichelman, G. L., 956
Tideman, J., 957-958
Tien Ju-kang, 820
Tillet, Gregory T., 1739
Tipon, Emmanuel S., 1498
Tiru, Muchi R., 759
Tiryakian, Edward A., 229-230
Toch, Hans, 231
Toliver, Ralph, 1270, 1274
T'ongil-gyo, 1740
Topley, Marjorie, 1303
Torbet, Robert G., 821
Traân Huân Nguyên. *See* Huân Nguyên T.
Tran Van Tuyen, 1390
Trinidad, Juan, 1500
Trinidad, R., 1501
Tripathy, Chandrabhal, 652
Trivino, J. F., 1271
Troisi, Joseph, 760-764
Trompf, Garry W., 232-233
Tuggy, Arthur L., 1272-1274, 1502-1504, 1697
Tumangday, Nick G., 1505
Tun, M. C. W., 822
Tupas, Rodolfo G., 1275
Turner, Harold W., 234-250, 344, 352, 1329
Turner, Victor W., 251-252
Tutay, Filemon V., 1276-1277

Unification Church, 1741
Unisala, E. R., 1506
United States Government, Department of the Army, 962, 988, 1278-1279, 1330, 1391

United States Government,
Department of the Navy,
1392-1393
Upadhyay, V. S., 765
Urgena, Cynthia B., 1280
Utrecht, Ernst, 960-961
Uyan, Vezancio, 1281

Vacas, Felix, 1698-1699
Valentine, Tom, 1282
Valjavek, Friedrich, 253
Valleser, Sebastian, 1700
Van Akkeren, Philip, 962-963
Van Den Berg, E. J., 964
Van Der Bent, Ans J., 965, 1283
Van Der Kroef, Justus M., 966-
974
Van Der Schueren, T., 766
Van Duuren, David A. P., 975
Van Exem, A., 767-769
Van Fossen, Anthony B., 400
Van Hien, Edward, 976
Van Naerssen, Fritz H., 977
Van Ufford, Ph. Quarles, 978
Vano, Manolo, 1284
Vasiljev, V. M., 397
Vatican, The, 254
Velez, Amosa L., 1285
Vengco, Sabino, Jr., 1507
Vera, Jose de, 1286
Verma, K. K., 770
Victoriano, Enrique L., 1701
Vidyarthi, L. P., 771-772
Vinginiano, G., 1394
Vinluan, Victor, 1508
Voget, F. W., 267
Von Der Mehden, Fred R., 1287,
1702
Vorren, Ørnulv, 383
Vos, Frits, 527
Vrooman, W. A., 1703

Waal Malefijt, A. de, 255

Wagan, Venancio P., 1288
Wahono, Oleh S. W., 980
Walker, Anthony R., 1331
Walker, Sheila S., 256
Wallace, Anthony F. C., 257-267
Wallace, Donald M., 398
Wallis, Roy, 268-269
Wallis, Wilson D., 270
Warren, Joseph, 773
Wasson, Alfred W., 528
Watkins, June E., 353
Watson, Lyall, 1289
Webster, John C. B., 774
Weems, Benjamin B., 529-530
Weiner, Myron, 775
Weisman, Steven R., 776
Welbourn, F. B., 271
Welch, Holmes, 452
Wentzel, Constance W., 1704
Werblowsky, R. J Zwi, 272-273
Werbner, R. P., 274
Werner, Jayne S., 1395-1396
Wertheim, Willem F., 981-982
Wherry, E. Morris, 777-779
Whitaker, Ian R., 384
White, E., 1016
White, John R., 1290
White, Peter T., 1397
Whitney, John R., 1705
Whittemore, L. B., 1706
Williams, Richard A. E., 780
Williams, Thomas R., 1017
Williams-Hunt, P. D. R., 1018
Wilson, Bryan R., 275-281, 354-
355, 1304
Wilson, John, 282-283
Wise, F. H., 1707
Wolf, Eric R., 284-285
Woods, Robert G., 1291-1292
Worcester, Dean C., 1293
Worm, Alfred, 1294
Worsley, Peter M., 286
Wright, Arnold, 689

Wuthnow, Robert, 287

Yi Pu-yong, 531
Yi Son-kun, 532
Yinger, J. Milton, 288
Yoder, Lawrence M., 942, 983-985
Young, Gordon, 1332
Young, William M., 823
Yü, Chün-fang, 452
Yug-Purush Guru Ghasi Das, 781
Yuson, Alfred A., 1295

Zaal, Wim, 401
Zafra, Nicolas, 1296
Zaide, Gregorio F., 1297-1300,
    1708
Zapanta, P. A., 1301
Zaretsky, Irving I., 356
Zidbäck, Aulis, 385-386
Zide, Norman H., 782
Zoetmulder, P. J., 986
Zykov, N. V., 399

Index of Main Movements and Individuals

The entry numbers of the main or more substantial or significant references are included here (i.e., those mentioned in the titles of the items or in the annotations). The list is therefore not exhaustive as to text references, but is fairly complete as to known named movements, apart from those that are designated only by general area or by dates. Founders, leaders, and other significant individuals appear under the most common form of names, but alternative spellings and names are also given or cross-referenced.

The materials on the three particular movements placed in three separate sections at the end of the volume refer primarily to the movement concerned. Where these movements are treated along with others, they may be found through the various other numbers also given at their names in this index.

Abangan, 861, 863, 881, 888
Abom, 564
Adam Makrifat, 885
Adivasi movements, 646, 714, 717, 725, 772
Adoracion Nocturna Filipina, 1163
African Watch Tower, 75
Agapito Illustrisismo, 1172
"Age of Gold," 1350
Aglipay, Gregorio, 1033, 1076, 1146, 1234, 1290, 1293, 1521-1526, 1535, 1565, 1512, 1514-1516, 1519-1520, 1576-1577, 1581-1582, 1590, 1615-1616, 1624, 1672, 1674, 1678-1679, 1682, 1685, 1692, 1696, 1706, 1708. *See also* Philippine Independent Church
Agpaoa, Tony, 1183, 1247, 1283
Ahmadia, 616
Aiyetoro (Nigeria), 354
Aladura movements (West Africa), 178, 354

Alagappa Nadan, 534, 687
Alangkat, 1135
Alaph Divine Temple, 565, 1125
Aleka cult, 565
All Free Group. *See* Thiang Lau
    Pawl
Almazar, V., 1257
Alvaneri Schism, 613
Ambedkar, 658, 757
Anting-Anting, 1032, 1062, 1090,
    1131, 1258
Apo Asiong, 1276
Apo Ipe, 1054, 1241
Apolinario de La Cruz, 1033,
    1043, 1066, 1114, 1179-1180,
    1096, 1103, 1116, 1153, 1176,
    1195, 1208, 1236, 1297, 1299,
    1300, 1708
Apostolic Church, 1733
Apostolic Lutheran Church, 373-
    374
Arigo (Brazil), 327
Ariya 813, 816
Arya Samaj, 207, 416, 632, 728

Babajaias, 750
Babaylanes. *See* Isio (Papa), 1235,
    1290
Baha'i, 454, 1379
Baitiangomg, 1005
Balangay, 1057
Balantac, Candida, 1110
Balitaan, Marie Bernarda, 1030
Bankaw's Revolt, 1053, 1199, 1297
"Banner of the Race." *See*
    Watawat Ng Lahi
Banten, 885, 887
Bastar Revolt, 690
Batak Independent Churches, 935,
    938
Batara Gowa, 957
Bathalismo, 1057, 1288

Baylan movements, 1067-1068,
    1073
Bekasi Revolt, 885
Bernabe, Mang, 1173
Bhachhi-Dan, 622
Bhagats, 565, 577, 622, 626-627,
    659, 662, 673, 709, 715, 729,
    735, 737-738
Bhausing Rajnegi, 540
Bhelwaragars, 750
Bhil movements, 590, 671, 685,
    735, 737
Bhima Bhoi, 565
Bhumij Kshatriya, 622, 738
Bible Mission, 696-697
"Big Candle." *See* Kuga Sorta
Binh-Xuyen, 1345
Bir Singh, 622
Birsa, 289, 550, 566, 571, 580-581,
    587, 590, 602-603, 610, 616,
    618, 622, 624-625, 630, 635,
    641, 655, 659, 662-663, 667-
    668, 678, 693-694, 702, 706-
    707, 712, 714, 718, 730, 733,
    743-748, 753-754, 759, 768-
    770, 775, 782
Bisanami, 673
Black Caribs (Caribbean), 199
Black Muslims (U.S.), 78-79, 134,
    295, 325
Bohol Revolt, 1043, 1077, 1094,
    1179, 1213
Bonga, 1065
Bonifacio, 1022, 1243, 1298
Bratakesawar, 867
Brotherhood of the Believers in
    the Apo, 1224
Brotherhood of the Love of God,
    1224
Bugarin, Joe and Romy, 1183
Bungan, 1006-1008, 1012-1014,
    1016
Bungan Malan, 1008

Burkhan, 318, 409, 418, 420-421, 426-431

Cabula, P., 1277
Cadak cult, 558
Calosa, Pedro, 1090, 1120, 1148, 1185, 1257, 1280
Cao Dai, 102, 295, 314, 321, 342, 1333-1338, 1342, 1344-1352, 1355-1359, 1362, 1364, 1366-1368, 1371-1372, 1374-1385, 1388-1393, 1395-1397
Cargo cults, 13, 35, 43, 55, 75, 148, 192, 231, 252, 272, 288, 290, 295, 300, 318, 321-322, 324-325, 533
Catholic Apostles Initiated by the Holy Spirit, 1106
Catholic Apostolic Church of Holy Spirit, 1230
Cekosi, 1316
Chattampillai-Aiya, 689
Ch'en Chien-fu, 440
Cherubim and Seraphim (West Africa), 321
Chet Rami, 609
Children of God, 269
Chondo-gwan, 521, 526
Ch'ondo-gyo, 456, 463, 466, 473, 480-489, 517-519, 529-530
Chonjin-gyo, 523
Ch'onsung-gyo, 523
Chot Chelpan. *See* Burkhan
Chota Nagpur Adivasi Maha Sabha, 772
Chota Nagpur Catholic Sabha, 772
Chota Nagpur Samaj, 772
"Christ Ashram," 677
Christian Catholic Apostolic Church (U.S.), 294, 313
Christianos Vivos Metodista, 1051
Chungsan-gyo, 514

Church of Eternal Gospel. *See* Yuo Mayam and Joseph, Justus
Church of Revealed Salvation. *See* Pratyaska Raksha Sasha
Church of the Messiah, 848
Church of the Muria. *See* Tunggul Wulung
Church of the Only Saviour, 689
Cian. *See* Djiung
Cofradia de San Jose, 1029, 1059, 1139-1140, 1157, 1266
Colaco, Miguel, 677
Colorums, 1022, 1032, 1043, 1054, 1068, 1083, 1090, 1093, 1095, 1120, 1123-1124, 1227, 1129, 1131, 1135, 1140, 1148, 1153, 1155, 1165, 1179, 1181-1182, 1185, 1229, 1232, 1243, 1257, 1260, 1263, 1276, 1279-1280, 1287, 1291-1293
Coolen's Church, 417, 848, 915, 963, 978
Coscino-Mancy, 442
Crusaders (World Army), 1047, 1050
Crusaders of the Divine Church of Christ, 118, 1097
Crusillo, 1178

Das, Ghasi, 688
Degan, Pedro. *See* Sapilada
Deima (Ivory Coast), 354
Dermadjaja, 888
Deva Dharma. *See* Deva Samaj
Deva Samaj, 588
Devadas, Mungamwi, 696-697
Dietz, 888
Dimas (Ma), 1163
Dionisio, P., 1257
Dios-Dios, 1052, 1054, 1228
Dipanagara Revolt, 840, 847, 885
Djasmani, 885

Djawa-Pasundan, 888, 949
Djiung, 993, 995
Djumadilkobra, 885
Do (Prophet, Ghana), 106
Donatism, 30
Donghak, *See* Tong Hak
Dravida Kazhagam, 636
Dupungay, 1228
Durnay, Thompson, 817

Eastern Learning. *See* Ch'ondo-
    gyo
Eglise Bouddhiste Phat-Giao-
    Hoa-Hao, 1361
Eglise Chretienne Universelle,
    400
Eight Trigrams, 443
Entrencherado, F., 1128, 1277
Equifrilibricum World Religion,
    1070, 1193
Espiritistas, 1088, 1184, 1281, 1285

Falam Revival, 799
Father Divine (U.S.), 321
Faustino (Pope), 1277
Filipino Christian Church, 1708
Filipino Federation of America.
    See H. C. Moncado and
    Moncadistas
Florencio, I., 1263
Full Gospel Central Church, 458

Gaidiliu, 549
Garing, 1017
Gedangan, 885
Geredta Kristen Protestant
    Indonesia, 938
Gerinda, 937
Ghost Dance (U.S.), 10, 75, 124,
    306, 309, 340, 342
Gnosticism, 113
Golongan Siradjabatak Indonesia,
    864, 898

Gond movements, 690, 772
Gospel Association of India, 647
Govindiri, 673
"Great Repentance." *See* Nias
    Revival
Guardia de Honor, 1044, 1081,
    1124, 1145, 1155, 1168, 1181-
    1182, 1250, 1259, 1261, 1263
Guarani (South America), 66, 306
G'uisha, 819, 1331-1332
Guisha, Ma-Heh, 819, 1331

Hallelujah Religion (Guyana), 236
Handsome Lake (U.S.), 13, 75,
    173, 221, 259, 264
"Happy Triumph Association,"
    1152
Haribaba, 780
Harris, W. W. (West Africa), 279
Hau Bong, 1385-1386
Haw Lay, 803
Hernandez, J., 1241
Hidup Betul, 885
Hindu Church of Lord Jesus, 613,
    695, 723
Hkli Bo Pa, 803
Ho-Phap, 1354
Ho Thai Bach, 1335
Hoa Hao, 102, 1336, 1342, 1345,
    1352, 1358, 1360-1361, 1364,
    1366-1368, 1372-1373, 1379,
    1381, 1383, 1391-1393
Holy Men's Rebellion, 1308-1309,
    1314-1315, 1318-1332
Holy Teaching of Heaven's
    Virtue, 452
Hpo Pai San, 817
Hsin Juchiao, 442
Hsuan-Yuan-Chiao, 442
Huria Kristen Indonesia, 417, 965
Huynh Phu So, 1360, 1373

IEMELIF. *See* Iglesia Evangelica
    Metodista
Iglesia Bundok Ng Kabanalan,
    1163
Iglesia Catolica Independencia
    Romana, 1165
Iglesia de Los Cristianos Filipinos
    (Presbyterian), 1051, 1234,
    1251, 1256
Iglesia del Cuidad Mistica de
    Dios, 1030, 1080, 1215, 1242
Iglesia Evangelica Metodista,
    1023, 1041, 1051, 1072, 1116,
    1126, 1136, 1189, 1196, 1203,
    1234, 1251, 1256, 1273, 1283
Iglesia Evangelica Unido de
    Cristo, 1051
Iglesia Ni Cristo, 102, 314, 322,
    415, 417, 1027-1028, 1051,
    1084, 1102, 1105, 1107, 1114-
    1116, 1130, 1152, 1163, 1164,
    1217, 1222-1233, 1249, 1256,
    1273-1274, 1278, 1399-1407,
    1532, 1612
Iglesiang Pilipina, 1110
I-Koan-Tao, 440-441
Ilsim-gyo, 456
Ina (Prophetess), 1036-1037
Inang Mahiwaga, 1163, 1288
Independent churches, 676
Indian Shakers (U.S.), 13
Isatai Sun Dance (U.S.), 342
Isio (Papa), 1054, 1235, 1290, 1293
Islamic movements (China), 438,
    731
Islamic movements (India), 533,
    632
Izhavas, 316, 692

Jainer, Marcelo, 1183
Jamaa (Central Africa), 69, 71-72,
    173

Japanese New Religions, 280, 290,
    319
Jarai Revolt, 1349-1350
Java Revival, 871
Java Sundra, 920
Jehovah Shammah, 647
Jehovah's Witnesses, 79, 116, 162,
    276, 512
Jharkhand, 660, 727, 739, 764, 770,
    772
Jharkhand Mukti Morcha, 665
Jindan Sects, 450
John Frum (Vanuatu), 318
Joria, 554, 655, 694
Joseph, Justus, 620, 634

Kabirpanthi, 622
Kabola, Pedro, 1257
Kach Naga, 549
Kai (monk), 987
Kalki Avatar, 873
Kannett Revival Church, 634
Kapatirang Pag-Ibig Sa Dios, 1057
Kapisanan Makabola Makasinag,
    1257
Kardecism (Brazil), 290
Karta Bhoja, 647
Kartowibowo, 917
Kasan Mukmin, 888
Katipunan, 1022, 1116, 1139, 1227,
    1243, 1297-1300, 1554, 1567,
    1609, 1675, 1682
Kau (prophet), 884
Kebatinan, 901, 908-909, 920-921,
    936, 939, 944, 947, 949, 986
Kejawen, 986
Kerapatan Protestant Church,
    833-834, 846
Kesar-Sage, 424
Kharia movements, 661
Khae Chae Uae, 1312, 1320
Kharwar. *See* Kherwar

Kherwar, 544, 553, 566, 615-616, 623, 643-644, 646, 691, 749-751, 760, 764
Khmu' movements, 993, 995, 1000
Khond Revolt, 690
Khruba Khao, 1316
Khuangtua Pawl, 576, 604-606
Kim, D. S. C., 1727
Kimbanguism (Central Africa), 9, 276, 279, 314-315, 342, 354
Kim Yum Paik, 463
King movement (Maori), 318
Kisan Sasha, 772
Kisar Revival, 902
Kitawala (Central Africa), 78, 134
Ko Pisan, 803
Kolan Revolt, 690
Korpela, Toivo, 367
Kota movement, 656
Kristen-Dlowo Church, 824, 963
Kuga Sorta, 387-388, 390-400
Kukas, 648
Kurangara (Australia), 340
Kwansong-gyo, 456

Laestadianism, 357-362, 364-368, 370-377, 379-386
Lahu Prophets, 810, 819, 822-823, 1318, 1320-1321, 1332
Laikai. *See* Ariya
Langkat, 1171
Lantayag, 1182
Lapiang Malaya, 1021, 1111, 1121, 1163, 1211-1212, 1216, 1218, 1238, 1259, 1267, 1275, 1277, 1301
Lasodia, 673
Leke, 802, 1313
Lenshina, Alice, 102, 111, 321, 354
Leyte Revolt, 1043, 1053, 1077, 1094, 1213
Li-Chiao, 442
Lisu movements, 436

"Little Flock," 417
Living Breath. *See* G'uisha
"Lola Maria," 1170
Lou (prophet, The Netherlands), 401
Lu Baung, 1305
Ludhiana Faqir movement, 773
"Ludovic I," 1228
Lungao, 1228, 1296
Lunk Phaw Yi, 1319
Lushai Church, 791
Lushai Revivals, 610, 614, 642, 686

Mabini, A., 1613-1614
Macanas, Felisa, 1183
Magliba, R. S., 1097
Mahdism, 97
Mahilom, R. (Jr.), 1125
Mahua Dev, 630-631, 670
Mai Chaza (Zimbabwe), 111
Maji Maji (Tanzania), 289, 309
Makanna (South Africa), 354
Malafela, 868
Malelaka, 855
Mallayya, Korra, 758
Mambu (Papua New Guinea), 309
Mampurok / Mamporok, 1171, 1204
Manalo, F. I., 1107, 1161, 1400, 1404, 1406, 1426-1427, 1455-1458, 1472, 1475, 1492, 1502. *See also* Iglesia Ni Cristo
Manasseh movement, 776
Mangal, 621
Mangkuwidjaja, 885
Manichaeism, 30
Manjhee, Bhagirath, 623
Manjhi, Bangam, 760
Manjhi, Bhegviath, 679
Manolay, 1250
Mansren, 318
Marang Buru, 562

Maranke, John (Central Africa), 114
Marching Rule (Solomon Islands), 318
Mashadi, 89
Mason (Mrs.), 786, 821
Mata, 616
Matswa, A. (Congo Republic), 354
Mau Mau (Kenya), 354
Mayuka, 417
Mejapi, 895, 897, 912, 948, 966
Meo Trinity, 989
Mercado, J., 1183, 1289
Meskinan (prophet), 1108, 1121
Methodist Episcopal Church, 1074, 1079
Mgijima (South Africa), 354
Midewiwin (North America), 306
Min-Tan, 1346
Min Thien, 1346
Misamis Occidental, F. M., 1106
Mizo Israel, 576, 776
Mizo Revivals, 607, 682
Mnao, J. (Mrs.), 843, 903
Moihen, 297
Moncadistas, 1070, 1098, 1142, 1186, 1226, 1240, 1244, 1269. *See also* Moncado, H. C.
Moncado, H. C., 1034, 1038, 1078, 1134, 1149, 1190-1194, 1225, 1244, 1269
Montanism, 80, 113
Mormons, 319, 512
Mpadi (Congo Republic), 354
Mt. San Cristobal "Holy Voices," 1234, 1279, 1293
Muhdi-Akbar, 417
Mukyokai, 417
Munda movements, 643, 661, 702, 766, 769-770. *See also* Birsa
Muria movements, 540
Murmu, R., 601

Muttukutty, 534, 617

Naga Revivals, 605, 639, 682
Naked cult (Vanuatu), 318
Narayan (Swami). *See* Sahajanand
Nat cults, 785, 809
National Church of Madras, 613
Naxalite movement, 756
Nemha, 622
New Age movements, 175
New Confucian Church, 439
New Gond Religion, 585
Nguyen Thanh Nam, 1369
Nias Revival, 848, 852, 871, 889, 912-914, 923-924, 948
Nichirenkyo, 442
Nishkalankis movement, 774, 777-779
Njuli, 858, 897, 899, 912, 948, 966
Noi-Dao, 1358
Nunkolo, 843, 902-903. *See also* Timor Revival

Obeah (Caribbean), 322
Olive Tree movement. *See* Pak Changno-gyo
O-Lot, 1144
Omelin, Elena, 178
Oraon movements, 590, 600, 622, 643, 661, 702, 708-709, 721, 770

Pa Chai Vue, 991, 997
Pabla (Pope), 1277
Pagal Panthis, 655
Pagujuban Sumarah, 867
Pai Marire (Maori), 289
Pak Changno-gyo, 499-500, 512, 520
Pak Taison, 521, 526
Paliau (Papua New Guinea), 173, 340
Pumumuwesto, 1253

Panay, 1297
Pangasinan, 1218, 1280, 1293
Pangestu, 862, 867, 873, 876, 945
Pansacula, 1124
Pantay-Pantay, 1167, 1268
Parha, 659
Parhudamdam, 912, 919, 956, 958, 964, 966, 975
Pau Cin Hau, 318, 785, 797, 801, 809
Paw Hku Lon, 1331
Paw Hku Yi, 1331
Pentecostalism, 85, 96, 103, 276, 290-291, 335, 605, 614, 638, 647, 898, 1004, 1011, 1173
Perfecto, Juan, 1198
Permai, 860, 863
Peyote (U.S.), 10, 55, 75, 156, 192, 236, 295, 321
Phalgunanda, 784
Phat Giao Hoa Hao, 1360, 1373
Phi Bun. *See* Phu-Mi-Bun
Philippine Benevolent Missionaries' Association, 1091-1092, 1186-1187
Philippine Independent Church, 322, 417, 1026, 1051, 1054, 1073, 1076, 1096, 1102, 1114, 1116, 1130-1131, 1153-1155, 1163-1164, 1181, 1217, 1222, 1235, 1249, 1251, 1256, 1273-1274, 1279, 1283, 1287, 1297, 1521-1708. *See also* Aglipay
Phu-Mi-Bun, 999, 1326
Phu Mi Kun, 1314
Poch'on-gyo, 463
Pontiac (U.S.), 279
Pormalin, 869, 904, 948, 958, 975
Pradjapangarsa, W. Hardjanto, 873
Pratyaska Raksha Sasha, 586, 640
Pravir Chandra (Maharajah), 597
Pravir Chandra Bhanjodeo, 540

Prayer Mountain movements, 476
Protestant Fellowship Church, 844
Puharich, Andrija, 327
Pulahan / Pulajanes, 1032, 1135, 1165, 1198, 1277
Puma Zai, 556, 576, 637
Purwoko, 962

Raj Gond, 540, 584, 592
Raj Mohini, 540, 627, 630, 654
Rajayogi. *See* Verabramham
Ramabai, Pandita, 682
Ramakrishna, 684
Ramasamy, P. E. V., 636
Ramba Revolt, 690
Ramos, B., 1257
Rastafarians (Caribbean), 13, 134, 231
"Red Swastika," 1357
"Red Turban," 1031
Religion of Adam, 831
Religion of the Heavenly Way. *See* Ch'ondo-gyo
"Revival Church," 620
Reyes, Isabelo, de los, Sr., 1526, 1553-1557, 1561, 1593, 1632, 1672, 1681, 1690, 1701
Rifangi, 885
Rios (prophet), 1140, 1277
Rizal, Jose, 1039, 1056, 1058, 1100, 1117, 1122, 1132-1133, 1167, 1202, 1209-1210, 1221, 1237, 1284, 1545
Rizalistas, 1068, 1100, 1110, 1140, 1163, 1167, 1182, 1206, 1220, 1243, 1248, 1255, 1259
Rock Christ (sect), 1042
Rosicrucians, 296

"Sacred Grove." *See* Sarna
Sadrach, 824-825, 845, 848, 877-878, 943, 950-951, 978
Sagrada Familia de Rizal, 1057

Sahajanand, 685
Sai Baba, 1010
Sakay, M. L., 1241
Sakdalista, 415, 1131, 1134, 1162, 1257, 1262, 1265, 1277
Salvador, Felipe, 1054, 1099, 1223, 1241
Sam, A. C. (U.S.), 232
Sam Bam / Bram, 1300, 1387
Samahan, 1163
Samahan Ng Tatlong Persona Solo Dios. See Tatlong Persona Solo Dios 1172, 1175
Samarah. See Sumarah, 945-947
Samat, 954
Samin, 415, 831, 836, 872, 875, 879, 890, 893, 897, 900, 907, 910, 953-955, 961, 979, 981-983
Samojeden, 422, 431, 433
San Hpo Pai, 817
Sangje-gyo, 456
Santa Iglesia, 1099, 1124, 1140, 1154, 1241
Santal movements, 535, 547-548, 551, 555, 558, 561-562, 566-570, 575, 590, 601, 615, 619, 622-623, 643, 655, 661-663, 665, 679, 681, 690, 694, 700, 703-705, 724, 740, 760, 762-764
Santissima, Maria, 1228
Santos, Antonio José dos, 315
Santos, Valentin de los, 1021, 1239
Sapha Hor, 566, 623, 700, 750
Sapilada, 1044, 1057, 1082, 1144, 1150, 1250
Sapta Darma, 867, 945
Sarasvati, Dayananda, 632
Sardar, 622, 644, 646, 707, 770
Sarekat Islam, 940
Sari Dharma, 562, 681

Sarna, 601, 629, 739
Sarna Dharam Samlet, 601, 680-681, 739
Satampillai. *See* Hindu Church of the Lord Jesus
Satnami, 552, 563, 621, 688, 711, 781
Satya Hangma, 784
Sawito Kartowibowo, 835
Saya San, 289, 324, 415, 788-790, 792-793, 798, 806, 808, 811, 814-815
Scientology, 269
Seventh Day Adventism, 79, 226
Sgaw-Karen, 1307, 1321
Shandong Independent Church, 446
Shango (Caribbean), 322
Shembe (South Africa), 342, 354
Shenism, 1302, 1304
Shin-Ma-Le, 795
Shiv Sena, 672
Shong Lue Yang, 991-992, 996, 998, 1002
Shouters (Caribbean), 322
Sich'on-gyo, 510
Sido-Kanhu, 664
Singaman- Garadja, 882, 927, 948
Singh, Hakim, 774
Sison, Josefine, 1183
Soka Gakkai, 78, 102, 314, 321, 521, 526
Solo Dios, 1140
Sombadan, 752
Sonat Santal Samaj, 724
Songdok-to, 526
Spirit movements (Timor), 842-843. *See* Timor Revival
Spiritism (Brazil), 321
Spiritualism, 463
Subba Row, 536, 647
Subud, 838, 841, 856, 859, 906, 933, 939, 945, 976

Subuh, Pak, 832
Suhada, Ahmad, 885
Sukino, 857
Suku Water movement (Zaire),
   121
Sumarah, 857, 945-947
Sun Myung Moon, 1709, 1712,
   1714, 1732. *See also*
   Unification Church
Surigao, 1277
Suryadipura, Paryana, 867

Taborites, 81
Taejong-gyo, 490, 518, 521
Taiping, 13, 102, 134, 284, 292,
   300, 524, 1309
Takia Pawl, 605
Tamblot's Revolt, 1053, 1077,
   1199, 1297
Tamil movement, 514
Tana Bhagat, 565, 573, 580-582,
   659, 690-691, 694, 706, 709,
   714, 715, 718, 768, 770, 775
Tanggerang Revolt, 885
Tangulan, 1257
Tan'gun movements, 526
Tan'gun-gyo, 463, 523
Tao Yuan, 1357
Tapar, 1228
Tapara, 1222
Tatang, 1218-1219, 1277
Tatlong Persona Solo Dios, 1084,
   1172, 1175, 1215
Tayabas Revolt, 1179-1180, 1266
Tayon-gyo, 469
Telakhon, 786, 795, 810, 816, 1306,
   1310, 1312-1313, 1316, 1320,
   1330
Tenrikyo, 442, 521, 526
Tenskwatawa (U.S.), 279
Thanliana, Lal, 791
Thang Lau Pawl, 576
Thiangzau. *See* Khuangtua Pawl

Tigare (Ghana), 354
Timor Revival, 849, 871, 891, 916,
   923, 930, 952. *See also* Mnao,
   J. (Mrs.) and Nunkolo
T'in movement, 1311
Tong Hak, 455, 461-462, 466-467,
   470, 472, 475, 477-480, 490,
   495-496, 498, 503, 506-508,
   510, 524, 527-528, 532. *See
   also* Ch'ondo-gyo
Tong-I-Shen-Ling-Chiao, 442
Tongil-gyo; T'ongil-gyo; T'ong-il-
   gyo. *See* Unification Church
Tres Personas Solo Dios. *See*
   Tatlong Persona Solo Dios,
   1215
True Jesus Church, 417
Tsimshian, 15
Tunggul Wulung (or Wuling),
   824, 850, 870, 942, 978, 983-
   985
Tungud, 948, 1108, 1119, 1155,
   1231
Tuvinsty cults, 423

Umbanda (Latin America), 78,
   290, 314
Unambul, 340
Unification Church, 162, 314, 417,
   458, 459, 512, 520-521, 1709-
   1741
Union Cristiana Espiritista, 1057,
   1184, 1281
Upi Espiritistas, 1245

Vailala Madness (Papua New
   Guinea), 74, 292, 309, 318,
   340
Valentin (Tatang), 1277
Verabramham, 583, 698
Vodou (Haiti), 28, 296-297, 302

Watawat Ng Lahi, 1026, 1032,
    1058-1059, 1061, 1063, 1084,
    1102, 1137-1138, 1140, 1143,
    1158, 1186, 1268, 1271, 1532
Watchman Nee, 416
Wetu Telu, 928
White Lotus, 443-444, 450
"White Monk." *See* Khae Chae
    Uae
Wi Maung, 1305

Yakan cult (Uganda), 354
Yaruro, 340
Yellow Cliff, 445
"Yellow Thread." *See* Lu Baung
Yohannan, 617, 620
Yonghwa Samdok-to, 526
Yuomayam, 634
Ywa, 795, 1312, 1320, 1332

Zakaia Pawl, 576, 604
Zamora, N., 1019, 1041, 1051,
    1072-1073, 1116, 1126, 1136,
    1189, 1203, 1234, 1251, 1273,
    1283, 1286
Zionism (African), 314
"Zionist" movement, 614

AAJ2941   4/16/92

BL
80
A1
TB
———
V.4